Teach

Yourself

Visual Basic

PROPERTY OF
DAMARIS BLANCO

**Bob Albrecht
and Karl Albrecht**

Berkeley New York St. Louis San Francisco Auckland Bogotá Hamburg London Madrid
Milan Montreal New Delhi Panama City Paris São Paulo Singapore Sydney Tokyo Toronto

Osborne **McGraw-Hill**
2600 Tenth Street
Berkeley, California 94710
U.S.A.

For information on translations or book distributors outside the U.S.A., or
to arrange bulk purchase discounts for sales promotions, premiums, or
fundraisers, please contact Osborne **McGraw-Hill** at the above address.

Teach Yourself Visual Basic

1234567890 DOC 99876

ISBN 0-07-882078-2

Acquisitions Editor: Joanne Cuthbertson
Project Editor: Nancy McLaughlin
Copy Editor: Ann Krueger Spivack
Proofreader: Stefany Otis
Indexer: David Heiret
Computer Designer: Jani Beckwith
Illustrator: Rhys Elliot
Quality Control Specialist: Joe Scuderi

About the Authors...

Bob Albrecht writes the "Power Tools for Math and Science" column for *Learning and Leading with Technology*. He has written over 20 books about Basic, including Osborne's **Using QuickBASIC, QBASIC Made Easy,** and **QuickBASIC Made Easy.**

Karl Albrecht has been a Basic programmer for 12 years. He currently writes shareware games and utility programs, and has developed freeware utilities. He is also the publisher of *Visual Basic Backpack,* a newsletter for Visual Basic beginners.

Contents

A Byte of Basic History

Bob Albrecht

O n May 1, 1964, at 4:00 A.M., Professor John Kemeny and student simultaneously entered and ran Basic programs on the Dartmouth College Time-Sharing System. Thus was born Basic, the first computer programming language designed to be used by just about anyone. On that day, Basic's creators, John G. Kemeny and Thomas E. Kurtz, realized their dream of providing easy computer access for all Dartmouth students and faculty. Basic was destined to become the "People's Computer Language," used by more people than any other programming language.

I learned about Basic soon after its creation, and immediately switched from FORTRAN to Basic as the best language for teaching kids how to program. I printed cards and buttons with the message SHAFT (Society to Help Abolish FORTRAN Teaching) and traveled the country, spreading the word about Basic to teachers and students in elementary and secondary schools. Since Basic's birth in 1964, I've been author or coauthor of more than 20 beginner's books about various versions of Basic.

As I got older, Basic got better, evolving to meet the needs of its users. Along the way, my greatest pleasure was helping son Karl start using Basic at about age 13. For awhile, I moved to newer and better versions of Basic and Karl followed. One day this scenario flipped-flopped--Karl leaped up, up, and away while I was stuck writing QBasic books. Karl had discovered Visual Basic.

Serendipity! The student became the teacher, the teacher became the student. For Karl and me, all those old versions of Basic are like earth-bound vehicles. Visual Basic is like a starship, a quantum leap beyond its progenitors. We wanted to share our adventure with beginners, people who have *no* programming experience, so we wrote *Teach Yourself Visual Basic*, my 30-somethingth book, Karl's first book.

Acknowledgments

WE would like to say a few words of acknowledgment to the people who made this book easier to write. We'd like to thank Joanne Cuthbertson for keeping everything together and helping us not to lose our way. Many thanks to Nancy McLaughlin for her stupendous job managing the editing and production of our work and putting up with all our errors and author notes. Also much thanks to John Heilborn (Dr. John to his multitude of readers) for his technical editing skills, which helped pull out all those little bugs that like to crawl in. Thanks to Heidi Poulin for her ever vigilant morning progress calls. We would also like to thank Traisa Albrecht, Karl's wife, for putting up with all of Karl's "computer time." Of course, our warmest thanks go out to the beginning Visual Basic application designer, without whom our work would have little meaning.

Introduction

WELCOME, Windows 95 users. Would you like to create your own Windows applications? In the millennia BVB (Before Visual Basic), that would have been a daunting task, requiring countless hours of nitpicky programming using the tools available in those ancient times.

Now there is Visual Basic, a quantum leap forward, a super power tool that you can use to create Windows applications for yourself, your friends, people on the net, or—well, you choose your audience. You can use Visual Basic to create a visual interface that looks and feels like the ones you see in your favorite Windows applications. You can write code that makes your visual interface respond to users the way you want it to respond. You can create friendly software that interacts dynamically with users.

Perhaps the most personal way to use a computer is to learn an applications development language, apply it to interesting problems, and produce useful solutions—your solutions. With a little help from this book, you can teach yourself to design Windows applications that look good, feel good, and work well.

In just a few hours, a high school student can use Visual Basic to create a Windows application that would have taken seven professional programmers seven days to do in the programming languages of a few years ago. We know this is true because we build learning environments where kids teach themselves Visual Basic, and we watch them do it. It's beautiful and wonderful--they experiment, try this, try that, share their discoveries, teach each other. Occasionally they'll ask a patiently waiting mentor for help. Sometimes we mentors feel like the Maytag repairman--nothing to do but watch students take responsibility for their own learning. If you are a teacher or parent of a teenager, we'd love to communicate with you about this. Contact us at

▼ *Visual Basic Backpack*
Post Office Box 478
San Lorenzo, CA 94580
Karl25@aol.com

▼ *DragonSmoke*
Post Office Box 1635
Sebastopol, CA 95473-1635
DragonFun@aol.com

About This Book

Teach Yourself Visual Basic is a task-oriented tutorial for beginners. It has 11 chapters, each divided into a number of short sections. Chapters 1 through 10 present end-of-section and end-of-chapter exercises so that you can try out your new skills. Chapter 11 is a descriptive chapter with no exercises. In all, the book has 289 exercises and an appendix with answers to about half of the exercises.

Chapter 1 is a brief exploration of Visual Basic's friendly environment. In Chapter 2, you will design several tiny Visual Basic applications called *projects*. You'll design visual interfaces and write code to make these interfaces respond to events initiated by users. Each project requires only a few minutes of your time from starting the project to producing a finished application.

Each subsequent chapter introduces new projects and new Visual Basic tools and toys. There are several project strands that begin with an absurdly simple project and continue with projects that slowly build in complexity, flexibility, and usefulness. Some of these strands extend over several chapters and provide a comfortable context for learning and using new tools.

This book describes about 200 Visual Basic projects. Many of these are small and straightforward; you can create them in a few minutes. Other projects are larger and more complex; they might require many minutes of your time to create. We have put most of the book's projects on a *Teach Yourself Visual Basic* disk that you can use to quickly load projects. The disk also contains answers to exercises in files that can be read by most word processors. You can read answers on the screen or print an answer book on your computer's printer. If you want to order this disk, look for the coupon at the end of this book (just beyond the Index).

And now, grab your backpack and move on up the road—its time to teach yourself Visual Basic.

1

Explore the Visual Basic Environment

chapter objectives

1.1 Launch Visual Basic and look around

1.2 Make things disappear and reappear

1.3 Create the Do Nothing project

1.4 Run the Do Nothing project

1.5 Save the Do Nothing project

1.6 Open and load the Do Nothing project

RELAX, make yourself comfortable. You can learn Visual Basic and use it to make great-looking Windows applications—**your** applications. You will learn to understand and use Visual Basic in the same way you learn a language such as English or Spanish or Japanese:

▼ Learn a little bit and use it.

▼ Learn a little more and use it.

▼ And so on. Becoming fluent in Visual Basic takes some time, but you can enjoy every moment.

▼ Be confident. Visual Basic is a simple language, much more easily learned than English, Spanish or Japanese.

Visual Basic is a **computer power tool** that you can use to make the computer do what you want, the way you want it done. You can use this book to teach yourself to understand Visual Basic, and how to create your own original Visual Basic applications.

You will create many Visual Basic projects as you work and play through this book. Think about where you will save them. We installed Visual Basic in a folder called "Vb" and then created a folder called "Teach Yourself Visual Basic" in which to save projects. Windows 95 allows the use of long, descriptive filenames. Terrific! No longer are we limited to eight-character filenames.

You may wish to create the Teach Yourself Visual Basic folder in the folder where your copy of Visual Basic resides.

 NOTE *The figures and illustrations in this book are from Visual Basic running in Windows 95. Since computer systems vary, your screens may look somewhat different than those shown in this book.*

Your exploration begins. You will collect Visual Basic tools and toys along the way, so grab a backpack and move on up the road.

1.1   *LAUNCH VISUAL BASIC AND LOOK AROUND*

Every exploration begins somewhere, usually in a well-stocked base camp. Your exploration begins in base camp Windows. Karl is up-to-date with Windows 95, as shown in Figure 1-1.

Visual Basic is ready to launch from Karl's Windows 95 base camp.

▼

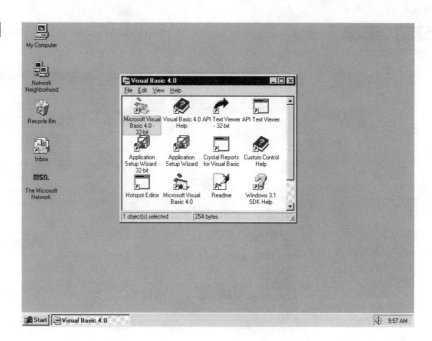

We belong to a mouse-users clique, so we use the mouse as much as possible, and use the keyboard as little as possible. We launch Visual Basic double-clicking the Visual Basic icon:

Microsoft Visual
Basic 4.0 -
32-bit

The Visual Basic Work Space

Go ahead—launch Visual Basic. You will soon see a screen titled Project1 - Microsoft Visual Basic [design]. That's quite a mouthful, so we'll call this screen the *design screen*. Figure 1-2 shows the design screen.

You will use the design screen to design **your** Visual Basic applications. Identify the following features of the design screen in Windows 95.

▼ The *title bar* is at the top of the screen.

▼ The *design screen title,* Project1 - Microsoft Visual Basic [design] is near the left end of the title bar.

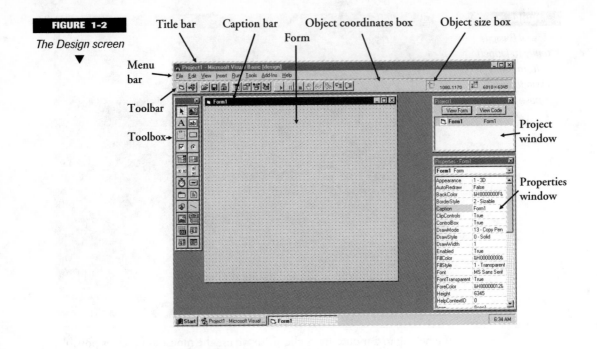

FIGURE 1-2

The Design screen

▼

▼ The *menu bar* is directly below the title bar.

▼ The *toolbar* resides just below the menu bar.

▼ The *object coordinates box* is to the right of the toolbar.

▼ The *object size box* is to the right of the object coordinates box.

▼ The *form* dominates the center of the screen. Its default *background color* is gray, and it has a grid of dots.

▼ The form's *caption bar* is at the top of the form. Its current *caption* is "Form1."

▼ The *toolbox* is to the left of the form.

▼ The *project window* is to the right of the form.

▼ The *Properties window* is to the right of the form and below the Project window.

The design screen is your canvas, the space in which you will create projects. The title bar across the top of the design screen contains the full title of the screen, "Project1 - Microsoft Visual Basic [design]." You can see the Windows 95 controls on the title bar, the *control-menu icon* on the left end, and the *minimize button,* *maximize button,* and *close button* on the right end.

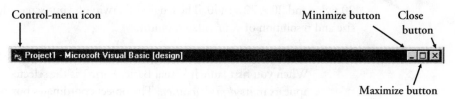

Control-menu icon

Minimize button   Close button

Maximize button

Directly below the title bar is the menu bar:

File Edit View Insert Run Tools Add-Ins Help

The menu bar contains the names of menus that you can pull down and use. You may have used menus similar to File, Edit, View, Insert, Tools, and Help in other applications. You will learn how to use the Run and Add-Ins menus when you need them to perform tasks.

The toolbar is just below the menu bar:

The toolbar provides instant access to frequently used tools. You may have used similar toolbars in applications such as Microsoft Word or Excel. If you move the mouse pointer to a tool (don't click) and wait a moment, Visual Basic will display the name of the tool. You will learn how to use toolbar tools as you need them in your Visual Basic work and play.

To the right of the toolbar are the object coordinates box and the object size box:

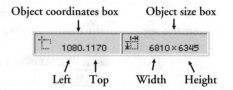

Object coordinates box   Object size box

1080.1170   6810 × 6345

Left   Top   Width   Height

Objects in Visual Basic are measured in weird units called *twips.* If you print a line on your printer and measure the line, you'll find that there are about 1440 twips to an inch (567 twips to a centimeter).

Why does Visual Basic use this strange unit of measurement? Twips are based upon the measurement used for fonts. Font size (the size of text characters in a selected font) is measured in points. 72 points equals one inch; one point equals 20 twips and $20 \times 72 = 1440$. The length of a twip on your screen depends on the size and resolution of your video monitor.

▼ The *object coordinates box* displays the coordinates of a selected object. When you first launch Visual Basic, Form1 is the selected object and appears in its *default location.* The object coordinates box displays the distance of the left edge of Form1 from the left edge of the design screen and the distance of the top of Form1 from the top of the design screen. In Figure 1-2, these values are: Left = 1080 twips and Top = 1170 twips. The object coordinates box displays: 1080, 1170.

▼ The *object size box* displays the width and height of a selected object. The first number is the width in twips; the second number is the height in twips. When you launch Visual Basic, Form1 is the selected object and appears in its *default size.* In Figure 1-2, the default size is: Width = 6810 twips and Height = 6345 twips. The object size box displays: 6810×6345.

▼ The *toolbox* is to the left of the form. Move the mouse pointer to a tool (don't click) and wait a moment—Visual Basic will display the name of the tool. In Chapter 2, you will use the toolbox to design Visual Basic projects. You will select toolbox objects, put them on the form, and endow them with interesting, useful, and fun properties.

▼ The *project window* and the *Properties window* are to the right of the form. If one of these windows is partially covered on your screen, click it to bring it up front.

Visual Basic assumes that you are beginning a project to create an application. It cleverly calls it "Project1" and displays this wisdom in the Project window's title bar. In its continuing cleverness, Visual Basic names the form "Form1." This information also appears in the project window, which now looks like this:

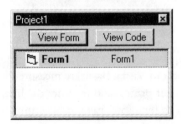

NOTE *Your project window may contain the names of other files. For now, just ignore them.*

The appearance and behavior of forms and other Visual Basic objects are determined by the settings of *properties*. Properties can specify an object's name, caption, size, location, and how it responds to events. The Properties window displays the properties of Form1, lots of properties! The setting of the Caption property is "Form1." This is the caption that you can see in Form1's caption bar. Form1's name appears in the object box. Here is the Properties window with the Caption property highlighted:

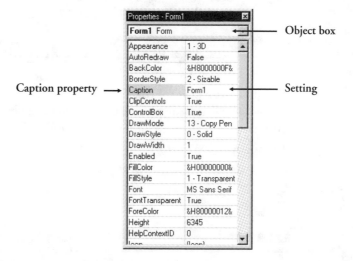

If the project window and Properties window overlap Form1, click Form1 to bring it up front again. Our design screen now looks much like it did when we first launched Visual Basic, as shown in Figure 1-2. Of course, we don't know where you wandered during your exploration!

How to Exit from Visual Basic

That's enough exploration for now. Make a graceful exit from Visual Basic and return to Windows, your well-stocked base camp, by clicking the close button on the right end of the design screen's title bar.

NOTE *Although Visual Basic usually provides more than one way to accomplish a task we will usually show only one way—our favorite way. For example, you can exit Visual Basic in one of three ways:*

▼ *Double-click the control-menu icon on the left end of the title bar*

▼ *Choose Exit from the File menu*

▼ *Press the ALT and F4 keys together on the keyboard*

In your rambunctious ramblings in the Design screen, you may do something that Visual Basic interprets as a change to Form1 or Project1. Just to be sure that you don't lose something you might want to save, helpful Visual Basic displays this dialog box:

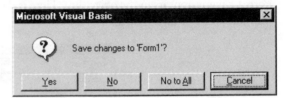

Notice the *command buttons* captioned "Yes," "No," "No to All," and "Cancel." In Chapter 2, you will create projects that use command buttons like these. For now, click the "No" command button. You leave Visual Basic and return to Windows. Now review what you have learned and get ready for another adventure.

EXERCISES

1. The Visual Basic design screen is shown in Figure 1-3 as it appears in Windows 95.

   Locate and identify the following elements of the design screen:

   a. The title bar

   b. The design screen title

   c. The menu bar

   d. The toolbar

   e. The object coordinates box

   f. The object size box

   g. The form

   h. The form's caption bar

    i. The toolbox

    j. The project window

    k. The Properties window

2. What are the coordinates of Form1 in Figure 1-3? Left = _____ and Top = _____. What are the coordinates on your screen?

3. What is the size in twips of Form1 in

    a. Figure 1-3? Width = _____ and Height = _____

    b. What is the size on your screen?

4. How do you exit Visual Basic and return to Windows?

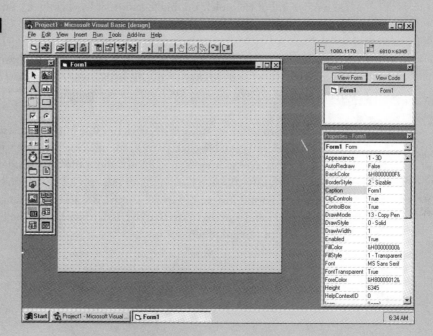

FIGURE 1-3

As you can see, the design screen is organized for easy learning. Form1, the toolbox, the project window, and the Properties window are all visible.

▼

1.2 — *MAKE THINGS DISAPPEAR AND REAPPEAR*

If Visual Basic is not running, launch it now and practice some sleight of hand—make things disappear and reappear while intoning "abracadabra," "alakazam," "shazam," or **your** favorite incantation. As we work and play in Visual Basic, we like to see the form, the toolbox, the Properties window, and the project window that you saw in Figure 1-3.

Some Common Mistakes and How to Recover from Them

As you explore Visual Basic, mysterious events may happen. Things in the Design screen may disappear or strange dialog boxes and windows may appear. We'll try to anticipate the problems you may encounter and show you how to cope with them. Here are a few of them.

If you click capriciously or if your fingers stumble on the keyboard, an unexpected dialog box may appear. If you see one, it will display a way for you to remove it. For example, you might remove it by clicking a Cancel or OK command button.

CAUTION   *Some OK buttons do things that may not be what you want done. For example, if you choose to overwrite a file accidentally and Visual Basic asks if you really want to do this, clicking OK can be a big mistake.*

If a wayward window wanders by, click its close button to close it. For example, if you inadvertently double-click Form1, you may see the code window—click its close button to send it away. You will learn about the code window in Chapter 2.

If you curiously click the Form tool on the left end of the toolbar, you will suddenly see Form2 instead of Form1. Form1 is still there, hiding under Form2. If this happens and you see Form2 on the design screen, use the File menu's Remove File command to remove it:

Abracadabra, etc.

You can make many of the elements in Visual Basic appear and disappear as you need. Here's how:

1. Close Form1 by clicking the close button on the right end of its caption bar. Form1 disappears and takes the contents of the Properties window with it. The Properties window shows no properties or settings. Our screen looks like the one shown in Figure 1-4.

2. To open Form1 and the Properties window (which will make them reappear), double-click "Form1" in the project window.

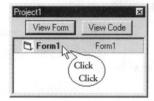

Another way to make Form1 disappear is to minimize it, instead of closing it:

1. Click the minimize button near the right end of Form1's caption bar. While Form1 is minimized, its icon and name remain on the taskbar.

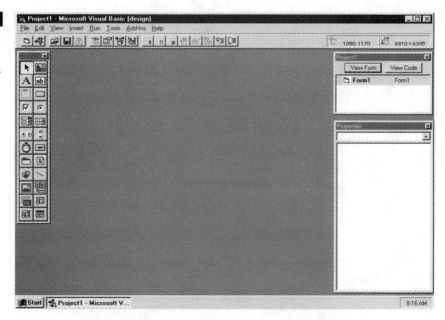

NOTE *The taskbar is a built-in feature new to Windows 95. Usually it appears on the bottom of your screen and it contains icon buttons of all applications that are running on your system. The currently active application will have its icon button depressed. Clicking on any of the icon buttons will bring that application's window to the front and ready for use.*

    2. To make the minimized Form reappear, double-click "Form1" in the project window.

Before moving on, try the above ways to make Form1 and the Properties window disappear and reappear. Then truck on up the road and work your magic on other design screen items.

    1. To close the Properties window, click its close button on the right end of its title bar. The Properties window disappears, but Form1 remains for your viewing pleasure.

    2. To retrieve the Properties window, click the Properties tool on the toolbar.

    3. To close the project window, click the close button on the right end of its title bar.

    4. To reopen the project window, click the Project tool on the toolbar.

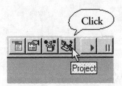

    5. To close the toolbox, click its close button.

    6. To reopen the toolbox, Select the Toolbox command on the View menu.

Changing the Size and Location of Visual Basic's Windows

Perhaps you would like to change the size and location of the design screen. To change the location of Form1, click its title bar and drag it where you want it. After you're done, take a look at the object coordinates box to see Form1's location.

You can adjust the size of Form1's window by clicking and dragging its border. When you put the mouse pointer on a window's border, it changes to a double-headed arrow:

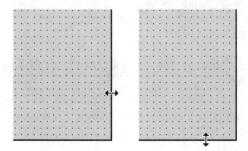

Click and drag a vertical border of the Form1 window to make its width the size you want. Adjust the height of Form1 to the height you like. The object size box displays Form1's width and height in twips.

If necessary, click anywhere in the project window to bring it up front, then click its title bar and drag it to where you want it. Adjust its width and height. Leave room below the project window for the Properties window.

Click the Properties window, adjust its size so that it will fit neatly below the project window, and move it into position just below the project window.

Is the toolbox where you want it? If not, click the bar across its top and drag it to its proper place.

You know how to make things disappear and reappear. You know how to arrange things and make them the sizes you want. Now review all this new information by dallying with these delightful exercises.

EXERCISES

1. Describe how to make Form1, the Properties window, or the project window disappear.

2. Suppose that Form1 is closed and does not appear on the screen. Describe how to open Form1 so that it reappears on the design screen.

3. Suppose that the Properties window is closed and does not appear on the screen. Describe how to open it so that it reappears on the design screen.

4. How do you make the toolbox disappear and reappear?

5. How do you change the size of Form1, the Properties window, or the project window?

6. How do you move Form1, the Properties window, the project window, or the toolbox?

1.3 CREATE THE DO NOTHING PROJECT

The Do Nothing project is absurdly simple. It does nothing and you do almost nothing to create it. You can quickly create, run, and save the Do Nothing project, then clear it from the design window, and then load it from the disk where you saved it.

This project has one form and nothing else. The form is a Visual Basic *object*. As you move on through this book, you will learn about and use other Visual Basic objects, such as command buttons, labels, text boxes, and picture boxes.

The appearance and behavior of the form is determined by the settings of its properties. The form has lots of properties. You can see these properties and their settings in the Properties window. You can use the Properties window's scroll bar to browse the properties and settings. Table 1-1 shows a few properties and their settings as they appear on our design screen.

When you launch Visual Basic, it assigns values to property settings. You can see these *default settings* in the Properties window. Project Do Nothing accepts Form1's default settings, except for its *Caption property*. You will change the caption from "Form1" to "Do Nothing." That's it—there is nothing more to do.

Property	Setting	Comment
Caption	Form1	You can see this caption in Form1's caption bar.
Height	6345	The height of Form1 in twips.
Left	1080	Distance of the left edge of Form1 from the left edge of the design screen (800 × 600 Super VGA).
Name	Form1	You can see this name in the Properties window and the project window.
Picture	(none)	There is no picture on Form1.
Top	1170	The distance of the top of Form1 from the top of the design screen.
Width	6810	The width of Form1 in twips (800 × 600 Super VGA).

TABLE 1-1 *Properties and Their Settings on Our Design Screen* ▼

Table 1-2 shows the specifications for the Do Nothing project, listing the name of its single object (Form1), the single property to change (Caption), the default setting (Form1), and the new setting for that property (Do Nothing).

Your job is to complete the Do Nothing project as specified in Table 1-2. Start in the design window:

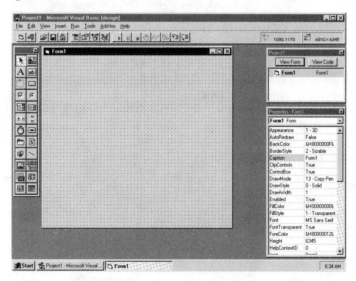

Object Type	Object Name	Property	Default Setting	Change Setting To
Form	Form1	Caption	Form1	Do Nothing

TABLE 1-2 *Specifications for Project Do Nothing* ▼

The caption of the form is "Form1." Change that caption to "Do Nothing" in three easy steps:

1. In the Properties window, click the Caption property:

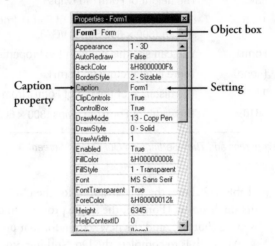

The object box displays the name of the currently selected object, Form1. The Caption property is highlighted.

2. Type **Do Nothing**.

    As soon as you begin typing, the previous setting (Form1) disappears. As you type the new setting, it immediately appears in the form's caption bar. The Properties window now looks like this:

The cursor is to the right of "Do Nothing" in the Caption property setting. If you made any typing mistakes, pleaze fix them now.

3. When everything is A-OK, press ENTER.

That's it—you have completed the Do Nothing project shown in Figure 1-5. While you are in Do Nothing land, here are some thoughts to munch on:

▼ The name of this project is Project1, as you can see in the project window's title bar.

▼ Project1 has one form. The name of a form is one of its properties. The name of Project1's form is Form1, as you can see in the Properties window's object box and in the project window's list of files.

▼ Since the name of an object is a property, it appears in the Properties window's list of properties. You can scroll down the properties list and see that the Name property still has the setting "Form1." In Chapter 2, you will change the setting of the Name property.

▼ Form1's Caption property now has the setting "Do Nothing" because you made it so. Remember, Name and Caption are different properties. The Name property setting identifies the form. The Caption property setting appears in the form's caption bar.

While project Do Nothing is doing nothing, please do the following mild exercises.

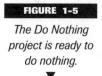

FIGURE 1-5

The Do Nothing project is ready to do nothing.
▼

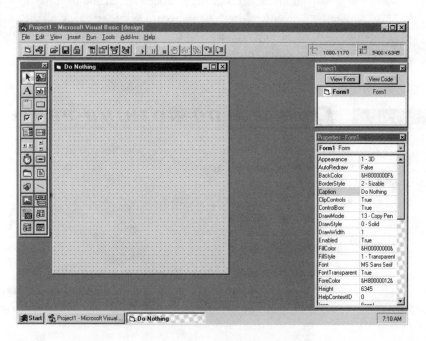

EXERCISES

1. What Visual Basic object is described in this section?

2. When you launch Visual Basic, it assigns default settings to all of the form's properties. What are the default settings of:

   a. the Caption property?

   b. the Height property?

   c. the Left property?

   d. the Name property?

   e. the Picture property?

   f. the Top property?

   g. the Width property?

3. How do you change the setting of the Caption property?

4. Suppose that you want to make Form1 exactly 6000 twips wide and 3600 twips high. Do this by changing the settings of the Width and Height properties in the same way that you changed the setting of the Caption property.

5. Suppose you want to locate Form1 so that its left edge is exactly 1200 twips from the left edge of the design screen and its top is 1300 twips from the top of the design screen. Do this by changing the settings of the Left and Top properties in the same way that you changed the setting of the Caption property.

1.4 ***R*UN THE DO NOTHING PROJECT**

Well, now that Do Nothing is done, why not run it? To run a project, click the Start tool on the toolbar:

When you run the Do Nothing project, the *run-time screen* appears, as shown in Figure 1-6. The title bar now reads "Project1 - Microsoft Visual Basic [run]."

FIGURE 1-6

The Do Nothing project is running in the run-time screen.

▼

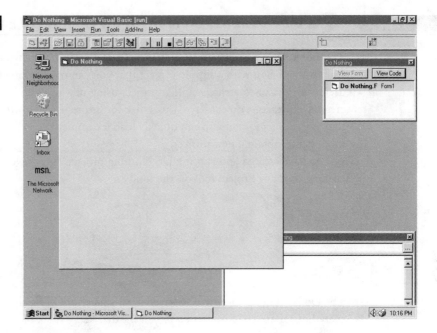

You can see part of the Debug window peeking out from under the form. You will learn about the Debug window in Chapter 7. The Do Nothing project is running and doing just what it was designed to do—nothing.

To end a run and return to the design screen, click the End tool on the toolbar:

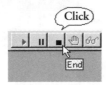

Use the above method to end the run and stop Do Nothing from doing nothing. You return to the design screen and the title bar again reads "Project1 - Microsoft Visual Basic [design]."

EXERCISES

1. Describe how to run a project.

2. Describe how to stop a project that is running.

1.5	# SAVE THE DO NOTHING PROJECT

This book describes more than 200 Visual Basic projects. There are several project strands that begin with a simple project that you can modify later to create a more useful version, or to create a similar project using new tools and methods. After creating a project, you can save it to a disk for future use. We strongly recommend that you do this so that you can quickly load a completed project and use it or modify it to obtain a new project.

You have created and run the Do Nothing project. Now save it to a disk by clicking the Save Project tool on the toolbar:

The Do Nothing project will be saved as two files, a *form file* that contains everything about the form and a *project file* that keeps track of all the bits and pieces of the project.

Using the Save Project command or the Save Project tool starts a process that saves both the form file and the project file. Since the project has neither been saved nor given a filename before this, the Save File As dialog box appears with a suggested filename (Form1) in the File name box:

You will create many Visual Basic projects as you wend your way through this book. Think about where you will save them. Where do you want to save the Do Nothing project? In the default folder shown in the Save In box (Vb in the above illustration)? On a removable disk in drive A? Elsewhere? While writing this book, we saved projects in the Teach Yourself Visual Basic folder on disk drive C. As you can see, our Save File As dialog box shows this folder in the list of folders and files. We double-click Teach Yourself Visual Basic to display it in the Save In box.

What will you name this file? Windows 95 allows long filenames with both uppercase and lowercase letters, and embedded spaces. We suggest the filename Do Nothing.frm. The filename extension .frm identifies this file as a form file. If you enter Do Nothing as the filename, Visual Basic automatically appends .frm as the filename extension. Choose your folder and then follow these steps:

1. Type **Do Nothing** in the File name box.

2. Press ENTER, or click the command button captioned Save.

The form file is saved with the filename Do Nothing.frm. Next you see the Save Project As dialog box with a suggested filename (Project1) in the File name box:

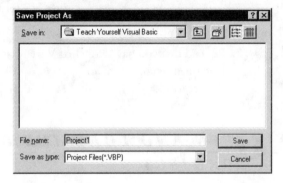

You are now saving the project file that knows everything about your project. We suggest the filename Do Nothing.vbp. The filename extension .vbp identifies this file as a Visual Basic project file. If you enter Do Nothing as the filename, Visual Basic automatically appends .vbp as the filename extension. Our Save As dialog box already displays Teach Yourself Visual Basic, which is the folder we want. Choose your folder, and then follow these steps:

1. Type **Do Nothing** in the File name box.

2. Press ENTER or click the Save command button.

The Do Nothing project is now saved. It consists of two files, a project file called Do Nothing.vbp and a form file called Do Nothing.frm. The project window now displays the project name Do Nothing in its title bar and the form file's name (Do Nothing.frm) in its list of form files:

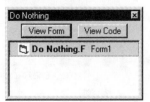

NOTE *Names may be truncated in the project window, especially if you get carried away and create very long names. You can enlarge the project window if you wish to see any part of the filename that may be truncated.*

Now that Do Nothing is safely tucked away, project your problem-solving skills toward these simple exercises.

EXERCISES

1. The Do Nothing project consists of a form file and a project file.

    a. What is the filename extension of a form file?

    b. What is the filename extension of a project file?

2. Pretend that you have launched Visual Basic and created a project. Describe the procedure for saving the project with the filenames My Project.frm for the form file and My Project.vbp for the project file.

1.6 *O*PEN AND LOAD THE DO NOTHING PROJECT

Now that Do Nothing is saved to a disk, you can load it, run it, modify it, and, if it actually did something, you could also even use it. Before you load Do Nothing from a disk, first remove it from the design screen. That way you can be sure that the Do Nothing project you see in the design screen later is the one you loaded from disk. Use the New project command on the File menu to clear the current project from the design screen:

File		
New Project		
Open Project...		Ctrl+O
Save File		Ctrl+S
Save File As...		Ctrl+A
Save Project		
Save Project As...		
Add File...		Ctrl+D
Remove File		
Print Setup...		
Print...		Ctrl+P
Make EXE File...		

Click

FIGURE 1-7

The New Project command clears any old project from the design screen.
▼

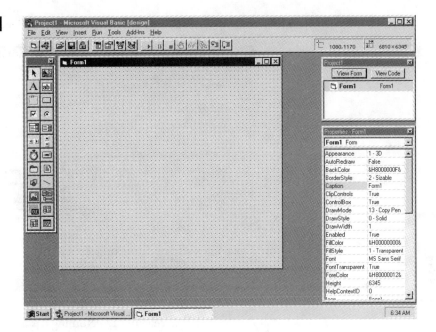

1. Click the File menu.

2. Click the New Project command.

3. If you see the Save Changes to 'Form1'? dialog box, click No to remove it.

4. If you see the Save Changes to 'Project1'? dialog box, click No to remove it. If all goes well, you should see a blank design screen, as shown in Figure 1-7.

Now open and load the Do Nothing project from its disk. There are two ways to open a project. We recommend that you click the Open Project tool on the toolbar:

The Open Project dialog box appears. On our screen, it looks like this:

1. Click Do Nothing to select it.

2. Click the Open button to open the project.

 NOTE *You can also double-click Do Nothing to open the project.*

Figure 1-8 shows the design screen after Do Nothing has been loaded. The form is absent and the Properties window is empty.

FIGURE 1-8

After Do Nothing has been loaded, Form1 is closed and the Properties window is empty.
▼

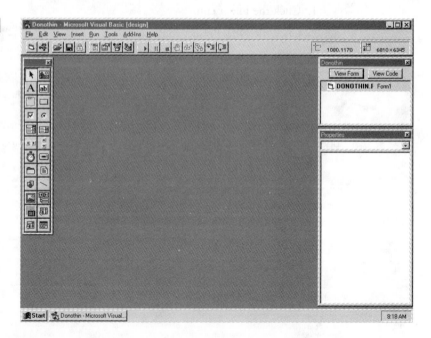

Open the form. We usually do this by double-clicking a form's filename (here, Do Nothing.frm) in the Project window. The form appears on the screen and its properties appear in the Properties window. The Do Nothing project is now fully loaded and visible. Run it and it will do exactly what it did the last time you ran it—nothing. That concludes your explorations in this chapter. Exit Visual Basic and return to Windows base camp.

EXERCISES

1. How do you close the project in the design screen and begin a new project?

2. Suppose someone has created a project called Doodle and saved it with the form filename Doodle.frm and the project filename Doodle.vbp. The project is stored on disk drive C, folder Visual Basic, folder Teach Yourself Visual Basic. How do you load this project into the design screen?

In this introductory exploration, you launched Visual Basic from Windows 95 and briefly browsed the Visual Basic environment. You used the Do Nothing project to learn how to do these things:

▼ Create a project

▼ Run a project

▼ Save a project

▼ Clear a project from the Design screen

▼ Load a saved project

Review the tools and toys you used in this chapter and stuff them into your Visual Basic backpack. Use the end-of-chapter exercises to check out your Visual Basic skills. In Chapter 2, you will create several absurdly simple projects that actually do things.

1. Figure 1-2 labels elements of the Visual Basic design screen. Without peeking at the figure, write the names of the design screen elements.

2. What Visual Basic object is described in this chapter?

3. Name three properties of Form1.

4. A twip is a measure of length. If you print a line of length 7200 twips on a classy laser printer, the line is five inches long. Its length on screen depends on the size and resolution of the video monitor. So try this: make the width of the form exactly 7200 twips and then measure it on your screen with a ruler or tape measure. What is its length in inches? In centimeters?

5. Describe how to make each of these design screen elements disappear and reappear:

   a. Form1

   b. Properties window

   c. project window

6. How do you make the toolbox disappear and reappear?

7. How do you move Form1, the Properties window, the project window, or the toolbox here, there, anywhere on the design screen?

8. How do you change the setting of the Caption property of Form1?

9. Describe two methods for changing the size of Form1.

10. How do you change the size of the Properties window and the project window?

11. Describe how to run a project and how to stop a project that is running.

12. While writing this book, we saved projects in the Teach Yourself Visual Basic folder of the Vb folder on disk drive C. Where do you save your projects? Describe the procedure for saving a project.

13. How do you close the project in the design screen and begin a new project?

14. Suppose that you have saved a project called My Project with the filenames My Project.frm for the form file and My Project.vbp for the project file. How do you load this project into the design screen? When it is loaded, is it entirely visible? If not, how do you make it entirely visible?

2

Use Forms and Command Buttons in Simple Projects

objectives

2.1 Design a project in a few easy steps

2.2 Design the Roadrunner project (Beep!)

2.3 Modify a project

2.4 Design some timely projects

2.5 Print your name and other things, such as strings

2.6 Learn more about forms

2.7 Add tools and toys to your Visual Basic backpack

N this chapter, you will work on several easy projects of gently increasing complexity. Each project requires only a few minutes of your time from starting the project to producing a finished application. You will also modify a project to get an enhanced version and then save it with a different name. In this way, you can build a sequence of applications in easy steps. A big application can evolve from a sequence of smaller ones.

A project can have two or more forms that are initially called Form1, Form2, Form3, and so on. You can use the Form tool on the left end of the toolbar to add forms to a project and you can use the File menu's Remove File command to remove a selected form. Each project in this chapter has one form initially called Form1. If you inadvertently put a second form (Form2) on the design screen, use the File menu's Remove File command to remove it and carry on with Form1. If a multitude of strange things happen and you become boggled—no problem—use the File menu's New Project command to start over. Ready? Grab your backpack and move on up the road.

2.1 DESIGN A PROJECT IN A FEW EASY STEPS

You can design a Visual Basic project in a few easy steps. Start in the Design screen. Use the File menu's New Project command to make sure that there is no old stuff that might interfere with your work and play. Begin a new project.

Draw the visual interface, the "look" of your application. Relax—you don't have to be Michelangelo, Picasso, or even an Art 101 student. Visual Basic has already done most of the work for you. You will select objects from the Toolbox, put them on the form, and arrange them to suit your aesthetic taste. Most of the objects in the Toolbox are *controls*. Each project in this chapter has one form and one or more *command buttons*. A command button is a control. Figure 2-1 shows the Toolbox, Form1, and a command button in the center of the form. The command button displays its default caption, "Command1."

After putting all of the visual pieces in place, adjust their properties. We suggest that you accept most of an object's default properties and change only one or two or a very few at first. In the next section you will change the Caption, Width, and Height properties of the form and the Caption property of a command button.

Some objects respond to *events*. For example, a command button captioned "Beep" might respond to a mouse click by sounding a beep on the computer's sound system. You will write *event procedures* that enable objects to respond to events. This is called *writing code*.

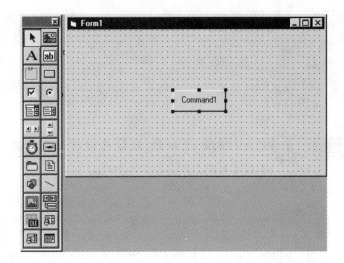

As you work on a project, save it now and then. This will be especially
important as your projects become somewhat longer and slightly more complex.
It's nice to have your project saved on a disk when your pet armadillo accidentally
disengages your computer's power cord from its electrical outlet.

Run it. We hope that every project runs perfectly the first time. We'll also be
very surprised! If a project doesn't do exactly what you thought you told it to do—
well, welcome to the real world of applications development. Carefully check each
piece of the project and fix any mistakes. This is called *debugging*.

Remember these seven simple steps that you will soon use to create a Visual
Basic project:

1. Start a new project.

2. Design the visual interface.

3. Adjust the properties of visual interface objects.

4. Write code. For example, write event procedures that enable objects to
   respond to events.

5. Save the project.

6. Run the project.

7. If necessary, debug the project and make it work.

As you work on projects and build applications, you will add several tools and
toys to your Visual Basic backpack. Briefly dally with this easy exercise before you
move on.

Review the seven simple steps that you use to create a Visual Basic project. Keep these easy steps in mind as you approach your first project oasis.

2.2 **D**ESIGN THE ROADRUNNER PROJECT (BEEP!)

As you trek toward Visual Basic literacy, perhaps you will encounter Roadrunner and marvel at his skill in eluding Coyote. We remember many happy hours watching Roadrunner cartoons. Beep, there he goes!

Project Beep #1 is very simple. It has one form named Form1 and captioned "Beep #1." You put one control, a command button, on Form1. When you run it, Beep #1 appears in a run-time screen, as shown in Figure 2-2. You may see the Debug window in the lower right corner of the screen—you will learn about it in Chapter 7.

Here are your seven easy steps for creating project Beep #1:

1. Start a new project.

FIGURE 2-2

When you click the command button captioned "Beep," it beeps.
▼

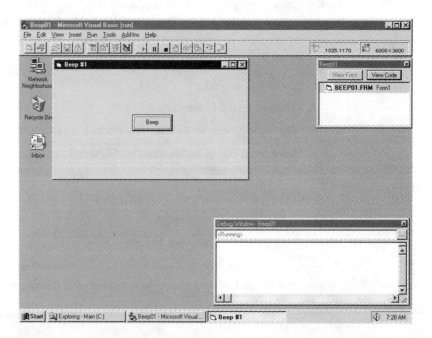

2. Draw the visual interface. Make the form the size you want and put a command button on the form.

3. Adjust properties of the visual interface objects, the form and the command button.

4. Write code for the command button's event procedure.

5. Save the project with the filenames Beep #1.frm for the form file and Beep #2.vbp for the project file.

6. Run the project.

7. If necessary, debug the project and make it work.

Table 2-1 shows the visual interface specifications for project Beep #1. The visual interface consists of two objects, a form named Form1 and a command button named Command1. The specifications list the objects that comprise the visual interface, and show the default and final settings of their Caption, Name, Width, and Height properties.

Table 2-2 lists the event procedure specifications for project Beep #1. It lists events that objects respond to and the nature of the response. Form1 does not respond to any events. The command button (Command1) responds to a mouse click by sounding a beep.

Drawing the visual interface is easy. First change Form1's caption and size. Change Form1's caption from "Form1" to "Beep #1" like this:

1. Click Form1 to select it.

2. Click the Caption property in the Properties window. This selects and highlights it.

Object	Property	Default Setting	Final Setting	Comment
Form1	Caption	Form1	Beep #1	
	Name	Form1	Form1	No change
	Width	6810	6000	
	Height	6345	3600	
Command1	Caption	Command1	Beep	
	Name	Command1	Command1	No change
	Width	1215	1215	No change
	Height	495	495	No change

TABLE 2-1   *Visual Interface Specifications for Project Beep #1*   ▼

Object Name	Event	Response
Form1	None	None
Command1	Click	Sounds a beep

TABLE 2-2 *Event Procedure Specifications for Project Beep #1* ▼

3. Type **Beep #1** and press ENTER. As soon as you begin typing, the previous setting disappears. As you type the new setting, it immediately appears as the Caption property's setting and in the form's caption bar.

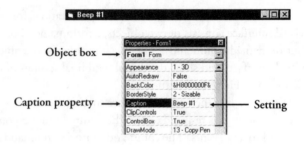

 NOTE *If you make a typing mistake, you can click the setting and edit it.*

Although the caption of the form is now "Beep #1," the setting of its Name property remains "Form1." To see this, scroll down to the Name property in the Properties window:

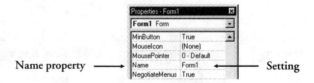

 REMEMBER *Caption and Name are different properties of an object. The setting of the form's Name property identifies the form. The setting of the form's Caption property appears in the form's Caption bar.*

You can change the width and height of Form1 the same way that you changed its caption. Do it like this:

1. Click Form1 to select it.

2. In the Properties window, scroll to the Width property and click it.

3. Type **6000** and press ENTER. Form1's width shrinks to 6000 twips.

4. Scroll to the Height property and click it.

5. Type **3600** and press ENTER. Form1's height shrinks to 3600 twips.

We chose 6000 twips as the width and 3600 twips as the height of Form1 because (take your pick):

▼ The ratio of height to width is 3600/6000 = 0.6, the same as a 3-by-5 card.

▼ The ratio of width to height is 6000/3600 = 1.667, close to the *golden ratio*, thought by ancient Greek mathematicians, artists, and others to be the most pleasing shape of a rectangle. The golden ratio is exactly $\frac{1}{2}(\sqrt{5} + 1)$, which is about 1.618.

▼ The numbers 6000 and 3600 are both multiples of 120, the spacing between gridpoints in the design screen.

▼ We like the numbers 6000 and 3600.

That completes the look of Form1. Now put one command button on the form by double-clicking the CommandButton tool in the toolbox.

Presto! A command button captioned "Command1" appears in the center of Form1. The command button is selected—it has eight selection handles (tiny black squares). Don't do it now, but remember that you can change the size of a command button by clicking and dragging a selection handle.

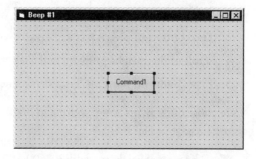

Because Command1 is the selected object, the object coordinates box displays its location on the form and the object size box displays its size. On our screen, Command1's coordinates are 2400, 1320. Command1's left edge is 2400 twips from the left edge of Form1 and its top is 1320 twips down from the top of Form1. The first coordinate (2400) appears in the Properties window as the setting of Command1's Left property and the second coordinate (1320) appears as the setting of the Top property. These values may be different on your design screen, so compare the values in your object coordinates box with the settings of Command1's Left and Top properties.

NOTE *Command1's Left property is measured from the inside of Form1's left border. Command1's Top property is measured from the bottom of Form1's caption bar (or menu bar if there is one). If you move Command1 to the left-upper corner of Form1, its coordinates are Left = 0 and Top = 0.*

Our object size box displays Command1's size as 1215 twips wide and 495 twips high. These values are also the settings of Command1's Width and Height properties, respectively. Check out these values on your design screen.

You have drawn the visual interface. It has two objects, Form1 and Command1. Now change the setting of Command1's Caption property from "Command1" to "Beep":

1. Click Command1 to select it. You will see the selection handles.

2. Click the Caption property in the Properties window.

3. Type **Beep** and press ENTER.

After doing this, you will see the new caption in the Caption property's Setting box and in the command button on the form:

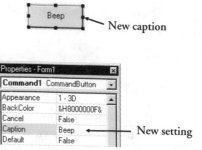

New caption

New setting

You have completed the design of the visual interface. Next you will write code to instruct command button Command1 how to respond to a mouse click. You will write an *event procedure* called Command1_Click. The name of this procedure consists of the name of the object that will respond to the event, the underscore character (_), and the name of the event:

Object Type	Object Name	Event Name	Event Procedure Name
command button	Command1	Click	Command1_Click

An event procedure is a set of *statements* that instructs a Visual Basic object how to respond to an event. In this case, the object is command button Command1 and the event occurs when someone clicks the command button at run time. You write each statement using Visual Basic's vocabulary (words that it knows) and *syntax* (rules of grammar that it understands). If you construct a statement that Visual Basic doesn't understand, it will let you know so that you can fix the problem.

You write code in the *code window.* The quickest way to open the code window is to double-click the object for which you wish to write code.

▼ Double-click command button Command1, which is captioned "Beep."

The code window opens, ready for you to complete an event procedure called Command1_Click.

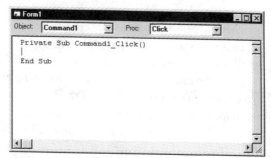

The code window displays the first and last lines (a *template*) of event procedure Command1_Click:

```
Private Sub Command1_Click()
|
End Sub
```

A **Private Sub** procedure is one of several types of Visual Basic procedures. It is attached to a specific object, hence "private" to that object and not available to other objects. Later in this book, you will learn about other types of procedures.

Event procedure Command1_Click begins with a **Private Sub** statement and ends with an **End Sub** statement. The name of the procedure appears in the **Private Sub** statement. This procedure is for the object named "Command1." The event to which it will respond is a mouse click. Your job is to write one or more statements that tell Command1 how to respond to the click. The cursor (|) is blinking between the **Private Sub** statement and the **End Sub** statement, waiting for you to write code. To complete the procedure, you type a **Beep** statement to sound a beep on the computer's speaker. It is good programming style to indent statements between the **Private Sub** statement and the **End Sub** statement in order to make the procedure easier to read and understand. We usually indent such statements two spaces.

Okay, do it—type an indented **Beep** statement, but do not press ENTER. The event procedure now has three lines of code:

```
Private Sub Command1_Click()
  Beep
End Sub
```

The **Private Sub** statement begins the event procedure and contains the name of the procedure, Command1_Click. The empty parentheses at the right end of the **Private Sub** statement tell Visual Basic that no additional data are needed for this procedure.

The **Beep** statement sounds a beep on the computer's internal speaker or on its fancy sound system. The sound heard on different computers might range from an anemic squeak to a robust clarion call. Notice that **Beep** is indented two spaces.

The **End Sub** statement marks the end of the event procedure.

That's it. You have completed the event procedure. Now close the code window by clicking the close button on the right end of the code window's title bar.

You are cruising up the road and have completed most of the work for this project, easy steps 1 through 4. All that's left is to save it (step 5), run it (step 6), and hope that step 7 (debugging) is unnecessary. Save the project with the filename Beep #1.frm for the form file and Beep #1.vbp for the project file.

Terrific! Another step done. With luck, only one to go—run the project by clicking the toolbar's Start tool. If all goes well, you see the run time screen shown in Figure 2-3. Notice that the title bar now reads "Beep #1 - Microsoft Visual Basic [run]."

Does it work? Let's find out. Click the command button captioned "Beep."

We hope you heard a beep. Click again to hear another beep. Click twice to hear beep, beep. There goes Roadrunner!

When you tire of beeping, stop the run and return to the design screen. You can select the Run menu's End command, or you can click the End tool on the toolbar. You return to the design screen. In the next section, you will modify project Beep #1 to obtain project Beep #2. If you haven't saved Beep #1, please do so now.

If you don't hear a beep, or if you see a mysterious error dialog box on the screen, carefully check each piece of the project, especially the event procedure. For example, suppose someone's mind was wandering and he or she entered "Boop" instead of "Beep" in event procedure Command1_Click:

```
Private Sub Command1_Click()
  Boop
End Sub
```

FIGURE 2-3

Project Beep #1's run time screen awaits your command click.
▼

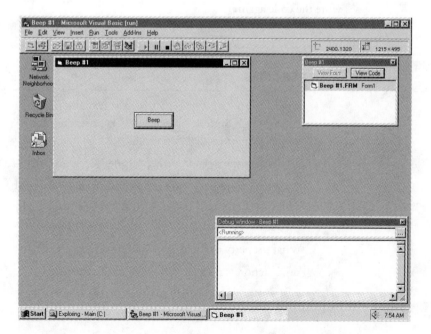

We tried it, ran the project, clicked "Beep," and saw this:

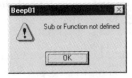

Visual Basic understands **Beep**, but is boggled by **Boop**. It opens the code window, highlights **Boop**, displays the Sub or Function not defined box, and waits patiently for someone to fix the problem. Do it like this:

1. Click OK to remove the Sub or Function not defined box.

2. Change Boop to Beep in the code window.

3. Close the code window.

4. Click the "Beep" button to hear a beep.

Sorry we can't be there to help. We trust that you will find any problems, fix them, and move on up the road. If problems persist, try deleting the entire code for event procedure Command1_Click. To do so, use the mouse to select (highlight) all of the code and then press DELETE. After deleting the code, close the code window, double-click the command button to open the code window, and write the code again.

EXERCISES

1. Project Beep #1's visual interface has two objects, a form and a command button. Each of these objects has default settings for all properties, except for any properties that you changed.

   a. What is the default setting for the Name property of the form?

   b. What properties of the form did you change? To what settings?

   c. What is the default setting of the Name property of the command button?

2. What property of the command button did you change? To what setting?

3. What action is performed by a **Beep** statement?

4. Project Beep #1 has one event procedure.

   a. What is the event?

   b. What object responds to the event?

c. What is the name of the event procedure?

d. The code for the event procedure consists of three statements. Show these statements here:

First statement: _____

Second statement: _____

Third statement: _____

2.3   *M*ODIFY A PROJECT

In this section, you will modify project Beep #1 to obtain project Beep #2, which looks like this in the design screen:

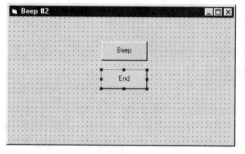

Project Beep #2 has three objects, Form1 and command buttons Command1 and Command2. Table 2-3 shows the visual interface specifications for project Beep #2 and Table 2-4 shows the event procedure specifications.

Start with project Beep #1 in the design screen. If Beep #1 is not already in the design screen, load it from the disk where you saved it. You did save it, didn't you? A save in time saves time later. Here is Beep #1:

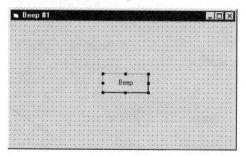

When you double-click the toolbox's CommandButton tool, a command button appears in the default position near the center of the form. That's where

Object	Property	Default Setting	Final Setting	Comment
Form1	Caption	Form1	Beep #2	
	Name	Form1	Form1	No change
	Width	6810	6000	
	Height	6345	3600	
Command1	Caption	Command1	Beep	
	Name	Command1	Command1	No change
	Width	1215	1215	No change
	Height	495	495	No change
Command2	Caption	Command2	End	
	Name	Command2	Command2	No change
	Width	1215	1215	No change
	Height	495	495	No change

TABLE 2-3   *Visual Interface Specifications for Project Beep #2* ▼

Command1 is in project Beep #1's form. To make room for Command2, move Command1 up a little by clicking and dragging Command1 upward a few gridpoints.

Now there is room in the center of the form for Command2. Put it on the form by double-clicking the CommandButton tool in the toolbox. Make Form1 the size you want and then move the two command buttons where you want them. Now the form might look like this:

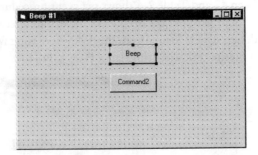

Object Name	Event	Response
Form1	None	None
Command1	Click	Sounds a beep
Command2	Click	Ends the run and returns to the Design screen

TABLE 2-4   *Event Procedure Specifications for Project Beep #2*

To change Form1's caption, follow these steps:

1. Click Form1.
2. Click the Caption property in the Properties window.
3. Type **Beep #2.**
4. Press ENTER.

Next, change the caption of the second command button from "Command2" to "End."

1. Click Command2.
2. Click the Caption property in the Properties window.
3. Type **End.**
4. Press ENTER.

This completes the visual interface design. Remember, Name and Caption are different properties. The command buttons still have the names "Command1" and "Command2," but their captions are "Beep" and "End."

You will now write code for Command2 and learn a new way to begin event procedure Command2_Click. Open the Code window like this:

▼ Click the View Code button in the Properties window.

The code window opens. It has an Object box and a Procedure (Proc) box:

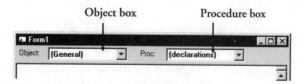

Click the arrow on the right end of the code window's Object box to drop down the Object menu:

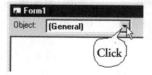

This pulls down a list of objects. You can see (General), Command1, Command2, and Form in the list. The Procedure (Proc) box displays "declarations."

To begin an event procedure for Command2, click Command2 in the Object list:

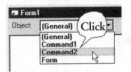

The Object box now displays "Command2," the Procedures box shows "Click," and the code window displays the first and last lines of event procedure Command2_Click:

```
Private Sub Command2_Click()
|
End Sub
```

To complete this procedure, type an **End** statement that tells Command2 to respond to a mouse click by ending the run in progress and returning to the design screen. Type two spaces and an **End** statement between the **Private Sub** statement and the **End Sub** statement. Do not press ENTER after typing the **End** statement.

The event procedure now has three lines of code:

```
Private Sub Command2_Click()
  End
End Sub
```

That's it. You have completed the event procedure. Close the code window (click its close button).

You have now written your second event procedure. The name of the procedure, Command2_Click, consists of the name of the object that will respond to the event, the underscore character (_), and the name of the event:

Object Type	Object Name	Event Name	Event Procedure Name
command button	Command2	Click	Command2_Click

If you began with project Beep #1 and have modified it to get Beep #2, then Visual Basic thinks that this project is still Beep #1. To save it as Beep #2, first use the File menu's Save File As... command to save the form with a new filename, and then use the File menu's Save Project As... command to save the project file with a new filename:

1. Select the File menu's Save File As... command to display the Save File As dialog box.

2. In the File name box, type **Beep #2.**

3. Press ENTER or click Save.

4. Select the File menu's Save Project As... command to display the Save Project As dialog box.

5. In the File name box, type **Beep #2.**

6. Press ENTER or click Save.

Run the project. Click the toolbar's Start tool and run time begins. The design screen is replaced by the run time screen shown in Figure 2-4.

Click the command button captioned "Beep" to hear a beep. Do it a few times. When you are all beeped out, click the command button captioned "End" to end the run and return to the design screen.

FIGURE 2-4

Project Beep #2's run time screen awaits. Click Beep to beep or click End to end the run.
▼

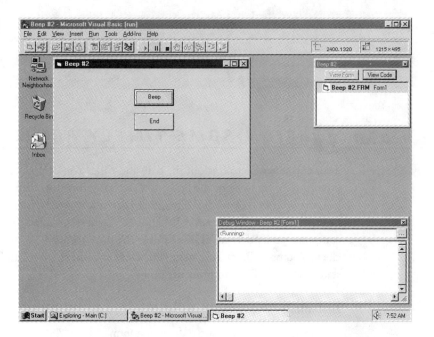

1. After completion of project Beep #2, what are the settings for the following objects and their properties in your design screen?

Object	Property	Setting
Form1	Caption	_____
Form1	Name	_____
Form1	Width	_____
Form1	Height	_____
Command1	Caption	_____
Command1	Name	_____
Command1	Left	_____
Command1	Top	_____
Command2	Caption	_____
Command2	Name	_____
Command2	Left	_____
Command2	Top	_____

2. What action is performed by an **End** statement?

3. Suppose that you have begun a new project and placed Command1 on the form. Describe how to begin an event procedure called Command1_Click.

2.4 *DESIGN SOME TIMELY PROJECTS*

Your computer keeps track of the date and time. You can include statements in an event procedure to print the date, time, or both, directly on the form. Visual Basic has two *functions,* **Date** and **Time,** that keep track of the date and time. A Visual Basic function returns a *value.* When used, **Date** returns the date according to the computer's calendar, and **Time** returns the time according to the computer's clock. You use a **Print** statement with **Date** to print the date, and you use a **Print** statement with **Time** to print the time:

Statement	Action	Example
Print Date	Prints the date on the form.	11/9/95
Print Time	Prints the time on the form.	10:25:37 AM

Your next project is a timely task. Project Kronos #1 - Date and Time has four objects, the form and three command buttons. Once they've been placed in the design screen, it looks like this:

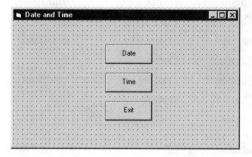

You have probably guessed that you can click "Date" to print the date, click "Time" to print the time, and click "Exit" to end the run. From now on, we'll frequently use "Exit" or "Quit" as the caption of the command button that ends a run.

The default names of objects are not conveniently descriptive. This project has three command buttons. It would be nice if they had names that describe what they do, so let's change the setting of the Name property for each command button. While we're at it, let's also change the setting of the form's Name property. Visual Basic has conventions for naming names. A name consists of a standard prefix followed by your suffix, whatever you want to call the object. The standard prefix for a form is "frm," and the standard prefix for a command button is "cmd." We invented the following names for objects in project Kronos #1:

Object	Prefix	Our Suffix	Complete Name
Form1	frm	Kronos1	frmKronos1
Command1	cmd	Date	cmdDate
Command2	cmd	Time	cmdTime
Command3	cmd	Exit	cmdExit

NOTE *A name cannot have embedded spaces. For example, the name of the form cannot be frm "Kronos1."*

Table 2-5 shows the visual interface specifications for project Kronos #1. Notice that both the caption and the name are changed for each object. The new name is used in the event procedure specifications. Table 2-6 lists the event procedure specifications.

Object	Property	Default Setting	Final Setting	Comment
Form1	Caption	Form1	Date and Time	Appears in the Caption bar.
	Name	Form1	frmKronos1	Identifies the form.
Command1	Caption	Command1	Date	Appears on the button.
	Name	Command1	cmdDate	Identifies the button.
Command2	Caption	Command2	Time	Appears on the button.
	Name	Command2	cmdTime	Identifies the button.
Command3	Caption	Command3	Exit	Appears on the button.
	Name	Command3	cmdExit	Identifies the button.

TABLE 2-5   *Visual Interface Specifications for Project Kronos #1 - Date and Time* ▼

Start a new project, make the form the size you want, and design the visual interface:

1. Double-click the CommandButton tool to put Command1 on the form.

2. Click and drag Command1 upward to make room for two command buttons below it.

3. Double-click the CommandButton tool to put Command2 on the form.

4. Click and drag Command2 upward to make room for one command button below it.

5. Double-click the CommandButton tool to put Command3 on the form.

Object Name	Event	Response
frmKronos1	none	none
cmdDate	Click	Prints the date on the form (**Print Date**).
cmdTime	Click	Prints the time on the form (**Print Time**).
cmdExit	Click	Ends the run and returns to the Design screen.

TABLE 2-6   *Event Procedure Specifications for Project Kronos #1 - Date and Time* ▼

All of the visual objects are in place and the project looks like this:

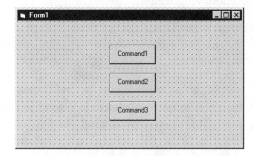

Now change selected properties. You already know how to change the Caption property. To change the Name property, scroll down the Properties window to the Name property, click it, type the new name in the Setting box, and press ENTER. Change the Caption property and the Name property for each object.

1. Click Form1 to select it.
2. Click the Caption property, type **Date and Time**, and press ENTER.
3. Click the Name property, type **frmKronos1**, and press ENTER.
4. Click Command1 to select it.
5. Click the Caption property, type **Date**, and press ENTER.
6. Click the Name property, type **cmdDate**, and press ENTER.
7. Click Command2 to select it.
8. Click the Caption property, type **Time**, and press ENTER.
9. Click the Name property, type **cmdTime**, and press ENTER.
10. Click Command3 to select it.
11. Click the Caption property, type **Exit**, and press ENTER.
12. Click the Name property, type **cmdExit**, and press ENTER.

That completes the appearance of the visual interface. Kronos #1 is looking good—now make it do something. Write code. Begin with the command button named "cmdDate" and captioned "Date." Double-click it to open its code window. The first and last statements (the template) of the event procedure appear:

```
Private Sub cmdDate_Click()
|
End Sub
```

Complete the event procedure by typing a **Print Date** statement so that the code looks like this:

```
Private Sub cmdDate_Click()
  Print Date
End Sub
```

Write the event procedure for cmdTime, now captioned "Time." Click the Object box arrow to pull down the object list, and then click cmdTime in the object list to begin the event procedure. The finished procedure should look like this:

```
Private Sub cmdTime_Click()
  Print Time
End Sub
```

Two done and one to go. Click the Object box and then click cmdExit to begin event procedure cmdExit_Click. Complete the procedure:

```
Private Sub cmdExit_Click()
  End
End Sub
```

That's it. Project Kronos #1 is complete. Run it. Click "Date" and then click "Time." If all goes well, you will see the date and time printed like this in the upper-left corner of the form:

```
11/9/95
10:25:37 AM
```

Click merrily away. Click "Date" to print the date; click "Time" to print the time; click the form instead of a button—nothing happens; click "Exit" to escape all this chronological clickety-clacking.

▼ Save project Kronos #1. We suggest the filename Kronos #1 - Date and Time.

It would be nice to click a button and clear any dates and times from the form. Easy—add a command button with an event procedure that uses a **Cls** statement. The **Cls** statement clears all text from the form. The specifications for this add-on command button are shown below. Since the existing command buttons have been renamed cmdDate, cmdTime, and cmdExit, this command button will appear as Command1. The visual interface and event procedure specifications for Command1 are:

Object	Property	Default Setting	Change Setting To
Command1	Caption	Command1	Clear form
	Name	Command1	cmdClearForm

Object Name	Event	Response
cmdClearForm	Click	Clears the form (**Cls**)

Here is event procedure cmdClearForm_Click:

```
Private Sub cmdClearForm_Click()
  Cls
End Sub
```

Add command button cmdClearForm to project Kronos #1. Change the name of the form to "frmKronos2" and save the modified project as Kronos #2 - Date and Time. Remember to save the form file first by using the File menu's Save File As... command; then save the project file by using the File menu's Save Project As... command. When run, the finished project might look like this:

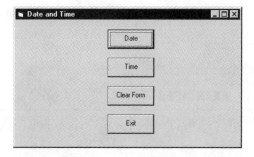

Try it. Click Date to print the date; click Time to print the time; click Clear Form to clear all text from the form; click Exit to make a timely escape.

We like to use the mouse to select and activate the button we want. If you are a keyboard aficionado, you may be pleased to know that you can use TAB to move to the button you want and then press ENTER to activate it. This activity is controlled by the TabIndex settings of the buttons on the form. The button whose TabIndex setting is zero (0) is selected at run time and looks different than the other buttons. Press ENTER to activate it. Press TAB to move to the button whose TabIndex setting is one (1). Press ENTER to activate it. And so on. In project Kronos #2, our TabIndex settings are:

Object Name	Property	Setting
cmdDate	TabIndex	0
cmdTime	TabIndex	1
cmdClearForm	TabIndex	2
cmdExit	TabIndex	3

Make these settings in your project Kronos #2, run the project, and press ENTER to print the date. Press TAB to move to the "Print Time" button and press ENTER to print the time. Et cetera, et cetera.

The **Now** function returns both the date and the time. You can use a **Print Now** statement to print both the date and the time on the form. The **Timer** function returns the number of seconds since midnight on the computer's clock. You can use a **Print Timer** statement to display the value of **Timer** on the form.

Statement	Action	Example
Print Now	Prints the date and the time on the form	11/9/1995 10:25:37 AM
Print Timer	Prints the number of seconds since midnight	37587.86

Now is the time to use the **Now** and **Timer** functions in these timely exercises.

EXERCISES

1. Briefly describe the action performed by each of the following statements:

   a. Cls

   b. Print Date

   c. Print Time

   d. Print Now

   e. Print Timer

   f. End

2. Design project Kronos #3 - Date, Time, Now, and Timer according to the specifications in Tables 2-7 and 2-8.

Object	Property	Default Setting	Final Setting
Form1	Caption	Form1	Date, Time, Now, and Timer
	Name	Form1	frmKronos3
Command1	Caption	Command1	Date
	Name	Command1	cmdDate
	TabIndex	0	0 (selected at run time)
Command2	Caption	Command2	Time
	Name	Command2	cmdTime
	TabIndex		1
Command3	Caption	Command3	Now
	Name	Command3	cmdNow
	TabIndex		2
Command4	Caption	Command4	Timer
	Name	Command4	cmdTimer
	TabIndex		3
Command5	Caption	Command5	Clear Form
	Name	Command5	cmdClearForm
	TabIndex		4
Command6	Caption	Command6	Quit
	Name	Command6	cmdQuit
	TabIndex		5

TABLE 2-7 *Visual Interface Specifications for Project Kronos #3 - Date, Time, Now, and Timer* ▼

Object Name	Event	Response
frmKronos3	none	none
cmdDate	Click	Prints the date on the form (**Print Date**).
cmdTime	Click	Prints the time on the form (**Print Time**).
cmdNow	Click	Prints the date and time on the form (**Print Now**).
cmdTimer	Click	Prints the number of seconds since midnight on the form (**Print Timer**).
cmdClearForm	Click	Clears all text from the form.
cmdQuit	Click	Ends the run.

TABLE 2-8 *Event Procedure Specifications for Project Kronos #3 - Date, Time, Now, and Timer* ▼

2.5 PRINT YOUR NAME AND OTHER THINGS, SUCH AS STRINGS

A *string* is a bunch of characters all strung together. A string can be:

▼ A name, such as "Laran Stardrake"

▼ A telephone number, such as "707-555-1212"

▼ A message, such as "Reality expands to fill the available fantasies."

▼ Gibberish, such as "2#3bZ@%W&"

You can use a **Print** statement to print a string on the form.

Statement	Action	String That Appears
Print "Laran Stardrake"	Prints Laran Stardrake's name.	Laran Stardrake
Print "707-555-1212"	Prints the telephone number.	707-555-1212
Print "2#3bZ@%W&"	Prints gibberish.	2#3bZ@%W&

In each of the above **Print** statements, quotation marks enclose the string that is printed. The quotation marks enclose the string, but they are not part of the string. They tell Visual Basic where the string begins and ends. These quotation marks are not printed on the form.

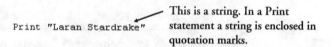

```
Print "Laran Stardrake"
```
This is a string. In a Print statement a string is enclosed in quotation marks.

There is even an *empty string*, a string that has no characters. It can be represented by a pair of quotation marks with nothing between them (""). Do not confuse the empty string ("") with a string that has one space enclosed in quotation marks (" "). You use spaces to separate words. If you used empty strings instead of spaces to separate words, your text might be somewhat hard to read. For example:

Ifyouusedemptystringstoseparatewordsitwouldlooklikethis.

You can use a **Print** statement with strings to print most anything on the form. Project Fortune Cookie #1 has one form and three command buttons. Here is a sample run after someone clicked "Fortune #1":

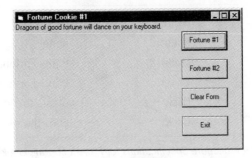

The event procedure for the command button captioned "Fortune #1" prints "Dragons of good fortune will dance on your keyboard." The event procedure for the command button captioned "Fortune #2" prints "Reality expands to fill the available fantasies." The Clear Form and Exit buttons do their usual things. Table 2-9 shows the visual interface specifications for project Fortune Cookie #1 and Table 2-10 lists the event procedure specifications. We don't show the TabIndex settings, so set them the way you want them.

We suspect that you have become quite adept at drawing the visual interface, so we won't bore you with a long list of detailed instructions. In case you may need some reminding, here are distilled directions:

1. Put Command1 on the form; click and drag it to where you want it.

2. Put Command2 on the form.

3. Click and drag both buttons to where you want them.

4. Put Command3 on the form.

Object	Property	Default Setting	Final Setting
Form1	Caption	Form1	Fortune Cookie #1
	Name	Form1	frmFortune1
Command1	Caption	Command1	Fortune #1
	Name	Command1	cmdFortune1
Command2	Caption	Command2	Fortune #2
	Name	Command2	cmdFortune2
Command3	Caption	Command3	Clear Form
	Name	Command3	cmdClearForm
Command4	Caption	Command4	Exit
	Name	Command4	cmdExit

TABLE 2-9   *Visual Interface Specifications for Project Fortune Cookie #1* ▼

Object Name	Event	Response
frmFortune1	none	none
cmdFortune1	Click	Prints Fortune #1.
cmdFortune2	Click	Prints Fortune #2.
cmdClearForm	Click	Clears the form.
cmdExit	Click	Ends the run.

TABLE 2-10 *Event Procedure Specifications for Project Fortune Cookie #1*   ▼

5. Move all three buttons to where you want them.

6. Set the properties for all objects as specified in Table 2-9.

You already know how to write event procedures cmdClearForm_Click and cmdExit_Click. Here are event procedures cmdFortune1_Click and cmdFortune2_Click:

```
Private Sub cmdFortune1()
  Cls
  Print "Dragons of good fortune will dance on your keyboard."
End Sub

Private Sub cmdFortune2()
  Cls
  Print "Reality expands to fill the available fantasies."
End Sub
```

We saved the project with the filenames Fortune Cookie #1.frm for the form file and Fortune Cookie #1.vbp for the project file.

Move on boldly and try it! Run the project, click "Fortune #1" and, with luck, see "Dragons of good fortune will dance on your keyboard." printed in the upper-left corner of the form. Click "Fortune #2" and see "Reality expands to fill the available fantasies." printed in the upper-left corner of the form.

First, the bad news. After someone sees both fortunes, there's not much fun in continued clicking. And now the good news. In Chapter 10, you will create a fortune cookie application in which the fortune is chosen randomly from a bunch of fortunes—as many as you want to enter in the fortune cookie database.

EXERCISES

1. Write a **Print** statement to print each of these strings on the form.

    a. Twinkle Starr

    b. Remember that a command button is a control.

    c. ---<MMMMMM@

2. Create project Letterhead #1 to print Laran Stardrake's name, address, and whimsical choice of a phone number on the form. When you run it and click the "Letterhead" button, project Letterhead should look like this:

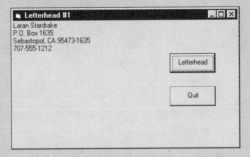

Tables 2-11 and 2-12 list the visual interface specifications for project Letterhead #1 and show the event procedure specifications.

Object	Property	Default Setting	Final Setting
Form1	Caption	Form1	Letterhead #1
	Name	Form1	frmLetterhead1
Command1	Caption	Command1	Letterhead
	Name	Command1	cmdLetterhead
Command2	Caption	Command2	Quit
	Name	Command2	cmdQuit

TABLE 2-11   *Visual Interface Specifications for Project Letterhead #1* ▼

Object Name	Event	Response
frmLetterHead	none	none
cmdLetterhead	Click	Clears the form and prints the letterhead (four **Print** statements).
cmdQuit	Click	Ends the run.

TABLE 2-12   *Event Procedure Specifications for Project Letterhead #1* ▼

Each time you click "Letterhead," blink—the form is cleared and the letterhead is printed in the same place.

2.6 *L*EARN MORE ABOUT FORMS

Start a new project. You will do a bunch of activities with Form1 in this section. Form1's caption bar has a control-menu icon, a maximize button, a minimize button, and a close button:

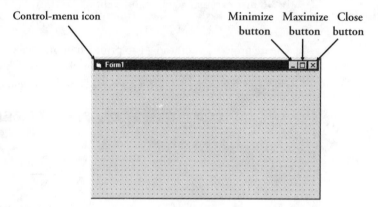

Control-menu icon   Minimize Maximize Close
                                      button   button   button

You can use these controls at design time to close Form1, maximize it, or minimize it:

▼ **Close Form1** Click its close button or double-click its control-menu icon. Poof! It's gone. To open Form1, double-click "Form1" in the project window.

▼ **Maximize Form1** Click its maximize button. Form1 grows to fill the entire screen and the maximize button changes to a restore button. To restore Form1 to its previous size, click the restore button.

▼ **Minimize Form1** Click its minimize button. Form1 disappears; its icon remains on the taskbar. To retrieve Form1, click its icon on the taskbar or double-click "Form1" in the project window.

You can use Form1's control-menu icon, maximize button, minimize button, and close button at run time too. If you close Form1 at run time, you return to the Design screen. Go ahead—run this do-nothing project. During the run, maximize Form1 and restore it, minimize it and restore it, and then close it. When you close Form1, you return to the design screen.

Form1's ControlBox, MaxButton, and MinButton properties determine whether the control-menu icon, maximize button, minimize button, and close button appear **at run time**. The default setting for each of these properties is True, so you usually see the icon and the three buttons at run time. Set the ControlBox property to False:

1. Click Form1 to select it.

2. Click the ControlBox property. A *Properties button* appears in the Settings box:

Properties button

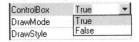

3. Click the Properties button to open a menu of possible selections:

4. Click the False choice. It appears in the Settings box.

Well, that's the slow way to change a setting that has True or False values. Use the quick way to change the MaxButton and MinButton settings from True to False:

▼ Double-click the MaxButton property. Its setting changes from True to False.

▼ Double-click the MinButton property. Its setting changes from True to False.

Run the project. At run time with the ControlBox, MaxButton, and MinButton settings set to False, Form1 looks like this:

Oops! At run time, you can't maximize Form1, you can't minimize it, and you can't close it. What can you still do to Form1? Well, you can move it by clicking and dragging the caption bar. You can resize it by clicking and dragging a border. You can end the run, return to the design screen and give back Form1's handy run time controls.

Click the End tool in the toolbar to end the run and return to the design screen. Form1 has a control-menu icon, maximize button, minimize button, and close button in the design screen and they all work just fine. The settings of the ControlBox, MaxButton, and MinButton properties affect only the run time appearance and behavior of Form1. Now return Form1 to its more controllable condition:

1. Set the ControlBox property to True.

2. Set the MaxButton property to True.

3. Set the MinButton property to True.

The default setting of Form1's BorderStyle property is 2 - Sizable. This setting lets you resize Form1 at run time. BorderStyle has six possible settings:

0	None
1	Fixed Single
2	Sizable
3	Fixed Dialog
4	Fixed ToolWindow
5	Sizable ToolWindow

You know about 2 - Sizable, so try each of the other settings, run the project, and see what happens. You have probably guessed that you can't resize a form at run time if its BorderStyle property is set to 1 - Fixed Single or 3 - Fixed Dialog. Or can you? Try it and find out.

Suppose that you put some controls on a form exactly where you want them in an aesthetically pleasing arrangement. The form is exactly the shape and size you want. Each control is the distance from the left edge of the form that suits you and the distance from the top of the form is precisely correct. You can set the BorderStyle to 1 - Fixed Single so that the user cannot undo your good work at run time by changing the size of the form.

A form can respond to an event. The default event for a form is Load and the name of its event procedure is Form_Load. When you run a project, Visual Basic loads the form and displays it in the run time screen. If you have written event procedure Form_Load, it is executed. Let's write event procedure Form_Load. It prints "I'm loaded!" and then beeps.

Double-click Form1 to open the code window. Visual Basic displays the first and last lines of event procedure Form_Load. Add a **Print** statement and a **Beep** statement to complete this event procedure for project Form Load #1:

```
Private Sub Form_Load()
  Print "I'm loaded!"
  Beep
End Sub
```

Close the code window and run the project. Form1 appears in the run time screen and beeps, but doesn't print the string "I'm loaded!" In order to see the result of a **Print** statement executed in the Form_Load procedure, you must set Form1's AutoRedraw property to True. So do it now—stop the run, return to the design screen, and set the AutoRedraw property to True.

Now run the project. You hear a beep and see this:

Well, that worked! Because the AutoRedraw property is set to True, the string "I'm loaded!" was printed on the form. When AutoRedraw is set to True the form is saved as an image in the computer's memory and anything printed to the form is saved to this image as well. If we print to the form before it's visible our text still remains because the image in the computer's memory remembers what was printed on the form. To make sure that AutoRedraw is set to True, you can do it in the Form_Load procedure for project Form Load #2 as shown here:

```
Private Sub Form_Load()
  AutoRedraw = True
  Print "I'm loaded!"
  Beep
End Sub
```

Perhaps you have noticed that text is printed beginning at the upper-left corner of the form. You can use the CurrentX and CurrentY properties to locate text anywhere in the form. These properties do not appear in the Properties window—you use code to set them.

▼ The value of CurrentX is the distance from the inside left edge of the form.

▼ The value of CurrentY is the distance down from the form's caption bar.

Project Form Load #3 prints "I'm loaded!" near the center of the form, thanks to this event procedure:

```
Private Sub Form_Load()
  AutoRedraw = True
  CurrentX = 2520
  CurrentY = 1440
  Print "I'm loaded!"
  Beep
End Sub
```

Run this project to see "I'm loaded!" printed near the center of the form and hear a beep.

A form can respond to a Click event, a double-click (DblClick) event, and a bunch of other events. Start a new project and make Form1 the size you want, then try these steps:

1. Click the View Code button in the project window to open the code window.

2. Click the Object box arrow to get a list of objects. The only object is "Form."

3. Click "Form." The Form_Load event procedure template appears and "Load" appears in the Procedure box.

4. Click the Procedure (Proc) box arrow to get a list of events for Form.

5. Scroll to the top of the list. The top three events are Activate, Click, and DblClick.

6. Click "Click." The Form_Load event procedure changes to Form_Click.

7. Click the Procedure box's arrow to get the list of events.

8. Click "DblClick." The Form_Click event procedure template changes to Form_DblClick.

Load your backpack and trundle on down to the exercises. In one of them, you will write event procedures Form_Click and Form_DblClick.

EXERCISES

1. For each property and its setting, describe the effect of the setting on the form at run time.

Property	Setting	Comment
AutoRedraw	True	
	False	
ControlBox	True	
	False	
CurrentX	2400	This property does not appear in the Properties window.
CurrentY	1200	This property does not appear in the Properties window.
MaxButton	True	
	False	
MinButton	True	
	False	

2. If you click the control-menu icon *once* at run time, you pull down its menu of commands. The commands that you see depend on the settings of the ControlBox, MaxButton, and MinButton properties. For each of the following combinations of settings, list the commands that appear in the menu.

	ControlBox	MaxButton	MinButton	Control-Menu Commands
	True	True	True	Restore, Move, Size, Minimize, Maximize, Close, Switch To
a.	True	False	True	
b.	True	True	False	
c.	True	False	False	

3. The appearance or nonappearance of control-menu commands also depends on the setting of the BorderStyle property. List the border style settings and show the control-menu commands for each setting.

4. Design project Form Load #4 - Click and DblClick. Event procedure Form_Load prints "Experiment! Click me and double-click me." Event procedure Form_Click prints "You clicked." and beeps. Event procedure Form_DblClick prints "You double-clicked." and beeps. Explain the perhaps unexpected thing that happens when you double-click the form.

2.7 ADD TOOLS AND TOYS TO YOUR VISUAL BASIC BACKPACK

Take a break. Sit under a tree, lean back, and think about the things you learned in this chapter. You worked on several projects.

▼ You saw that each project has at least one **form** and can have one or more **command buttons**. Forms and command buttons are Visual Basic **objects**. A command button is a Visual Basic **control**.

▼ You designed a project's **visual interface** by putting command buttons on the form, dragging them to their proper places, and changing the **settings** for selected **properties** of the form and the command buttons.

▼ You **wrote code**. You wrote **event procedures** that enabled objects to respond to **events**. You wrote code that enabled command buttons and the form to respond to mouse clicks. You wrote code to make things happen when the form is loaded at run time.

▼ You saved projects to a disk. Perhaps you used the filenames we suggested, or maybe you coined your own filenames. By whatever names, you now have a small portfolio of Visual Basic projects in your backpack.

▼ You ran each project. We hope that they all worked the first time. We trust that you carefully examined any bug-infested project, gently removed the bugs, and made the project work.

In writing event procedures, you used several Visual Basic **statements**. Here are some examples:

Statement	Action
Private Sub *Object_Event*( )	Begins an event procedure called *Object_Event* (such as Command1_Click).
Beep	Sounds a beep on the computer's sound system.
Cls	Clears all text from the form.
End	Ends a run and returns to the design screen.
Print Date	Prints the date on the form.
Print Time	Prints the time on the form.
Print Now	Prints the date and the time on the form.
Print Timer	Prints the number of seconds since midnight on the form.
Print "Laran Stardrake"	Prints the string enclosed in quotation marks on the form.
End Sub	Ends an event procedure.

Statement	Action
AutoRedraw = True	Sets the form's AutoRedraw property to True.
CurrentX = 2520	Sets the horizontal coordinate for printing on the form.
CurrentY = 1440	Sets the vertical coordinate for printing on the form.

Date, **Time**, **Now**, and **Timer** are Visual Basic **functions**. When used, a function returns a **value**. **Date** returns the date according to the computer's calendar and **Time** returns the time according to the computer's clock. **Now** returns both the date and time. **Timer** returns the number of seconds after midnight, from 0 at midnight to 86,399 at one second before midnight.

You can use Visual Basic's Help system to learn more about Visual Basic. Click the Help menu on the Menu bar to pull down the Help menu:

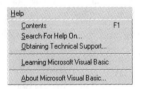

To learn more about Visual Basic, click "Learning Microsoft Visual Basic" and cruise the online tutorial. To get help on a specific topic, click "Search for Help On..." and use its dialog box to look for help. For example, look for help about the form, command button, event, Print, Date, Cls, and anything else you are curious about. To see what's available, click "Contents" and then hypertext your way along this path, that path, another path.

Well, your Visual Basic backpack is getting heavier, but that's okay 'cause you are getting stronger.

mastery skills check

1. List the seven easy steps that you use to create a Visual Basic project.

2. What two types of objects are used in this chapter's projects?

3. How do you change:

   a. The setting of the Caption property of an object?

   b. The setting of the Name property of an object?

   c. The size of the form?

   d. The size of a command button?

4. Visual Basic has conventions for naming objects. An object name consists of a standard prefix and a suffix that you select.

   a. What is the standard prefix for a form?

   b. What is the standard prefix for a command button?

5. Complete this sentence: The name of an event procedure consists of _____, the underscore character, and _____.

6. Project Kronos #4 - Start and Stop Times is shown here at run time after someone has clicked the Start Time button, waited a few seconds, and then clicked the Stop Time button. You click Start Time to print the string "Start time:" and the value of **Timer**. Click Stop Time to print the string "Stop time:" and the value of **Timer**. The difference between the two times is the elapsed time between the two clicks. Think of Kronos #4 as a primitive stopwatch. Later in this book, you will create more elegant stopwatches. Click Clear Form to clear the form and click The End to end the run.

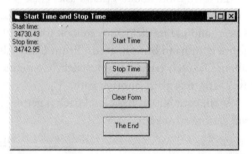

   First write a table of specifications for project Kronos #4 and then create the project according to your specifications.

7. Create Fortune #3 and add it to the fortune cookie project. Update the table of specifications and call this project Fortune Cookie #2.

8. Visual Basic has functions that operate on a date function such as **Date** or **Now** and return the year, month (1 to 12), day of the month (1 to 31), and the day of the week (1 to 7). Suppose that your computer thinks that it is Monday, October 23, 1996. You can use these **Print** statements to print the date (10/23/96), year (1996), month (10), day of the month (23), and day of the week (2) on the form:

The Statement	Prints	Comment
Print Date	10/23/96	Prints the value of the **Date** function.
Print Year(Date)	1996	Prints the year in the value of **Date**.
Print Month(Date)	10	Prints the month in the value of **Date**.
Print Day(Date)	23	Prints the day of the month in the value of **Date**.
Print Weekday(Date)	2	Prints the day of the week in the value of **Date.**

Project Kronos #5 - Year, Month, Day, and Weekday has buttons "Date," "Year," "Month," "Day," and "Weekday" that you click to print on the form the value of the function whose name is on the button. Write the specs and create project Kronos #5.

9. Visual Basic has functions that operate on a time function such as **Time** or **Now** and return the hour of a day (0 to 23), minute of the hour (0 to 59), and second of the minute (0 to 59). Suppose that your computer thinks that it is 2:37:45 P.M. You can use these **Print** statements to print the time (2:37:45 PM), hour (14), minute (37), and second (45) on the form:

The Statement	Prints	Comment
Print Time	2:37:45 PM	Prints the value of the **Time** function.
Print Hour(Time)	14	Prints the hour in the value of **Time.**
Print Minute(Time)	37	Prints the minute in the value of **Time.**
Print Second(Time)	45	Prints the second in the value of **Time.**

Project Kronos #6 - Hour, Minute, and Second has buttons "Time," "Hour," "Minute," and "Second" that you click to print on the form the value of the function whose name is on the button. Write the specs and create project Kronos #6.

10. Combine projects Kronos #5 and Kronos #6 into a single project called Kronos #7 - Demonstrate Date and Time Functions. Instead of using **Date** or **Time**, use **Now** to supply both the date and time. For example: Print Year(Now), Print Month(Now), Print Hour(Now), and Print Minute(Now). The function buttons are captioned: Now, Year, Month, Day, Weekday, Hour, Second, and Minute. Write the specs and create project Kronos #7.

11. Keep up the good work.

3

Road Signs And Trail Markers

chapter objectives

3.1 Display timely text in a text box

3.2 Design a factory reject stopwatch

3.3 Fix the factory reject stopwatch

3.4 Display strings in text boxes

3.5 Enter strings into text boxes from the keyboard

3.6 Add scroll bars to text boxes

3.7 Add a little pizazz to forms and labels

3.8 Use the QBColor function to add color to your projects

3.9 Use the RGB function to add color to your projects

YOU can put neat little boxes here, there, anywhere on a form and then display information in them. You can display text in *text boxes* and put *labels* next to boxes to inform viewers about what they are viewing. Look for the tools you need near the top of the toolbox. You can double-click the Label tool to put a label on the form, and you can double-click the TextBox tool to put a text box on the form:

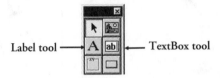

Label tool ——→   ←—— TextBox tool

Most of the objects that you can select from the toolbox are controls. A command button is a control. Labels and text boxes are also controls. Figure 3-1 shows a design screen form with two labels and two text boxes. Label1 and Text1 are shown as they appear when first placed on the design screen, before any properties are changed. Label1 does not have a visible border in the design screen; we selected it so that you can see the position of its caption inside its invisible border. Label1's BorderStyle property has the default setting, 0 - None. Text box Text1 contains its default text "Text1". Its border is visible in the design screen and looks three-dimensional. Text1's BorderStyle property has the default setting, 1 - Fixed Single.

FIGURE 3-1

Label1 and Text1 are shown in their default border styles. We changed the BorderStyle property settings of Label2 and Text2.
▼

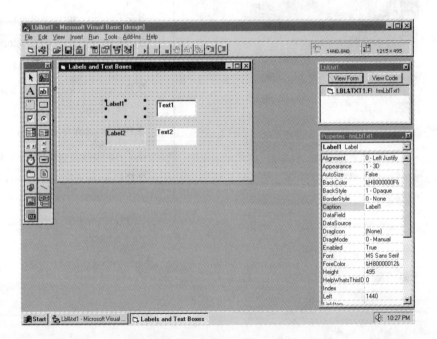

We changed the BorderStyle settings of Label2 and Text2. Label2's BorderStyle setting is 1 - Fixed Single and Text2's BorderStyle setting is 0 - None. You can see Text2's boundary because its background color is white, different from Form1's background color, which is gray.

3.1 *D*ISPLAY TIMELY TEXT IN A TEXT BOX

You already know how to print the values of **Date**, **Time**, **Now**, and **Timer** directly on the form. Now explore another way to display timely text. You can put text boxes wherever you want them on the form and then display the values of **Date**, **Time**, **Now**, or **Timer** inside the text boxes.

Project Kronos #8 - Time in a Text Box has one form, one text box, and two command buttons. When you run it and click the Time button, you will see the current time displayed in the text box:

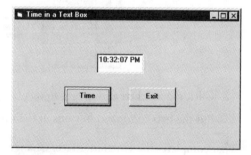

Tables 3-1 and 3-2 list the specifications for project Kronos #8. In Table 3-1, notice that the Text property of the text box is empty. To do this, you delete the default "Text1" that appears when you place the text box on the form.

Object	Property	Default Setting	Final Setting	Comment
Form1	Caption	Form1	Time in a Text Box	
	Name	Form1	frmKronos8	
Text1	Text	Text1		Empty. Delete "Text1."
	Name	Text1	txtTime	
Command1	Caption	Command1	Time	
	Name	Command1	cmdTime	
Command2	Caption	Command2	Exit	
	Name	Command2	cmdExit	

TABLE 3-1 *Visual Interface Specifications for Project Kronos #8* ▼

Object Name	Event	Response
frmTime	None	None
txtTime	None	None
cmdTime	Click	Displays the time in text box txtTime.
cmdExit	Click	Ends the run.

TABLE 3-2 *Event Procedure Specifications for Project Kronos #8* ▼

Start in the design screen and place the text box on the form like this:

1. Double-click the Text box tool in the toolbox. The text box appears near the center of the form with "Text1" inside the box:

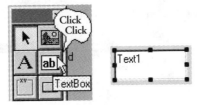

2. Click the text box and drag it to its place on the form.

3. Put the two command buttons in their places on the form.

That completes the visual interface. Change the property settings as specified in the specifications. You already know how to change the property settings of the form and the two command buttons. A text box does not have a Caption property. Instead, it has a Text property. You can see the default setting "Text1" inside the box. Change the settings for the text box like this:

1. Click the text box to select it. The selection handles appear.

2. In the Properties window, click the Text property. Its default setting is "Text1."

3. Press BACKSPACE to erase "Text1" from the Settings box.

If all goes well, the Text property setting will now be empty. On the form, the text box is also empty. If these are not both empty, click the Text property, erase any text you see in the Settings box, and press ENTER.

The default setting of the text box's Name property is "Text1." We prefer something more descriptive. The standard prefix for the name of a text box is "txt." Let's name this text box "txtTime."

Object	Prefix	Our Suffix	Complete Name
Text1	txt	Time	txtTime

4. Click the Name property and change the setting to "txtTime."

Now install the event procedures for the command buttons, cmdTime and cmdExit. You already know the code for cmdExit. The event procedure for command button cmdTime is:

```
Private Sub cmdTime_Click()
   txtTime.Text = Time
End Sub
```

Keep in mind that "cmdTime" is the name of the command button captioned "Time." During a run, if you click the Time button, event procedure cmdTime_Click executes the following statement:

```
txtTime.Text = Time
```

This statement assigns the value of **Time** as the new value of the Text property of txtTime. Oops, what was that again? Well, the statement tells Visual Basic to peek into the area in the computer's memory where the value of **Time** is stored and copy that value as the new value of the Text property of the text box named "txtTime." Every object and property combination has a name that consists of the name of the object, a period, and the name of the property:

Object Name	Property	Object.Property Name
txtTime	Text	txtTime.Text

Once more we remind you to save the project. From now on, it's up to you to save or not save the project.

Run the project and click the Time button, and the time should appear in the text box. Click the Time button again to see another time. Time is moving on, so click the Exit button and reinforce your new know-how by browsing some ToolTalk and working a couple of easy exercises.

 TOOLTALK *We usually double-click a toolbox tool to put a control on the form, drag it to where we want it, and resize it if we want a size other than the default size. On our screen, the default size for a label, text box, or command button is 1215 x 495 twips. You can see an object's dimensions by first selecting the object and then viewing its Width and Height properties in the Properties window or viewing its size in the object size box.*

You can also draw a control such as a command button, label, or text box on the screen like this:

1. Click the control's tool *once* to select it.

2. Move the mouse pointer to the form—it changes to a cross-hair.

3. Put the cross-hair where you want the control to appear.

4. Click and drag to draw the control the size you want.

You can use a control's Width and Height properties to set its width and height to specific numerical values, expressed in twips. For example, to make a text box 2400 twips wide and 600 twips high, follow these steps:

1. Click the text box to select it.

2. Click the Width property to select it.

3. Type **2400** and press ENTER.

4. Click the Height property to select it.

5. Type **600** and press ENTER.

You may need to draw objects in non-default sizes as you munch on these easy exercises.

EXERCISES

1. What is the standard prefix for the name of a label? the name of a text box?

2. Describe how to put a label or a text box on the form in the location and size you want.

3. Tables 3-3 and 3-4 show the specifications for project Kronos #9 - Date and Time in a Text Box.

Object	Property	Default Setting	Change Setting To	Comment
Form1	Caption	Form1	Date and Time in a Text Box	
	Name	Form1	frmKronos9	
Text1	Text	Text1		Empty. Delete "Text1."
	Name	Text1	txtNow	
Command1	Caption	Command1	Date and Time	
	Name	Command1	cmdNow	
Command2	Caption	Command2	Exit	

TABLE 3-3 *Visual Interface Specifications for Project Kronos #9 - Date and Time in a Text Box* ▼

Object Name	Event	Response
frmNow	None	None
txtNow	None	None
cmdNow	Click	Displays the date and time (value of **Now**) in txtNow.
cmdExit	Click	Ends the run.

TABLE 3-4 *Event Procedure Specifications for Project Kronos #9 - Date and Time in a Text Box* ▼

A sample run is shown here with the date and time in a text box. The text box is wider than the default width. Draw the visual interface, set properties, and install the code for event procedure cmdNow_Click.

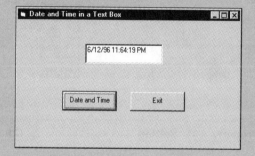

3.2 **D**ESIGN A FACTORY REJECT STOPWATCH

Project Kronos #10 - Factory Reject Stopwatch almost makes it as a stopwatch, but it has a major problem. You click the Start button to start the stopwatch and display the starting time in a labeled text box. You click the Stop button to stop the stopwatch and display that time in another labeled text box. So you see the starting and stopping times, both displayed as the number of seconds after midnight (value of **Timer**). The problem is that you don't see the elapsed time. We'll fix that problem later in the next section. Here is a sample run of Kronos #10:

Tables 3-5 and 3-6 show the specifications for project Kronos #10. It has one form, two text boxes, two labels, and three command buttons. From now on, we will no longer show the default settings in a specifications table. In the Setting column in Table 3-5, we show the final setting for any property that is changed from the default setting. In Table 3-6, we show only objects that respond to events. Notice that event procedure cmdStart_Click displays the starting time (value of **Timer**) in txtStart and then clears txtStop. Therefore, txtStop is empty until you click the Stop button.

Draw the visual interface by following these steps:

1. Put label Label1 on the form and move it up and left to its place. (To put a label on the form, double-click the Label tool.)

Object	Property	Setting	Comment
Form1	Caption	Factory Reject Stopwatch	
	Name	frmKronos10	
Text1	Text		Empty. Delete "Text1."
	Name	txtStart	
Text2	Text		Empty. Delete "Text2."
	Name	txtStop	
Label1	Caption	Start time:	
	Name	lblStart	The standard prefix for a label is "lbl."
Label2	Caption	Stop time:	
	Name	lblStop	The standard prefix for a label is "lbl."
Command1	Caption	Start	
	Name	cmdStart	
Command2	Caption	Stop	
	Name	cmdStop	
Command3	Caption	Exit	
	Name	cmdExit	

TABLE 3-5 *Visual Interface Specifications for Project Kronos #10 - Factory Reject Stopwatch* ▼

Object Name	Event	Response
cmdStart	Click	Displays the value of **Timer** in txtStart, clears txtStop, and beeps.
cmdStop	Click	Displays the value of **Timer** in txtStop and beeps.
cmdExit	Click	Ends the run.

TABLE 3-6 *Event Procedure Specifications for Project Kronos #10 - Factory Reject Stopwatch* ▼

2. Put text box Text1 on the form and move it just to the right of Label1.

3. Put label Label2 on the form and move it below Label1.

4. Put text box Text2 on the form and move it just to the right of Label2.

5. Put Command1 on the form and position it to the right of Text1.

6. Put Command2 on the form and place it to the right of Text2.

7. Put Command3 on the form and move it below Command2.

Set the properties of the form and the controls. For both text boxes, the Text property should be empty.

Write code. Command button cmdStart responds to a click by displaying the value of **Timer** in text box txtStart. It then clears text box txtStop by displaying the empty string ("") in it. Remember, the empty string is empty—it has no characters. The procedure beeps to remind you that time is marching on.

The code for event procedure cmdStart_Click is shown below. Two lines contain comments to help you understand what is happening. A comment consists of an apostrophe (') followed by text. Comments are for people. Visual Basic ignores any text following an apostrophe in a line of code. From now on, we will frequently use comments to help you read and understand code.

```
Private Sub cmdStart_Click()
    txtStart.Text = Timer        ' Assign Timer to txtStart.Text
    txtStop.Text = ""            ' Clear txtStop
    Beep
End Sub
```

 REMEMBER txtStart.Text *is the name of the Text property of text box txtStart and* txtStop.Text *is the name of the Text property of text box txtStop.*

Object Type	Object Name	Property	Object.Property Name
Text box	txtStart	Text	txtStart.Text
Text box	txtStop	Text	txtStop.Text

In event procedure cmdStart_Click, *txtStart.Text* and *txtStop.Text* are assigned values like this:

Statement	Action
txtStart.Text = Timer	Assigns the value of **Timer** to txtStart.Text. It appears in txtStart.
txtStop.Text = ""	Assigns the empty string to txtStop.Text. Clears txtStop.

Event procedure cmdStop_Click is:

```
Private Sub cmdStop_Click()
    txtStop.Text = Timer          ' Assign Timer to txtStop.Text
    Beep
End Sub
```

Finish the project and run it. The form should appear with both text boxes empty. Click the Start button to display the start time in text box txtStart. Click the Stop button to display the stop time in text box txtStop. Click Start again. Event procedure cmdStart_Click should display the new start time in txtStart and clear txtStop. Click Exit to end the run.

Do the labels "Start Time:" and "Stop Time:" seem a little far left? We think so. The labels in lblStart and lblStop are *left-justified*—they begin at the left edge of the label box. To see this, click a label to display its selection handles:

You can control a label's alignment by setting its Alignment property to 0 - Left Justify, 1 - Right Justify, or 2 - Center. The default setting is 0 - Left Justify:

Object Name	Property	Default Setting
lblStart	Alignment	0 - Left Justify

Change lblStart's Alignment setting first to 1 - Right Justify and then to 2 - Center like this:

1. Click lblStart to select it. The selection handles appear.

2. In the Properties window, click the Alignment property. A *Properties button* appears in the Setting box:

   3. Click the Properties button to open a menu of possible settings:

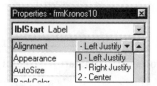

   4. Click the setting that you want. It appears in the Setting box and the text
      in the label moves to that alignment.

   Try all three alignments and see what happens to the label. Here are all three
alignments shown with selection handles so that you can see the position of the
label inside its box:

   As you drive up the road in a vehicle, keep it right-justified, except when
passing. When you walk up the road, do it left-justified so that you are facing
traffic and can quickly leap onto the ditch to avoid approaching danger.

EXERCISE

   1. Modify the visual interface and rewrite the specifications table for project
      Kronos #10 - Factory Reject Stopwatch using right-justified labels.

3.3 FIX THE FACTORY REJECT STOPWATCH

   How can we fix the factory reject stopwatch and display the elapsed time?
Easy—subtract the start time from the stop time and put the difference in a text
box labeled "Elapsed time:". The visual interface for project Kronos #11 -
Stopwatch looks like this:

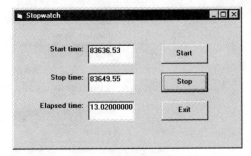

Event procedures cmdStart_Click and cmdStop_Click are:

```
Private Sub cmdStart_Click()
  txtStart.Text = Timer
  txtStop.Text = ""
  txtElapsed.Text = ""
  Beep
End Sub

Private Sub cmdStop_Click()
  txtStop.Text = Timer
  txtElapsed.Text = txtStop.Text - txtStart.Text
  Beep
End Sub
```

In event procedure cmdStop_Click, the statement

```
txtElapsed.Text = txtStop.Text - txtStart.Text
```

subtracts the start time in txtStart from the stop time in txtStop and puts the difference (the elapsed time) in txtElapsed. The value of **Timer** is stored in the text boxes as text strings with up to two decimal places. The computer's clock ticks away at the rate of 18.2 *ticks* per second, so the value of **Timer** is accurate to about $1/18.2 = 0.055$ seconds, or about 55 milliseconds (1 millisecond = 0.001 second). The value of the elapsed time may appear with up to eight decimal places. Here are some values of the stop, start, and elapsed times that we saw during a run:

Stop Time	Start Time	Elapsed Time	Comment
21482.34	21469.11	13.22999999	Why eight decimal places? See discussion.
23406	23402.32	3.68000000	Why eight decimal places? See discussion.
24250.7	24240.7	10	
23666.73	23659.48	7.25	
24300.19	24275.69	24.5	

The elapsed time usually appears with eight decimal places, such as 13.22999999 or 3.68000000. Only the first two decimal places are significant. The other six occur because Visual Basic converts the text strings in the text boxes to *binary* (base 2) numbers before doing the arithmetic. When converted to binary, a start time or stop time that has a decimal fraction may have a tiny error. Therefore, their difference may also have a tiny error that appears when the number is converted to a string and stuffed into text box txtElapsed. It would be nice to round off numbers such as 13.22999999 and 3.68000000 so that they are displayed as 13.23 and 3.68, respectively. You can use the **Format** function to do this.

Project Kronos #12 - Stopwatch is the same as project Kronos #11, except for event procedure cmdStop_Click, which is modified as shown here:

```
Private Sub cmdStop_Click()
  Dim Elapsed As Variant
  txtStop.Text = Timer
  Elapsed = txtStop.Text - txtStart.Text
  txtElapsed.Text = Format(Elapsed, "####0.##")
  Beep
End Sub
```

The statement

```
Dim Elapsed As Variant
```

declares *Elapsed* to be a *variable* of data type *Variant*. This "invents" a variable that can store a number or a string along with information that tells Visual Basic the data type of the value. The Variant data type is very flexible—you can use it without worrying about whether its value is a string, a number, a date, a time, or some other type of data. You will learn more about Variant and other data types in Chapters 7 and 8.

The statement

```
Elapsed = txtStop.Text - txtStart.Text
```

computes the elapsed time and assigns it to the variable *Elapsed*. Since this value is the result of an arithmetic operation, it is stored in Variant variable *Elapsed* as a number. Clever!

The statement

```
txtElapsed.Text = Format(Elapsed, "####0.##")
```

formats the value of *Elapsed*, converts it to a string, and stuffs it into txtElapsed. It will appear with up to five digits to the left of the decimal point, the decimal point, and rounded to two digits to the right of the decimal point. This formatting is specified by the *format string* "####0.##". The zero (0) in the format string causes a zero to be displayed before the decimal point for a number that is less than one. You will learn much more about the **Format** function in Chapters 7 and 8.

EXERCISES

1. Create project Kronos #11 - Stopwatch. Write the specifications table, design the visual interface, set properties, write code, save it, run it, and make it work.

2. Create project Kronos #12 - Stopwatch. Write the specifications table, design the visual interface, set properties, write code, save it, run it, and make it work.

3.4 DISPLAY STRINGS IN TEXT BOXES

You can display a string in a text box by assigning it to the text box's Text property. The following assignment statement will be used in a fortune cookie project:

```
txtFortune.Text = "Dragons of good fortune will dance on your keyboard."
```

This statement assigns the string "Dragons of good fortune will dance on your keyboard." to the Text property of txtFortune. When the statement is executed, the string immediately appears in the text box, replacing its previous contents.

Project Fortune Cookie #3 has one form, one text box, one label, and three command buttons. Here is a sample run showing Fortune #1 in the text box:

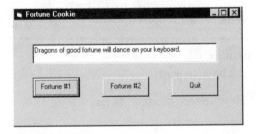

Object	Property	Setting	Comment
Form1	Caption	Fortune Cookie	
	Name	frmFortune3	
Text1	Text		Empty. Delete "Text1."
	Name	txtFortune	
Command1	Caption	Fortune #1	
	Name	cmdFortune1	
Command2	Caption	Fortune #2	
	Name	cmdFortune2	
Command3	Caption	Exit	
	Name	cmdExit	

TABLE 3-7 *Visual Interface Specifications for Project Fortune Cookie #3* ▼

Click the Fortune #1 button and "Dragons of good fortune will dance on your keyboard." appears in the text box. Click the Fortune #2 button and "Reality expands to fill the available fantasies." appears in the text box. Tables 3-7 and 3-8 list the specifications for project Fortune Cookie #3.

Draw the visual interface and set the properties. Event procedures cmdFortune1_Click and cmdFortune2_Click are:

```
Private Sub cmdFortune1_Click()
  txtFortune.Text = "Dragons of good fortune will dance on your keyboard."
End Sub

Private Sub cmdFortune2_Click()
  txtFortune.Text = "Reality expands to fill the available fantasies."
End Sub
```

After you install the event procedures for all three command buttons, run the project and try it. Later in this book, you will expand the fortune cookie project to lots of fortunes that you can view sequentially or randomly.

Object Name	Event	Response
cmdFortune1	Click	Displays Fortune #1 in txtFortune.
cmdFortune2	Click	Displays Fortune #2 in txtFortune.
cmdExit	Click	Ends the run.

TABLE 3-8 *Event Procedure Specifications for Project Fortune Cookie #3* ▼

Every object has a bunch of properties. Each property has a setting. You can display some of these settings in a text box. For example, you can use the following statement to display the width in twips of the form named frmExperiment1 in the text box named txtFormWidth:

```
txtFormWidth.Text = frmExperiment1.Width
```

This statement assigns the current setting of the Width property of frmExperiment1 to the Text property of txtFormWidth. This value immediately appears in the text box for anyone to see. The names *txtFormWidth.Text* and *frmExperiment1.Width* are constructed like this:

Object Name	Property	Object.Property Name
txtFormWidth	Text	txtFormWidth.Text
frmExperiment1	Width	frmExperiment1.Width

You can use project Experiment #1 - Show Form Location and Size to display the values of the form's Left, Top, Width, and Height properties in text boxes during a run. For this and later experiments, we'll omit the Exit button. You can click the End tool on the toolbar to end a run. Here is a sample run:

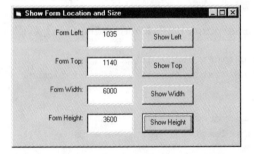

Move the form, change its size, and click the buttons to show the new values of the form's Left, Top, Width, and Height properties. Partial specifications for project Experiment #1 are shown in Tables 3-9 and 3-10.

NOTE *Moving or resizing the form at run time does not change the numbers in the object coordinates box and the object size box. These values are for the object in the design screen that was selected when you ran the project.*

Object	Property	Setting	Comment
Form1	Caption	Show Form Location and Size	
	Name	frmExperiment1	
Label1	Caption	Form Left:	
	Name	lblFormLeft	
	Alignment	1 - Right Justify	
Text1	Text		Empty. Delete "Text1."
	Name	txtFormLeft	
Command1	Caption	Show Left	
	Name	cmdShowLeft	

TABLE 3-9 *Partial Visual Interface Specifications for Project Experiment #1 - Show Form Location and Size* ▼

Event procedure cmdShowLeft_Click is small and simple:

```
Private Sub cmdShowLeft_Click()
  txtFormLeft.Text = frmExperiment1.Left
End Sub
```

Go ahead—design the project and run it.

The default setting of a text box's Alignment property is 0 - Left Justify. To change the alignment of text in a text box, you change the Alignment setting and you must also set the Multiline property to True. Change the alignment of project Experiment #1's text boxes to 2 - Center like this:

1. Click a text box to select it.

2. Click the Multiline property. The Properties button appears.

3. Click the Properties button to open a menu of possible settings (True or False).

4. Click True.

5. Click the Alignment property. The Properties button appears.

Object	Event	Response
cmdShowLeft	Click	Displays the value of the form's Width property in txtFormLeft.

TABLE 3-10 *Partial Event Procedure Specifications for Project Experiment #1 - Show Form Location and Size* ▼

6. Click the Properties button to open a menu of possible settings.

7. Click 2 - Center.

Run the project and click a button. The number it displays should appear centered in the text box.

 NOTE *You can change the Multiline property or the Alignment property more quickly by double-clicking the property until the value you want appears in the Settings box.*

Well, once again it is time to align those neurons and synapses by doing some low-impact exercises.

EXERCISES

1. Add a third fortune to the Fortune Cookie project. We suggest "Your computer will understand you today." Save the modified project as Fortune Cookie #4.

2. Complete Tables 3-9 and 3-10 for project Experiment #1 - Show Form Location and Size. Show the specifications for the project's form and all of its labels, text boxes, and command buttons.

3. Design project Experiment #2 - Show Text Box Location and Size to print the values of text box Text1's Left, Top, Width, and Height properties directly on the form. Write the specifications and design the visual interface or use this one:

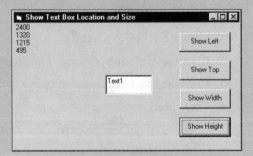

Use the **Print** method to print the value of Text1's Left, Top, Width, or Height property directly on the form. For example, you can use the following statement to print the value of *Text1.Width* on the form:

```
Print Text1.Width
```

You cannot move or resize a text box at run time. Position and size the text box in the design screen, select it and jot down its Left, Top, Width, and Height values shown in the Properties window or in the object coordinates and object size boxes.

Run the project and click the buttons—you should see the same values. Stop the run, move and resize the text box, run the project, click the buttons, et cetera, et cetera.

4. Start a new project. Put text box Text1 on Form1. Leave the text box's Text property set to "Text1".

a. Set Text1's Multiline property to True.

b. Set the Alignment property to 1 - Right Justify. What happens to the text in the text box?

c. Set the Alignment property to 2 - Center. What happens to the text in the text box?

d. Set the Alignment property to 0 - Left Justify. What happens to the text in the text box?

3.5 ENTER STRINGS INTO TEXT BOXES FROM THE KEYBOARD

During a run, you can click a text box to select it. The blinking cursor (|) appears in the text box. When the cursor is in a text box, you can type a string on the keyboard and it appears in the text box. An event procedure can select a text box by using the **SetFocus** method. The following statement uses the **SetFocus** method to select text box txtEnter:

```
txtEnter.SetFocus
```

A **SetFocus** statement consists of the name of an object, a period, and the **SetFocus** method:

Object Name	Method	Statement
txtEnter	SetFocus	txtEnter.SetFocus

Project Copycat #1 allows you to enter a string from the keyboard into one text box and then copy it to another text box with a mouse click. The visual interface is:

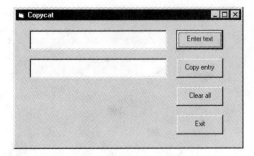

Click the Enter Text button to select the upper text box and clear it. You will see the cursor blinking in the upper text box. Type any old nonsense on the keyboard and it appears in the text box. Click Copy Entry to copy the contents of the upper text box into the lower text box. Click Clear All to erase everything from both text boxes. Tables 3-11 and 3-12 list the specifications for project Copycat #1.

In the event procedures, you will see two Object.Property names. Each name consists of the name of the object, a period, and the name of the property:

Object Name	Property	Object.Property Name
txtEnter	Text	txtEnter.Text
txtCopyEntry	Text	txtCopyEntry.Text

When you run the project and click Enter Data, event procedure cmdEnterText_Click clears text box txtEnter and then selects it with the **SetFocus** method. You see the cursor (|) blinking in txtEnter, ready to accept whatever you type on the keyboard.

```
Private Sub cmdEnterText_Click()
   txtEnter.Text = ""     ' Clear txtEnter
   txtEnter.SetFocus      ' Select txtEnter (cursor appears)
End Sub
```

Whatever wisdom you type becomes the new setting of the Text property of txtEnter, the value of *txtEnter.Text*. When you click Copy Entry, event procedure cmdCopyEntry_Click copies this value to the Text property of text box txtCopyEntry where it becomes the value of *txtCopyEntry.Text*.

```
Private Sub cmdCopyEntry_Click()
   txtCopyEntry.Text = txtEnter.Text    ' Copy the string
End Sub
```

Object	Property	Setting	Comment
Form1	Caption	Copycat	
	Name	frmCopycat1	
Text1	Text		Empty. Delete "Text1."
	Name	txtEnter	
Text2	Text		Empty. Delete "Text2."
	Name	txtCopyEntry	
Command1	Caption	Enter text	
	Name	cmdEnterText	
Command2	Caption	Copy entry	
	Name	cmdCopyEntry	
Command3	Caption	Clear all	
	Name	cmdClearAll	
Command4	Caption	Exit	
	Name	cmdExit	

TABLE 3-11 *Visual Interface Specifications for Project Copycat #1* ▼

The statement

```
txtCopyEntry.Text = txtEnter.Text
```

copies the value of txtEnter.Text to txtCopyEntry.Text. Whatever you entered into the upper text box appears in the lower text box. You can click Clear All to erase everything from both text boxes:

```
Private Sub cmdClearAll_Click ()
  txtEnter.Text = ""        ' Clear txtEnter
  txtCopyEntry.Text = ""    ' Clear txtCopyEntry
End Sub
```

Object Name	Event	Response
cmdEnterText	Click	Clears txtEnter and then sets focus in it.
cmdCopyEntry	Click	Copies txtEnter.Text to txtCopyEntry.Text.
cmdClearAll	Click	Clears both txtEnter and txtCopyEntry.
cmdExit	Click	Ends the run.

TABLE 3-12 *Event Procedure Specifications for Project Copycat #1* ▼

Try it. Run the project and follow these steps:

1. Click Enter Text to select the upper text box and clear it.

2. Type your name, message, or any string into the upper text box. You don't need to press ENTER. If you do, Visual Basic will beep.

3. Click Copy Entry to see your string copied into the lower text box.

Here is what Laran Stardrake saw:

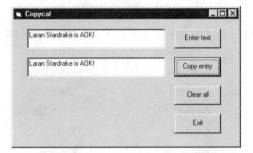

Run Copycat #1, click Enter Text, and type a long message that is wider than the text box. Oops! the beginning of your message scrolls out of sight to the left as you type. You can fix the problem easily—just set the text box's Multiline property to True. Project Copycat #2 - Multiline Text Boxes has tall multiline text boxes:

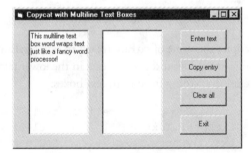

Modify project Copycat #1 to create project Copycat #2. Move the various objects to their new places, resize the text boxes, and set their Multiline properties to True:

Object Name	Property	Setting
txtEnter	Multiline	True
txtCopyEntry	Multiline	True

Run the project. Type a bunch of stuff in the left text box and watch it word wrap. Click Copy Entry to copy it properly wrapped into the right text box. Then wrap up these exercises and move on to explore more text box tricks.

EXERCISES

1. Complete the following visual interface specifications for project Copycat #2 - Multiline Text Boxes:

Object	Property	Setting
Form1	Caption	
	Name	
Text1	Text	
	Name	txtEnter
	Multiline	
Text2	Text	
	Name	txtCopyEntry
	Multiline	

2. In project Copycat #2, set txtEnter's Multiline property to True and set txtCopyEntry's Multiline property to False. Run the project, enter several lines of text in txtEnter and then click Copy Entry. How does the text in txtEnter appear in txtCopyEntry?

3.6   *A*DD SCROLL BARS TO TEXT BOXES

You know about scroll bars. Visual Basic's Properties window has a vertical scroll bar and its code window has both vertical and horizontal scroll bars. You can easily attach a scroll bar to a text box. Project Copycat #3 - Text Boxes with Scroll Bars has text boxes with vertical scroll bars. In the sample run shown here, someone entered more text than the upper text box can display, copied it to the lower text box, and then used the scroll bars to show the top of the text in the upper text box and the bottom of the text in the lower text box, with a one-line overlap:

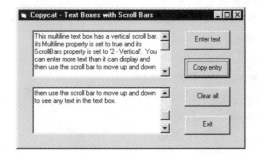

Project Copycat #3 is similar to project Copycat #2 except for the location and size of the text boxes and command buttons, and the setting of the ScrollBars property for the two text boxes. For both text boxes, set the ScrollBars property to:

Object Name	Property	Setting
txtEnter	ScrollBars	2 - Vertical
txtCopyEntry	ScrollBars	2 - Vertical

As soon as you set the ScrollBars property to 2 - Vertical, the scroll bar appears on the right side of the text box. Tables 3-13 and 3-14 list the specifications for project Copycat #3.

Object	Property	Setting	Comment
Form1	Caption	Copycat - Text Boxes with Scroll Bars	
	Name	frmCopycat3	
Text1	Text		Empty.
	Name	txtEnter	
	Multiline	True	Will word wrap.
	ScrollBars	2 - Vertical	Vertical scroll bar.
	Width	3600	Both text boxes are the same size.
	Height	1200	Both text boxes are the same size.
Text2	Text		Empty
	Name	txtCopyEntry	
	Multiline	True	Will word wrap.
	ScrollBars	2 - Vertical	Vertical scroll bar.
	Width	3600	Both text boxes are the same size.
	Height	1200	Both text boxes are the same size.
Command1	Caption	Enter text	
	Name	cmdEnterText	
Command2	Caption	Clear all	
	Name	cmdClearAll	
Command3	Caption	Copy Entry	
	Name	cmdCopyEntry	
Command4	Caption	Exit	
	Name	cmdExit	

TABLE 3-13 *Visual Interface Specifications for Project Copycat #3* ▼

Object Name	Event	Response
cmdEnterText	Click	Clears txtEnter and sets focus in it.
cmdClearAll	Click	Clears txtEnter and txtCopyEntry.
cmdCopyEntry	Click	Copies txtEnter.Text to txtCopyEntry.Text.
cmdExit	Click	Ends the run.

TABLE 3-14 *Event Procedure Specifications for Project Copycat #3* ▼

Create project Copycat #3, try out its scroll bars, and then scroll on down to the exercises.

EXERCISES

1. Experiment with project Copycat #3. Here are some things that you might try:

   a. Reduce the height of txtEnter and increase the height of txtCopyEntry. Run the project, enter more text in txtEnter than it can display, then copy your entry to txtCopyEntry.

   b. Make the widths and heights of the two text boxes different.

   c. Remove the scroll bar from one of the text boxes. To do so, set its ScrollBars property to 0 - None. Try various combinations of height, width, scroll bar, and no scroll bar.

2. Create project Copycat #4 - Vertical and Horizontal Scroll Bars. Make txtEnter large (ours is 3600 x 1920) and make txtCopyEntry wide and short (ours is 3600 x 600). Put a vertical scroll bar on txtEnter and a horizontal scroll bar on txtCopyEntry (ScrollBars = 1 - Horizontal). Run the project. Enter several lines of text into txtEnter and copy it into txtCopyEntry. Use txtCopyEntry's horizontal scroll bar to scroll right and left to view its text. As you scroll leisurely along in txtCopyEntry, compare its text with the text in txtEnter.

3.7 ADD A LITTLE PIZAZZ TO FORMS AND LABELS

Our labels have been quite ordinary with most of their properties set to the default values. The forms, too, are monotonously mundane. So let's add a little pizazz to the forms and the labels! In the next section we'll do the same for text boxes.

Start a new project and take a look at good old Form1. It is mostly gray, the *default background color*, with a grid of lots of dots in black, the *default foreground color*. The foreground color is controlled by the setting of the ForeColor property and the background color by the setting of the BackColor property. The default settings are strange-looking *hexadecimal numbers*:

Property	Setting	Comment
BackColor	&H8000000F&	This hexadecimal number specifies gray.
ForeColor	&H80000012&	This hexadecimal number specifies black.

Hexadecimal numbers are *base 16* numbers. If you grow three more fingers on each hand and then label your 16 fingers 0 to 9, A, B, C, D, E, and F, you can soon learn to count in hexadecimal. Fortunately, you don't need to know anything about hexadecimal numbers to change the settings of the BackColor and ForeColor properties.

Instead of black dots on a gray form, let's get colorful. First, change Form1's background color to something pizazzy. Do it like this:

1. Click Form1 to select it.

2. Click the BackColor property. The Properties button appears in the Settings box:

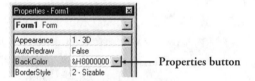 —— **Properties button**

3. Click the Properties button to get a palette of colors:

4. What color do you want? Pick and click. Form1 becomes that color.

Try several colors. Pick and click, pick and click. We like the textured-looking colors in the top row, especially the peach flavor (fourth from the left) and the lime flavor (sixth from the left). The hexadecimal numbers for these selections are &H00C0E0FF& for peach and &H00C0FFC0& for lime.

You can probably see foreground colors best on a white background, so change BackColor's setting to white. Click BackColor, click the Properties button, and click any of the white squares on the palette. Then change ForeColor's setting and watch the form's grid dots change color:

1. Click the ForeColor property. The Properties button appears.

2. Click the Properties button to get the palette of colors.

3. Pick and click the color you want. The dots change to that color.

Some of the colors in the third row of the palette show well against a white background. Also try assorted foreground colors on a black background, including white dots on black. Pick the foreground and background colors that you like and move on.

Double-click the Label tool so that Label1 appears on the form. Set its BorderStyle property to 1 - Fixed Single, its Alignment property to 2 - Center, and its BackColor and ForeColor properties to the colors you like. We tried several combinations—magenta on green is nice. We also like blue on orange, yellow, or cyan. Some color combinations don't have enough contrast and the caption is hard to read. Here is blue on orange (shown in gorgeous black on gray):

Label1's caption appears in the default font, 8-point MS Sans Serif. Let's first change the size of the font, and then try other fonts:

1. Click Label1 to select it.

2. Click the Font property. The Properties button appears.

3. Click the Properties button to get the Font dialog box:

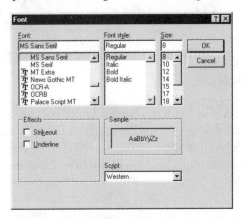

4. Scroll to the bottom of the Size box. The largest size is 24 points. Click it.

5. Click the OK button to complete the font size change and remove the Font dialog box.

Oops! Label1's caption is now too big to fit in its box. That's okay—easy to fix. You can tell Label1 to automatically adjust its size to fit the caption. Change the setting of the AutoSize property to True:

1. Click Label1 to select it.

2. Click the AutoSize property. The Properties button appears.

3. Click the Properties button to open a tiny menu of choices: False and True.

4. Click True.

Snap! Label1's border expands expeditiously so that its caption fits neatly in its box:

 NOTE *You can double-click the AutoSize property to quickly* toggle *its setting from False to True or from True to False.*

 EXPERIMENT *Get the Font dialog box and try assorted fonts, font styles, and font sizes. Scroll down the list of fonts and try a bunch of them. Type* **Symbols** *as the caption and then change the font to Symbol. Type* **WingDings** *as the caption and then change the font to WingDings. We did it:*

A label has 32 properties. In this book, you have explored these 12 properties of a label: Alignment, AutoSize, BackColor, BorderStyle, Caption, Font, ForeColor, Height, Left, Name, Top, and Width. Brief descriptions of three additional properties of a label are shown here. Experiment with them.

Property	Default Setting	Description
Appearance	1 - 3D	The default look is three-dimensional with a gray BackColor. Try the other setting, 0 - Flat.
BackStyle	1 - Opaque	Determines whether the background is opaque or transparent. Try both settings and move the label over another object.
WordWrap	False	If you set AutoSize to True and then set WordWrap to True, the label will expand vertically and word wrap a long caption.

EXERCISES

1. Font sizes are measured in points, where 72 points equals one inch. How many twips equals one point?

2. Put Label1 on the form in its default size and enter this caption: "Alas, this caption is too long to fit in a default-sized label box." What happens? Now set the AutoSize property to True. What happens?

3. Put Label2 on the form. Set the AutoSize property to True. What happens? Click the label and widen it to the default size of 1215 twips. Set the WordWrap property to True, then Click Caption and enter this caption: "Alas, this caption is too long to fit in a default-sized label box." What happens?

3.8 USE THE QBCOLOR FUNCTION TO ADD COLOR TO YOUR PROJECTS

During the millennia BVB (Before Visual Basic), we were quite happy writing books about Neanderthal BASIC, Cro-Magnon BASIC, GW-BASIC, and QBasic. Much of QBasic exists within Visual Basic, including QBasic's simple way of selecting background and foreground colors. Table 3-15 lists QBasic's 16 colors and their color numbers.

Color	Color Number
Black	0
Blue	1
Green	2
Cyan	3
Red	4
Magenta	5
Yellow	6
White	7
Gray	8
Light Blue	9
Light Green	10
Light Cyan	11
Light Red	12
Light Magenta	13
Light Yellow	14
Bright White	15

TABLE 3-15 *QBasic Color Numbers* ▼

You can use Visual Basic's **QBColor** function to assign a QBasic color to an object's BackColor or ForeColor property:

Assignment Statement	Action Performed
Form1.BackColor = QBColor(1)	Sets Form1's BackColor to blue.
Form1.ForeColor = QBColor(14)	Sets Form1's ForeColor to light yellow.
Text1.BackColor = QBColor(13)	Sets Text1's BackColor to light magenta.
Text1.ForeColor = QBColor(2)	Sets Text1's ForeColor to green.
Text3.BackColor = QB(Text1.Text)	Sets Text3's BackColor to the color number in Text1.
Text3.ForeColor = QB(Text2.Text)	Sets Text3's ForeColor to the color number in Text2.

Project QBColor #1 - Text Box Colors Using QBColor has three text boxes. Enter color numbers into txtBackColor and txtForeColor, and then click txtShowColors to set its BackColor and ForeColor to the colors specified in the other two text boxes. Tables 3-16 and 3-17 lists the project's specifications.

Object	Property	Setting
Form1	Caption	Text Box Colors Using QBColor
	Name	frmQBColor1
Label1	Caption	Click and then enter BackColor (0 - 15):
	Name	lblBackColor
	Wordwrap	True
Text1	Text	
	Name	txtBackColor
Label2	Caption	Click and then enter ForeColor (0 - 15):
	Name	lblForeColor
	Wordwrap	True
Text2	Text	
	Name	txtForeColor
Label3	Caption	Click to show colors:
	AutoSize	True
	Name	lblShowColors
Text3	Text	Foreground text
	Name	txtShowColors
Command1	Caption	Exit
	Name	cmdExit

TABLE 3-16 *Visual Interface Specifications for Project QBColor #1* ▼

Object Name	Event	Response
txtBackColor	Click	Clears itself and accepts focus.
txtForeColor	Click	Clears itself and accepts focus.
txtShowColors	Click	Sets its BackColor and ForeColor to the colors specified in txtBackColor and txtForeColor.
cmdExit	Click	Ends the run.

TABLE 3-17 *Event Procedure Specifications for Project QBColor #1* ▼

In the sample run shown here, imagine that txtShowColors is displaying Foreground Text in green (QBasic color 2) on a light yellow background (QBasic color 14).

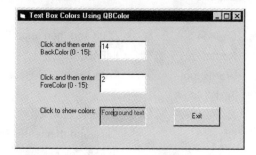

Event procedures for the three text boxes are:

```
Private Sub txtBackColor_Click()
  txtBackColor.Text = ""   ' Clear txtBackColor
End Sub

Private Sub txtForeColor_Click()
  txtForeColor.Text = ""   ' Clear txtForeColor
End Sub

Private Sub txtShowColors_Click()
  txtShowColors.BackColor = QBColor(txtBackColor.Text)
  txtShowColors.ForeColor = QBColor(txtForeColor.Text)
End Sub
```

When you double-click an object to open the code window, Visual Basic automatically assigns a default procedure for that object. For example, the default procedure for a command button is Click. The default procedure for a text box is Change, which is not the one we want just now. If you double-click text box txtBackColor to open the code window, you see the beginning of event procedure txtBackColor_Change:

```
Private Sub txtBackColor_Change()
|
End Sub
```

The code window's Object box displays the name of the object (txtBackColor) and the Procedures box shows the name of the procedure (Change). Change is not the procedure we want. Click is the procedure we want. Convert the procedure's name to txtBackColor_Click:

1. Click the Procedure box's arrow to pull down a list of possible procedures.

2. Click the procedure you want. In this case, click Click.

NOTE *You can also modify the name of a procedure by editing the name in the* Private Sub *statement. For example, click Change and change it to Click.*

Design the project, run it, and try some color combinations. What happens if you enter a color number that is not an integer from 0 to 15? Try it and find out. Try integers greater than 15, try negative integers, and try 3.14. Try this: click txtBackColor and don't enter a number, then click txtShowColors. You will see a "Type mismatch" error message because Visual Basic doesn't know what to do with the empty string in the text box. We'll fix this type of problem in Chapters 7 and 8.

Instead of using text boxes to acquire color numbers, use scroll bars. Project QBColor #2 - Text Box Colors Using Scroll Bars provides scroll bars that you can use to select color numbers 0 to 15. As you scroll, you see the color number displayed in the text box to the right of the scroll bar. The background or foreground color in the text box below the scroll bars changes as you drag a scroll button right or left. In the sample run shown here, notice the positions of the scroll buttons and the numbers in the corresponding text boxes. The background color is blue (1) and the foreground color is light yellow (14):

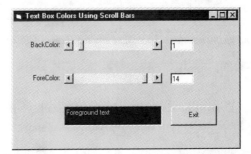

To place a horizontal scroll bar on the form, use the Toolbox's HScrollBar tool:

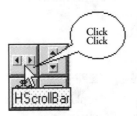

While creating project QBColor #2, you will place two horizontal scroll bars on the form, widen them, and adjust their Max, Min, and Value properties. Look for these properties in Tables 3-18 and 3-19, which list partial specifications for project QBColor #2.

Object	Property	Setting	Comment
Form1	Caption	Text Box Colors Using Scroll Bars	
	Name	frmQBColor2	
Label1	Caption	BackColor:	
	Alignment	1 - Right Justify	
	AutoSize	True	
	Name	lblBackColor	
HScrollBar1	Name	hsbBackColor	The standard prefix is hsb.
	Max	15	Maximum value - scroll button far right.
	Min	0	Minimum value - scroll button far left.
	Value	0	Position of the scroll button.
Text1	Text		
	Name	txtBackColor	
Text3	Text	Foreground text	
	Name	txtShowColors	
Command1	Caption	Exit	
	Name	cmdExit	

TABLE 3-18 *Partial Visual Interface Specifications for Project QBColor #2 - Text Box Colors Using Scroll Bars* ▼

Design the visual interface and install event procedure hsbBackColor_Scroll. One way to begin is by following these steps:

1. Double-click scroll bar hsbBackColor to open the code window. Oops! That begins the hsbBackColor_Change procedure, not the one you want.

Object Name	Event	Response
hsbBackColor	Scroll	Displays its Value in txtBackColor and sets BackColor of txtShowColors.
hsbForeColor	Scroll	Displays its Value in txtForeColor and sets ForeColor of txtShowColors.
cmdExit	Click	Ends the run.

TABLE 3-19 *Partial Event Procedure Specifications for Project QBColor #2 - Text Box Colors Using Scroll Bars* ▼

2. Click the Procedures box and scroll down to Scroll at the very bottom.

3. Click Scroll and you should see the template you want:

```
Private Sub hsbBackColor_Scroll()
  |
End Sub
```

Complete the event procedure like this:

```
Private Sub hsbBackColor_Scroll()
  txtBackColor.Text = hsbBackColor.Value
  txtShowColors.BackColor = QBColor(hsbBackColor.Value)
End Sub
```

The statement

```
txtBackColor.Text = hsbBackColor.Value
```

displays hsbBackColor's Value in txtBackColor. The scroll bar's Value depends on the position of the scroll button. It is an integer from 0 when the button is far left (the Min setting) to 15 when the button is far right (the Max setting).

The statement

```
txtShowColors.BackColor = QBColor(hsbBackColor.Value)
```

uses hsbBackColor's Value setting to set the background color of txtShowColors. This happens in real time as you drag the scroll button right or left.

Install the event procedure and run the project. Drag the BackColor scroll button right and left to see the background color change, then mosey on down to the exercise that asks you to complete the project.

EXERCISES

1. Complete the visual interface specifications table for project QBColor #2. Add the specs for the foreground color label, scroll bar, and text box. Write and install event procedure hsbForeColor_Scroll.

2. Create project QBColor #3 - Text Box Colors Using Scroll Bars. It is similar to project QBColor #2, but uses vertical scroll bars. In the toolbox, look for the VScrollBar tool.

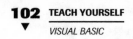

3.9 | USE THE RGB FUNCTION TO ADD COLOR TO YOUR PROJECTS

Give an artist a glob each of red, green, and blue paint and she can mix dollops of them to get any color you want. She may also use white and black to lighten or darken the mixed colors. You can use the **RGB** function to mix red, green, and blue to produce 16,777,216 colors. To perform this amazing feat, you assign an integer from 0 to 255 to each primary color, red, green, and blue, with 0 specifying the least intensity (darkest) and 255 the greatest intensity (brightest). You use these three numbers in an **RGB** function:

RGB(*red, green, blue*)

Here, *red, green,* and *blue* are color numbers in the range 0 to 255.

You can use the **RGB** function in an assignment statement to set the BackColor or ForeColor of an object:

Assignment Statement	Action Performed
Form1.BackColor = RGB(255, 0, 0)	Sets Form1's BackColor to the most intense (brightest) red.
Form1.BackColor = RGB(0, 128, 0)	Sets Form1's BackColor to medium-intensity green.
Form1.BackColor = RGB(0, 0, 64)	Sets Form1's BackColor to low-intensity (dark) blue.
Form1.BackColor = RGB(255, 255, 0)	Sets Form1's BackColor to yellow (mixes red and green).
Text1.BackColor = RGB(128, 128, 0)	Sets Text1's BackColor to—well, it looks olive drab to us.
Text1.BackColor = RGB(128, 0, 128)	Sets Text1's BackColor to purple (mixes red and blue).
Text1.ForeColor = RGB(255, 255, 255)	Sets Text1's ForeColor to bright white.
Text1.ForeColor = RGB(0, 0, 0)	Sets Text1's ForeColor to black.

For each primary color, red, green, or blue, there are 256 intensity numbers, so there are $256 \times 256 \times 256$ combinations of these numbers for a grand total of 16,777,216 colors. Use project RGB #1 - Form BackColor Using RGB to try a few million of these possibilities. In the sample run shown here, someone entered 0 for red, 192 for green, 192 for blue, and then clicked the Form BackColor button to put a blue-green background on the form. Aqua? Turquoise?

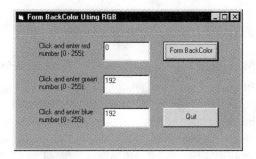

 NOTE *Most computers can't display all 16,777,216 colors—that requires an expensive 24-bit video graphics card. A 4-bit graphics card can display 16 colors and an 8-bit graphics card can display 256 colors. The manual for our 16-bit graphics card claims that it can display 65,536 colors.*

We'll ask you to construct the specifications table for project RGB #1 in the exercises. We named the form frmRGB01 and the labels lblRed, lblGreen, and lblBlue. We called the text boxes txtRed, txtGreen, and txtBlue. The monikers of the command buttons are cmdBackColor and cmdQuit. Here are the event procedures for cmdBackColor and the text boxes:

```
Private Sub cmdBackColor_Click()
  Dim red, green, blue As
  red = txtRed.Text
  green = txtGreen.Text
  blue = txtBlue.Text
  frmRGB01.BackColor = RGB(red, green, blue)
End Sub

Private txtRed_Click()
  txtRed.Text = ""    ' Clear txtRed
End Sub

Private txtGreen_Click()
  txtGreen.Text = "" ' Clear txtGreen
End Sub

Private txtBlue_Click()
  txtBlue.Text = ""   ' Clear txtBlue
End Sub
```

For event procedure cmdBackColor, we invented three *variables* called *red*, *green*, and *blue*. Each variable is assigned a value from an appropriate text box.

The three variables are used in the **RGB** function in an assignment statement to set the background color of form frmRGB01:

Statement	Action Performed
Dim red, green, blue	Creates variables *red*, *green*, and *blue*
red = txtRed.Text	Assigns the value of *txtRed.Text* to *red*
green = txtGreen.Text	Assigns the value of *txtGreen.Text* to *green*
blue = txtGreen.Text	Assigns the value of *txtBlue.Text* to *blue*
frmRGB01.BackColor = RGB (red, green, blue)	Sets frmRGB01's BackColor to RGB (*red*, *green*, *blue*)

The statement

```
Dim red, green, blue
```

declares *red, green,* and *blue* to be variables of data type Variant. If you omit this line of code, that's okay. When Visual Basic encounters a name in your code that is not the name of an existing variable, it creates a new variable with that name. We prefer declaring variables in a **Dim** statement. You will learn more and more about variables as you travel farther and farther up the road to Visual Basic literacy. We used variables in cmdBackColor_Click because we don't like long assignment statements. The event procedure can also be written without the variables *red, green,* and *blue* like this:

```
Private Sub cmdBackColor_Click()
    frmRGB01.BackColor = RGB(txtRed.Text, txtGreen.Text, txtBlue.Text)
End Sub
```

EXERCISES

1. Construct the specifications table for project RGB #1 - Form BackColor Using RGB. Complete the project, run it, and try a bunch of values for *red, green,* and *blue.*

2. The beginning of a run of project RGB #2 - Text Box Colors Using RGB appears as follows. Enter RGB numbers for *red, green,* and *blue* under BackColor and ForeColor. Then click Show Colors to see your background and foreground colors appear in the text box. Of course, to make it so, you must design the visual interface and write the event procedures.

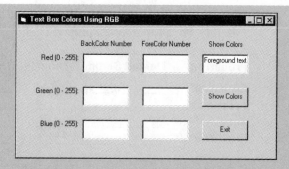

3. Create project RGB #3 - RGB Color Mixing with Scroll Bars. The visual interface is:

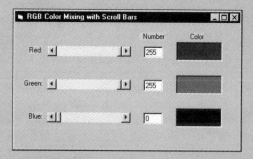

When you scroll a scroll bar, you see its Value setting and color in the text boxes to its right. The colors specified by the three scroll bars are mixed and appear as the form's BackColor.

mastery skills check

1. A form is a Visual Basic object. Is a form a control? Name three types of objects that are controls.

2. Describe two ways to put a control on the form in the location and with the size that you want.

3. Labels and text boxes have some of the same properties. The default settings of these properties may be the same or different. A label has properties that a text box doesn't have, and a text box has properties that a

label doesn't have. Below are properties of a label or text box or both or neither. For all appropriate properties, show the default setting.

Property	Default Setting – Label	Default Setting – Text box
Alignment	_____	_____
Appearance	_____	_____
AutoSize	_____	_____
BackColor	_____	_____
BackPack	_____	_____
BackStyle	_____	_____
BorderStyle	_____	_____
Caption	_____	_____
Font	_____	_____
ForeColor	_____	_____
Height	_____	_____
HitchHike	_____	_____
MultiLine	_____	_____
Name	_____	_____
Text	_____	_____
Width	_____	_____
WordWrap	_____	_____

4. What is the standard prefix for the name of a form? a command button? a text box? a label? a horizontal scroll bar? a vertical scroll bar?

5. For each combination of object and property, construct the *Object.Property* name:

   a. The Text property of text box txtFortune.

   b. The Width property of form frmExperiment1.

   c. The Left property of Text1.

   d. The BackColor property of text box txtShowColors.

   e. The Value property of horizontal scroll bar hsbBackColor.

6. If you double-click an object, the code window appears with a template of the default event procedure for that object. The default event procedure for a command button is Click; if you double-click command button Command1, you see the following template:

```
Private Sub Command1_Click()
|
End Sub
```

    a. What is the default event procedure for a form? a text box? a label? a horizontal scroll bar?

    b. If the default event procedure is not the one you want, how do you change it to the one you want?

7. Describe the action performed by each statement:

    a. txtStart.Text = Timer

    b. txtStop.Text = Timer

    c. txtElapsed.Text = txtStop.Text - txtStart.Text

8. Describe the action performed by each statement:

    a. Dim Elapsed As Variant

    b. Elapsed = txtStop.Text - txtStart.Text

    c. txtElapsed.Text = Format(Elapsed, "####0.##")

9. Describe the action performed by each statement:

    a. txtEnter.SetFocus

    b. txtCopyEntry.Text = txtEnter.Text

10. The default alignment for a text box is 0 - Left Justify. How do you make a text box's text appear right-aligned or centered? How do you make it word wrap?

11. A text box can have a vertical scroll bar, a horizontal scroll bar, or both. Experiment with these three possibilities and write a tiny essay describing your experience.

12. Describe the action performed by each statement:

    a. Text1.BackColor = QBColor(1)

    b. Text1.ForeColor = QBColor(14)

    c. Form1.BackColor = RGB(255, 0, 0)

    d. Form1.ForeColor = RGB(0, 0, 255)

    e. Dim red, green, blue As Variant

    f. red = txtRed.Text

    g. green = hsbGreen.Value

13. For each of the following actions, write a statement to perform the action:

    a. Place Label1 600 twips from the left edge of the form.

    b. Place Label1 900 twips from the top of the form.

    c. Make Label1 exactly 1440 twips tall.

    d. Make Label1 exactly 1800 twips wide.

    e. Print Label1's width and height on the form.

    f. Set Form1's BackColor to QBasic color number 13.

    g. Set Form1's ForeColor to QBasic color number 2.

    h. Set Form1's BackColor to the RGB color specified by text boxes txtRed, txtGreen, and txtBlue.

    i. Set Form1's BackColor to the setting of hsbBackColor's Value property. Use **QBColor**.

    j. Assign to the variable *green* the value in text box txtGreen.

    k. Assign to the variable *blue* the setting of hsbBlue's Value property.

14. Design project Tickle #1 - Tickle and Double-Tickle using the visual interface shown here:

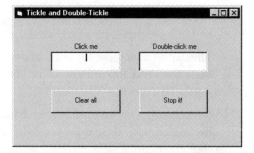

Click the text box under the label "Click me" and "That tickles!" appears in the box on a light yellow background. Double-click the text box under the label "Double-click me" and "That double-tickles!!" appears on a bright red background. Click the Clear All button to clear both text boxes and change their BackColors to white. For the text box on the right, write a DblClick event procedure. Design the visual interface, set the properties, and write good code. Try both **QBColor** and **RGB** to set the text box BackColors.

15. Design an original project that uses one or more of these controls: command button, label, text box, horizontal scroll bar, and vertical scroll bar. Include the use of **Variant** variables and the **Format**, **QBColor**, and **RGB** functions. We'll watch for the fruit of your labor in our favorite Windows magazines.

4

Take the Scenic Route

chapter objectives

4.1 Display bitmaps, icons, and metafiles on a form

4.2 Display scenic icons in image boxes

4.3 Make icons appear and disappear

4.4 Make image boxes shrink or grow to fit the show

4.5 Display pictures in picture boxes

4.6 Print text in picture boxes

4.7 If you don't like the scenery, draw your own

4.8 Make things move

ONE of the joys of traveling is admiring the scenery. Provide that joy by putting scenery into your projects for users to admire. Visual Basic has boxes and tools especially designed to help you put pictures anywhere on a form. You can display pictures directly in a form or in containers called *image boxes* and *picture boxes,* controls that are designed especially for displaying images. If you can't find just the image you want, use the Shape and Line controls to draw your own objets d'art. Look for the tools you need in the toolbox:

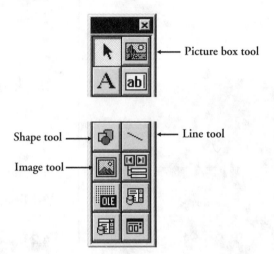

Picture box tool

Shape tool ——— ←— Line tool

Image tool ———

You can load three types of picture files onto a form or into image and picture boxes:

▼ **Bitmaps** A bitmap file represents a picture as a pattern of pixels (square dots) and specifies the color of each pixel. If you enlarge a bitmap enough, it looks "grainy" because you can see the individual pixels. The conventional filename extension for a bitmap file is *.bmp.* Visual Basic gives you more than 200 ready-to-use bitmap files. You also can create pictures with Windows Paintbrush and other Windows-compatible paint programs and then save your art as bitmap files.

▼ **Icons** An icon is a bitmap with a maximum size of 32 pixels by 32 pixels. The conventional filename extension for an icon file is *.ico.* Visual Basic includes more than 450 icons for your viewing pleasure.

▼ **Metafiles** A metafile contains a recipe for drawing a picture using lines, curves, and geometric shapes. Because it is drawn to fit its container each time it is displayed, a metafile picture never appears grainy. The conventional filename extension for a metafile is *.wmf.*

You create metafiles using a Windows-compatible draw program such as CorelDRAW.

Visual Basic has hundreds of images ready for your use. If you can't find just the picture you want, use the Shape and Line controls to draw pictures consisting of lines and assorted geometric shapes. Oh, you want still more? You can import pictures from other applications—Microsoft Word for Windows, Microsoft Publisher, and other Windows applications have libraries of clip art that you can import into your projects.

4.1 DISPLAY BITMAPS, ICONS, AND METAFILES ON A FORM

In the spirit of worldwide adventuring, let's display the earth, the sun, clouds, rain, lightning, and other elements as icons on a form. Here is the Earth icon displayed in the upper-left corner of Form1:

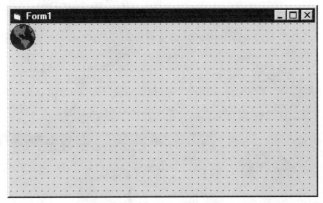

To add a picture to a form, click the form's Picture property and then select the picture you want from Visual Basic's portfolio of picturesque possibilities. If you haven't moved this folder, you'll find the Earth icon in the Icons folder of the Vb folder. The Icons folder contains several folders, one of which is Elements. That's where you'll find the Earth icon—its full filename is Earth.ico. Put the Earth icon on Form1 in six easy steps:

1. Click Form1 to select it.

2. Click the Picture property. The Properties button pops into view.

3. Click the Properties button. The Load Picture dialog box appears:

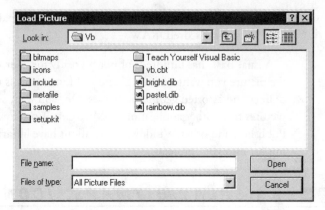

4. Double-click the Icons folder to obtain a list of its folders:

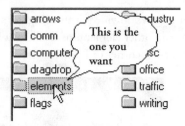

5. You're getting close! The Elements folder contains the Earth icon that you're after. Double-click Elements to get its list of files. The Load Picture dialog box might now look like this:

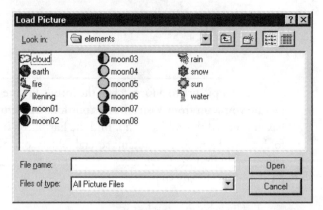

6. Double-click Earth to load the Earth icon and display it on Form1:

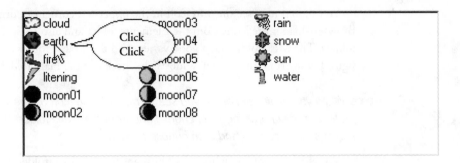

If all goes well, and we hope it does, you will see the Earth icon in the upper-left corner of Form1 and the setting of Form1's Picture property is: (Icon). If something goes awry, try again. Look in the folder where you installed Visual Basic, find the Icons folder and its Elements folder. There you should find the Earth.ico file.

When you load a picture directly onto Form1, the picture appears in the upper-left corner of the form and replaces any picture that was previously there. Replace the Earth icon with another icon from the Elements folder. If you are sauntering up the trail in a mellow mood, perhaps you'd like a sunny day:

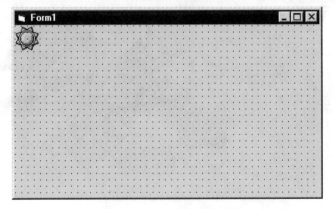

Use this quick method to load the Sun icon onto Form1:

1. Click Form1 to select it.

2. Double-click the Picture property. The Load Picture dialog box appears. It should already display the names of files in the Elements folder. If not, double-click Elements.

3. Double-click Sun to load the Sun icon.

You should now see the Sun icon in the upper-left corner of Form1. Browse—load more icons from the Elements folder and also try icons from other folders. The Misc folder has a good variety and the Traffic folder has lots of road signs. If you cruise the World Wide Web, check out the Flags folder.

 NOTE *When you minimize Form1, you see its rather bland icon on the Taskbar. If you prefer a more interesting icon, choose one from the Icons folder. Double-click Form1's Icon property and then choose an icon.*

Visual Basic provides many small bitmaps in its Bitmap folder. Our Bitmap folder contains folders called Assorted, Gauge, Outline, and Toolbar3. You display a bitmap just as you displayed an icon. Try one or two or more from each folder. Many will look familiar because they are used in numerous Windows applications. You can use them in your projects too.

Metafiles are different. Metafiles love space. When you load a metafile onto Form1, it occupies the entire form. Our Metafile folder has folders in it called Arrows and Business. The arrow with the filename Multarw4.wmf reminds us of a freeway intersection we were once trapped in for several hours:

Load the Multarw4.wmf metafile picture onto Form1 like this:

1. Click Form1 to select it.

2. Double-click the Picture property. The Load Picture dialog box appears.

3. Double-click the Metafile folder.

4. Double-click the Arrows folder to get its list of files.

5. Double-click the metafile named Multarw4.wmf.

Your metafile picture appears on Form1, taking it over entirely. If you resize Form1, you resize the metafile picture that it contains. Try this: load your favorite metafile picture onto Form1, then resize Form1. Make a square picture, then make it wide and short, then make it tall and thin. Make the picture look the way **you** want it to look. Try it with several metafile pictures—some look good square, some look good wide and short, some look good tall and thin. Of course, looking good is in the eye of the beholder.

After putting as many pictures as you want on the form, you may wish to delete the current picture and see an empty Form1. Do it like this:

1. Click Form1 to select it.

2. Click the Picture property to select it. The Properties button appears.

3. **DON'T** click the Properties button. Instead, click anywhere in the Settings box except the Properties button.

4. Press DELETE .

The picture should disappear from Form1, and the Picture property setting should now be: (None). Remember this way of deleting a picture--it works with image boxes and picture boxes too.

Load a Picture in an Event Procedure

You can use the **LoadPicture** function in event procedure Form_Load to load a picture onto the form at run time. Table 4-1 shows examples of statements using the **LoadPicture** function to load a picture onto Form1 from a folder in the Vb folder on disk drive C.

The Object.Property name "Form1.Picture" names both the object and the property. If the object name is omitted in a Form_Load event procedure, Visual Basic obligingly uses the name of the form as the default object name. You can use either of these Form_Load event procedures to load the "freeway" metafile (Multarw4.wmf) at run time:

```
Private Sub Form_Load()
```

Statement	Action Performed
Form1.Picture = LoadPicture("c:\vb\icons\elements\earth.ico")	Loads Earth icon.
Form1.Picture = LoadPicture("c:\vb\bitmaps\assorted\fish.bmp")	Loads Fish bitmap.
Form1.Picture = LoadPicture("c:\vb\metafile\arrows\multarw4.wmf")	Loads "freeway" metafile.
Picture = LoadPicture("c:\vb\icons\elements\earth.ico")	Loads Earth icon.

TABLE 4-1 *Statements Using the LoadPicture Function to Display a Picture on the Form* ▼

```
   AutoRedraw = True
   Picture = LoadPicture("c:\Vb\metafile\arrows\multarw4.wmf")
End Sub

Private Sub Form_Load()
   AutoRedraw = True
   Form1.Picture = LoadPicture("c:\Vb\metafile\arrows\multarw4.wmf")
End Sub
```

If you load a picture onto a form and then print text over the picture, the text may erase a rectangular strip of the picture, as shown here:

You can superimpose text on the picture without erasing any part of it by using the FontTransparent property. Use project Form Load #5 - Print Text on a Picture to demonstrate the effects of the two FontTransparent settings. Install this Form_Load procedure:

```
Private Sub Form_Load()
   AutoRedraw = True
   Form1.Picture = LoadPicture("c:\Vb\metafile\arrows\multarw4.wmf")

   Form1.CurrentX = 0      ' Left inside edge of form
   Form1.CurrentY = 1200   ' 1200 twips (10 gridpoints) down

   Form1.Print "The way this looks depends on the FontTransparent setting."
End Sub
```

The procedure sets the form's AutoRedraw property to True. This is required to make the picture loaded onto the form visible at run time. Run the project twice, first with the form's FontTransparent property set to its default value, True. Then set FontTransparent to False and run the project again. Because

FontTransparent is False, the text superimposed on the picture takes a rectangular bite out of the picture. Forms and picture boxes have the FontTransparent property. The default setting is True. Now get up, move around a bit, stretch a little, and try these exercises, which we hope you'll find transparent instead of opaque.

EXERCISES

1. Binoculars might be a handy item for your backpack. You'll find one in the Misc folder of the Icons folder of the Vb folder. The filename is Binocular.ico. What is the path of this file if the Vb folder is on disk drive C? Describe how to load the Binocular icon onto Form1 if:

   a. You have just started a new project and have not previously displayed a picture file on Form1.

   b. You have just finished displaying an icon from the Elements folder.

   c. You have just finished displaying an icon from the Misc folder.

2. Suppose that you have just finished displaying an icon from the Misc folder on Form1. Describe how to next load a bitmap onto Form1. Make it the one called Camcord in the Assorted folder of the Bitmaps folder.

3. Write a Form_Load procedure to load a bitmap, icon, or metafile (your choice) onto the form.

4.2 DISPLAY SCENIC ICONS IN IMAGE BOXES

Image boxes are great containers for pictures. Move an image box anywhere on a form and its picture goes along for the ride. You can use an image box to contain a bitmap, icon, or metafile, make it the size you want, then put it where you want it. Project Icons #1 - Icons in Image Boxes displays eight image boxes on the project's form. Two image boxes are empty and labeled "Image box." The other six contain icons from the Elements folder and are labeled with the filenames and filename extensions (.ico) of the icon files:

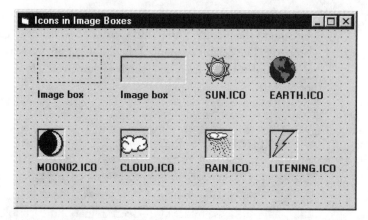

To put an image box on the form in its default size, double-click the Image tool on the Toolbox. The first image box in the top row of the form shows how an image box looks when you put it on the form with its default BorderStyle setting of 0 - None. The dashed-line border is invisible at run time. The second empty image box's BorderStyle is 1 - Fixed Single. The border is visible at run time. The other six image boxes contain images.

When you load an icon into an image box, the image box shrinks to the size of the icon and the dashed-line border disappears. You can see this for the icons labeled "SUN.ICO" and "EARTH.ICO." In the second row, we changed the BorderStyle of all the image boxes to 1 - Fixed Single. For these image boxes, you see a three-dimensional border around each icon in the Design screen. You will see the same border when you run the project. When you design this project and run it, you should see the run-time screen shown here:

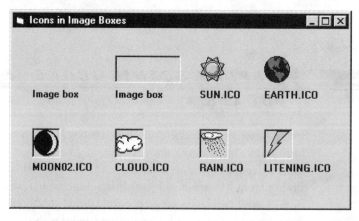

Please notice the following things in this run-time screen:

▼ The upper-left image box is empty and invisible. Its BorderStyle setting is 0 - None.

▼ The second image box in the top row is empty and visible. Its BorderStyle setting is 1 - Fixed Single.

▼ The Sun and Earth icons appear inside their invisible image boxes.

▼ The Moon, Cloud, Rain, and Litening icons appear inside their visible image boxes.

Project Icons #1 has many objects, so the specifications table for the entire project is quite long. Table 4-2 shows the specs for the form, the first three image boxes in the top row, and the first three image boxes in the bottom row. We left the specs for the fourth image box in each row for you to write in during the exercises. We are confident that you know how to add labels, so we omitted the specs for the labels. Table 4-2 includes the Height and Width settings for the image boxes. These settings change automatically when you set the BorderStyle property and then use the Picture property to load an icon.

Each image box first appeared in its default width and height, 1215×495 twips. Image boxes imgEmpty1 and imgEmpty2 do not contain icons and remain default size. When you load an icon into an image box, the box shrinks to the size of the icon. In Table 4-2, notice that the size of an image box with an invisible border is 480×480 and the size with a visible border is slightly larger, 540×540. How wide is the visible border? There are *two* horizontal borders and *two* vertical borders. A little arithmetic produces the answer: 30 twips.

What happens if you click an image box that contains an icon, grab a selection handle, and enlarge the image box? It depends on the setting of the image box's Stretch property. If Stretch has its default setting of False, the icon simply remains in the upper-left corner of the image box as you stretch it:

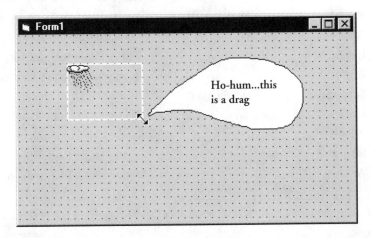

Object	Property	Setting	Comments
Form1	Caption	Icons in Image Boxes	
	Name	frmIcons01	
Image1	BorderStyle	0 - None	Dashed at design time, invisible at run time.
	Name	imgEmpty1	The standard prefix for an image box is img.
	Picture	(none)	Empty—no picture.
	Height	1215	Default size.
	Width	495	Default size.
Image2	BorderStyle	1 - Fixed Single	Visible at design time and run time.
	Name	imgEmpty2	The standard prefix for an image box is img.
	Picture	(none)	Empty—no picture.
	Height	1215	Default size.
	Width	495	Default size.
Image3	BorderStyle	0 - None	Invisible after picture is loaded.
	Name	imgSun	The standard prefix for an image box is img.
	Picture	(Icon)	Sun.ico from the Vb\Icons\Elements folder.
	Height	480	It shrunk to fit the icon.
	Width	480	It shrunk to fit the icon.
Image5	BorderStyle	1 - Fixed Single	Visible at design time and run time.
	Name	imgMoon02	The standard prefix for an image box is img.
	Picture	(Icon)	Moon02.ico from the Vb\Icons\Elements folder.
	Height	540	Slightly larger than with an invisible border.
	Width	540	Slightly larger than with an invisible border.
Image6	BorderStyle	1 - Fixed Single	Visible at design time and run time.
	Name	imgCloud	The standard prefix for an image box is img.
	Picture	(Icon)	Cloud.ico from the Vb\Icons\Elements folder.
	Height	540	Slightly larger than with an invisible border.
	Width	540	Slightly larger than with an invisible border.
Image7	BorderStyle	1 - Fixed Single	Visible at design time and run time.
	Name	imgRain	The standard prefix for an image box is img.
	Picture	(Icon)	Rain.ico from the Vb\Icons\Elements folder.
	Height	540	Slightly larger than with an invisible border.
	Width	540	Slightly larger than with an invisible border.

TABLE 4-2 *Partial Visual Interface Specifications for Project Icons #1 - Icons in Image Boxes* ▼

If you change the setting of an image box's Stretch property to True and enlarge the image box, then the icon expands with it. Change an image box's Stretch property setting with these steps:

1. Click the image box to select it.

2. Click the Stretch property. The Properties button appears.

3. Click the Properties button to get a list of settings—there are only two, False and True.

4. Click True.

Here are stretched icons, a wide earth and a tall thunderstorm in image boxes with their BorderStyles set to 1 - Fixed Single:

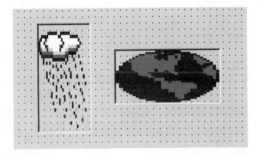

As you enlarge an icon, each of its pixels becomes larger and the image becomes grainier. The same thing happens when you enlarge a photographic image. As you make it larger and larger, it gets grainier and grainier. This is especially evident in the Rain icon's raindrops. Put the Rain icon in an image box, set the Stretch property to True, and make it big. Ouch! Those raindrops have square corners.

EXERCISES

1. Complete Table 4-2. Add specifications for image box imgEarth in the top row and imgLitening in the bottom row. Then create project Icons #1 on your Design screen.

2. What happens to an icon in an image box if you:

   a. Set the image box's Stretch property to False and then enlarge the box?

   b. Set the image box's Stretch property to True and then enlarge the box?

3. At design time, you can delete a picture from an image box in the same way that you delete a picture from a form. Describe the procedure for deleting the current picture from Image1 so that the image box is empty and its Picture setting is (None).

4.3 MAKE ICONS APPEAR AND DISAPPEAR

At run time, an image box and its picture can be visible or invisible. An event can make an invisible picture visible or make a visible picture invisible. You can use an image box's Visible property to make pictures disappear and reappear. Project Light Bulb #1 - Light Bulb Off or On is shown here at the beginning of a run, before either of its command buttons has been clicked.

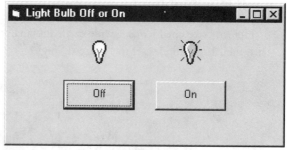

Click the Off button. The turned-off light bulb appears and the turned-on light bulb disappears. (Of course, you don't see the turned-off light appear because it was already visible at the beginning of the run.) Click the On button. The turned-off bulb disappears and the turned-on bulb appears. Click the Off button to make the turned-off bulb appear and the turned-on bulb disappear. When you click the On button, the run-time screen looks like this:

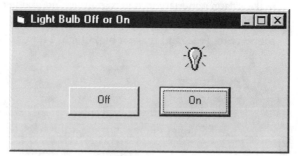

Tables 4-3 and 4-4 list the specifications for project Light Bulb #1. The Visible property for image boxes imgLightOff and imgLightOn is True (the default value) in the Design screen. You use event procedures to make one visible and the other invisible at run time.

Object	Property	Setting	Comment
Form1	Caption	Light Bulb Off or On	
	Name	frmLtBulb1	
Image1	Picture	(Icon)	Lightoff.ico from the Vb\Icons\Misc folder.
	Name	imgLightOff	
	Visible	True	Default setting.
Image2	Picture	(Icon)	Lighton.ico from the Vb\Icons\Misc folder.
	Name	imgLightOn	
	Visible	True	Default setting.
Command1	Caption	Off	
	Name	cmdLightOff	
Command2	Caption	On	
	Name	cmdLightOn	

TABLE 4-3 *Visual Interface Partial Specifications for Project Light Bulb #1 - Light Bulb Off or On* ▼

These are the event procedures for cmdLightOff_Click and cmdLightOn_Click:

```
Private Sub cmdLightOff_Click()
   imgLightOff.Visible = True    ' Makes imgLightOff visible
   imgLightOn.Visible = False    ' Makes imgLightOn invisible
End Sub

Private Sub cmdLightOn_Click()
   imgLightOn.Visible = True     ' Makes imgLightOn visible
   imgLightOff.Visible = False   ' Makes imgLightOff invisible
End Sub
```

Object Name	Event	Response
cmdLightOff	Click	Makes imgLightOff visible and imgLightOn invisible.
cmdLightOn	Click	Makes imgLightOn visible and imgLightOff invisible.

TABLE 4-4 *Partial Event Procedure Specifications for Project Light Bulb #1 - Light Bulb Off or On* ▼

Create the project and make it work. You will modify it to get project Light Bulb #2 - Light Bulb Off or On. When you run Light Bulb #2, it begins with one turned-off bulb visible, as shown here:

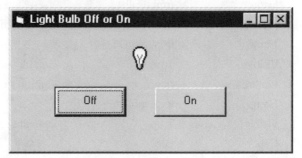

Click the Off button and you'll see that nothing happens because the bulb is already turned off. Click the On button and the bulb turns on. Click the Off button to turn it off again. Here it is turned on:

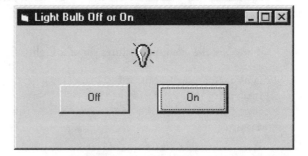

It is easy to modify Light Bulb #1 to get Light Bulb #2. You just move image boxes imgLightOff and imgLightOn to the same place on the form so that they are superimposed. You can do this by clicking and dragging them to the same place. Perhaps a better way is to set their Left and Top properties to the same values. Then you set imgLightOn's Visible property to False so that it is invisible when you run the project. Leave imgLightOff's Visible setting at the default setting of True so that it is visible at run time. The event procedures are the same as for project Light Bulb #1.

Use Event Procedures to Make Things Visible or Invisible

You can "stack" image boxes and then control their visibility with event procedures. If you put image box Image1 on a form, put a second image box Image2 on the form, load pictures into them, and move either image box on top of the other, Image2 will appear to be on top. You may see part of Image1 shining through. Try this:

1. Put Image1 on the form and load it with the Cloud icon (Cloud.ico).

2. Put Image2 on the form and load it with the Litening icon (Litening.ico).

3. Move either image box on top of the other. Here is what we saw when we did it:

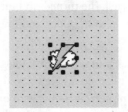

If two or more image boxes are stacked and only one is visible, the visible image box can respond to a click. If two or more image boxes are visible in a stack of image boxes, the visible box "on top" can respond to a click. You can control this by using the Enabled property. When Enabled is set to True, an image box can respond to an event. Change the setting to False and the image box cannot respond to an event. Suppose that the Cloud, Litening, and Rain icons are in stacked image boxes and that imgCloud is visible and is the only enabled box in the stack. Event procedure imgCloud_Click makes imgCloud and imgLitening both visible, makes imgRain invisible, disables imgCloud and imgRain, and enables imgLitening. Image box imgLitening can then respond to an event, but imgCloud and imgRain cannot.

```
Private Sub imgCloud_Click()
   imgCloud.Visible = True      ' Makes cloud visible
   imgCloud.Enabled = False     ' Can't respond to event
   imgLitening.Visible = True   ' Makes lightning visible
   imgLitening.Enabled = True   ' Can respond to event
   imgRain.Visible = False      ' Makes rain invisible
   imgRain.Enabled = False      ' Can't respond to event
End Sub
```

If you click the cloud, you will then see lightning superimposed on the cloud. Litening is enabled and Cloud is disabled, so if you click the cloud and lightning combination, the lightning's image box can respond to the event. You may find imgCloud_Click useful in Exercise 2.

EXERCISES

1. An image box can respond to a click. Create project Light Bulb #3 - Light Bulb Off or On. It has no command buttons. You click the light bulb directly to turn it off or on. The visual interface is easy—it is the same as Light Bulb #2, except that there are no command buttons. You see only the light bulb, initially off at run time. Click the turned-off bulb to turn it on; click the turned-on bulb to turn it off. Write event procedures imgLightOff_Click and imgLightOn_Click to make it so.

2. As the Wizard of the Elements, design project Storm #1. Three image boxes containing the Cloud (Cloud.ico), Litening (Litening.ico), and Rain (Rain.ico) icons are stacked in the same place on the form. When you run the project, it begins with only the cloud visible. Click the cloud and you see lightning superimposed on the cloud. Click that combination and you next see only rain. Click Rain to stop the rain and make the cloud reappear. Do all these things and you will see the following sequence of images:

3. Project Bang #1 - Chinese New Year and 4th of July is not the big bang that began the universe, but provides a quiet bang that won't burn your fingers. It begins like this:

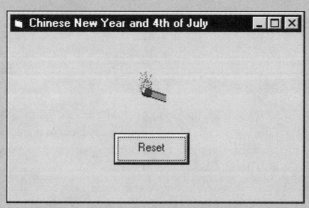

Click the match (Elements\Fire.ico) and a firecracker (Misc\Misc39a.ico) appears. Click the firecracker and it goes bang (Misc\Misc39b.ico). You don't hear the bang, but you see "Bang!" in a label above the exploding firecracker. Click the Reset button to start over. Here is the sequence of images that you see as you click merrily away:

4.4 *M*AKE IMAGE BOXES SHRINK OR GROW TO FIT THE SHOW

When you load a picture into an image box, the box shrinks or grows to fit the size of the picture. A default-sized image box shrinks to fit an icon or one of the tiny bitmaps in Visual Basic's Bitmaps folder. You can set an image box's Stretch property to True and then change the size of the image box and its picture. We put three image boxes on Form1 and loaded them all with the same picture, a fish from the Assorted folder of the Bitmaps folder of the Vb folder. The filename is easy to remember: Fish.bmp. Our Design screen displays these piscatorial possibilities:

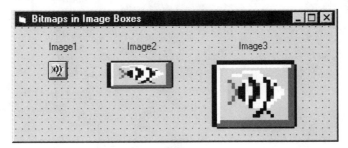

Image1's Stretch property is set to False. When we plopped a fish into it, Image1 immediately shrunk to the size of the fish. We first set Image2's Stretch property to True and then gave it a fish. Well, the fish sure liked that environment—

it immediately grew to the size of the image box. We did the same with Image3, then clicked a selection handle and enlarged the image box—the fish grew with it.

If you set an image box's Stretch setting to False and then load a picture, the image box changes size to fit the picture. If you set an image box's Stretch property setting to True and then load a picture, the picture changes size to fit the box. Let's try it with a metafile:

1. Put Image1 on Form1 and make it the size you want.

2. Set Image1's BorderStyle property to 1 - Fixed Single.

3. Set Image1's Stretch property to True.

4. Load a metafile picture into Image1.

We loaded the intertwingled arrows metafile (Multarw4.wmf). It's the one that looks like a freeway intersection designed to boggle, befuddle, and bewilder unwary travelers. Since Image1's Stretch property is True, the picture changed size to fit neatly into Image1:

Now change Image1's Stretch property to False. Shazam! The metafile expands to its true size—very big—and Image1 expands with it. On our screen, most of Image1 and its picture expanded off of the form and we see only the upper-left part of the picture:

EXERCISES

1. Draw image boxes Image1, Image2, and Image3 on the form, make them the sizes you want, and set their Stretch properties to False. What happens when you:

    a. Load an icon into Image1?

    b. Load a bitmap into Image2?

    c. Load a metafile into Image3?

2. Draw image boxes Image1, Image2, and Image3 on the form, make them the sizes you want, and set their Stretch properties to True. What happens when you:

    a. Load an icon into Image1?

    b. Load a bitmap into Image2?

    c. Load a metafile into Image3?

4.5 DISPLAY PICTURES IN PICTURE BOXES

Picture boxes are awesome! A picture box has 45 properties. Fortunately, you already know how to use many picture box properties that are the same as the properties of a form, text box, or image box. These are Appearance, AutoRedraw, AutoSize, BackColor, BorderStyle, Enabled, Font, ForeColor, Height, Left, Name, Picture, Top, Visible, and Width. An image box is great for displaying a picture and responding to certain events. A picture box can do much more. You can print text in it and use it as a container for controls. For example, you can put controls such as command buttons, labels, and image boxes in a picture box and then move the whole shebang anywhere on the form by moving the picture box.

Picture boxes, like image boxes, are great containers for pictures. You draw a picture box on a form and load it with a picture the same way that you draw an image box and load it with a picture. We drew three square picture boxes and loaded them with pictures. The left picture box contains a bitmap (Cup.bmp), the middle box contains a road sign icon (Traffic07.ico), and the box on the right displays a metafile (Laptop1.wmf). The laptop is not a recent model—it looks a bit bulky and heavy for backpack duty.

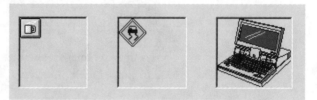

A picture box does not have a Stretch property, as does an image box. Instead, a picture box has an AutoSize property. In the illustration, the AutoSize property setting is False for all three picture boxes, so they do not automatically resize to fit the picture. The bitmap and the icon appear in the upper-left corner of their boxes. The metafile is drawn to exactly fit the box. If you resize a picture box that contains a bitmap or icon, the picture remains the same size nestled in its corner. If you resize a picture box that contains a metafile, the picture is redrawn to fill the box.

If you set AutoSize to True, the picture box will shrink or grow to the size of the picture. A picture box that contains a bitmap or icon will shrink to the size of the picture, and a box that contains a metafile will grow to the inherent size of the metafile, a size determined by the way the metafile is drawn and saved on the disk where it resides. Try it with default picture boxes, except for size—make each picture box about 1215 × 1215 twips:

1. Draw Picture1 on Form1 and put it where you want it.

2. Load a bitmap into Picture1.

3. Draw Picture2 on Form1 and move it to where you want it.

4. Load an icon into Picture2.

5. Draw Picture3 on Form1 and locate it where you want it.

6. Load a metafile into Picture3.

Now set the AutoSize property of each box to True and watch it shrink or grow. Also try changing the BackColor setting for each picture box. Some of the metafiles in the Arrows folder look good on light green, cyan, blue, or magenta.

We are using Microsoft Word for Windows 6 to write this book, so we can tap into it for lots of metafiles. They are in the Clipart folder of the Winword folder. Here are two that we like, a compass to help you navigate the road to Visual Basic literacy and a pretty butterfly:

You can use the **LoadPicture** function in an event procedure to load a picture into a picture box at run time. The standard prefix for the name of a picture box is "pic." Table 4-5 shows examples of statements using the **LoadPicture** function to load a picture into a picture box picDisplay from the Vb folder on disk drive C.

Project Picture Box #1 - Picture in a Picture Box looks like this at run time:

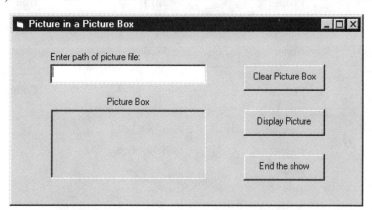

Statement	Action Performed
picDisplay.Picture = LoadPicture("c:\vb\icons\elements\earth.ico")	Loads the Earth icon.
picDisplay.Picture = LoadPicture("c:\vb\bitmaps\assorted\fish.bmp")	Loads the Fish bitmap.
picDisplay.Picture = LoadPicture("c:\vb\metafile\arrows\multarw4.wmf")	Loads the "freeway" metafile.
picDisplay.Picture = LoadPicture(txtPath.Text)	Path is specified by txtPath.Text.
picDisplay.Picture = LoadPicture( )	Clears picture from picDisplay.

TABLE 4-5 *Statements Using the LoadPicture Function to Display a Picture in a Picture Box* ▼

At run time, you can load a picture into the picture box by supplying the path of the picture you want to display. The path specifies the disk drive, the folder where Visual Basic is stored, the folders where the picture file is stored, and the filename of the picture file. Load a picture like this:

1. Click the text box and enter the path of the picture file that you want. For the Earth icon, our path is C:\Vb\Icons\Elements\Earth.ico. The "freeway" metafile path is C:\Vb\Metafile\Arrows\Multarw4.wmf.

2. Click the Display Picture button to display the picture in the picture box.

3. Click the Clear Picture Box button to clear a picture from the picture box.

When you click the text box, any old text disappears. If you mistype the path, you may see a "Path not found" or "File not found" error message. If that happens, remove the dialog box and try again. You don't have to clear the picture box before entering another picture. A new picture will replace any existing picture.

Object	Property	Setting	Comments
Form1	Caption	Picture in a Picture Box	
	Name	frmPicBox1	
Picture1	Name	picDisplay	The standard prefix is "pic."
	Picture	(None)	Default setting—no picture.
Label1	AutoSize	True	
	Caption	Picture Box	
	Name	lblPictureBox	
Text1	Name	txtPath	
	Text		
Label2	AutoSize	True	
	Caption	Enter path of picture file:	
	Name	lblPath	
Command1	Caption	Clear Picture Box	
	Name	cmdClearPic	
Command2	Caption	Display Picture	
	Name	cmdDisplay	
Command3	Caption	End the show	
	Name	cmdEndShow	

TABLE 4-6 *Visual Interface Specifications for Project Picture Box #1 - Picture in a Picture Box* ▼

Object Name	Event	Response
txtFilename	Click	Clears itself and accepts focus (cursor appears).
cmdClearPic	Click	Clears picture from picture box picDisplay.
cmdDisplay	Click	Loads into picDisplay the picture specified in txtPath.
cmdEndShow	Click	Ends the run.

TABLE 4-7 *Event Procedure Specifications for Project Picture Box #1 - Picture in a Picture Box* ▼

Tables 4-6 and 4-7 list specifications for project Picture Box #1. Make the text box the size you want, but wide enough to hold the text of the path. The standard prefix for a picture box is "pic."

Event procedure cmdClearPic_Click uses the **LoadPicture** function to clear any picture from picDisplay:

```
Private Sub cmdClearPic_Click()
  picDisplay.Picture = LoadPicture()    ' Clear picture from picDisplay
End Sub
```

Event procedure txtPath_Click clears txtPath and accepts focus. At run time, you click the text box and enter the complete path of the picture file you want to display, such as C:\Vb\Icons\Elements\Earth.ico:

```
Private Sub txtPath_Click()
  txtPath.Text = ""          ' Clear txtPath
End Sub
```

Event procedure cmdDisplay_Click uses **LoadPicture** to load a picture into picDisplay. The path of the picture is the value of txtPath.text.

```
Private Sub cmdDisplay_Click()
  ' Display the picture whose path is in txtPath
  picDisplay.Picture = LoadPicture(txtPath.Text)
End Sub
```

Now picture yourself on the path to these exercises.

EXERCISES

1. Draw picture boxes Picture1, Picture2, and Picture3 on Form1. Leave the AutoSize property at its default setting of False.

   a. Click Picture1 to select it and then load the horizontal thermometer (Horz.bmp) from the Gauge folder of the Bitmaps folder. What is the path? Describe the appearance of the picture in Picture1.

   b. Click Picture2 to select it and then load the bicycle (Bicycle.ico) from the Industry folder of the Icons folder. What is the path? Describe the appearance of the picture in Picture2.

   c. Click Picture3 to select it and then load the second satellite (Satelit2.wmf) from the Business folder of the Metafile folder. What is the path? Describe the appearance of the picture in Picture3.

2. After completing Exercise 1, set the AutoSize property to True for all three picture boxes.

   a. What happened to Picture1 and its picture?

   b. What happened to Picture2 and its picture?

   c. What happened to Picture3 and its picture?

3. Modify project Light Bulb #2 - Light Bulb Off or On from Section 4.3 to use picture boxes instead of image boxes. Name this project Light Bulb #4 - Light Bulb Off or On.

4.6 **PRINT TEXT IN PICTURE BOXES**

You have used the **Print** method to print text directly on a form and you have used the **Cls** method to clear a form. You can use **Print** to print text in a picture box and **Cls** to clear a picture box of text that was entered at run time. To do so, you use an *Object.Method* statement that consists of the name of the object, a period, and the name of the method. Here are Object.Method statements using the **Cls** and **Print** methods with picture box picDisplayText:

Statement	Action Performed
picDisplayText.Cls	Clears picture box picText of text entered at run time.
picDisplayText.Print "qwerty"	Prints the string "qwerty" in picture box picDisplayText.

At run time, project Picture Box #2 - Text in a Picture Box looks like this after someone clicks the Display Text button:

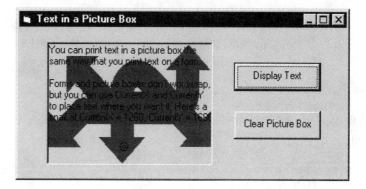

Click Display Text to print text in the picture box. Click Clear Picture Box to clear the picture box of the text entered at run time. Tables 4-8 and 4-9 list the specifications for project Picture Box #2.

Object	Property	Setting	Comment
Form1	Caption	Text in a Picture Box	
	Name	frmPicBox2	
Picture1	Name	picDisplayText	The standard prefix is "pic."
	Picture	(Metafile)	The "freeway" metafile.
	FontTransparent	True	Default setting.
	Height	2160	Make it big enough to hold the text printed by cmdDisplayText_Click.
	Width	3000	
Command1	Caption	Clear Picture Box	
	Name	cmdClearPic	
Command2	Caption	Display Text	
	Name	cmdDisplay	

TABLE 4-8 *Visual Interface Specifications for Project Picture Box #2 - Text in a Picture Box* ▼

Object Name	Event	Response
cmdClear	Click	Clears picture box picDisplay of text entered at run time.
cmdDisplay	Click	Prints text in picture box picDisplay.

TABLE 4-9 *Event Procedure Specifications for Project Picture Box #2 - Text in a Picture Box* ▼

Event procedure cmdDisplayText_Click uses the **Print** method to print text in the picture box. Event procedure cmdClearPic_Click uses the **Cls** method to clear the picture box of text entered by cmdDisplay_Click at run time:

```
Private Sub cmdClearPic_Click()
   picDisplayText.Cls        ' Clear text
End Sub

Private Sub cmdDisplayText_Click()
   picDisplayText.CurrentX = 0
   picDisplayText.CurrentY = 0
   picDisplayText.Print "You can print text in a picture box the"
   picDisplayText.Print "same way that you print text on a form."
   picDisplayText.Print
   picDisplayText.Print "Forms and picture boxes don't word wrap,"
   picDisplayText.Print "but you can use CurrentX and CurrentY"
   picDisplayText.Print "to place text where you want it. Here's a"
   picDisplayText.Print "snail at CurrentX = 1260, CurrentY = 1680."
   picDisplayText.CurrentX = 1260
   picDisplayText.CurrentY = 1680
   picDisplayText.Print "@"
End Sub
```

The statements

```
picDisplayText.CurrentX = 0
picDisplayText.CurrentY = 0
```

position the cursor at the upper-left inside corner of picDisplayText. Printing of text begins there.

The statements

```
picDisplayText.CurrentX = 1260
picDisplayText.CurrentY = 1680
```

position the cursor 1260 twips from the left edge and 1680 twips down from the top of picDisplayText. The snail (@) is printed there.

Design project Picture Box #2 and run it. Click Display Text to see text printed on the picture. Click Clear Picture Box to clear the text that was printed at run time. This does not clear the picture that was loaded at design time. We hope that all this is clear to you so that you can quickly display the answers to these exercises.

EXERCISES

1. Describe the action performed by each statement if it is executed in an event procedure:

   a. Cls

   b. Print "Be nice to the driver who just cut across your bow."

   c. Form1.Cls

   d. Form1.Print "Dance, sing, and whistle to banish the blues."

   e. Picture1.Cls

   f. Picture1.Print "Honk if you understand Visual Basic."

   g. Print Time

   h. Form1.Print Time

   i. Picture1.Print Time

2. Experiment with project Picture Box #2 - Text in a Picture Box.

   a. Set the picture box's FontTransparent property to False, run the project, and click the Display Text button. What do you see? Click the Clear Picture Box button. What happens?

   b. Set the picture box's width to 2400 twips, run the project, and click Display Text. What do you see?

3. Design project Kronos #13 - Time in a Picture Box. Here is the run-time snapshot after someone has clicked Show Time:

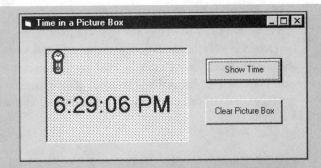

For the clock image, we used C:\Vb\Icons\Misc\Clock04.ico. For the picture box's BackColor, we selected the light peach color, fourth from the left in the top row of the palette. In event procedure cmdShowTime_Click, we set picShowTime's FontSize to 24 and set its CurrentX and CurrentY properties to position the printed time where we wanted it.

4.7 *IF YOU DON'T LIKE THE SCENERY, DRAW YOUR OWN*

The Toolbox has two tools that you can use to draw pictures on a form or in a picture box. You use the Line tool to draw lines and the Shape tool to draw any of six geometric shapes:

Shape tool ⟶  ⟵ Line tool

Well, what first, the Line control or the Shape control? The coin is in the air—heads for Line, tails for Shape. Oops, it fell through a crack in the big rock we are sitting on. Okay, we'll start with the Line control. Starting with an empty form draw a line on the form using these steps:

1. Click the Line tool once to select it.

2. Move the mouse pointer to the form. The pointer changes to a cross-hair.

3. Move the cross-hair to the place on the form where you want to draw the line.

4. Click and drag to draw the line. When it looks right, release the mouse button.

Here is our line on Form1:

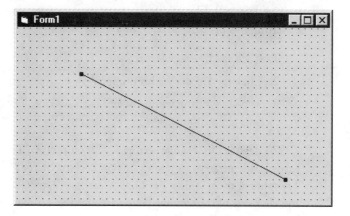

Move the line elsewhere on Form1 and then change its length and slope with these steps:

1. Click the line anywhere except on an endpoint and drag the line elsewhere.

2. Click an endpoint and drag it elsewhere. The other endpoint remains in place. Make the line longer or shorter. Move the endpoint you are dragging around the fixed endpoint. Enjoy.

3. Draw another line on Form1 and introduce the two lines to each other.

4. Draw a bunch of lines, pretend that they are Tinkertoys, and build something.

Change some properties. The default BorderColor setting is black. Change it to another color with these easy steps:

1. Click the line to select it. You see the selection handles.

2. Double-click the BorderColor property. The palette of colors pops into view.

3. Click the color you want. The line changes to that color.

The default BorderStyle setting is 1 - Solid. Seven styles are available. Try them:

1. Click the line to select it.

2. Click the BorderStyle property. The Properties button appears.

3. Click the Properties button to pull down a list of settings.

4. Click a setting. Try 2 - Dot or 3 - Dash or 4 - Dash-Dot. Try 'em all and watch the line change.

The default BorderWidth setting is 1, quite thin. You can make the line thicker by setting this property to 2, 3, or a higher setting:

1. Click the line to select it.

2. Click the BorderWidth property.

3. Type the setting you want and press ENTER. Try 2 or 4 or 8 or whatever setting **you** want.

The default DrawMode setting is 13 - Copy Pen. The other 15 possible settings have equally mysterious names such as 2 - Not Merge Pen and 10 - Not Xor Pen. Try some of them—click the DrawMode property, click the Properties button, and click one of the settings. Some settings seem to have no effect; others make the line disappear. We won't get into this unless there is a task that requires one of these settings. When you finish experimenting, set the DrawMode property to its default setting, 13 - Copy Pen.

You already know about the Name and Visible properties, which you have used with other controls. Ignore the Index and Tag properties for now and experiment with the X1, X2, Y1, and Y2 properties.

The settings of the X1 and Y1 properties are the coordinates of the line's first endpoint, the one that you put on the form when you begin to draw the line. The settings of the X2 and Y2 properties are the coordinates of the second endpoint. An X setting is the number of twips from the inside left edge of the form and a Y setting is the number of twips down from the form's caption bar. When the line is selected, you can see the values of X1 and Y1 in the object coordinates box. Change X1's setting:

1. Click the line to select it.

2. Click the X1 property.

3. Type the setting you want and press ENTER. The line's first endpoint moves horizontally to that X-coordinate.

Try a variety of settings for X1, X2, Y1, and Y2 and watch the line jump around. Click an endpoint, drag it and drop it (release the mouse button). Notice the new settings for that endpoint's coordinates. Click the middle of the line and move it to a new location—the X and Y settings of both endpoints change.

Whew! We're all lined out, so let's move on and experiment with shapes. You can double-click the Shape tool to put a Shape control on the form and then move it to where you want it, or draw the Shape control yourself with these steps:

1. Click the Shape tool once to select it.

2. Move the mouse pointer to the form. The pointer changes to a cross-hair.

3. Move the cross-hair to the place on the form where you want to draw the Shape control.

4. Click and drag to draw it the size you want. When it looks right, release the mouse button.

The Shape control appears on the form in its default shape, a rectangle. You can use the Shape property to select one of six shapes, listed here:

0 - Rectangle (the default shape—you see it as soon as you draw the shape control)

1 - Square

2 - Oval

3 - Circle

4 - Rounded Rectangle

5 - Rounded Square

Select the shape you want with these steps:

1. Click the shape (the rectangle) to select it.

2. Click the Shape property. The Properties button appears.

3. Click the Properties button to pull down a list of settings.

4. Click a setting. Try 'em all and watch the shapes appear.

Project Shapes #1 - The Shape Control's Six Shapes shows all six shapes in their default sizes and appearances:

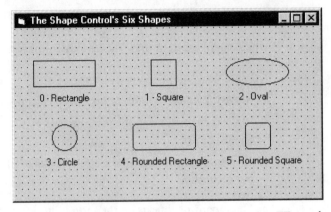

Put the six shapes on your screen and change some properties. We made a bunch of changes and saved the project as Shapes #2 - The Six Shapes with Changed Properties. At run time, our screen looks like this:

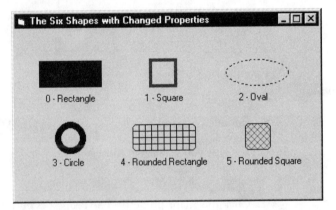

Table 4-10 shows the changes we made in the six shapes. Make these changes slowly and watch what happens to the shape as you change its property settings. Experiment—try other settings.

You can draw a line or a shape in a picture box and then move the picture box and its picture anywhere on the form. In order to show off our amazing artistic skills, we drew a picture of Adam in a picture box. As you can see, Adam is not completely created—we're still learning how to do Garden of Eden art:

Object	Property	Setting	Comments
Shape1	Shape	0 - Rectangle	Default setting (not changed).
	BackColor	Blue	Selected from the BackColor palette.
	BackStyle	1 - Opaque	If set to 0 - Transparent, you won't see the color.
Shape2	Shape	1 - Square	
	BorderColor	Red	Selected from the BorderColor palette.
	BorderWidth	4	
Shape3	Shape	2 - Oval	
	BorderStyle	3 - Dot	A dotted curve. Try other styles.
Shape4	Shape	3 - Circle	
	BorderWidth	8	
Shape5	Shape	4 - Rounded Rectangle	
	FillStyle	6 - Cross	Checkerboard pattern. Try other styles.
Shape6	Shape	5 - Rounded Square	
	FillColor	Green	Selected from the FillColor palette.
	FillStyle	6 - Diagonal Cross	Diamond pattern. Try other styles.

TABLE 4-10   *Project Shapes #2 - The Six Shapes with Changed Property Settings* ▼

Draw a line in a picture box like this:

1. Click the Line tool once to select it.

2. Move the mouse pointer inside the picture box. The pointer changes to a cross-hair.

3. Move the cross-hair to the place in the picture box where you want to draw the line.

4. Click and drag to draw the line. When it looks right, release the mouse button.

Draw a shape in a picture box like this:

1. Click the Shape tool once to select it.

2. Move the mouse pointer inside the picture box. The pointer changes to a cross-hair.

3. Move the cross-hair to the place in the picture box where you want to draw the Shape control.

4. Click and drag to draw it until it's the size you want. When it looks right, release the mouse button. You will see the default shape, a rectangle.

5. Click the Shape property. The Properties button appears.

6. Click the Properties button to pull down a list of shape settings.

7. Click the shape setting you want.

After drawing a line or a shape in a picture box, you can move or resize it the same way that you resized a line or shape on a form.

EXERCISES

1. Draw Eve on the form. Eve might look like this:

This picture shows Eve wearing a dress after she and Adam were expelled from the Garden of Eden into the cold, cruel world and forced to wear clothes.

2. Draw Eve in a picture box.

4.8 # ***M**AKE THINGS MOVE*

You can move an object left or right by changing the value of its Left property. You can move it up or down by changing the value of its Top property. Project Move It #1 - Move It Up, Down, Left, or Right provides arrows that you click to move a ball in the direction the arrow points:

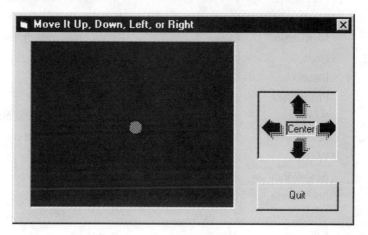

This project has these entities:

▼   A picture box that contains a ball (shape).

▼   A picture box that contains four arrows in image boxes and a label captioned "Center."

▼   A command button.

When you click an arrow, the ball moves 120 twips in the direction the arrow points. Tables 4-11 and 4-12 list the specs for project Move It #1.

A picture box's ScaleHeight and ScaleWidth property settings are the *inside* dimensions of the picture box. ScaleHeight is the vertical height inside the top and bottom borders. ScaleWidth is the horizontal width inside the left and right borders. The ScaleMode property specifies the unit of measurement for ScaleHeight and ScaleWidth. ScaleMode's default setting is 1 - Twip, exactly what we want for this project. Height, Width, ScaleHeight, and ScaleWidth are measured in twips.

Object	Property	Setting	Comment
Form1	Caption	Move It Up, Down, Left, or Right	
	Name	frmMoveIt1	
	BorderStyle	1 - Fixed Single	At run time, you can't change the form's size.
	MaxButton	False	At run time, you can't maximize the form.
	MinButton	False	At run time, you can't minimize the form.
Picture1	Name	picPoolTable	Contains the ball.
	BackColor	&H00FF0000&	Blue.
	BorderStyle	1 - Fixed Single	
	Height	2910	Outside height of the pool table.
	ScaleHeight	2880	Inside height of the pool table.
	Width	3630	Outside width of the pool table.
	ScaleWidth	3600	Inside width of the pool table.
	ScaleMode	1 - Twips	
Shape1	Shape	3 - Circle	Drawn inside picPoolTable.
	FillColor	&H000080FF&	Orange.
	FillStyle	0 - Solid	The ball is a solid color.
	Height	240	
	Width	240	
	Left	1680	From the inside left edge of picPoolTable.
	Top	1320	From the inside top of picPoolTable.
Picture2	Name	picMoveControls	Contains the arrows and "Center" label.
Label1	Caption	Center	Drawn inside picMoveControls.
	Name	lblCenter	
	BorderStyle	1 - Fixed Single	
Image1	Name	imgUp	Drawn inside picMoveControls.
	Picture	(Icon)	Arw04up.ico from Vb\Icons\Arrows.
Image2	Name	imgRight	Drawn inside picMoveControls.
	Picture	(Icon)	Arw04rt.ico from Vb\Icons\Arrows.
Image3	Name	imgDown	Drawn inside picMoveControls.
	Picture	(Icon)	Arw04dn.ico from Vb\Icons\Arrows.
Image4	Name	imgLeft	Drawn inside picMoveControls.
	Picture	(Icon)	Arw04lt.ico from Vb\Icons\Arrows.

TABLE 4-11 *Visual Interface Specifications for Project Move It #1 - Move It Up, Down, Left, or Right* ▼

Object Name	Event	Response
lblCenter	Click	Moves the ball to the center of picPoolTable.
imgUp	Click	Moves the ball up 120 twips.
imgRight	Click	Moves the ball right 120 twips.
imgDown	Click	Moves the ball down 120 twips.
imgLeft	Click	Moves the ball left 120 twips.

TABLE 4-12   *Event Procedure Specifications for Project Move It #1 - Move It Up, Down, Left, or Right* ▼

When you set the Height and Width properties, Visual Basic automatically sets the ScaleHeight and ScaleWidth properties. We set Height = 2910 and Visual Basic set ScaleHeight = 2880. We set Width = 3630 and Visual Basic set ScaleWidth = 3600. Good, exactly what we wanted. The ScaleHeight and ScaleWidth are both multiples of 120 twips, the distance between gridpoints (2880 = 24 × 120 and 3600 = 30 × 120). Be sure to notice the Height, Width, ScaleHeight, ScaleWidth, and ScaleMode settings in Table 4-11.

REMEMBER *To draw a control such as a shape or an image box inside a picture box, click the control once to select it—it will look "pushed in" and be highlighted. Move the mouse pointer (it changes to a cross-hair) inside the picture box and then click and drag to draw the control.*

Design the visual interface as specified by Table 4-11, or do it your way. Event procedure lblCenter_Click moves the ball to the center of picture box picPoolTable:

```
Private Sub lblCenter_Click()
  ' Move the ball to the center of picPoolTable
  shpBall.Left = 1680
  shpBall.Top = 1320
End Sub
```

The dimensions of picPoolTable are ScaleWidth = 3600 and ScaleHeight = 2880. The ball is 240 × 240. Do a little arithmetic and verify that the coordinates 1680, 1320 put the *center* of the ball at the *center* of the picture box.

Here are the event procedures for the four image boxes inside picMoveControls:

```
Private Sub imgUp_Click()
  ' Move it 120 twips up
  shpBall.Top = shpBall.Top - 120
End Sub
```

```
Private Sub imgRight_Click()
  ' Move it 120 twips to the right
  shpBall.Left = shpBall.Left + 120
End Sub

Private Sub imgDown_Click()
  ' Move it 120 twips down
  shpBall.Top = shpBall.Top + 120
End Sub

Private Sub imgLeft_Click()
  ' Move it 120 twips left
  shpBall.Left = shpBall.Left - 120
End Sub
```

If you want the ball to move upward, decrease the value of shpBall.Top.
The statement:

```
shpBall.Top = shpBall.Top - 120
```

grabs the value of *shpBall.Top*, subtracts 120 from it, and stuffs the result back into
shpBall.Top. The ball jumps up to the new setting of its Top property.

You can modify project Move It #1 to get project Move It #2 - Move it in
Eight Compass Directions. Easy—change the form's caption, add four image
boxes to picMoveControls, and write their event procedures. Here's Move It #2
at run time:

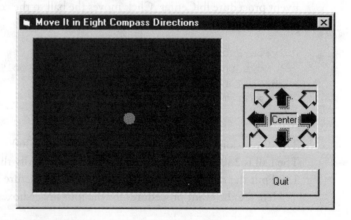

Notice the new images in picture box picMoveControls, arrows that point
northeast, southeast, southwest, and northwest. Tables 4-13 and 4-14 list specs for
the four additional image boxes.

Object	Property	Setting	Comment
Image1	Name	imgNE	Drawn inside picMoveControls.
	Picture	(Icon)	Arw10ne.ico from Vb\Icons\Arrows.
Image2	Name	imgSE	Drawn inside picMoveControls.
	Picture	(Icon)	Arw10se.ico from Vb\Icons\Arrows.
Image3	Name	imgSW	Drawn inside picMoveControls.
	Picture	(Icon)	Arw10sw.ico from Vb\Icons\Arrows.
Image4	Name	imgNW	Drawn inside picMoveControls.
	Picture	(Icon)	Arw10nw.ico from Vb\Icons\Arrows.

TABLE 4-13   *Visual Interface Specifications, Added Image Boxes for Project Move It #2 - Move It in Eight Compass Directions* ▼

One way to write event procedure imgNE_Click is to change the setting of imgNE's Left property and then change the setting of its Top property, like this:

```
Private Sub imgNE_Click()
  ' Move it 120 twips right, then move it 120 twips up
  imgNE.Left = imgNE.Left + 120
  imgNE.Top = imgNE.Top - 120
End Sub
```

This causes the ball to zig right and then zag up. We didn't do it that way because we want the ball to move diagonally to its new location. Fortunately, Visual Basic

Object Name	Event	Response
lblCenter	Click	Moves the ball directly to the center of picPoolTable.
imgNE	Click	Moves the ball diagonally to the northeast.
imgSE	Click	Moves the ball diagonally to the southeast.
imgSW	Click	Moves the ball diagonally to the southwest.
imgNW	Click	Moves the ball diagonally to the northwest.

TABLE 4-14   *Event Procedure Specifications, Added Image Boxes for Project Move It #2 - Move It in Eight Compass Directions* ▼

provides the means to perform this task. You can use the **Move** method to move an object to a new location. For example:

Statement	Action Performed
shpBall.Move 1680, 1320	Moves it to 1680, 1320 (center of picPoolTable).
shpBall.Move NewLeft, NewTop	Moves it to the location specified by *NewLeft* and *NewTop*.

Revised event procedure lblCenter_Click uses the **Move** method to move the ball directly to the center of picPoolTable:

```
Private Sub lblCenter_Click()
   ' Move the ball to the center of picPoolTable
   shpBall.Move 1680, 1320
End Sub
```

Event procedures imgNE_Click, imgSE_Click, imgSW_Click, and imgNW_Click use the **Move** method to move the ball diagonally to its new location:

```
Private Sub imgNE_Click()
   ' Move it NE (120 twips right and 120 twips up)
   Dim NewLeft As Integer, NewTop As Integer
   NewLeft = shpBall.Left + 120
   NewTop = shpBall.Top - 120
   shpBall.Move NewLeft, NewTop
End Sub

Private Sub imgSE_Click()
   ' Move it SE (120 twips right and 120 twips down)
   Dim NewLeft As Integer, NewTop As Integer
   NewLeft = shpBall.Left + 120
   NewTop = shpBall.Top + 120
   shpBall.Move NewLeft, NewTop
End Sub

Private Sub imgSW_Click()
   ' Move it SW (120 twips left and 120 twips down)
   Dim NewLeft As Integer, NewTop As Integer
   NewLeft = shpBall.Left - 120
   NewTop = shpBall.Top + 120
   shpBall.Move NewLeft, NewTop
End Sub
```

```
Private Sub imgNW_Click()
  ' Move it NW (120 twips left and 120 twips up)
  Dim NewLeft As Integer, NewTop As Integer
  NewLeft = shpBall.Left - 120
  NewTop = shpBall.Top - 120
  shpBall.Move NewLeft, NewTop
End Sub
```

Your turn—move directly on to the exercises.

EXERCISES

1. Suppose that picture box picPoolTable's inside dimensions are 3000 × 2400 (ScaleWidth × ScaleHeight) and the diameter of the ball is 180 twips (Width = 180 and Height = 180).

   a. Modify event procedure lblCenter_Click in project Move It #1 so that it puts the resized ball in the center of the resized picPoolTable.

   b. Modify event procedure lblCenter_Click in project Move It #2 so that it puts the resized ball in the center of the resized picPoolTable.

2. Whatever its size, picPoolTable's dimensions are available as the values of its ScaleWidth and ScaleHeight properties. The diameter of the ball is available, too, as the settings of its Width and Height properties, if they are the same. What is the ball's diameter if these are different? Use picPoolTable's ScaleWidth and ScaleHeight settings and shpBall's diameter to perform these algebraic alakazams:

   a. Modify event procedure lblCenter_Click in project Move It #1 so that it puts the ball in the center of the picPoolTable.

   b. Modify event procedure lblCenter_Click in project Move It #2 so that it puts the resized ball in the center of the resized picPoolTable.

3. Design project Move It #3 - Move It in Eight Compass Directions. Instead of putting the ball in a picture box, put it directly on the form. What happens at run time when you move the ball so that it collides with picMoveControls or cmdQuit?

You are moving well. Now it is time for you to collide with the following end-of-chapter recreations.

1. Describe the procedure for loading:

   a. The pay phone metafile (Vb\Metafile\Business\Payphone.wmf) onto Form1.

   b. The rocket icon (Vb\Icons\Industry\Rocket.ico) into image box Image1.

   c. The heart bitmap (Vb\Bitmaps\Assorted\Heart.bmp) into picture box Picture1.

2. Suppose you draw image control Image1 and picture box control Picture1 on friendly Form1. What happens if you:

   a. Leave Image1's Stretch property set to its default value of False and load a bitmap or an icon into Image1?

   b. Leave Image1's Stretch property set to its default value of False and load a metafile into Image1?

   c. Set Image1's Stretch property to True and then load a bitmap or an icon into Image1?

   d. Set Image1's Stretch property to True and then load a metafile into Image1?

   e. Leave Picture1's AutoSize property set to its default value of False and load a bitmap or an icon into Picture1?

   f. Leave Picture1's AutoSize property set to its default value of False and load a metafile into Picture1?

   g. Set Picture1's AutoSize property to True and then load a bitmap or an icon into Picture1?

   h. Set Picture1's AutoSize property to True and then load a metafile into Picture1?

3. Forms and picture boxes have some of the same properties. The default settings of these properties may be the same or different. Forms have properties that picture boxes don't have, and picture boxes have properties

that forms don't have. Below are selected properties of a form or
picture box or both or neither. For all appropriate properties, show the
default setting.

Property	Default Setting—Form	Default Setting—Picture Box
Appearance		
AutoRedraw		
AutoSize		
BackColor		
BorderStyle		
Caption		
ControlBox		
DrawBridge		
DrawMode		
DrawStyle		
DrawWidth		
Enabled		
FillColor		
FillStyle		
Font		
FontTransparent		
ForeColor		
Icon		
MaxButton		
MinButton		
Picture		
Visible		

4. An *Object.Property* variable consists of the name of an object, a period, and
   the name of a property of the object. Complete the following table of
   Object.Property variables and show a possible value for each variable:

Object Name	Property Name	Object Property Variable	Possible Value
Form1	DrawStyle	Form1.DrawStyle	0 - Solid
frmIcons01	BackColor	_____	_____
Image1	Stretch	_____	_____
imgEmpty	BorderStyle	_____	_____
Picture1	Picture	_____	_____
picEarth	Visible	_____	_____
Line1	BorderWidth	_____	_____
linLeftArm	X1	_____	_____
Shape1	Shape	_____	_____
shpAnyShape	FillStyle	_____	_____

5. Describe the action performed by each statement:

   a. Image1.BorderStyle = 0

   b. Form1.DrawStyle = 0

   c. Picture1.DrawStyle = 1

   d. Picture1.DrawWidth = 4

   e. Form1.FillColor = QBColor(3)

   f. Picture1.FillColor = RGB(255, 0, 0)

   g. Form1.Caption = "A statement can change a caption."

   h. Form1.FillStyle = 6

   i. Picture1.FillStyle = 7

   j. Image1.Enabled = True

   k. Image1.Stretch = True

   l. Picture1.AutoSize = False

   m. Image1.Picture = LoadPicture("vb\icons\misc\misc42")

   n. Picture1.Picture = LoadPicture()

   o. Image1.Picture = LoadPicture(txtFilename.Text)

   p. Picture1.Print "When tools become toys, then work becomes play."

   q. Picture1.Cls

   r. Picture1.Print Picture1.BorderStyle

   s. Picture1.Picture = Image1.Picture

    t. Line1.X1 = 1000

    u. Shape1.Shape = 3

    v. Shape1.Move 1200, 600

6. For each action, write a statement or statements to perform the action.

    a. Make imgLightOff visible.

    b. Make imgLightOn invisible.

    c. Enable imgLitening so that it can respond to an event.

    d. Disable imgCloud so that it cannot respond to an event.

    e. Load the Earth icon into picDisplay (use the **LoadPicture** function).

    f. Set picDisplay's AutoSize property to True.

    g. Print your name on Form1.

    h. Print your name in picture box Picture1.

    i. Clear picDisplay.

    j. Set the DrawWidth property of frmCanvas to 4.

    k. Set the coordinates of Line1 to X1 = 240, Y1 = 360, X2 = 1200, and Y2 = 1320.

    l. Make Shape1 a rounded square.

    m. Move Shape1 to 960, 1440.

7. Draw a picture box on the form and make it somewhat large. Load it with the "freeway" metafile (Multarw4.wmf). Draw a small image box directly on the "freeway" and load it with the cars icon (Cars.ico). Save the project as Freeway #1 - Cars on a Freeway. Ours looks like this:

8. As Wizard of the Elements, modify project Storm #1 to get project Storm #2 - Storm with a Happy Ending. At run time, Storm #2 begins with the cloud visible. Click the cloud and you see lightning superimposed on it. Click that combination and it rains. Click the rain and the sun comes out. Click the sun to start over with the cloud. Here is the sequence of pictures that you see when you run the project and click in your wizardly way:

9. Design project Storm #3 - Storm with a Happy Ending. It is the same as project Storm #2 in Exercise 8, except that you build it in a picture box instead of on the form. Draw a picture box on the form and make it big enough to hold four image boxes. Draw the four image boxes directly in the picture box and load them with the icons for the cloud, lightning, rain, and sun:

Write the event procedures and stack the four image boxes in the same place in the picture box. Run the project—it should respond to clicks in exactly the same way as project Storm #2. Because the image boxes are drawn in a picture box, in the Design screen, you can move everything anywhere on the form by moving the picture box. Click the picture box anywhere away from the stacked image boxes and drag everything around the screen.

10. Use the Line control to draw one or more triangles:

   a. On the form.

   b. In a picture box.

11. Design project Freeway #2 - Drive Vehicles. Load the "freeway" metafile into a picture box, then draw an image box on the freeway and load it with the cars icon (Cars.ico) or the bicycle icon (Bicycle.ico)—your choice. Port the arrow controls over from project Move It #2 and use them to drive the cars or the bicycle on the freeway. Try not to go off the road!

The next exercise is a Visual Basic Backpack Challenge that is offered without an answer. You can do it because your computer understands you when you speak Visual Basic.

12. Design project Garden of Eden #1. It has one picture box and three command buttons, as shown here:

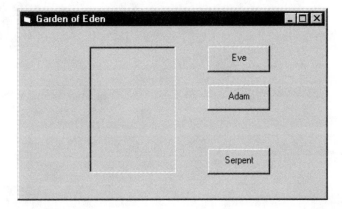

Click the Eve button and Eve appears in the picture box. Click the Adam button and Adam appears in the picture box. Click Serpent and you leave the Garden of Eden. Suddenly we feel hungry. Fortunately, we are approaching a rest stop. Hey, look! There's a restaurant called "Garden of Eating." We could really go for some apple pie about now.

5

Hone Your Tools and Add a Few More

chapter objectives

5.1 Look back on a road well-travelled

5.2 Create projects that use two or more forms

5.3 Learn about modal forms and cancel buttons

5.4 Combine the Light Bulb and Storm projects into one

5.5 Print your project

5.6 Print information from your project

5.7 Make an .exe file of your project

5.8 Add message boxes and input boxes to your backpack

Y O U have travelled well on the road to Visual Basic literacy. Now relax, rest by a lake, stream, or ocean, and reflect on what you have learned. Refreshed, hit the road again and add more tools to your Visual Basic backpack.

5.1 *L OOK BACK ON A ROAD WELL-TRAVELLED*

Here are some elements of Visual Basic that you have encountered during your exploration.

▼ **Objects** You have used two types of Visual Basic objects: forms and controls. You have designed projects that have one form. You will learn more about forms in this chapter, and design projects that have more than one form. You have used these controls: command button, horizontal scroll bar, image, label, line, picture box, shape, text box, and vertical scroll bar.

▼ **Properties** A form or a control has a portfolio of properties. You know how to use many properties and you will use more properties in this chapter.

▼ **Events and event procedures** Objects can respond to events such as a mouse click or double-click. You write an event procedure for an object to tell it how to respond to an event. An event procedure name is of the form *Object_Event*. For example: Form_Load, Command1_Click, txtEnter_Click, imgCloud_Click, and hsbBackColor_Scroll. You have written event procedures that consist of three or more lines of code. Each line of code is a *statement* constructed from object names, event names, property names, methods, functions, and variables.

▼ **Object names** Every object has a default name when it first appears on the screen. For example: Form1, Command1, and Text1. You can invent more descriptive names by using a standard prefix followed by the suffix of your choice. The standard prefixes for objects described so far in this book are:

Object	Prefix	Example
Form	frm	frmStorm01
Command button	cmd	cmdExit
Horizontal scroll bar	hsb	hsbBackColor
Image	img	imgEarth
Label	lbl	lblRed

Object	**Prefix**	**Example**
Line	lin	linLeftArm
Picture box	pic	picDisplay
Shape	shp	shpBall
Text box	txt	txtFortune
Vertical scroll bar	vsb	vsbRed

▼   **Functions**   A function returns a value. You have used these functions:

Date	Hour	Month	RGB	Timer
Day	Load Picture	Now	Second	Weekday
Format	Minute	QBColor	Time	Year

▼   **Methods**   You have used the methods **Cls**, **Move**, **Print**, and **SetFocus**. A method performs an action upon an object. A method statement is of the form *Object.Method* and may include other information. If you omit the object name and the period, the method acts on the form. For example, suppose that your project has the form Form1 and picture box Picture1. The statement **Cls** or **Form1.Cls** clears the form; **Picture1.Cls** clears the picture box. **Print Time** or **Form1.Print Time** prints the time on Form1 while **Picture1.Print Time** prints the time in Picture1.

▼   **Variables**   You have used many variables of the form *Object.Property*. For example: *Form1.BackColor, txtFortune.Text, imgCloud.Visible, hsbBackColor.Value*, and *shpBall.Left*. You can use a **Dim** statement to invent variables as we did in several event procedures. We used **Dim** statements to declare *Elapsed, red, green, blue, NewLeft*, and *NewTop* as variables of **Variant** type. We were careful not to use a Visual Basic *reserved word* (also called a *keyword*) as an invented variable. The Microsoft Visual Basic *Language Reference* contains a long list of reserved words.

▼   **Statements**   A statement is a complete line of code. You have used the **Beep**, **Dim**, **End**, **End Sub**, and **Private Sub** statements, statements of the form *Object.Method*, and assignment statements of the form *variable = value*. Here are some examples:

```
Private Sub Command1_Click()
Beep
Dim red As Variant, green As Variant, blue As Variant
End Sub
Print "This is a string."
Form1.Print "This is a string."
Picture1.Print "This is a string."
```

```
Text1.Text = Time
Text1.Text = Text2.Text
Text1.Text = ""
Image1.Visible = True
green = hsbGreen.Value
Form1.BackColor = RGB(red, green, blue)
```

You can find much information in Visual Basic's Help System. Click the Menu bar's Help menu and then click the Contents command to get the table of contents. Browse—click one of these topics under Programming Language Summary:

Functions	Properties
Methods	Statements
Events	Objects
Keywords by Task	

After meandering in this part of the Help system, also try the main headings Using Visual Basic and Reference Information. Click and browse, click and browse. There are no exercises in this section. When you are well-rested and ready to go, move on to the next section and learn more about forms.

5.2 ▮ *CREATE PROJECTS THAT HAVE TWO OR MORE FORMS*

A project can have one form, two forms, or many forms. A large application may have many forms, each designed and optimized for a particular task. When you run a project, Visual Basic displays at least one form called the *startup form*. This opening window (form) might have buttons or icons that you can click to open other windows (forms) in which you work or play.

The startup form is usually the first form in the project, Form1 or whatever you name the first form. You write code in event procedures to show the other forms. You can also use code to hide a form and remove it from view. Let's start in a slow and easy way with simple projects that have two forms.

Project Forms #1 - Show or Hide Form2 has two forms, Form1 and Form2. Form1 is the startup form. At run time you see only Form1. Click the Show Form2 button to display Form2. After you click Show Form2, you see both forms:

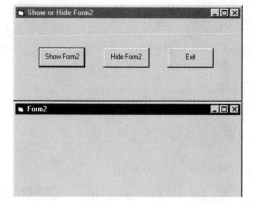

Click Hide Form2 to remove Form2 from view and again see only Form1. Click
Exit to end the run. Tables 5-1 and 5-2 list the specifications for project Forms #1.

Object	Property	Setting
Form1	Caption	Show or Hide Form2
	Name	Form1
	Left	1200
	Top	1200
	Width	6000
	Height	2400
Form2	Caption	Form2
	Name	Form2
	Left	1200
	Top	3600
	Width	6000
	Height	2400
Command1	Caption	Show Form2
	Name	cmdShowForm2
	Left	600
	Top	720
Command2	Caption	Hide Form2
	Name	cmdHideForm2
	Left	2280
	Top	720
Command3	Caption	Exit
	Name	cmdExit
	Left	3960
	Top	720

TABLE 5-1   *Visual Interface Specifications for Project Forms #1 - Show or Hide Form2* ▼

Object Name	Event	Response
cmdShowForm2	Click	Displays Form2 (makes it visible).
cmdHideForm2	Click	Hides Form2 (removes it from view).
cmdExit	Click	Ends the run.

TABLE 5-2 *Event Procedure Specifications for Project Forms #1 - Show or Hide Form2* ▼

First design the visual interface for Form1. Start a new project with Form1 and add its three command buttons. After designing Form1, you are ready to put Form2 on the design screen:

▼ Click the Form tool on the left end of the toolbar:

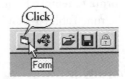

Form2 covers Form1. Make Form2 the size you want (ours is 6000 × 2400) and then click its caption bar and drag it down below Form1 (ours is at 1200, 3600). Our screen now appears as shown here:

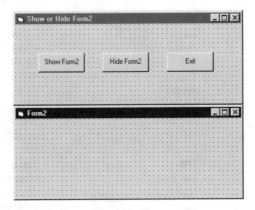

 REMEMBER *To remove a form from a project, select the form and then use the File menu's Remove File command.*

The event procedures are very simple. You use the **Show** method to show (display) a form and the **Hide** method to hide (remove from view) a form. A **Form2.Show** statement shows Form2 and a **Form2.Hide** statement hides it. Install the following event procedures:

```
Private Sub cmdShowForm2_Click()
  Form2.Show
End Sub

Private Sub cmdHideForm2_Click()
  Form2.Hide
End Sub

Private Sub cmdExit_Click()
  End
End Sub
```

That's it. Now save the two forms and the project:

1. Save Form1 with the filename Forms #1 - Form1, Show or Hide Form2.

2. Save Form2 with the filename Forms #1 - Form2, Show or Hide Form2.

3. Save the project file with the filename Forms #1 - Show or Hide Form2.

Run project Forms #1 and try it. It begins with Form1 and its three command buttons—Form2 is nowhere to be seen. Click the Show Form2 button and Form2 obediently appears. Click Hide Form2 to make it go away. Click Exit to return to the design screen where you can modify project Forms #1 to create project Forms #2.

Event procedure cmdShowForm2_Click can do much more than merely show Form2. It can also set a bunch of Form2's properties. Project Forms #2 - Show or Hide Form2 has event procedure Form_Load that positions and sizes Form1 and also positions its three command buttons. Event procedure cmdShowForm2_Click positions and sizes Form2, and then shows it:

```
Private Sub Form_Load()

  ' Position and size Form1
  Form1.Left = 1200
  Form1.Top = 1200
  Form1.Width = 6000
  Form1.Height = 2400
  cmdShowForm2.Left = 600
  cmdShowForm2.Top = 720
  cmdHideForm2.Left = 2280
  cmdHideForm2.Top = 720
  cmdExit.Left = 3960
  cmdExit.Top = 720

End Sub
```

```
Private Sub cmdShowForm2_Click()

  Form2.Left = 1200
  Form2.Top = 3600
  Form2.Width = 6000
  Form2.Height = 2400
  Form2.Show

End Sub
```

Before you run the project, make Form1's and Form2's sizes other than 6000 × 2400 and move both forms to strange places in the design screen. Move Form1's command buttons to weird places on Form1. Run the project to see Form1 and Form2 appear in the locations and sizes determined by the event procedures with Form1's command buttons neatly lined up. Save the project:

1. Save Form1 with the filename Forms #2 - Form1, Show or Hide Form2.

2. Save Form2 with the filename Forms #2 - Form2, Show or Hide Form2.

3. Save the project file with the filename Forms #2, Show or Hide Form2.

You have created and saved project Forms #2. The names of its form files appear in the project window. Click the Close button of either form to close it and then double-click its filename in the project window to open it.

The **Hide** method hides a form by setting the form's Visible property to False. The **Show** method shows a form by setting its Visible property to True. Alternative ways to hide and show Form2 are demonstrated by these event procedures:

```
Private Sub cmdShowForm2_Click()
  Form2.Visible = True
End Sub

Private Sub cmdHideForm2_Click()
  Form2.Visible = False
End Sub
```

Now hone your new skills by formulating answers to the following exercises.

EXERCISES

1. Modify project Forms #1 to create project Forms #3 - Show or Hide Form2. The visual interface is:

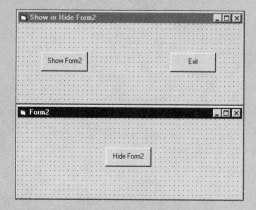

At run time, Form1 appears. Click the Show Form2 button and Form2 appears with its command button. Click the Hide Form2 button and Form2 disappears. To write code for Form1's command buttons, select Form1 and then open its code window. To write code for Form2's command button, select Form2 and then open its code window. Each code window displays only the event procedures for its form.

2. Modify project Forms #2 to create project Forms #4 - Show or Hide Two Forms. It has three forms: Form1, Form2, and Form3. The visual interface looks like this:

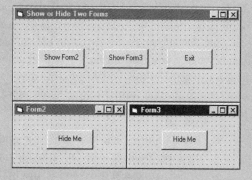

Position and size Form1 in its Form_Load event procedure. Position and size Form2 and Form3 in event procedures cmdShowForm2_Click and cmdShowForm3_Click. Run the project and experiment:

a. Click the Show Form2 button to show Form2 and then click Form2's close button to close it. Click the Show Form2 button to show it again.

b. Click the Show Form3 button to show Form3 and then minimize Form3. Click the Show Form3 button again. Does Form3 reappear? If not, how do you get it back?

c. Maximize Form2 and then click its Hide Me button to make it go away. Click the Show Form2 button to get it back. When it reappears, is it still maximized?

3. Experiment with project Forms #3 - Show or Hide Two Forms. Change the BorderStyles of Form2 and Form3 to something other than 2 - Sizable. Run the project and show Form2 and Form3. Note the appearance of their borders and the existence or nonexistence of a control-menu icon, maximize button, and minimize button. Some BorderStyles set the MaxButton and MinButton properties to False. To return the BorderStyle to 2 - Sizable and make it effective, you may have to reset the MaxButton and MinButton settings to True.

5.3 *L*EARN ABOUT MODAL FORMS AND *C*ANCEL BUTTONS

You have probably encountered forms that lock you in and won't allow you to use another form. Dialog boxes are like this—you can't use another form until you close the dialog box. Forms that won't let go are called *modal forms*. They are handy when you want your user to pay attention to information presented or action requested in the modal form. He or she must close or hide a modal form in order to use another form. You can show a form as a modal form by using **Show 1** instead of **Show**. For example:

▼ **Form2.Show 1** shows Form2 as a modal form. If you try to use a control on another form, it doesn't respond and you hear a beep. You must close or hide Form2 in order to use another form.

▼ **Form2.Show** or **Form2.Show 0** shows Form2 as an unselfish *modeless* form that lets you use other forms.

Object	Property	Setting	Comment
Form1	Caption	Demonstrate a Modal Form	
	Name	Form1	
Command1	Caption	Show Form2	On Form1.
	Name	cmdShowForm2	
Command2	Caption	Hide Form2	On Form1.
	Name	cmdHideForm2	
Command3	Caption	Exit	On Form1.
	Name	cmdExit	
Form2	Caption	Form2	
	Name	Form2	
Command1	Caption	Hide me	On Form2.
	Name	cmdHideMe	

TABLE 5-3 *Visual Interface Specifications for Project Forms #5 - Modal Form* ▼

Create project Forms #5 - Modal Form. Tables 5-3 and 5-4 show the caption, name, and command button specifications for both forms. The design screen visual interface looks like this:

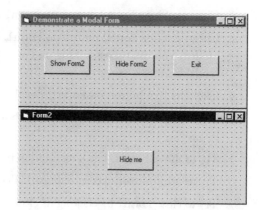

Object Name	Event	Response
cmdShowForm2	Click	Shows Form2 as a modal form.
cmdHideForm2	Click	Hides Form2 but can't be used when Form2 is showing.
cmdExit	Click	Ends the run but can't be used when Form2 is showing.
cmdHideMe	Click	Hides Form2.

TABLE 5-4 *Event Procedure Specifications for Project Forms #5 - Modal Form* ▼

Form1's event procedures are:

```
Private Sub cmdShowForm2_Click()
  Form2.show 1   ' Shows Form2 as a modal form
End Sub

Private Sub cmdHideForm2_Click()
  Form2.Hide
End Sub

Private Sub cmdExit_Click()
  End
End Sub
```

Form2's event procedure is:

```
Private Sub cmdHideMe_Click()
  Form2.Hide
End Sub
```

Design the visual interface, install the event procedures, run the project, and try these things:

1. Click the Show Form2 button on Form1 to show Form2 as a modal form.

2. Click the Hide Form2 button on Form1. Beep! Form2 is still there, not hidden. You can't use anything on Form1 while Form2 is showing as a modal form.

3. Click the Exit button on Form1. Beep! Form1 and Form2 are still there.

4. Try to resize Form1. Click and drag a border. Beep! You can't change its size.

5. Try to move Form1. Click its Caption bar and drag. Beep! It's drag-proof.

6. Try to minimize or maximize Form1. Beep! Form1 doesn't change size.

7. Try to close Form1 by clicking its close button. Beep! Form1 is not closed.

Well, you get the picture. As long as Form2 is showing as a modal form, you can't play with the tools on Form1. Click the Hide Me button on Form2 to hide it.

While wandering about in Windows, you have likely seen forms that have a Cancel button. You can click the Cancel button or press ESC to hide the form. Project Forms #6 - Use a Cancel Button to Hide Form2 is a revision of project Forms #5. Form2's Hide Me button has been changed to a Cancel button:

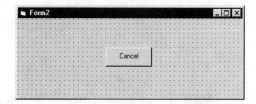

We changed the name of Form2's command button to cmdCancel. To make the cmdCancel respond to pressing the ESC key, set the button's Cancel property to True:

Property	Setting
Name	cmdCancel
Cancel	True

Then install its event procedure:

```
Private Sub cmdCancel_Click()
  Form2.Hide
End Sub
```

Run the project and test the Cancel button. You should be able to hide the form by clicking Cancel or pressing ESC.

 NOTE *Only one command button on a form can have its Cancel property set to True. Pressing ESC causes this button to respond and run its event procedure. The normal use of this feature is to cancel the form that contains the Cancel button.*

If your project has two or more forms, you can write code on one form that modifies controls on another form. To do this, you use the name of the remote form, an exclamation point, and the name of the control on that form (no spaces). For example, in project Forms #6, you can use the following statements in event procedure cmdShowForm2_Click to change the position of command button cmdCancel in Form2:

```
Form2!cmdCancel.Left = 2280
Form2!cmdCancel.Top = 720
```

This is very handy. You can write an event procedure in Form1 that partially designs Form2 (or the form of your choice) and then shows it. Keep this in mind and show, don't hide, your skills as you do these exercises.

EXERCISES

1. Design project Forms #7 - Modeless and Modal Forms. Here is a run-time view after someone clicked the Show Form2 button on the startup form (frmForms07), then clicked the Print My Mode button in Form2, then clicked the Show Form3 button in frmForms07, and then clicked the Print My Mode button in Form3:

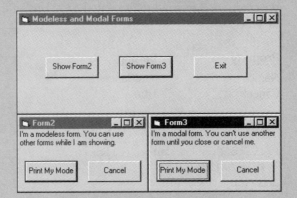

   Run the project and try all the buttons in assorted sequences. For example, click the Show Form2 button and then click the Show Form3 button. This should lock out all the buttons on Form1 and Form2. Try them—beep!

2. Modify event procedure cmdShowForm2_Click in project Forms #5 so that the procedure sizes and positions Form2 (to the size and location that you want), and also locates Form2's command button where you want it.

5.4

COMBINE THE LIGHT BULB AND STORM PROJECTS INTO ONE

In Chapter 4 you created projects Light Bulb #2 - Light Bulb Off or On and Storm #1. Of course you did. You did, didn't you? We saved the form files with the filenames Light Bulb #2 - Light Bulb Off or On.frm and Storm #1.frm. We hope that you saved these projects so that their forms reside happily and conveniently on your hard disk. If you didn't save them, you can quickly recreate them for use in the projects described in this section.

Each of these projects has one form. Both forms are shown here modified for use in a new project. The forms are resized, objects have been moved, and Cancel buttons have been added:

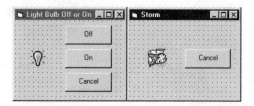

Project Light Bulb and Storm #1 combines the light bulb project and the storm project into a single project with three forms. At run time you see project Light Bulb and Storm #1's startup form:

Click the Light Bulb button and the light bulb form appears—in that form, you can clickly turn the light bulb off or on. Click the Storm button and the storm form appears—click the cloud to see lightning, click lightning to see rain, and click rain to see the cloud. Click the Cancel button or press ESC to hide the light bulb form or the storm form.

You can create project Light Bulb and Storm #1 like this:

1. Start a new project.

2. Draw the visual interface for the startup form and write the event procedures for its command buttons.

3. Add the form file from project Light Bulb #2 to the project.

4. Add the form file from project Storm #1 to the project.

Tables 5-5 and 5-6 list the specifications for project Light Bulb and Storm #1's startup form.

Object	Property	Setting
Form1	Caption	Light Bulb and Storm
	Name	frmLtBlbStorm
Command1	Caption	Light Bulb
	Name	cmdLightBulb
Command2	Caption	Storm
	Name	cmdStorm
Command3	Caption	Exit
	Name	cmdExit

TABLE 5-5 *Visual Interface Specifications for Project Light Bulb and Storm #1's Startup Form* ▼

Event procedures for the startup form, frmLtBlbStorm are:

```
Private Sub cmdLightBulb_Click()
 frmLtBulb2.Show
End Sub

Private Sub cmdStorm_Click()
  frmStorm01.Show
End Sub

Private Sub cmdExit_Click()
  End
End Sub
```

Our project window tells us that Project1 has one form with the name frmLtBlbStorm. Now let's add the form files from projects Light Bulb #2 and Storm #1 to this project. Since we don't know what you called their form files, we'll go with our filenames, Light Bulb #2 - Light Bulb Off or On.frm and

Object Name	Event	Response
cmdLightBulb	Click	Shows the light bulb form, named frmLtBulb2 in Chapter 4.
cmdStorm	Click	Shows the storm form, named frmStorm01 in Chapter 4.
cmdExit	Click	Ends the run.

TABLE 5-6 *Event Procedure Specifications for Project Light Bulb and Storm #1's Startup Form* ▼

Storm #1.frm. To add a file to a project, you use the Add File command on the
File menu. Add Light Bulb #2 - Light Bulb Off or On.frm like this:

1. Pull down the File menu and select the Add File command:

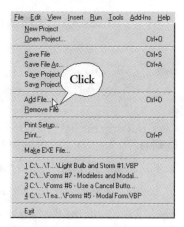

2. Behold the Add File dialog box. It displays a list of form files. Find the
    filename you want and double-click it:

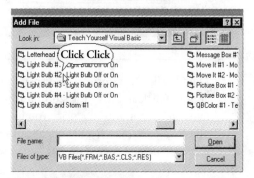

Visual Basic loads the file, but does not display it. The project now has two
forms and the project window lists them like this:

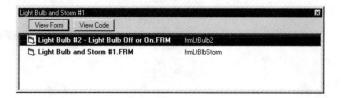

NOTE *We have enlarged the project box so you can see the whole file name.*

3. Double-click frmLtBulb2 to display the added form. See the light bulb form appear in the design screen, perched on frmLtBlbStorm:

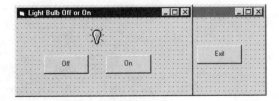

4. Click and drag the light bulb form down below the startup form or drag it to wherever you want it, then add the storm form:

   a. Pull down the File menu and select the Add File command.

   b. Locate the Storm #1.frm file and load it.

5. Visual Basic loads the file but does not display it. The project now has three forms and the project window lists them like this:

6. Double-click frmStorm01 to display it. Do it and see the storm form appear. Click and drag the storm form down below or to the right of the light bulb form or to the place you like. We resized the forms, moved their objects to new places, and added Cancel buttons to both forms. The three forms peacefully coexist on our design screen:

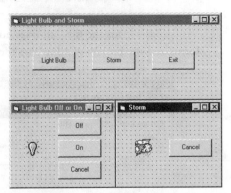

The Light Bulb and Storm forms already have event procedures. Click the Light Bulb form and open a code window to view its code. Click the Storm form and open a code window to view its code. Add event procedures for the two Cancel buttons. Project Light Bulb and Storm #1 is complete and ready to run, so do it.

▼ At run time, the startup form appears with its three command buttons.

▼ Click the Light Bulb button to show the Light Bulb form. It appears in the place where you put it in the design screen. You can drag it elsewhere.

▼ Click the Off and On buttons a few times to make sure that the Light Bulb form works. Click the Cancel button to hide the form.

▼ Click the Storm button to show the Storm form. It appears in the place where you put it in the design screen. You can drag it elsewhere.

▼ In the Storm form, click the cloud to see lightning, click lightning to see rain, and click rain to see the cloud. Click the Cancel button to hide the form.

When you add a file to a project, Visual Basic adds its name and location on your hard drive to the project file. Therefore, a single file can be included in two or more projects. If you change a file in one project, you change it in all projects in which it is included. If you move a form file to another folder and then try to load a project that includes that file, the project may be unable to locate the moved file. In this case you will see a File Not Found error message box with the path and filename of the file that wasn't found.

After building a project by adding files, you can save all of its files with filenames related to the project name. Use the File menu's Save File As... command to save the form files and the Save Project As... command to save the project file:

1. Click the startup file to select it and then save it with the filename Light Bulb and Storm #1.

2. Click the light bulb form to select it and then save it with the filename Light Bulb and Storm #1 - Light Bulb.

3. Click the storm form to select it and then save it with the filename Light Bulb and Storm #1 - Storm.

4. Save the project file with the filename Light Bulb and Storm #1.

After you complete these steps, the project window's title bar displays: Light Bulb and Storm #1. The file list displays the form filenames and form names:

Now use your recently-acquired enlightenment to take these exercises by storm.

1. Modify project Light Bulb and Storm #1 to obtain project Light Bulb and Storm #2. Here are desired features of project Light Bulb and Storm #2:

   a. Use the startup form's Form_Load event procedure to position it at 1200, 1200, make its size 6000 × 2400, and place its command buttons where you want them.

   b. Use event procedure cmdLightBulb_Click to position the light bulb form at 1200, 3600 and make its size 3000 × 2400.

   c. Use event procedure cmdStorm_Click to position the storm form at 4200, 3600 and make its size 3000 × 2400.

2. Combine project Picture Box #1 - Picture in a Picture Box and project Picture Box #2 - Text in a Picture Box into a single project called Picture Box #5 - Picture or Text. Design a startup form with command buttons to show the forms from Picture Box #1 and Picture Box #2. Add the form files from Picture Box #1 and Picture Box #2. For each of these, change the End the Show button to a Cancel button. Save the project with the filenames Picture Box #5 - Picture or Text for the startup form, Picture Box #5 - Picture for the Picture in a Picture Box form, Picture Box #5 - Text for the Text in a Picture Box form, and Picture Box #5 - Picture or Text for the project file.

5.5   *P*RINT YOUR PROJECT

After spending your precious time creating a project, it's often nice to print hard copy of the project itself, or information about the project. You can use the File menu's Print command to print the visual image of a form, a text description of the form, and the form's event procedure code. Load project Light Bulb and Storm #1 and print information about its startup form:

1. Click the startup form to select it.

2. Select the Print command on the File menu. Visual Basic displays the Print dialog box:

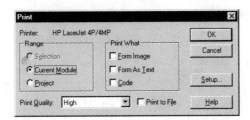

In the Range box, Current Module is selected. Good—that's the one we think you want. If you click Project, Visual Basic will print information about *all* of the forms in the project. Your choice—we'll stay with Current Module and save trees by saving paper.

The Print What box lets you choose exactly what you want to print. You must select at least one item.

3. Click Form Image (an X appears in its check box) to select a graphical image of the visual contents of the form.

4. Click Form As Text to select a list of property settings of the form and its controls. For a busy form, this list can be quite long.

5. Click Code to select the code in all of the form's event procedures.

6. Select all three choices in the Print What box and then click OK.

Our printer chugged out three pages with the event procedures on the first page, the list of properties on the second page, and the form image on the third page. The form image showed the three command buttons but not the form's caption bar or borders. It looks like this:

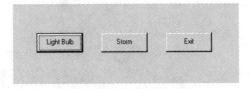

Our Form As Text list is many lines long and includes items we haven't yet covered. We are quite sure you will recognize the following visual interface items:

```
Begin VB.Form frmLtBlbStorm
   Caption         =    "Light Bulb and Storm"
   Height          =    2400
   Left            =    1200
   Top             =    1200
   Width           =    6000
   Begin VB.CommandButton cmdLightBulb
      Caption      =    "Light Bulb"
      Height       =    495
      Left         =    600
      Top          =    720
      Width        =    1215
   End
End
```

The event procedures were printed like this:

```
Private Sub cmdExit_Click()
   End
End Sub

Private Sub cmdLightBulb_Click()
   frmLtBulb2.Show
End Sub

Private Sub cmdStorm_Click()
   frmStorm01.Show
End Sub
```

Another tool for your backpack—check it out by doing these exercises:

EXERCISES

1. Print the Form Image, Form As Text, and Code for Light Bulb and Storm #1's light bulb form. From the Form As Text printout, list the Cancel button's properties and settings.

2. Print only the Form As Text listing for Light Bulb and Storm #1's storm form. What property settings are printed for image box imgCloud?

5.6   *P*RINT INFORMATION FROM YOUR PROJECT

You have used the **Print** method to print information on a form or in a Picture box. You can use the **Print** method with the **Printer** object to print the same type of information on the printer. The statement

```
Printer.Print "Your computer will understand you today."
```

sends the text enclosed in quotation marks to a buffer, ready to be printed on the Printer. Following one or two or more **Printer.Print** statements, a **Printer.EndDoc** statement tells the printer to print the previously delivered information. The **Printer.Print** and **Printer.EndDoc** statements are both of the form *Object.Method*:

Object	Method	Object.Method Statement
Printer	Print	Printer.Print
Printer	EndDoc	Printer.EndDoc

Try the **Printer.Print** and **Printer.EndDoc** statements and see for yourself how they work. Start a new project, put command button Command1 on the form, and install:

```
Private Sub Command1_Click()

  Printer.Print "ABCDEFGHIJKLMNOPQRSTUVWXYZ1234567890"
  Printer.Print "abcdefghijklmnopqrstuvwxyz1234567890"
  printer.enddoc

End Sub
```

Run the project and click Command1. If all goes well, you will see one page containing the two lines of text printed on your printer:

```
ABCDEFGHIJKLMNOPQRSTUVWXYZ1234567890
abcdefghijklmnopqrstuvwxyz1234567890
```

The two lines will be printed in your printer's current font. Yours may look different than the lines shown here. You can specify the font, its size, and its style by using some of the **Printer** object's properties in the event procedure that prints the information. Properties include:

Property	Possible Setting
Font	A font name such as "Times New Roman" or "Courier."
FontSize	Size in points. For example: 12.
FontBold	True or False.
FontItalic	True or False.

Try some of these properties. Modify event procedure Command1_Click so that it prints information in the fonts, Times New Roman and Courier:

```
Private Sub Command1_Click()

    Printer.Font = "Times New Roman"
    Printer.FontSize = 12
    Printer.Print "This is printed in 12-point Times New Roman, a"
    Printer.Print "proportional font in which different characters"
    Printer.Print "may be printed in different column widths."
    Printer.Print
    Printer.Font = "Courier"
    Printer.Print "This is printed in Courier, a monospace font in which"
    Printer.Print "each character occupies the same column width."
    Printer.Print "Here's the alphabet in Courier and Times New Roman:"
    Printer.Print
    Printer.Print "ABCDEFGHIJKLMNOPQRSTUVWXYZabcdefghijklmnopqrstuvwxyz"
    Printer.Font = "Times New Roman"
    Printer.FontSize = 12
    Printer.Print "ABCDEFGHIJKLMNOPQRSTUVWXYZabcdefghijklmnopqrstuvwxyz"
    Printer.EndDoc

End Sub
```

Run the project. If your printer supports Times New Roman and Courier, you will see information printed in 12-point Times New Roman, a *proportional* font, and Courier, a *monospace* font. In a proportional font, different characters may be printed in different column widths, so there is no correlation between the number of characters and the number of columns. In a monospace font, each character occupies the same column width—one character is printed in one printer column.

If you are printing two or more pages of information on the printer, you can use the **NewPage** method to start a new page. The event procedure shown here prints two lines on one page, and then starts a new page and prints one line on that page:

```
Private Sub Command1_Click()

    Printer.NewPage
    Printer.Print "This procedure wastes paper because a Printer.NewPage"
    Printer.Print "statement starts a new page after this line."
    Printer.NewPage
    Printer.Print "If you try it, be sure to recycle!"
    Printer.EndDoc

End Sub
```

And now, quickly recycle this exercise.

EXERCISE

1. Imagine what will be printed by this event procedure and how it will look on paper, then install the procedure and use it to verify your conjecture:

    ```
    Private Sub Command1_Click()

        Printer.Font = "Arial"
        Printer.FontSize = 24
        Printer.FontBold = False
        Printer.FontItalic = True
        Printer.Print "Go, Team, Go!!!"
        Printer.EndDoc

    End Sub
    ```

5.7   *MAKE AN .EXE FILE OF YOUR PROJECT*

You may wish to make your good work available to any Windows user. Alas, for some unfathomable reason, not all Windows users have Visual Basic installed on their systems. No problem—you can create an .exe file of your project that will run directly from anybody's Windows. An .exe file is an *executable program file* that will run without Visual Basic.

Creating an .exe file is absurdly simple—you simply load the project into the design screen, select the File menu's Make EXE File command, and click the OK button in the Make EXE File dialog box—Visual Basic does the rest.

We'll demonstrate by creating an .exe file for a really simple project, the one called Beep #2 from Chapter 2. We saved Beep #2 with the filenames Beep #2.frm for the form file and Beep #2.vbp for the project file.

1. Open project Beep #2. If you didn't save it, quickly create it. We loaded Beep #2, resized the form, and moved the command buttons. It looks like this:

2. Pull down the File menu and select the Make EXE File command:

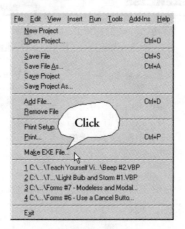

Visual Basic displays the Make EXE File dialog box:

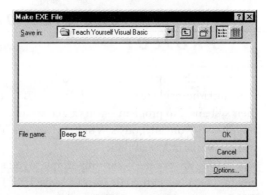

The Save In box contains a suggested folder (in this case, *Teach Yourself Visual Basic*) and the File Name box contains the filename (Beep #2). If these are okay, click the OK button to complete your task and Visual Basic does the rest. For the example shown in the illustration, Visual Basic creates an .exe file with the filename Beep #2.exe and saves it in the *Teach Yourself Visual Basic* folder of the *Vb* folder on disk drive C. If you want to save the .exe file in a different place with a different filename, use the Save In box and the File Name box to assert yourself.

Well, the reason for doing all of the above is to create a stand-alone application that can be run directly from Windows, so let's try it. One way is to run Windows Explorer, find the Beep #2.exe file, and run it. Using the taskbar, you can do it like this:

1. Click the start button on your taskbar.

2. Click the Programs icon to open the Programs list.

3. Find the Windows Explorer icon and click it.

4. Using the folder tree, find the Teach Yourself Visual Basic folder in the Vb folder on drive C (or find the folder in which *you* saved the .exe file).

   Aha! There it is:

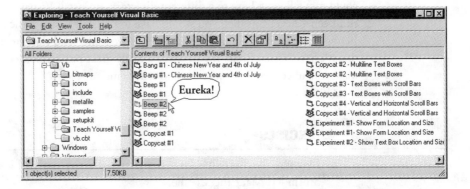

 NOTE *The way that you have set your Windows Explorer options determines the appearance of filenames. You may see anything from a large icon with the filename below it to a list of files with small icons to their left and file attributes (size, date, etc.) to their right. By default, Windows 95 does not show file extensions, so Beep #2.exe will appear as Beep #2. If you did not change it, Beep #2's icon will look just like a Visual Basic form icon.*

5. Double-click Beep #2's icon. Windows, noting the .exe filename extension, loads the project and runs it without consulting Visual Basic. Beep #2's run-time screen appears:

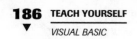

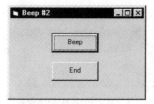

6. Click the Beep button to hear a beep. Click twice to hear beep beep—there goes Roadrunner! Click the End button to end the run.

 NOTE *The .exe files created in Visual Basic are not truly stand-alone files. They require a file named Vb40016.dll to be in the user's Windows\System folder. If you want to send an .exe file to a friend who doesn't have Visual Basic, send the Vb40016.dll file as well.*

Perhaps you are skeptical about this. After all, we didn't close Visual Basic; we simply switched to the Windows Explorer to run Beep #2.exe. How do we know that Windows isn't secretly using Visual Basic to run the .exe file? Well, to convince yourself, close Visual Basic and then run Beep #2.exe. Still skeptical? You could move Beep #2.exe to a different directory, uninstall Visual Basic, and then run Beep #2.exe. But then you would have to reinstall Visual Basic to continue. Better to create .exe files of your favorite projects and send them to a friend who doesn't have Visual Basic. If you create a really great project that everyone wants, make lots of copies of the .exe file and sell them!

EXERCISES

1. Describe the procedure for making an .exe file of project Light Bulb and Storm #1. Make the .exe file.

2. Describe a procedure for running the .exe file of project Light Bulb and Storm #1 that you made in Exercise 1.

5.8 *A*DD MESSAGE BOXES AND INPUT BOXES TO YOUR BACKPACK

Visual Basic has a handy ready-to-use modal form called a *message box*. You can use a **MsgBox** statement in an event procedure to display a message box with whatever information you want to present. A **MsgBox** statement consists of the keyword **MsgBox** followed by the message enclosed in quotation marks:

```
MsgBox "This is a message box."
```

Start a new project (Project1), put command button Command1 on the form, and install its event procedure:

```
Command1_Click()
  MsgBox "This is a message box."
End Sub
```

Run the project and click Command1 to see the message box and its message:

This message box has a title bar with the title "Project1," the message "This is a message box.", and an OK button. A message box is a modal form, so you must close or hide it before you can use another form. Click the OK button to remove the message box.

There are four special types of message boxes. Each type displays an icon that hints at the nature of its message. The icon can be the letter "i," an exclamation point, a question mark, or a cross that looks like the letter "X." You use a type number in the **MsgBox** statement to select the icon you want. The type number follows the message and is separated from it by a comma:

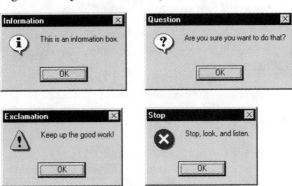

A **MsgBox** statement can specify a title to appear in the message box's title bar. The title is enclosed in quotation marks and follows the type number. The message, type number, and title are separated by commas:

```
MsgBox "Keep up the good work.", 48, "Exclamation"
```

Project Message Box #1 - Four Types of Message Boxes shows off the four types of message boxes:

Click a button, see a message box. For example, click the Question button to see its message box. Notice the title (Question), the icon (a large question mark in a balloon), and the message (Are you sure you want to do that?):

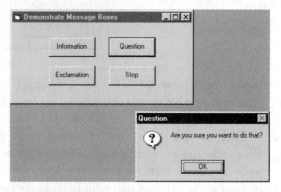

Design project Message Box #1 and install these event procedures for the project's four command buttons:

```
Private Sub cmdInformation_Click()
  MsgBox "This is an information box.", 64, "Information"
End Sub

Private Sub cmdExclamation_Click()
  MsgBox "Keep up the good work!", 48, "Exclamation"
End Sub

Private Sub cmdQuestion_Click()
  MsgBox "Are you sure you want to do that?", 32, "Question"
End Sub

Private Sub cmdStop_Click()
  MsgBox "Stop, look, and listen.", 16, "Stop"
End Sub
```

The message can be quite long and the title usually has several characters. We like to assign them to **Variant** variables called *Msg* and *Title*, and then use these variables in the **MsgBox** statement. We'll demonstrate for event procedure cmdInformation_Click:

```
Private Sub cmdInformation_Click()

 Dim Msg As Variant, Title As Variant

  Msg = "This is an information box."
  Title = "Information"
  MsgBox Msg, 64, Title

End Sub
```

Message boxes are handy objects for sending messages out to the happy user of your friendly project. Input boxes are handy for acquiring information from your contented user. You use an **InputBox** function to acquire a value of a variable, as shown in this code:

```
Variable = InputBox("Please enter something.")
```

The **InputBox** function displays this input box:

This input box has a title bar with the title "Project1," the message "Please enter something.", a text box in which you can enter something, and command buttons OK and Cancel. An input box is a modal form. You must remove it before you can use another form. The usual way is to enter something and then click the OK button or press ENTER. You can also click the Cancel button to hide the input box.

NOTE *The message displayed in an input box is called a* prompt *in Microsoft's documentation.*

To experience an input box, start a new project (Project1), put command button Command1 on the form and install its event procedure:

```
Private Sub Command1_Click()

  Dim Variable As Variant

  Variable = InputBox("Please enter something.")
  Print Variable

End Sub
```

Run the project, click the Command1 button to open the input box, enter something, and click the OK button or press ENTER Whatever you entered is assigned as the value of *Variable* and then printed on the form.

Now put another command button (Command2) and a text box (Text1) on the form. Install event procedure Command2_Click:

```
Private Sub Command2_Click()
  Text1.Text = InputBox("Please enter something.")
End Sub
```

Run the project, click the Command2 button to open the input box, enter something, and click the OK button or press ENTER Whatever you entered appears in Text1 as the value of Text1.Text.

You can include the title that you want in the **InputBox** function:

```
Text1.Text = InputBox("Please enter something.", "My Title")
```

You can assign the message (prompt) and the title to variables and then use the variables in the **InputBox** function:

```
Private Sub Command2_Click()

  Dim Msg As Variant, Title As Variant

  Msg = "Please enter something."
  Title = "My Title"
  Text1.Text = InputBox(Msg, Title)

End Sub
```

Although input boxes are handy for acquiring values of variables, use them sparingly. When you use Windows itself and Windows applications designed by code wizards, notice that text boxes are the primary objects used to acquire information from users. As an apprentice code wizard, you too can use text boxes to acquire information in your projects.

And now: **MsgBox** "Whiz on down and do the exercises!", 48, "Advice"

EXERCISES

1. Rewrite event procedures cmdExclamation_Click, cmdQuestion_Click, and cmdStop_Click in project Message Box #1 to use variables *Msg* and *Title* as we did in event procedure cmdInformation_Click.

2. Write event procedure Command3_Click to use an input box to acquire something and print whatever is entered in picture box Picture1.

mastery skills check

1. How do you add a form to a project? How do you remove a form from a project?

2. We have shown two or more forms *tiled*, touching but not overlapping. You can *cascade* (overlap) forms in the design screen, as shown here:

Design project Forms #8 - Cascaded Forms. It has Form1 and Form2. Form1 has command buttons Show Form2, Hide Form2, and Exit. Form2 has a Cancel button. The forms are overlapped, as you can see above. Run the project and experiment.

3. Write a statement used in Form1 to perform each of these tasks:

a. Locate text box Text1 on Form2 at the coordinates 600, 360.

b. Move image box Image1 on Form3 to 720, 240. Use the **Move** method.

    c. Load the Earth icon (*Vb\Icons\Elements\Earth.ico*) into image box imgEarth on form frmPlanets.

    d. Load the "freeway" metafile (*Vb\Metafile\Arrows\Multarw4.wmf*) into Picture box picFreeway on form frmCongestion.

4. Suppose that a project has three forms, Form1, Form2, and Form3. How do you

    a. Print only the Form Image for Form1?

    b. Print only the Form As Text for Form2?

    c. Print only the Code for Form3?

    d. Print the Form Image, Form As Text, and Code for the entire project?

5. Write event procedure Command1_Click to print "Visual Basic is AOK!" on the printer in 24-point, bold, italic Times New Roman.

6. Describe the procedure for making an .exe file. After making an .exe file, how do you run it from Windows?

7. Complete event procedure Command4_Click. It uses an input box to acquire the value of the variable called *InputMsg* and then displays this value in a message box.

```
Private Sub Command4_Click()
  Dim InputMsg As Variant
  _____

  _____

End Sub
```

8. Combine any two or three projects from previous chapters into a single multiform project.

9. Design an original project that uses three or more forms. We'll call 'em Form1, Form2, Form3, and so on, but encourage you to give them more interesting names. For example, at run time your project might start with Form1. You click a button to show Form2. Perhaps an event on Form2 shows Form3. And so on. Your startup form might be a title screen that includes your name and tells people how to get to the form that does the real work or play. We'll watch for you on the Net.

6

Loops, Switchbacks, and Forks in the Road

chapter objectives

6.1 The Timer control repeats code periodically

6.2 Use the **If...Then** structure to make decisions

6.3 Use the **If...Then...Else** structure to make decisions

6.4 Check boxes and option buttons allow click choices

6.5 Use the **Select Case** structure to select code

6.6 Use the **For...Next** loop structure to repeat code

6.7 The **DoEvents** statement can tame a selfish **For...Next** loop

6.8 Use the **Do...Loop** structure for repetitive operation

YOU have designed visual interfaces and written event procedures. You can write code. A code wizard uses three fundamental logic structures: *sequential structures*, *decision structures*, and *loop structures*. In Chapters 2 through 5, you wrote code using sequential structures. In this chapter you will learn how to use decision structures and loop structures so that you can become a code wizard.

A sequential structure is a set of statements that are executed sequentially, from the first statement to the last statement, from top to bottom. The event procedures in Chapters 2 through 5 use sequentially structured code. For example, the code in event procedure cmdSequentialCode_Click is sequential code:

```
Private Sub cmdSequentialCode_Click()
  Cls
  Print "Sequential code is executed from top to bottom."
  Beep
End Sub
```

The code in cmdSequentialCode_Click is executed sequentially from top to bottom, from **Cls** to **Beep**.

A *decision structure* makes a decision based on a *condition*. Execution of the code continues one way or another, depending on the outcome of the decision. In this chapter, you will learn how to use the **If...Then**, **If...Then...Else**, and **Select Case** decision structures.

A *loop structure* is a structure that executes a block of code repetitively. In this chapter, you will learn how to use the Timer control, **For...Next** loop, and **Do...Loop** structures.

6.1 ▐ *T*HE TIMER CONTROL REPEATS CODE PERIODICALLY

Suppose that you want something to happen repetitively once a minute or once a second or once every time interval that you specify. The Timer control has the right stuff for this task. Look for it on the toolbox:

Timer ———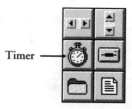

You can use Timer and its event procedure to repeat code periodically. You set the time interval in milliseconds (thousandths of a second), write code to do what you want done periodically, and turn Timer loose. Sure enough, at the end of the time interval you specified, Timer runs your code, does it again at the end of the next time interval, and so on. If you want your code to be executed every second, set the time interval to 1000 milliseconds. If you want your code to run every 10 seconds, set the interval to 10,000 milliseconds. Want ten times a second? Set the interval to 100 milliseconds, which works out to a tenth of a second. The time interval's maximum setting is 65,535 milliseconds (65.535 seconds = 1.09225 minutes).

Project Metronome #1 is absurdly simple. All it does is beep once every second. Drag out that old guitar, harmonica, or whatever, and play along while Metronome #1 beeps the seconds away. In the design screen, the visual interface looks like this:

The Timer control is visible in the design screen, but invisible at run time—you see an empty form and hear a beep every second. When you tire of harmonizing with this rather expensive metronome, click the toolbar's End tool to end the run.

The Timer control has seven properties and one event, also called Timer. For this project, the pertinent properties are Enabled, Interval, and Name, listed in Table 6-1. Table 6-2 shows the project's event procedure specifications.

Event procedure Timer_Timer is very simple:

```
Private Sub Timer1_Timer()

    Beep

End Sub
```

Object	Property	Setting	Comment
Form1	Caption	Metronome	
Timer1	Enabled	True	Default setting. Timer begins automatically at run time.
	Interval	1000	Time interval in milliseconds. 1000 milliseconds = 1 second.
	Name	Timer1	Default setting.

TABLE 6-1   *Visual Interface Specifications for Project Metronome #1* ▼

Object	Event	Response
Timer1	Timer	Beeps once every 1000 milliseconds (once every second).

TABLE 6-2 *Event Procedure Specifications for Project Metronome #1* ▼

Design the project and run it. Because the Timer control is invisible at run time, you see an empty form captioned "Metronome." Timer1's Enabled property setting is True, so event procedure Timer1_Timer begins its work at run time. After one second you hear the first beep and then you hear a beep every second. Experiment by trying these options:

▼ Change the Interval setting to 100 to hear a beep every 100 milliseconds (0.1 second).

▼ Change the Interval setting to 56 to hear a beep every 56 milliseconds (0.056 second).

▼ Try lowering the Interval setting to less than 56. Try 55, 20, or 1. What do you hear?

We hear a distinct difference between settings of 55 and 56. Settings below 56 all sound alike to our ears. That's because the time interval is really measured in the computer's clock *ticks*. There are 18.2 ticks per second, so one tick is about 0.055 second, or 55 milliseconds.

We also hear some irregularity in the interval—a slight hitch now and then. Sometimes the beeps are a little faster, sometimes a little slower. This happens because Windows is running in the background and occasionally fussing with something just as Timer1_Timer wants to do its thing. The beep is delayed a bit now and then.

▼ What happens if you set the interval to 65,536 or to a noninteger such as 123.45 or to a negative number? Try it and find out.

▼ Set the Interval property to 0 and run the project. You will hear no beeps. For Timer to do its task, the setting of the Interval property must be an integer in the range 1 to 65,535.

Project Metronome #2 provides more control at run time. This is the visual interface:

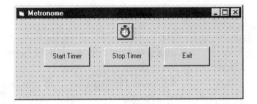

Tables 6-3 and 6-4 show the specifications for project Metronome #2. Timer1's Enabled property is set to False. Therefore, its event procedure does not begin automatically at run time. To start it, click the Start Timer button to set Enabled to True. To stop it, click the Stop Timer button to set Enabled to False.

Here are the event procedures for cmdStartTimer, cmdStopTimer, and Timer1:

```
Private Sub cmdStartTimer_Click()
  Timer1.Enabled = True
End Sub

Private Sub cmdStopTimer_Click()
  Timer1.Enabled = False
End Sub

Private Sub Timer1_Timer()
  Beep
End Sub
```

Run the project and click cmdStartTimer. Its event procedure enables Timer1, and event procedure Timer1_Timer starts working. Click cmdStopTimer. Its event procedure disables Timer1, and event procedure Timer1_Timer stops working.

Object	Property	Setting	Comment
Form1	Caption	Metronome	
Command1	Caption	Start Timer	
	Name	cmdStartTimer	
Command2	Caption	Stop Timer	
	Name	cmdStopTimer	
Command3	Caption	Exit	
	Name	cmdExit	
Timer1	Enabled	False	Timer1 will not start automatically at run time.
	Interval	1000	1000 milliseconds = 1 second.
	Name	Timer1	Default name.

TABLE 6-3 *Visual Interface Specifications for Project Metronome #2* ▼

Object	Event	Response
cmdStartTimer	Click	Starts the metronome. (Sets Timer1.Enabled to True.)
cmdStopTimer	Click	Stops the metronome. (Sets Timer1.Enabled to False.)
cmdExit	Click	Ends the run.
Timer1	Timer	If Enabled is True, sounds one beep each second.

TABLE 6-4 *Event Procedure Specifications for Project Metronome #2* ▼

Now it's time for you to start working on these timely exercises.

EXERCISES

1. Complete this sentence: Event procedure Timer1_Timer runs its code periodically if its Enabled property is set to _____ and its Interval property is set to an integer in the range _____ to _____.

2. Create project Metronome #3. This is the design screen visual interface:

Click the text box and enter the time interval. Click the Start Timer button to set Timer1's Interval property to the number you entered in the text box, set Timer1's Enabled property to True, and start the metronome. Click Stop Timer to set Timer1's Enabled property to False and stop the metronome.

6.2 *USE THE IF...THEN STRUCTURE TO MAKE DECISIONS*

You can include a *decision structure* in an event procedure. A decision structure is like a fork in the road. It tests a *condition*, an expression that has one of two possible values, True or False. The path through the code then proceeds one way or another depending on the value of the condition. Something might happen or not happen depending on the condition's value. A condition is usually a *relation*, or *comparison*, between two values, or between a variable and a value, or between two variables. To create a condition, you use a *relational operator*. Relational operators are shown in Table 6-5.

Operator	Meaning	Example Condition	Comment About the Condition
=	Equal to	Text1.Text = 0	True if Text1.Text is 0 (zero).
<>	Not equal to	Text1.Text <> 7	True if Text1.Text is not 7.
>	Greater than	Text1.Text > 0	True if Text1.Text is greater than zero.
<	Less than	Text1.Text < 0	True if Text1.Text is less than zero.
>=	Greater than or equal to	Text1.Text >= 3	True if Text1.Text is a number greater than or equal to 3.
<=	Less than or equal to	Text1.Text <= 10	True if Text1.Text is a number less than or equal to 10.

TABLE 6-5 *Relational Operators* ▼

The simplest decision structure is the **If...Then** statement. It tells the computer to do a certain operation if a given condition is true. If the condition is false, the computer skips the operation. The way that a statement is constructed is called *syntax*. The **If...Then** statement has the following syntax:

If *condition* **Then** *statement*

If the *condition* is True, then the *statement* following **Then** is executed. If the *condition* is False, then the *statement* following **Then** is not executed. Here is an example that we'll soon use in a project:

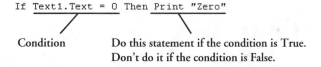

```
If Text1.Text = 0 Then Print "Zero"
```

Condition   Do this statement if the condition is True.
                   Don't do it if the condition is False.

This **If...Then** statement instructs the computer as follows:

▼ If the condition *Text1.Text = 0* is True, then print the string "Zero" on the form.

▼ If the condition *Text1.Text = 0* is False, then don't print anything.

Here is another way to think about it:

▼ If the condition *Text1.Text = 0* is True, then execute the statement, Print "Zero".

▼ If the condition *Text1.Text = 0* is False, then don't execute the statement, Print "Zero".

Project Negative, Zero, or Positive #1 demonstrates **If...Then** statements with three types of conditions. You click the text box, enter a number, and then click the Negative, Zero, or Positive button. The command button's event procedure looks at the number in the text box and prints an appropriate message directly on the form. Tables 6-6 and 6-7 show the project's specifications. Here is a sample run:

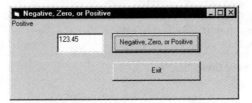

Here is the event procedure code for button cmdNegZerPos and text box Text1:

```
Private Sub cmdNegZerPos_Click()

    Cls    ' Clear the form

    If Text1.Text < 0 Then Print "Negative"
    If Text1.Text = 0 Then Print "Zero"
    If Text1.Text > 0 Then Print "Positive"

    Beep

End Sub

Private Sub Text1_Click()
    Cls                ' Clear the form
    Text1.Text = ""    ' Clear the text box
End Sub
```

Event procedure Text1.Text_Click clears the form and then clears Text1. Event procedure cmdNegZerPos_Click also clears the form so that only one message

Object	Property	Setting
Command1	Caption	Negative, Zero, or Positive
	Name	cmdNegZerPos
Command2	Caption	Exit
	Name	cmdExit
Text1	Text	

TABLE 6-6   *Visual Interface Specifications for Project Negative, Zero, or Positive #1* ▼

Object	Event	Response
cmdExit	Click	Ends the run.
cmdNegZerPos	Click	Prints a message that depends on the value of Text1.Text. Beeps.
Text1	Click	Clears the form, clears itself, and accepts focus.

TABLE 6-7 *Event Procedure Specifications for Project Negative, Zero, or Positive #1* ▼

appears on the form even though you click the button several times for the same number. The **If...Then** statements then test the value of Text1.Text and decide what message to print on the form:

▼ If you enter a negative number, the first **If...Then** statement prints "Negative" on the form.

▼ If you enter zero, the second **If...Then** statement prints "Zero" on the form.

▼ If you enter a positive number, the third **If...Then** statement prints "Positive" on the form.

For these **If...Then** statements to work properly, the value of Text1.Text must be a number. Run the project and try negative numbers, positive numbers, and zero. Enter some non-numbers and communicate with the Type Mismatch dialog box. Enter the empty string (just click the text box) and then click the "Negative, Zero, or Positive" button to further your friendship with the Type Mismatch dialog box. In Chapters 7 and 8 you will learn more about Visual Basic's various data types.

Well, here is a positive thing to do: Try these exercises before moving on to the next exciting section.

EXERCISES

1. An **If...Then** statement has the form **If** *condition* **Then** *statement.* What is the condition for each of the following? What is the statement?

   a. If Text1.Text < 0 Then Print "Negative"

   b. If Text1.Text = 0 Then MsgBox "Zero"

   c. If Text1.Text > 0 Then Text2.Text = "Positive"

2. Design project Negative, Zero, or Positive #2. Event procedure cmdNegZerPos should display the type of number (Negative, Zero, or Positive) in a text box.

6.3 USE THE IF...THEN...ELSE STRUCTURE TO MAKE DECISIONS

The **If...Then...Else** decision structure greatly expands the utility and readability of code that makes multiple decisions. An **If...Then...Else** decision structure has the syntax shown here:

```
If condition-1 Then
   [block of code - 1]
[ElseIf condition-2 Then
   [block of code - 2]]
   .
   .
   .
[Else
   [block of code - n]]
End If
```

Elements of the structure enclosed in square brackets [ ] are optional. You may include as many **ElseIf** chunks (also called *clauses*) as you want, or don't include them if none are needed. You may include one **Else** chunk (clause) or not include it if it isn't needed. In writing the **If...Then...Else** structure, remember these rules:

▼ The first line is an **If...Then** statement and the last line is an **End If** statement.

▼ A line beginning with **If** must end with **Then**. There is no statement following **Then** on this line.

▼ A line beginning with **ElseIf** can end with **Then**, or it can end with **Then** followed by a statement. In this book, an **ElseIf** clause will always end with **Then**.

▼ Each conditional clause (**If** *condition* **Then** or **ElseIf** *condition* **Then**) is followed by a block of code that is executed if the condition is true.

▼ If the conditions in the conditional clauses (**If** or **ElseIf**) are all false, then the block of code following **Else** is executed.

▼ **End If** includes a space; **ElseIf** does not.

Project Negative, Zero, or Positive #3 demonstrates the **If...Then...Else** structure. It is the same as project Negative, Zero, or Positive #1 except that event procedure cmdNegZerPos_Click sports an **If...Then...Else** structure that includes the structure's bells and whistles described above. Notice the indentations of lines in the **If...Then...Else** structure. This is an element of coding style intended to make the structure easy to read. The **If**, **End If**, **ElseIf**, and **Else** statements are indented two spaces inside **Private Sub** and **End Sub**. Each block of code is indented two spaces inside **If** and **End If**. These are arbitrary choices—indent the number of spaces you like.

```
Private Sub cmdNegZerPos_Click()

  Cls                              ' Clear the form.

  If Text1.Text < 0 Then           ' If this is True, then
    Print "Negative"               ' do this.
  ElseIf Text1.Text = 0 Then       ' If this is True, then
    Print "Zero"                   ' do this.
  Else                             ' If both the above are false, then
    Print "Positive"               ' do this.
  End If

  Beep

End Sub
```

Project Light Bulb #5 - Blinking Light Bulb uses a Timer control and an **If...Then...Else** structure to make a light bulb blink on and off. The visual interface looks like this in the design screen:

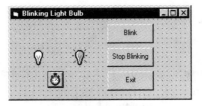

The Form_Load event procedure moves both light bulbs to the same place, makes the turned-off bulb visible, and makes the turned-on bulb invisible. At run time you see the turned-off bulb. Click the Blink button to enable event procedure tmrBlink_Timer. This **If...Then...Else** structure blinks the light:

```
If imgLightOff.Visible = True Then
  imgLightOff.Visible = False
  imgLightOn.Visible = True
ElseIf imgLightOn.Visible = True Then
  imgLightOn.Visible = False
  imgLightOff.Visible = True
End If
```

At each time interval, this structure looks at imgLightOff. If it is visible, the bulb appears turned off. The **If** clause makes imgLightOff invisible and makes imgLightOn visible so that the light appears turned on. On the other hand, if imgLightOff is not visible, then perhaps imgLightOn is visible so that the bulb appears turned on. In that case, the **ElseIf** clause makes imgLightOn invisible and makes imgLightOff visible. Blink, blink, blink. Tables 6-8 and 6-9 list the project's specifications.

The event procedures are shown here, except for cmdExit, which we are sure that you can write. The Form_Load procedure moves the turned-off and turned-on light bulbs to the same place on the form and disables the Timer control so that they don't blink:

```
Private Sub Form_Load()

  ' Move imgLightOff and imgLightOn to the same place
  imgLightOff.Left = 1200
  imgLightOff.Top = 720
  imgLightOn.Left = 1200
  imgLightOn.Top = 720

  ' Make the light bulb appear turned off
  imgLightOff.Visible = True
  imgLightOn.Visible = False

  ' Disable the Timer control
  tmrBlink.Enabled = False

End Sub
```

Object	Property	Setting	Comment
Form1	Caption	Blinking Light Bulb	
	Name	frmLtBulb5	
Command1	Caption	Blink	
	Name	cmdBlink	
Command2	Caption	Stop Blinking	
	Name	cmdStopBlink	
Command3	Caption	Exit	
	Name	cmdExit	
Image1	Name	imgLightOff	
	Picture	(Icon)	Vb\Icons\Misc\Lightoff.ico
Image2	Name	imgLightOn	
	Picture	(Icon)	Vb\Icons\Misc\Lighton.ico
Timer1	Enabled	False	
	Interval	1000	1000 milliseconds (1 second).
	Name	tmrBlink	The standard prefix is "tmr."

TABLE 6-8 *Visual Interface Specifications for Project Light Bulb #5 - Blinking Light Bulb* ▼

Object	Event	Response
frmLtBulb5	Load	Puts boxes in the same place and turns the light off.
cmdBlink	Click	Enables Timer1. The light starts blinking.
cmdStopBlink	Click	Disables Timer1 and turns the light off. The light stops blinking.
cmdExit	Click	Ends the run.
tmrBlink	Timer	If Enabled is True, blinks the light.

TABLE 6-9 *Event Procedure Specifications for Project Light Bulb #5 - Blinking Light Bulb* ▼

Click command button cmdBlink. Its event procedure enables the Timer control and causes the light bulb to blink:

```
Private Sub cmdBlink_Click()

   tmrBlink.Enabled = True

End Sub
```

Click command button cmdStopBlink. Its event procedure disables the Timer control, stops the blinking, and turns off the bulb:

```
Private Sub cmdStopBlink_Click()

   tmrBlink.Enabled = False
   imgLightOff.Visible = True
   imgLightOn.Visible = False

End Sub
```

When the Timer control is enabled, its event procedure blinks the light bulb on and off:

```
Private Sub tmrBlink_Timer()

   ' If the bulb is off, turn it on. If it is on, turn it off.
   If imgLightOff.Visible = True Then
     imgLightOff.Visible = False
     imgLightOn.Visible = True
   ElseIf imgLightOff.Visible = False Then
     imgLightOff.Visible = True
     imgLightOn.Visible = False
   End If

End Sub
```

There's always another way to make something happen. In the exercises, you are asked to make the light bulb blink another way, by alternately copying the light-off icon or the light-on icon into the image box where it is displayed. In preparation for that exercise, try project Light Bulb #6 - Copy an Icon. The visual interface has three image boxes and two command buttons:

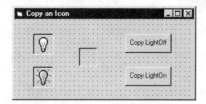

At run time, you see image box imgLightOff with the light-off icon, image box imgLightOn with the light-on icon, and an empty image box that we named imgLight. Click the Copy LightOff button and the light-off icon is copied from imgLightOff into imgLight. Click the Copy LightOn button and the light-on icon is copied from imgLightOn into imgLight, replacing its previous contents. Here are the event procedures that make it so:

```
Private Sub cmdLightOff_Click()

    imgLight.Picture = imgLightOff.Picture

End Sub

Private Sub cmdLightOn_Click()

    imgLight.Picture = imgLightOn.Picture

End Sub
```

Now jump up, aim well, and light on this exercise.

EXERCISE

1. Design project Light Bulb #7 - Blinking Light Bulb. At run time, you see only the turned-off bulb in imgLight and the three command buttons. This is the design screen visual interface:

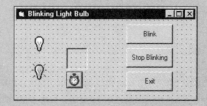

a. Event procedure Form_Load copies the icon in imgLightOff to imgLight.

b. Event procedure cmdBlink_Click enables tmrBlink and starts the light blinking in imgLight.

c. Event procedure cmdStopBlink_Click disables tmrBlink, stops the blinking, and makes sure that the light appears turned off.

d. Event procedure tmrBlink_Timer blinks the light by copying the icons in imgLightOff and imgLightOn alternately into imgLight.

6.4 *CHECK BOXES AND OPTION BUTTONS ALLOW CLICK CHOICES*

Option buttons provide a quick and easy way to select one option from a set of options. Check boxes allow multiple choices. You can draw option buttons and check boxes on a form, in a picture box, or in a frame. Look for the Option Button, Check Box, and Frame tools on the toolbox:

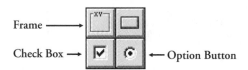

Project Check Box #1 - Mix Colors has check boxes for selecting any combination of red, green, and blue to be mixed as the form's BackColor:

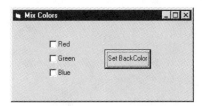

A check box has a Value property with three possible settings: 0 - Unchecked, 1 - Checked, and 2 - Grayed (disabled). Project Check Box #1 uses only 0 and 1 as Value settings. A checked check box (Value = 1) displays an X. An unchecked check box (Value = 0) is empty. Click an unchecked box to set its Value to 1 and display an X. Click a checked box to clear it and set its Value to 0. Check Tables 6-10 and 6-11 for project Check Box #1's specs.

Object	Property	Setting	Comment
Form1	Caption	Mix Colors	
	Name	frmChkBox1	
Command1	Caption	Set BackColor	
	Name	cmdBackColor	
Check1	Caption	Red	
	Name	chkRed	The standard prefix is "chk".
	Value	0	Unchecked at run time.
Check2	Caption	Green	
	Name	chkGreen	The standard prefix is "chk".
	Value	0	Unchecked at run time.
Check2	Caption	Blue	
	Name	chkBlue	The standard prefix is "chk".
	Value	0	Unchecked at run time.

TABLE 6-10 *Visual Interface Specifications for Project Check Box #1 - Mix Colors* ▼

Event procedure cmdBackColor uses an **If...Then...Else** decision structure to assign values to variables *red, green,* and *blue* that depend on the Value settings of the check boxes. For each of these variables, there are two possible values, 0 or 255. The values of red, green, and blue are then used in an RGB function to obtain the mixed color:

```
Private Sub cmdBackColor_Click()

Dim red As Variant, green As Variant, blue As Variant


If chkRed.Value = 1 Then
  red = 255
Else
  red = 0
End If


If chkGreen.Value = 1 Then
  green = 255
Else
  green = 0
End If


If chkBlue.Value = 1 Then
  blue = 255
Else
  blue = 0
End If
```

Object	Event	Response
cmdBackColor	Click	Mixes colors in checked boxes and sets the form's BackColor.

TABLE 6-11   *Event Procedure Specifications for Project Check Box #1 - Mix Colors* ▼

```
frmChkBox1.BackColor = RGB(red, green, blue)

End Sub
```

Design the project, run it, and try all checked/unchecked combinations of the three check boxes.

Project Option Button #1 - Select BackColor provides a set of five option buttons for selecting the form's BackColor. At run time, the project looks like this:

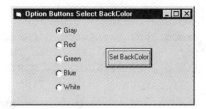

Only one option button can be selected. The selected option button's circle contains a bullet (•). Click an option button to select a color and then click the Set BackColor button to set the form's BackColor to the selected option. When you click an option button, the bullet appears in its circle and disappears from the previously selected button's circle. Table 6-12 lists specifications for project Option Button #1's form, command button, and the top two option buttons. Notice the setting of the Value property for both option buttons. The property settings for the rest of the option buttons are similar to those for option button optRed. Table 6-13 lists the event procedure specifications.

Object	Property	Setting	Comment
Form1	Caption	Option Buttons Select BackColor	
	Name	frmOption1	
Command1	Caption	Set BackColor	
	Name	cmdBackColor	
Option1	Caption	Gray	
	Name	optGray	The standard prefix is "opt."
	Value	True	On (selected) at run time.
Option2	Caption	Red	
	Name	optRed	The standard prefix is "opt."
	Value	False	Off (not selected) at run time.

TABLE 6-12   *Partial Visual Interface Specifications for Project Option Button #1 - Select BackColor* ▼

Object	Event	Response
cmdBackColor	Click	Sets the form's BackColor to the color specified by the "on" option button.

TABLE 6-13 *Event Procedure Specifications for Project Option Button #1 - Select BackColor* ▼

In a set of option buttons, only one button can be on; its Value setting is True. All other buttons in the set are off; their Value settings are False. Event procedure cmdBackColor uses an **If...Then...Else** decision structure to first find the option button whose value setting is True and then set the form's BackColor to the color specified by that option button:

```
Private Sub cmdBackColor_Click()

  If optGray.Value = True Then
     frmOption1.BackColor = RGB(192, 192, 192)   ' Gray
  ElseIf optRed.Value = True Then
     frmOption1.BackColor = RGB(255, 0, 0)        ' Red
  ElseIf optGreen.Value = True Then
     frmOption1.BackColor = RGB(0, 255, 0)        ' Green
  ElseIf optBlue.Value = True Then
     frmOption1.BackColor = RGB(0, 0, 255)        ' Blue
  ElseIf optWhite.Value = True Then
     frmOption1.BackColor = RGB(255, 255, 255)    ' White
  End If

End Sub
```

If you draw option buttons directly on the form, only one can be on. This is inconvenient if you want two or more independent sets of option buttons. No problem—draw each set in a picture box or in a frame. Project Option Button #2 - Select BackColor is the same as project Option Button #1 except that the five option buttons are drawn inside a frame:

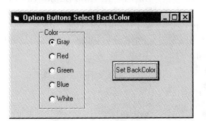

In creating project Option Button #2, do not double-click the Option Button tool and then drag the button inside the frame. Instead, first draw the frame on the form and then draw the option buttons inside the frame. Click the Option Button tool *once* to select it, then move the mouse pointer inside the frame and draw the button. We drew the frame, changed its caption to "Color", and changed its name to "fraColor." Yes, the standard prefix for a frame name is "fra".

Now check out these exercises and opt to do them.

EXERCISES

1. How are check boxes and option buttons alike? How are they different?

2. Design project Check Boxes and Option Buttons #1. Here is a run after someone selected the Green option button and both check boxes, and then clicked the Print Message button. The message is printed in a green, bold, italic, 12-point font:

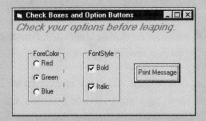

To make the font style bold or not bold, set the FontBold property to True for bold or False for not bold. To make the font style italic or not italic, set the FontItalic property to True for italic or False for not italic.

6.5 USE THE SELECT CASE STRUCTURE TO SELECT CODE

Select Case is a decision structure that selects and executes one block of code from two or more blocks of code. A **Select Case** structure begins with a **Select Case** statement, ends with an **End Select** statement, and can have one or more **Case** blocks in between. At most, one of the **Case** blocks in the structure is executed. In the following **Select Case** structure, what happens depends on the value of a number in text box Text1:

```
Select Case Text1.Text
  Case 1
    Print "one"
  Case 2, 3
    Print "two or three"
  Case Else
    Print "not one, two, or three"
End Select
```

This **Select Case** structure begins with the statement:

```
Select Case Text1.Text
```

There are three **Case** blocks that might be executed based on the value of *Text1.Text*: **Case** 1; **Case** 2, 3; or **Case Else**. For any numerical value of *Text1.Text*, only one **Case** block is executed.

- ▼ If the value of *Text1.Text* is 1, the **Case 1** block prints "one".

- ▼ If the value of *Text1.Text* is 2 or 3, the **Case 2, 3** block prints "two or three".

- ▼ For any value of *Text1.Text* other than 1, 2, or 3, the **Case Else** block prints "not one, two, or three".

The **Select Case** structure ends with an **End Select** statement. The **Case** blocks are indented two spaces inside of **Select Case** and **End Select**. The code that goes with a **Case** block is indented two spaces inside the **Case** clause. These indentations are elements of coding style intended to make the **Select Case** structure easy to read. Indent two spaces or the number of spaces you like, but do indent so that others can easily read and understand your code.

Project Negative, Zero, or Positive #4 - Select Case uses the **Select Case** structure in place of the **If...Then...Else** structure used in project Negative, Zero, or Positive #3. When you use relational operators in **Select Case**, each **Case** block is headed by **Case Is**. If you type **Case** only, Visual Basic inserts **Is** following **Case**. You can convert project Negative, Zero, or Positive #4 into project Negative, Zero, or Positive #5 by rewriting event procedure cmdNegZerPos_Click using a **Select Case** structure:

```
Private Sub cmdNegZerPos_Click()

  Cls                    ' Clear the form.

  Select Case Text1.Text
    Case Is < 0          ' If this is True, then
```

```
      Print "Negative"      ' do this.
   Case Is = 0              ' If this is True, then
      Print "Zero"          ' do this.
   Case Else                ' If both the above are False, then
      Print "Positive"      ' do this.
   End Select

   Beep

End Sub
```

One **Case** block is executed based on the value of *Text1.Text*:

▼ If the value of *Text1.Text* is a negative number, the **Case Is < 0** block is executed and the computer prints "Negative" on the form.

▼ If the value of *Text1.Text* is zero, the **Case Is 0** block is executed and the computer prints "Zero" on the form.

▼ If the value of *Text1.Text* is a number that is not negative and not zero, then it must be positive. The **Case Else** block is executed and the computer prints "Positive" on the form.

▼ For this structure to work, the value of *Text1.Text* must be a number. If the value of *Text1.Text* is a non-number, the Type mismatch dialog box appears with its jolly OK button.

Project Light Bulb #8 - Blink with Select Case is the same as project Light Bulb #5 - Blinking Light Bulb except that event procedure tmrBlink_Timer uses a **Select Case** structure instead of an **If...Then...Else** structure to blink the light bulb on and off:

```
Private Sub tmrBlink_Timer()

   Select Case imgLightOff.Visible
   Case True
      ' Turn the bulb off
      imgLightOff.Visible = False
      imgLightOn.Visible = True
   Case False
      ' Turn the bulb on
      imgLightOff.Visible = True
      imgLightOn.Visible = False
   End Select

End Sub
```

This **Select Case** structure has two cases that depend on the value of *imgLightOff.Visible*. If *imgLightOff.Visible* is True, the **Case** True clause makes the turned-off bulb invisible and the turned-on bulb visible. If *imgLightOff.Visible* is False, the **Case** False clause makes the turned-off bulb visible and the turned-on bulb invisible. Because True and False are the only possible values of *imgLightOff.Visible*, it is okay to use a **Case Else** block instead of the **Case False** block.

Here is the syntax of the **Select Case** structure:

```
Select Case test expression
  [Case list of expressions - 1
    [block of code - 1]]
  [Case list of expressions - 2
    [block of code - 2]]
        .
        .
        .
  [Case Else
    [block of code - n]]
End Select
```

A list of expressions can be a list of one or more values of the test expression. If there are two or more values, they are separated by a comma. If an expression is a condition, then **Case** becomes **Case Is**. If more than one **Case** has a value that matches the test expression, then only the first of these executes its code. **Case Else**, if present, is executed if none of the **Case** values match the value of the test expression.

Now case this exercise and select the solution that suits you.

1. Design project Negative, Zero, or Positive #6 - Ignite My Light. Use a **Select Case** structure in event procedure cmdIgniteLight_Click. This is the run-time visual interface:

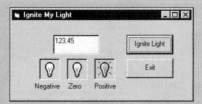

At run time, click the text box, enter a number, click the Ignite Light button and the appropriate light turns on.

6.6 **U**SE THE FOR...NEXT LOOP STRUCTURE TO REPEAT CODE

Suppose that you want to repeat a block of code 10 times or 23 times or any other number of times. The **For...Next** loop structure makes it easy to repeat a block of code a predetermined number of times. A **For...Next** loop begins with a **For** statement, ends with a **Next** statement, and can have a block of code between **For** and **Next**. The block of code is executed repetitively a number of times determined by the **For** statement. The **For...Next** loop shown next has a **Print** statement between the **For** statement and the **Next** statement.

```
For Number = 1 To 7
   Print Number
Next Number
```

This **For...Next** loop prints the integers from 1 to 7 on the form. To check it out, put Command1 on a form and install this event procedure:

```
Private Sub Command1_Click()

  Dim Number As Variant

  For Number = 1 To 7
    Print Number
  Next Number

End Sub
```

Run the project and click Command1. You should see the numbers 1 through 7 printed in a vertical column in the upper-left corner of the form. The **For...Next** loop tells the computer to count from 1 to 7:

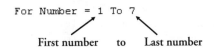

As the computer counts from 1 to 7, each value is assigned to the variable *Number*. This value of *Number* is printed by the **Print** statement inside the **For...Next** loop.

A **For...Next** loop begins with a **For** statement, ends with a **Next** statement, and can have any number of statements in between. A variable must follow **For**. The same variable follows **Next**. The variable may be used in statements between the **For** and **Next** statements.

A **For** statement defines a *sequence of values* for the variable that follows **For**, in steps of one (1) from the first number to the last number. Here are some examples:

For Statement	Sequence of Values
For Number = 1 To 7	1, 2, 3, 4, 5, 6, 7
For digit = 0 To 9	0, 1, 2, 3, 4, 5, 6, 7, 8, 9
For ColorNumber = 0 To 15	0, 1, 2, 3, ..., 15
For n = –1 To 1	–1, 0, 1
For x = 3 To 3	3

The last number must be greater than or equal to the first number. Later in this section you will learn how to construct **For...Next** loops that count down or that count by steps different than one.

Event procedure Command1_Click prints a line on Form1 in each QBasic color, color numbers 0 to 15:

```
Private Sub Command1_Click()

  Dim ColorNumber As Variant

  Cls

  For ColorNumber = 0 To 15
    Form1.ForeColor = QBColor(ColorNumber)
    Form1.Print "This is printed in QBColor"; ColorNumber
  Next ColorNumber

End Sub
```

Install the event procedure and try it. It prints 16 lines. The line printed in QBColor 7 (gray) is invisible because it is printed in the form's BackColor. Here are the first three lines and the last line:

```
This is printed in QBColor 0
This is printed in QBColor 1
This is printed in QBColor 2
 .
 .
 .
This is printed in QBColor 15
```

The **For** statement defines a sequence of values for *ColorNumber*. Each value is used to set Form1's ForeColor property and also appears in the line that is printed on the form. The statement

```
Form1.Print "This is printed in QBColor"; ColorNumber
```

prints the string "This is printed in QBColor" and then prints the value of the variable *ColorNumber* on the same line. A semicolon separates the string and the variable. You can also use a comma as a separator between two items in a **Print** statement. Try it and see what happens.

The **For...Next** loops that you have seen so far count up, from a lower number to a higher number. You can also count down, from a higher number to a lower number. To do so, include a **Step** clause.

```
For Number = 7 To 1 Step -1
  Print Number;
Next Number
```

Put this **For...Next** loop in an event procedure and try it. You will see the numbers from 7 to 1 printed. The semicolon at the end of the **Print** statement causes the numbers to be printed on one line like this:

```
 7  6  5  4  3  2  1
```

The **Step** clause defines the increment by which the variable following **For** changes each time. The next **For...Next** loop uses a positive noninteger **Step** size. The values of *x* are 0, 0.25, 0.50, 0.75, and 1:

```
For x = 0 To 1 Step 0.25
  Print x
Next x
```

Here are more examples showing the sequence of values defined by a **For...To...Step** statement:

For...To...Step Statement	Sequence of Values	Comment
For even = 2 To 10 Step 2	2, 4, 6, 8, 10	
For red = 0 To 255 Step 64	0, 64, 128, 192	255 is not attained.
For red = 255 To 0 Step –51	255, 204, 153, 102, 51, 0	
For x = –1 To 1 Step 0.5	–1, –0.5, 0, 0.5, 1	
For p = 0 To 1 Step 0.333	0, 0.333, 0.666, 0.999	1 is not attained.
For z = 0 To 2 Step 0.667	0, 0.667, 1.334	2 is not attained.

EXERCISES

1. For each of the following **For** statements, list the sequence of values that will be assigned to the variable:

   a. For n = 0 To 5

    b. For x = 0.5 To 2.5

    c. For y = 1 To 2.5

    d. For z = 1 To 2.5 Step 0.25

    e. For w = 100 To 200 Step 10

    f. For f = 3000 To 1000 Step –100

    g. For z = 10 To 11 Step 0.333

    h. For q = 10 To 12 Step 0.667

2. For each sequence of values, write a **For** statement that will generate the sequence.

    a. 0, 3, 6, 9

    b. 10, 8, 6, 4, 2, 0

    c. 1000, 2000, 3000

    d. 3, 2.5, 2, 1.5, 1

3. Write event procedure Command1_Click that uses a **For...Next** loop to rapidly display the numbers from 2000 to 1000 in picture box Picture1.

6.7   *T*HE DOEVENTS STATEMENT CAN TAME A SELFISH FOR...NEXT LOOP

Windows is a *multitasking* environment. It can manage several tasks simultaneously by moving from task to task, giving each a small slice of time. Visual Basic usually responds to events as they occur. Unfortunately, a **For...Next** loop presents a problem. While it is running, nothing else can happen. Visual Basic can't respond to events outside the **For...Next** loop and Windows can't do its normal multitasking. We'll first demonstrate the problem and then fix it.

Project For...Next #1 - Selfish For...Next Loop has a **For...Next** loop that rapidly counts from 1 to 3000 and displays each counting number in a text box. Start it running and it takes over—nothing else can happen until it finishes its egocentric enumeration. Run time begins like this:

Don't click the Count button yet. Click the Beep button and you hear a beep, click the Quit button and the run ends. Both events work. Run the project again. Click the Count button and its event procedure's **For...Next** loop begins. The numbers 1, 2, 3, and so on are rapidly displayed in the text box. While this is happening, nothing works. Click the Beep button and you don't hear a beep. Click the Quit button and it doesn't quit. You can wait until the count reaches 3000 or you can do this:

▼ Hold down CTRL and press BREAK. Look for BREAK on the top-right part of the keyboard. On some keyboards, BREAK and PAUSE are labels on the same key.

Don't take our word for it—design project For...Next #1 and try it. Tables 6-14 and 6-15 list the specs.

You know how to write event procedures cmdBeep_Click and cmdQuit_Click. Here's event procedure cmdCount_Click:

```
Private Sub cmdCount_Click()

  Dim Number As Variant

  ' Set Text1's font size and style, then clear it
  Text1.FontSize = 16
  Text1.FontBold = True
  Text1.Text = ""

  ' Display numbers from 1 to 3000 in Text1
  For Number = 1 To 3000
    Cls
    Text1.Text = Number
  Next Number

End Sub
```

Object	Property	Setting
Form1	Caption	Selfish For...Next Loop
	Name	frmForNext1
Text1	Name	Text1
	Text	
Command1	Caption	Count
	Name	cmdCount
Command2	Caption	Beep
	Name	cmdBeep
Command3	Caption	Quit
	Name	cmdQuit

TABLE 6-14 *Visual Interface Specifications for Project For...Next #1 - Selfish For...Next Loop* ▼

Object	Event	Response
cmdCount	Click	Counts from 1 to 3000 and displays each number in Text1.
cmdBeep	Click	Beeps.
cmdQuit	Click	Ends the run.

TABLE 6-15 *Event Procedure Specifications for Project For...Next #1 - Selfish For...Next Loop* ▼

Design the project, run it, and experience the problem. If you have the time, click the Count button and wait until it counts to 3000. While you are waiting, click the Beep button. When the count reaches 3000 you will hear a beep. What happens if you click the Quit button while waiting for the count to reach 3000? Try it and find out.

Visual Basic provides the solution to this problem. You can put a **DoEvents** statement inside the **For...Next** loop to tell it to pay attention to the outside world. Modify project For...Next #1 to obtain project For...Next #2 with **DoEvents**. Add a **DoEvents** statement to the **For...Next** loop as shown in this variation of cmdCount_Click:

```
Private Sub cmdCount_Click()

  Dim Number As Variant

  ' Set Text1's font size and style, then clear it
  Text1.FontSize = 16
  Text1.FontBold = True
  Text1.Text = ""

  ' Display numbers from 1 to 3000 in Text1
  For Number = 1 To 3000
    DoEvents                 ' Respond to outside events
    Cls
    Text1.Text = Number
  Next Number

End Sub
```

Run For...Next #2, and click the Count button to start its **For...Next** loop. While it is counting, click the Beep button and you hear a beep. Click the Quit button and the run ends even if the count hasn't reached 3000.

The next project contains a **For...Next** loop within a **For...Next**:

```
Private Sub cmdLoop_Click()

  Dim outer As Variant, inner As Variant

  For outer = 1 To 20          ' Begin outer loop
    DoEvents                   ' Respond to outside events
    picOuter.Cls
    picOuter.Print outer

    For inner = 1 To 100       ' Begin inner loop
      picInner.Cls
      picInner.Print inner
    Next inner                 ' End inner loop

  Next outer                   ' End outer loop

End Sub
```

For each value of the variable *outer* in the outer loop, the entire inner loop is executed. In other words, for each value of *outer*, the inner loop variable *inner* runs through its entire sequence of values from 1 to 100. There is no **DoEvents** statement in the inner loop so it does not respond to outside events. There is a **DoEvents** statement in the outer loop so it responds to outside events. Project For...Next #3 - Loop Within a Loop exercises this loop within a loop. Here is a snapshot of the project during a run:

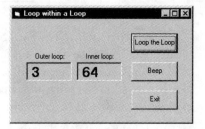

If you watch an entire run, you see the integers from 1 to 20 appear sequentially in the picture box labeled "Outer loop:." For each of these values, you see the integers from 1 to 100 flash by rapidly in the picture box labeled "Inner loop:". Click the Beep button while the inner loop is running. You hear the beep after the inner loop ends, thanks to **DoEvents** in the outer loop. Tables 6-16 and 6-17 list specs for project For...Next #3 - Loop Within a Loop's specifications.

Install event procedure cmdLoop_Click shown at the beginning of this section and run the project. You can think of a loop within a loop as a wheel within a wheel. Each time the inner wheel goes around once, the outer wheel moves a little. Wheel on down to the exercises and make your own loops.

Object	Property	Setting	Comment
Picture1	Name	picOuter	
	Font	18 points bold	Click Font and use the Font dialog box.
Picture2	Name	picInner	
	Font	18 points bold	Click Font and use the Font dialog box.
Command1	Caption	Loop the Loop	
	Name	cmdLoop	

TABLE 6-16 *Partial Visual Interface Specifications for Project For...Next #3 - Loop Within a Loop* ▼

Object	Event	Response
cmdLoop	Click	Runs a **For...Next** loop within a **For...Next** loop.

TABLE 6-17 *Partial Event Procedure Specifications for Project For...Next #3 - Loop Within a Loop* ▼

EXERCISES

1. Design Project RGB #4 with For...Next. This is the visual interface:

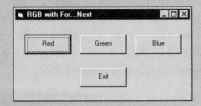

   Click the Red button and its **For...Next** loop sequentially displays all 256 shades of red from the darkest (0) to the brightest (255) as the form's BackColor. Click the Green or Blue buttons to see all 256 shades of those colors. Do not use a **DoEvents** statement in the **For...Next** loops. Run the project and answer these questions:

   a. What happens if you click the Red button and then quickly click the Green button?

   b. What happens if you rapidly click the Green button two times?

2. Modify project RGB #4. Put a **DoEvents** statement in each **For...Next** loop. Call this project RGB #5 with For...Next and DoEvents. Run the project and answer these questions:

   a. What happens if you click the Red button and then quickly click the Green button?

b. What happens if you rapidly click the Green button two times?

3. You can use the **Move** method in a **For...Next** loop to make an object travel from one place to another on the form. Make the form's size 6000×3600. Put an image box on the left edge of the form at coordinates 0, 1200 and name it imgArrow. Load a right-pointing arrow into imgArrow (we used Vb\Icons\Arrows\Arw08rt.ico). Install event procedure imgArrow_Click:

```
Private Sub imgArrow_Click()

  Dim NewLeft As Variant

  For NewLeft = 0 To 5400
    DoEvents
    imgArrow.Move NewLeft, 1200
  Next NewLeft

End Sub
```

a. Run the project, click the arrow, and watch it fly leisurely across the form. It should rest with its point touching the right edge of the form.

b. How can you make the arrow fly faster?

c. Save the project as Move It #4 - Shoot an Arrow.

4. Design projects Move It #5 - Launch a Rocket and Move It #6 - Fly a Plane:

a. Project Move It #5. Put imgRocket containing Vb\Icons\Industry \Rocket.ico at the bottom of the form and fly it to the top of the form.

b. Project Move It #6. Put imgPlane containing Vb\Icons\Industry \Plane.ico in the lower-left corner of the form and fly it to the upper-right corner.

6.8 USE THE DO...LOOP STRUCTURE FOR REPETITIVE OPERATION

You can use the **Do...Loop** structure to create a never-ending loop or a loop that stops when a condition is satisfied. A never-ending loop keeps going and going until someone presses CTRL - BREAK to stop the action.

The never-ending **Do...Loop** shown next begins with a **Do** statement, ends with a **Loop** statement, and has two statements between them.

```
Do
  Form1.Forecolor = QBColor(15 * Rnd)    ' Random foreground color
  Print "To stop, hold down Ctrl and press break"
Loop
```

Once you start this **Do...Loop**, it's like Mickey Mouse as the sorcerer's apprentice. Mickey knew how to start the broom fetching water, but he didn't know how to stop it. If you don't stop it, eventually Visual Basic may stop it and display an "out of memory" message.

Before you use this **Do...Loop** in a project, locate the BREAK key. You will need it to stop the runaway **Do...Loop**. Now put Command1 on the form and install event procedure Command1_Click. Postpone worrying about the **Rnd** function in the statement that sets Form1's ForeColor property. We'll tell you about it later.

```
Private Sub Command1_Click()

  Do
    Form1.ForeColor = QBColor(15 * Rnd)    ' Random foreground color
    Print "To stop, hold down Ctrl and press Break."
  Loop

End Sub
```

Ready? Run the project, click Command1, and watch as the form quickly fills with the **Print** statement's message printed in random foreground colors. You see the following in random colors:

```
To stop, hold down Ctrl-Break.
```

After awhile, strange things begin to happen as the project runs out of memory space and starts overprinting text already on the form. When you tire of watching this message endlessly repeated, hold down CTRL-BREAK to stop the run. Then add a **DoEvents** statement to the **Do...Loop** so that it can respond to outside events such as a Quit button or a Clear Form button:

```
Private Sub Command1_Click()

  Do
    DoEvents
```

```
      ForeColor = QBColor(15 * Rnd)    ' Random foreground color
      Print "To stop, hold down Ctrl and press Break."
   Loop

End Sub
```

The **Do...Loop** executes the block of code between **Do** and **Loop** repeatedly until you interrupt. The code between **Do** and **Loop** is indented in the hope of making the **Do...Loop** easier to read and understand. This statement

```
The statement:  ForeColor = QBColor(15 * Rnd)
```

uses the **Rnd** function to obtain random color numbers. **Rnd** is a Visual Basic function that returns a random number greater than 0 but less than 1:

```
0 < Rnd < 1
```

To get random color numbers in the range 0 to 15, use Visual Basic's multiplication operator (*) to multiply **Rnd** by 15:

```
0 < 15 * Rnd < 15
```

This generates a random number (**15 * Rnd**) between 0 and 15. Color numbers must be integers, so Visual Basic rounds the random number to the nearest integer. After rounding, any integer value from 0 to 15 is possible.

Here are some values of **Rnd**, 15 * **Rnd**, the rounded value, and the color selected:

Rnd	15 * Rnd	Rounded	Color
0.8298016	12.44702	12	Light red
0.1063697	1.595545	2	Green
0.9495566	14.24335	14	Yellow
0.9798294	14.69744	15	Bright white

Never-ending **Do...Loops** are not very useful. A more useful **Do...Loop** includes a condition that, when True, ends the **Do...Loop**. The following block of code acts as a brief time delay of 0.125 second:

```
start = Timer
Do While Timer < start + 0.125
Loop
```

The value of **Timer** is the number of seconds after midnight. This chunk of code sets the variable *start* equal to **Timer**. This value remains the same while **Timer** marches on. The **Do...Loop** loops **While** the condition *Timer < start + 0.125* is True. When the value of **Timer** becomes equal to or greater than *start + 0.125*, the condition becomes False and the **Do...Loop** ends. Try it. Put Command1 on Form1 and install this event procedure:

```
Private Sub Command1_Click()

  Dim green As Variant, start As Variant

  Cls

  For green = 0 To 255
    DoEvents
    BackColor = RGB(0, green, 0)
    start = Timer
    Do Until Timer >= start + 0.125
    Loop
  Next

End Sub
```

Run the procedure and click Command1. You will see Form1's background color slowly change from the darkest green to the brightest green. Since the time delay is 0.125 second and there are 256 shades of green, this will take about 32 seconds.

The time delay **Do...Loop** is an example of a **Do...While...Loop**. This type of **Do...Loop** has the following syntax:

Do While *condition*
 [block of code]
Loop

The block of code is repeated **While** the condition is True. The **Do...Loop** ends when the condition is False.

Another type of **Do...Loop** is the **Do...Until...Loop**:

Do Until condition
 [block of code]
Loop

The block of code is repeated **Until** the condition is True. The **Do...Loop** ends when the condition is False. You can put the **While** or **Until** clause in the **Loop** statement instead of the **Do** statement as shown in these two variations of the **Do...Loop**:

```
Do
    [block of code]
Loop While condition

Do
    [block of code]
Loop Until condition
```

Do try the following exercises.

EXERCISES

1. Suppose that the never-ending **Do...Loop** shown below is running:

```
Do
    ForeColor = QBColor(15 * Rnd)    ' Random foreground color
    Print "To stop, hold down Ctrl and press Break"
Loop
```

   a. Can you stop it by clicking the End tool on the toolbar?

   b. Can you stop it by using the Stop command on the Run menu?

   c. How do you stop it?

2. The time delay code is shown here:

```
start = Timer
Do While Timer < start + 0.125
Loop
```

   a. Rewrite the time delay using a **Do...Until...Loop** structure.

   b. Rewrite the time delay using a **Do...Loop While** structure.

   c. Rewrite the time delay using a **Do...Loop Until** structure.

3. For a short time delay it may be okay to omit a **DoEvents** statement. For a long delay, the **DoEvents** statement should be included. Write code for a 10-second delay that includes a **DoEvents** statement.

mastery
skills check

1. You have learned how to write code using three types of logic structures. Name and describe these three types of structures.

2. Put Timer1 on Form1, set Timer1's Interval property to 1000, and install these event procedures:

```
Private Sub Form_Load()

  Form1.BackColor = RGB(255, 0, 0)

End Sub

Private Sub Timer1_Timer()

  If Form1.BackColor = RGB(255, 0, 0) Then
    Form1.BackColor = RGB(0, 255, 0)
  ElseIf Form1.BackColor = RGB(0, 255, 0) Then
    Form1.BackColor = RGB(255, 0, 0)
  End If

End Sub
```

What will you see at run time? Describe the run-time behavior before you run the project, then run it to verify your conjecture.

3. Rewrite event procedure Timer1_Timer in Exercise 2 by using a **Select Case** structure instead of the **If...Then...Else** structure.

4. Modify event procedure Timer1_Timer of Exercise 2 so that the background color of Form1 changes from red to green to blue to red to green to blue and so on.

   a. Use an **If...Then...Else** structure.

   b. Use a **Select Case** structure.

5. Create project Alarm #1 - Turn Off the Oven!. When you click the Alarm button it beeps and blinks "Turn Off the Oven!". The message blinks on for one second, blinks off for one second, on for a second, off for a second,

and so on until you click the Stop it! button. Display the message in a text box in a bold 18-point font.

   a. Use an **If...Then...Else** structure.

   b. Use a **Select Case** structure.

6. For each of the following **For** statements, identify the sequence of values that will be assigned to the variable following **For**:

   a. For n = 0 To 5

   b. For x = 0.5 To 2.5

   c. For y = 1 To 2.5

   d. For z = 1 To 2.5 Step 0.5

   e. For w = 100 To 200 Step 10

   f. For f = 3000 To 1000 Step −100

   g. For a = 10 To 11 Step 0.333

   h. For b = 10 To 12 Step 0.667

7. Write a **For** statement to generate each sequence of values of the variable following **For**.

   a. 0, 3, 6, 9

   b. 10, 8, 6, 4, 2, 0

   c. 1000, 2000, 3000

   d. 1, 2, 3, 4,..., 365

   e. 365, 364, 363, 362,..., 1

   f. 0, 0.125, 0.25, 0.375,..., 1

   g. 3, 2.5, 2, 1.5, 1, 0.5, 0

   h. 0.5, 1.5, 2.5, 3.5, 4.5

8. The statement $n = n - 1$ decreases the value of the variable n by 1. What is printed by this block of code?

```
n = 10
Do While n >= 0
  Print n
  n = n - 1
Loop
End Sub
```

9. Rewrite the code in Exercise 8 three different ways so that the rewritten code prints exactly the same sequence of numbers:

   a. Use a **Do Until...Loop** structure.

   b. Use a **Do...Loop While** structure.

   c. Use a **Do...Loop Until** structure.

10. Assume that text box Text1 contains a positive integer. Write a **Do...Loop** to print on the form the integers from 1 to the integer in Text1.

11. Modify project Fortune Cookie #3 from Chapter 3 to obtain project Fortune Cookie #5. To do so, add check boxes captioned "Bold" and "Italic" so that the user can show Fortune #1 or Fortune #2 in bold, italic, both bold and italic, or neither.

12. Design project RGB #6 - Loop Within a Loop Within a Loop. At run time you see this:

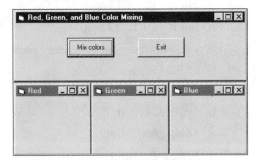

    Use a loop within a loop within a loop to do this:

    a. Outer loop: Display the 256 shades of red as the background color of the Red form.

    b. Middle loop: For each shade of red, display the 256 shades of green as the background color of the Green form.

    c. Inner loop: For each shade of red and green, display the 256 shades of blue as the background color of the Blue form. For each combination of red, green, and blue, display the mixed color as the background color of the Loop Within a Loop Within a Loop form.

13. Design projects Spin the Arrow #1, Spin the Arrow #2, and perhaps more spinning arrows. The *icons* folder has several sets of four arrows that point north, east, south, or west (or up, right, down, and left if you prefer). Put four image boxes in a picture box and load them with a set of arrows, one arrow per image box. Move all the image boxes to the same place in the

picture box. Write code to spin the arrow. Perhaps use a Timer event procedure to make one arrow visible at a time, first the north-pointing arrow, then the east-pointing arrow, then the south-pointing arrow, then the north-pointing arrow, and so on. You might provide command buttons such as Spin, Faster, Slower, and Stop Spinning! Do you want to spin the arrow clockwise or counterclockwise? Why not provide option buttons captioned Clockwise and Counterclockwise? Then the user can decide the spin direction.

The *icons* folder also has sets of arrows that point northeast, southeast, southwest, and northwest. You might use four of them to spin the arrow. You might also use eight arrows and spin them to all eight compass headings. Or you might...well, crank up your imagination and create your own animations.

14. Design project Inflation #1. Put metafile Money.wmf in a large picture box and make it slowly shrink as time marches on.

7

Number Crunching

chapter objectives

7.1 Create immediate statements in the Debug window

7.2 Use the Debug window to explore data types

7.3 Do arithmetic in the Debug window

7.4 Explore a number pattern in the Debug window

7.5 Learn more about variables

7.6 Build better calculating machines

7.7 Create computer "art" in the style of Zappy Artist

DURING the millenia BVB (Before Visual Basic), a code writer had to be very knowledgeable about the way data was represented deep down inside the computer. BVB programming languages were very nit-picky about this.

Fortunately, a few years ago a fortuitous burst of cosmic rays impinged on Redmond, Washington, the home of Microsoft. Unbelievably, this burst struck the area occupied by the junk food machines at exactly the time when a critical mass of code wizards were congregating to stoke up on their favorite brain food.

Serendipity! One high-energy particle triggered exactly the right neurons of one code wizard who leaped to his or her feet and exclaimed, "Eureka! Let's invent a smart data type!"

Thus was born Visual Basic's **Variant** data type. **Variant** is very flexible—it can represent several types of data, including dates, times, numbers, and strings. You blithely used these **Variant** data types in Chapters 2 through 6 without bothering about picky details. In this chapter, you will use the Debug window to experiment with data types, do arithmetic, and experiment with variables that represent Visual Basic's numeric data types. In Chapter 8 you will learn more about the data type that represents strings.

If you have used QBasic or QuickBasic, you already know about several data types and corresponding types of variables and you can quickly cavort through this and the next chapter. If you are a beginning coder, peruse these chapters and add new tools to your Visual Basic backpack.

7.1 CREATE IMMEDIATE STATEMENTS IN THE DEBUG WINDOW

You can use the Debug window as a powerful exploration tool. In the Debug window, you can enter statements that are executed immediately—let's call them *immediate statements*. To access the Debug window, you run a project and then click the Break tool on the toolbar. The Break tool is between the Start tool and the End tool. Let's do it:

1. Start a new project with Form1 and nothing else.

2. Run the project.

3. At run time, click the Break tool on the toolbar:

This activates the Debug window and brings it up front with its title bar highlighted. The design screen's title bar displays *Project1 - Microsoft Visual Basic [break]*. The Debug window awaits your command:

Get acquainted with the Debug window and identify these features:

▼ The title bar displays *Debug Window - Project1*.

▼ Below the title bar is a box containing the dimmed message <Break: Form1> and an ellipses (...) button off to the right. Ignore this box for now.

▼ Most of the Debug window is a big empty area called the *Immediate pane*. The cursor is blinking in the upper-left corner of the Immediate pane.

You can enter and execute immediate **Print** statements in the Immediate pane. It's easy—you just type a **Print** statement and press ENTER. Try it—enter an immediate **Print** statement to print the value of Form1's Caption property. You see your **Print** statement and its result in the Immediate pane:

```
Print Caption
Form1
```

You can print more than one thing in a **Print** statement if you separate items with commas or semicolons. For example, print both the width and the height of Form1 like this:

```
Print Width, Height
 6840            6435
```

The comma causes items to be printed in *standard print zones*. Each standard print zone is 14 characters wide in the font, font size, and font style that you are using. The values of *Width* and *Height* are printed in the first two print zones. If you use semicolons (;) instead of commas, the items are *concatenated* (joined together).

Use a semicolon to separate *Width* and *Height* in the following **Print** statement:

```
Print Width; Height
 6840   6435
```

These numeric values are concatenated. A positive number or zero is printed as a space, the digits of the number, and a space. Therefore, you see two spaces between the two numbers above, one following the first number and another preceding the second number.

The settings of the BackColor and ForeColor properties are hexadecimal numbers. Let's print them and see what they look like:

```
Print BackColor; ForeColor
-2147483633 -2147483630
```

Visual Basic converts these hexadecimal numbers to decimal numbers that happen to be negative. A negative number is printed as a minus sign (–), the digits of the number, and a space. Don't be boggled by hexadecimal numbers. You don't need to know anything about them to set the BackColor and ForeColor properties at design time, and you can use the **QBColor** and **RGB** functions to set them in event procedures.

If the Debug window becomes cluttered with **Print** statements and their results, click the one at the top, drag downward to highlight a bunch of them, and press DELETE to get rid of them. If statements scroll out of sight, use the scroll bars to scroll up, down, or sideways in the usual way.

You have used the **Date** and **Time** functions in earlier chapters. Use them here in an immediate **Print** statement:

```
Print Date, Time
11/30/95       7:30:09 AM
```

Enough experimenting for now. Click the Stop tool on the toolbar to end the run. You can learn even more about the Debug window by doing these exercises immediately.

EXERCISES

1. Start a new project, leave all of Form1's properties set to their default values, run the project, and click the Break tool to get the Debug window. Describe the result printed by each immediate **Print** statement:

   a. Print AutoRedraw

   b. Print BorderStyle

   c. Print DrawWidth

   d. Print Font

   e. Print MaxButton

2. Load up Form1 with objects: Label1, Text1, Image1, Picture1, Line1, Shape1, Timer1, and anything else you'd like. Put the Earth icon (Earth.ico) in Image1, the freeway intersection metafile (Multarw4.wmf) in Picture1, a circle in Shape1, and set Timer1's Interval property to 1000 milliseconds. For each object and property, write a **Print** statement to print the *Object.Property* variable's value:

	Object	**Property**	**Comment**
a.	Label1	Caption	
b.	Text1	Text	
c.	Form1	Picture	
d.	Image1	Picture	
e.	Picture1	Picture	
f.	Line1	X1 and Y1	Use a comma to separate the two items.
g.	Line1	X2 and Y2	Use a semicolon to separate the two items.
h.	Shape1	Shape	
i.	Timer1	Interval	

7.2

USE THE DEBUG WINDOW TO EXPLORE DATA TYPES

Visual Basic has many *data types*, including strings, dates, times, and several types of numbers. You can use the **VarType** function to find out what data type is lurking as the setting of a property, the value of a function, or the value of a variable. Table 7-1 lists several of Visual Basic's data types and shows the data type number returned by the **VarType** function for each data type.

Data Type	VarType Returns	Brief Description of Data Type
Empty	0	A special type that indicates no value has been assigned.
Null	1	Indicates missing or unknown data.
Integer	2	An integer in the range –32,768 to 32,767.*
Long	3	An integer in the range –2,147,483,648 to 2,147,483,647.*
Single	4	A *single-precision number* with up to 7 digits.**
Double	5	A *double-precision number* with up to 15 digits.**
Currency	6	Designed for fast and accurate monetary calculations.
Date/Time	7	Designed to represent date and time. For example, the value of **Now**.
String	8	Any string of Visual Basic characters.
Boolean	11	True or False. Standard numerical values are True = –1 and False = 0.

*A number without a fractional part.
**Can represent integers or nonintegers. A noninteger may have a decimal point and decimal fraction, as in 123.45 or 3.14.

TABLE 7-1   *Visual Basic Data Types and the Data Type Number Returned by the **VarType** Function* ▼

The **VarType** function has the syntax

VarType(*argument*)

where *argument* can be a variable, a function, or a specific data value.

You can use an immediate **Print** statement with the **VarType** function to print an argument's data type. Use it to print the data types of default values of Form1's properties. Start a new project, run it, click the Break tool to activate the Debug window, and use immediate **Print** statements with **VarType** to print the data types of property settings. Begin by discovering the data type of Form1's Caption setting:

```
Print VarType(Caption)
 8
```

Just what we expected. Form1's Caption setting is data type 8, String. We suspect that a label's Caption setting and a text box's Text setting are also strings. What other properties might be strings?

Next, let's print the data type of a property that might be a number. Enter an immediate **Print** statement to print the data type of Form1's Width property:

```
Print VarType(Width)
 4
```

The Width setting is stored as data type 4, Single—a single-precision number. It can have up to seven digits and can be an integer or a noninteger.

There are only a few possible settings of the BorderStyle property, and they appear to be small integers. Let's find out:

```
Print VarType(BorderStyle)
 2
```

As expected, BorderStyle's value is data type 2, Integer.

Recall that the BackColor and ForeColor properties are hexadecimal numbers, but were previously printed as rather large negative decimal integers. A **Print** statement confirms that they are of data type 3, Long:

```
Print VarType(BackColor), VarType(ForeColor)
 3                        3
```

Actually, all numbers are stored as *binary*, or *base 2*, numbers. People prefer decimal numbers, so Visual Basic obligingly converts numbers to decimal form when displaying or printing them. An exception is the way it displays the BackColor and ForeColor settings in the Properties window. These are shown as hexadecimal (base 16) numbers. You can recognize a hexadecimal number by the ampersand and H (&H) that begins the number and the ampersand (&) that ends the number. For example: &H8000000F&. (The trailing ampersand may be omitted.)

Some properties have only two possible settings, True or False. Let's discover the data type for AutoRedraw (the default setting is False) and ControlBox (the default setting is True):

```
Print VarType(AutoRedraw), VarType(ControlBox)
 11               11
```

Both of these settings are of data type 11, Boolean. The Boolean data type is named in honor of George Boole, a hyperlogical person who spent much of his life creating Boolean Algebra and writing college football fight songs such as "Boola Boola."

Next, let's check the data types of the **Date**, **Time**, and **Now** functions:

```
Print VarType(Date); VarType(Time); VarType(Now)
 7  7  7
```

These are all data type 7, Date/Time, which seems quite reasonable. What is **Timer**'s data type?

```
Print VarType(Timer)
 4
```

Timer's data type is 4, Single, a single-precision number with up to seven digits. **Timer**'s value is usually shown with one or two decimal places. You have probably seen values of **Timer** such as 32597.82, 53272.45, or 49606.06. There are 86,400 seconds in one day, so at one second before midnight the value of **Timer** is 86,399. At midnight, the value of **Timer** is set to 0.

While we're wandering off the road exploring these Visual Basic nooks and crannies, let's invent some data and apply **VarType** to our data. Hmmm...how about 32,767, which should be data type 2, Integer. 32,768 is slightly out of the range for Integer, so perhaps it is data type 3, Long. Let's check our conjectures. Notice that these numbers are typed without a comma separating the thousands digit and the hundreds digit:

```
Print VarType(32767); VarType(32768)
 2  3
```

Conjectures verified—we're on a roll! Now let's try a couple of nonintegers, one with fewer than seven digits (data type 4, Single?) and one with more than seven digits (data type 5, Double?):

```
Print VarType(123.45); VarType(123.456789)
 5  5
```

Well, that's a surprise. We thought that 123.45 might be data type 4, Single, but both numbers are data type 5, Double. Actually, that's good. Numbers are stored in the computer as binary (base 2) numbers. That's okay for integers—they can be represented exactly in either decimal or binary format. However, nonintegers that have a decimal fraction after the decimal point may have tiny errors introduced when converted to binary. These errors are much less if the numbers are converted to data type 5, Double, than if they are converted to data type 4, Single.

Why does Visual Basic have all of these number types? One reason is storage space; another is arithmetic speed. Data type 2, Integer, requires only two bytes of memory space, and arithmetic with integers is slightly faster than arithmetic with other data types. Data type 5, Double, and 6, Currency, require eight bytes of memory space; arithmetic with these data types is somewhat slower. You can coerce a number to be the type you want by appending a type designator to its right end. Here are the numeric data types, their type designators, examples, and the number of bytes of memory required to store one number of the type:

Data Type	Type Designator	Example	Bytes per Number
Integer	%	123%	2
Long	&	123&	4
Single	!	123!	4
Double	#	123#	8
Currency	@	123@	8

Do these designators work? It's easy to find out:

```
Print VarType(123%); VarType(123&); VarType(123!)
 2  3  4
Print VarType(123#); VarType(123@)
 5  6
```

They work! Now you can work on these exercises.

EXERCISES

1. Start a new project, leave Form1's properties set to their default values, run the project, and click the Break tool to get the Debug window. Show the result printed by each immediate **Print** statement:

   a. Print VarType(BorderStyle)

   b. Print VarType(DrawMode); VarType(DrawStyle); VarType(DrawWidth)

   c. Print VarType(FontSize); VarType(FontBold); VarType(FontItalic)

   d. Print VarType(MaxButton), VarType(MinButton)

   e. Print VarType(Name)

   f. Print VarType(Left), VarType(Top)

2. Load up Form1 with objects: Label1, Text1, Image1, Picture1, Line1, Shape1, Timer1, and anything else you'd like. Put the Earth icon (Earth.ico) in Image1, the freeway intersection metafile (Multarw4.wmf) in Picture1, a circle in Shape1, and set Timer1's Interval property to 1000 milliseconds. For each object and property, write a **Print** statement to print the data type of the *Object.Property* variable's value:

	Object	Property	Comment
a.	Label1	Caption	
b.	Text1	Text	
c.	Form1	ScaleWidth	
d.	Image1	Width	
e.	Picture1	ScaleHeight	
f.	Line1	X1 and Y1	Use a comma to separate the two items.
g.	Line1	X2 and Y2	Use a semicolon to separate the two items.
h.	Shape1	Shape	
i.	Timer1	Interval	

3. What is the data type of each number?

   a. 3.14

   b. 3.141592653589793#

   c. 365%

   d. 234567.89@

   e. –2147483648&

7.3 **D**O ARITHMETIC IN THE DEBUG WINDOW

You can use Visual Basic's *arithmetic operators* **+** (addition), **–** (subtraction), ***** (multiplication), and **/** (division) to do calculations. To do arithmetic, use **Print** followed by a *numeric expression* such as 3 + 4 or 3 – 4. Visual Basic *evaluates* the numeric expression (does the arithmetic) and then prints the result. A numeric expression is any expression that Visual Basic can evaluate to produce a number. Try these immediate statements. You may omit the comment following an apostrophe on each code line:

```
Print 3 + 4      ' addition
 7
Print 3 - 4      ' subtraction
-1
Print 3 * 4      ' multiplication
 12
Print 3 / 4      ' division
 0.75
```

The statement

```
Print 3 + 4
```

first evaluates the numeric expression 3 + 4 and then prints the result (7).
The statement

```
Print 3 - 4
```

first evaluates the numeric expression 3 – 4 and then prints the result (–1).
The statement

```
Print 3 * 4
```

first evaluates the numeric expression 3 * 4 and then prints the result (12).
The statement

```
Print 3 / 4
```

first evaluates the numeric expression 3 / 4 and then prints the result (0.75).
Recall that a **Print** statement can print more than one item. Use commas or semicolons to separate items:

```
Print 3 + 4, 3 - 4, 3 * 4, 3 / 4
 7              -1              12              0.75
Print 3 + 4; 3 - 4; 3 * 4; 3 / 4
 7 -1  12  0.75
```

Commas between items in a **Print** statement place items in *standard print zones*. Each zone is 14 columns wide (in the font, font size, and font style that you are using). Semicolons (;) cause items to be concatenated. A positive number or zero

is printed as a space, the digits of the number, and another space. A negative
number is printed as a minus sign, the digits of the number, and another space.
The number 0.75 is printed as a space, 0, the decimal point, two digits, and a
space. To learn more about Visual Basic arithmetic, review the following examples:

1. Mariko is 5 feet, 6 inches tall. A **Print** statement converts this height to
   inches:

   ```
   Print 5 * 12 + 6
    66
   ```

   Visual Basic first does the multiplication (5 times 12) and then the addition
   (plus 6). In evaluating an expression, the computer does multiplications
   and divisions first, then additions and subtractions.

2. Almost everyone gets a monthly bill from an energy company. Gas is
   measured in *therms* and electricity in *kilowatt-hours*. Our gas rate is
   $0.5265 per therm and our electric rate is $0.1195 per kilowatt-hour.
   Compute the amount paid for 82 therms and 789 kilowatt-hours:

   ```
   Print 82 * 0.5265 + 789 * 0.1195
    137.4585
   ```

   Visual Basic first does both multiplications left to right and then adds the
   two products to get the final result. Rounded to the nearest penny, the
   result is $137.46.

3. Before he reached full stature, King Kong was once 37 feet 8 inches tall.
   How tall was he in meters?

   ```
   Print (37 * 12 + 8) * 2.54 / 100
    11.4808
   ```

   Visual Basic does the arithmetic inside the parentheses first, getting Kong's
   height in inches. Then it multiplies the result by 2.54 centimeters per inch
   and divides by 100 to get the answer in meters.

4. At the beginning of an auto trip, the odometer showed 71,832 miles. At
   the end of the trip it read 72,219 miles. The car used 9.3 gallons of gas.
   How many miles per gallon did the car get on the trip?

   ```
   Print (72219 - 71832) / 9.3
    41.6129032258064
   ```

   Lots of digits! We'll just say 41.6 when we brag to friends who own
   gas-guzzlers.

5. Suppose that your favorite team has won 38 games and lost 24. Compute its win percentage like this:

```
Print 38 / (38 + 24)
 0.6129032
```

Visual Basic first does the arithmetic inside the parentheses, adding 38 and 24 to obtain 62. It then divides 38 by this result. Newspapers usually round the percentage to three places after the decimal point, so this result would be reported as 0.613. Your team is doing very well.

 NOTE *You use the exponentiation operation (^) to compute a power of a number. To type the exponentiation symbol (^), hold down SHIFT and hit 6.*

6. A room has a floor that is 12 feet square. The floor is a square and each side is 12 feet long. What is the area of the room in square feet? Here are two ways to compute the area, first using multiplication, and then using exponentiation:

```
Print 12 * 12    ' multiplication
 144
Print 12 ^ 2     ' exponentiation
 144
```

Now suppose that the room has a lofty ceiling, exactly 12 feet high. A fortuitous coincidence! The room is $12 \times 12 \times 12$. Therefore, the volume of the room is 12 times 12 times 12, or 12 cubed:

```
Print 12 * 12 * 12   ' multiplication
 1728
Print 12 ^ 3          ' exponentiation
 1728
```

In an expression such as 12 ^ 3, the number 12 is the *base*, and 3 is the *exponent*. The exponent tells how many times the base is used as a factor:

Expression	Base	Exponent	Using Multiplication
12 ^ 2	12	2	12 * 12
12 ^ 3	12	3	12 * 12 * 12
2 ^ 10	2	10	2 * 2 * 2 * 2 * 2 * 2 * 2 * 2 * 2 * 2

Exponents can be very useful. It is much easier to write

```
2 ^ 10
```

than to write

```
2 * 2 * 2 * 2 * 2 * 2 * 2 * 2 * 2 * 2
```

A few years ago, a computer might have had a meager 640K bytes of memory. *K* is an abbreviation of the metric term "kilo," which means 1,000. A kilogram is 1,000 grams; a kilometer is 1,000 meters; a kilobuck is $1,000. However, 1K bytes (1 *kilobyte*) is $2 \wedge 10$ bytes:

```
Print 2 ^ 10          ' 1K bytes (1 kilobyte)
 1024
Print 640 * 2 ^ 10    ' 640K bytes (640 kilobytes)
 655360
```

In evaluating $640 * 2 \wedge 10$, Visual Basic first computes the value of $2 \wedge 10$ and then multiplies the result by 640.

In mathematics, there is an accepted order of operations used to perform arithmetic. Visual Basic uses this same order of operations. If there are no parentheses in an expression, arithmetic operations are performed from the left to the right side of the expression in the following order:

1. Exponentiations ($\wedge$) are done first in left-to-right order.

2. Multiplications ($*$) and divisions ($/$) are done next in left-to-right order.

3. Additions ($+$) and subtractions ($-$) are done next in left-to-right order.

Here are some examples:

▼ $2 * 3 + 4 * 5 = 6 + 4 * 5 = 6 + 20 = 26$

▼ $2 * 3 - 4 / 5 = 6 - 4 / 5 = 6 - 0.8 = 5.2$

▼ $3 \wedge 2 + 4 \wedge 2 = 9 + 4 \wedge 2 = 9 + 16 = 25$

▼ $3.14 * 12 \wedge 2 = 3.14 * 144 = 452.16$

You can use parentheses to modify the order of operations. The operations within parentheses are performed first, using the previously defined rules. If an expression has more than one pair of parentheses, they are evaluated from left to right. For example:

```
(2 + 3) * (4 + 5) = 5 * (4 + 5) = 5 * 9 = 45
```

One parenthetical expression may be nested inside another. In this case, the innermost parenthetical expression is evaluated first, as shown here:

```
2 + 3 * (4 + 5 * (6 + 7)) = 2 + 3 * (4 + 5 * 13)
                         = 2 + 3 * (4 + 65)
                         = 2 + 3 * 69
                         = 2 + 207
                         = 209
```

EXERCISES

1. Write a Print statement to compute and display the answer for each of the following:

   a. Find the sum of 19.95, 6.59, and 2.50.

   b. Your checkbook balance is $123.45. What is the balance after subtracting checks in the amounts of $24.95 and $12.23?

   c. Convert 53 kilograms to pounds (1 kilogram = 2.2 pounds).

   d. Convert 1000 kilometers to miles (1 mile = 1.61 kilometers).

2. Write a **Print** statement to compute and display the answer for each of the following. Use parentheses where appropriate.

   a. Convert 23 pounds, 14 ounces to grams (1 ounce = 28.35 grams).

   b. Convert 8 hours, 37 minutes, 42 seconds to seconds.

   c. In his first three games, Christopher scored 19, 17, and 24 points. What is his average number of points per game?

   d. Suppose that your favorite hockey team has won 29 games, lost 12 games, and tied 5 games. What is the percentage of games won? (The winning percentage is the number of games won divided by the total number of games played.)

3. The Earth's population is increasing at the rate of about 1.7 percent per year. If this rate holds steady, the population 20 years from now can be estimated by multiplying the present population by the 20th power of $1 + 1.7/100$, like this: $(1 + 1.7/100)^{20}$. The current population is about 5.8 billion people. Write a **Print** statement to compute the projected population 20 years hence.

7.4 *EXPLORE A NUMBER PATTERN IN THE DEBUG WINDOW*

You will encounter several of Visual Basic's number types as you explore a simple number pattern. Start with the three immediate **Print** statements shown here:

```
Print 11 * 11
 121
Print 111 * 111
 12321
Print 1111 * 1111
```

Oops! The third **Print** statement provoked Visual Basic into displaying the
Overflow dialog box:

The numbers 11, 111, and 1111 are all less than 32,767, so Visual Basic stores
them as data type 2, Integer. **Print** 1111 * 1111 produced a result that is too large
to be represented by this data type. It would "overflow" the 2 bytes allowed for
integers. Press ENTER or click OK to remove the dialog box.

   This problem has a simple solution. Use a type designator to designate one of
the numbers as data type 3, Long. For example, 1111& is a long integer. Try this
Print statement:

```
Print 1111 * 1111&     ' 1111& is data type 3, Long
  1234321
```

   Add another **Print** statement that uses a long integer:

```
Print 11111 * 11111&   ' 11111& is data type 3, Long
  123454321
```

   If Visual Basic notices that one *operand* (number in a numeric expression) is a
long integer, it uses long integer arithmetic to multiply the two numbers and
produces a long integer result.

   The next numeric expression in this series of increasing digits is 111111 *
111111&, the result of which is 12345654321. That value exceeds the limit for long
integers and would cause an overflow. Visual Basic also has a solution: Instead of an
ampersand to designate a long integer, use a number sign (#) to designate the
number as data type 5, Double, a double-precision number with up to 15 digits:

```
Print 111111 * 111111#   ' 111111# is data type 5, Double
  12345654321
```

   If any operand in a numerical expression is a double-precision number, Visual
Basic treats the entire expression as double-precision. Continue increasing the
number of digits in the **Print** statement. Here is the next change in the pattern:

```
Print 111111111 * 111111111#   ' each operand has nine digits
  1.23456789876543E+16
```

This result is a *double-precision floating-point number*: 1.23456789876543E+16

Mantissa   E   Exponent

A double-precision floating-point number consists of a *mantissa* and an *exponent* separated by the letter *E*. The mantissa can have up to 15 digits and the exponent is a power of 10 in the range of −324 to +308. A double-precision number is stored in 8 bytes of memory. Visual Basic's floating-point notation is similar to scientific notation used in math, science, and engineering books:

Floating-point notation: 1.23456789876543E+16
Scientific notation: $1.23456789876543 \times 10^{16}$
Ordinary, everyday notation: 12,345,678,987,654,300

Table 7-2 shows examples of large numbers in ordinary notation, floating-point notation, and scientific notation.

Floating-point notation is useful in representing large numbers. It is equally useful in representing very small numbers. Suppose that a frightened snail moves at the speed of 1 inch every 4 seconds. How fast is that in feet per second and miles per second? The snail moves at 0.25 inches per second. Divide that number by 12 to get its speed in feet per second. Because there are 5280 feet in a mile, divide the snail's speed in feet per second by 5280 to get its speed in miles per second:

```
Print 0.25 / 12           ' feet per second
 2.08333333333333E-02
Print 0.25 / 12 / 5280   ' miles per second
 3.94570707070707E-06
```

Visual Basic prints very small numbers as floating-point numbers with a mantissa and a negative exponent. The mantissa and exponent are separated by the letter *E*.

Floating-point notation: 3.94570707070707E−06
Scientific notation: $3.94570707070707 \times 10^{-6}$
Ordinary notation: 0.00000394570707070707

Number	Ordinary	Floating-point	Scientific
Earth's population	5,800,000,000	5.8E+09	5.8×10^9
Four trillion	4,000,000,000,000	4E+12	4×10^{12}
One Light year (km)	9,460,000,000,000	9.46E+12	9.46×10^{12}
Avogadro's number	Too big to fit	6.022E+23	6.022×10^{23}

TABLE 7-2   *Large Numbers in Ordinary, Floating-point, and Scientific Notations* ▼

Hydrogen is universal stuff. It began with the big bang that created the universe and is now everywhere. The hydrogen atom is very small and light. Its mass is about 1.67×10^{-27} kilograms.

Floating-point notation:	1.67–27
Scientific notation:	1.67×10^{-27}
Ordinary notation:	0.00000000000000000000000000167

You can type this number much more quickly in floating-point than in ordinary notation, and with less chance of a typing mistake. Now float on down and crunch these exercises.

EXERCISES

1. Write each floating-point number as an "ordinary" number without using the letter E and without using an exponent. For example, write 1.23E6 as 1,230,000 and write 1.23E–6 as 0.00000123.

   a. Speed of light in meters per second: 2.9979E8

   b. Mass of an electron in kilograms: 9.11E-31

   c. Mass of the Earth in kilograms: 5.97E24

2. Write each number as a floating-point number:

   a. 123 billion

   b. 0.00000000123

   c. 6.3 trillion

   d. 123,456,789

   e. 0.00000123456789

3. Use data type 6, Currency, to continue exploring the number pattern. What result is printed by each **Print** statement?

   a. Print 111111111@ * 111111111@

   b. Print 11111111.1@ * 11111111.1@

   c. Print 11111111.11@ * 11111111.11@

LEARN MORE ABOUT VARIABLES

A *variable* is a name that represents data. You can assign a *value* to a variable and use the variable in expressions. You can invent variable names (subject to a few restrictions). A variable name:

▼ Is constructed using letters, digits, and the underscore character (_).

▼ Must begin with a letter.

▼ Cannot have an embedded space or period.

▼ Cannot be a Visual Basic reserved word. For example, you cannot use **Print** or **Cls** or **End** because they are the names of Visual Basic methods. However, a reserved word can be part of a variable name such as *EndOfData*.

Here are some valid variable names:

```
green    NewLeft    ElecRate    Kwh    pi    R2D2
```

You can type variable names in lowercase, uppercase, or a mixture of uppercase and lowercase letters. In this book, letters in variable names appear in lowercase or a mixture of lowercase and uppercase. We will try to use variables that relate to the type of data being represented. For example: *ElecRate* to represent electric rate and *Kwh* to represent kilowatt-hours.

Visual Basic has several types of variables, including the chameleon-like **Variant** type. A variable of **Variant** type is extremely flexible as it can be any of the data types listed previously in Table 7-1. Try out a **Variant** variable called *variable* in the Debug window. Assign it a value and then print the value and the data type of the variable. For assignments, try different types of numbers, a string, and the **Time** function:

```
variable = 123
Print variable, VarType(variable)
 123            2

variable = 123.45
Print variable, VarType(variable)
 123.45         5

variable = "A string"
Print variable, VarType(variable)
A string        8

variable = Time
Print variable, VarType(variable)
11:30:18 AM     7
```

Amazing! A **Variant** variable goes with the flow—it is whatever data type it needs to be to accept the data you assign to it.

Because Visual Basic has five types of numbers, it also has five types of numeric variables: Integer, Long, Single, Double, and Currency. You can use a type designator at the end of a variable to designate it as the type you want.

▼ A designated Integer variable is a variable name followed by a percent sign (%): *year%*, for instance.

▼ A designated Long variable is a variable name followed by an ampersand (&): *VoteTally&*

▼ A designated Single variable is a variable name followed by an exclamation point (!): *radius!*

▼ A designated Double variable is a variable name followed by a number symbol (#): *pi#*

▼ A designated Currency variable is a variable name followed by an "at" symbol (@): *LotsaBucks@*

Well, that's okay, but many computer science professors and real world code wizards claim that it is better to use a **Dim** statement to define the data type of a variable, as shown here:

```
Dim year As Integer
Dim VoteTally As Long
Dim radius As Single
Dim pi As Double
Dim LotsaBucks As Currency
```

Project Calculator #1 - Factory Reject Adding Machine uses default **Variant** variables to attempt to add two numbers entered into text boxes and display their sum in a third text box. It doesn't work. We entered the numbers 123 and 456 into the left two text boxes and clicked the + button, but the sum of the numbers (579) did not appear in the third text box:

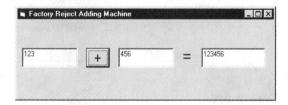

To understand why it didn't work, examine our factory reject event procedure cmdAdd_Click:

```
Private Sub cmdAdd_Click()

  Number1 = txtNumber1.Text
  Number2 = txtNumber2.Text
  Sum = Number1 + Number2
  txtSum.Text = Sum

End
```

We invented variables *Number1*, *Number2*, and *Sum* without using a type designator or a **Dim** statement to define their data types. So, by default, these are of **Variant** type. Data entered into a text box is data type 8, String, so string values are assigned to *Number1* and *Number2*. In the run, the value of *Number1* is the string "123" and the value of *Number2* is the string "456". If you use a plus sign (+) to connect two strings, they are concatenated, or joined together, so the value of *Number1* + *Number2* is the string, "123456". This string is assigned to *Sum* and then to *txtSum.Text* and displayed. You will learn more about strings in Chapter 8.

We fixed the event procedure so that it now looks like this:

```
Private Sub cmdAdd_Click()

  Dim Number1 As Integer
  Dim Number2 As Integer
  Dim Sum As Integer

  Number1 = txtNumber1.Text
  Number2 = txtNumber2.Text
  Sum = Number1 + Number2
  txtSum.Text = Sum

End Sub
```

Anticipating a successful run, we changed the form's caption to "Adding Machine - Integer," and saved the project as Calculator #2 - Adding Machine, Integer. We ran the project and enjoyed this view:

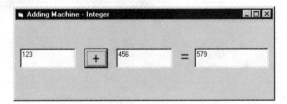

It works fine for integers in the range –32,768 to 32,767. If either number or their sum is outside this range, you will see the Overflow error message box. In the exercises, you will be asked to build better machines.

How does Calculator #2 work? Examine Table 7-3 to see what happens after you enter 123 in txtNumber1, enter 456 in txtNumber2, and then click the + button. After doing so, examine the exercise.

 NOTE *In Table 7-3, it is assumed that txtNumber1.Text = "123" and txtNumber2.Text = "456".*

You can define more than one variable in a single **Dim** statement. The statement

```
Dim Number1 As Integer, Number2 As Integer, Sum As Long
```

defines *Number1* and *Number2* as Integer variables, and defines *Sum* as a variable of type Long.

EXERCISE

1. Integer addition is rather limiting. Modify project Calculator #2 to create projects Calculator #3 - Adding Machine, Double and Calculator #4 - Adding Machine, Currency:

   a. Project Calculator #3 - Adding Machine, Double. Use double-precision variables, data type 5, Double.

   b. Project Calculator #4 - Adding Machine, Currency. Use variables of data type 6, Currency.

Statement	Action Performed
Dim Number1 As Integer	Defines *Number1* as a variable of Integer type.
Dim Number2 As Integer	Defines *Number2* as a variable of Integer type.
Dim Sum As Integer	Defines *Sum* as a variable of Integer type.
Number1 = txtNumber1.Text	Converts "123" to an integer and assigns it to *Number1*.
Number2 = txtNumber2.Text	Converts "123" to an integer and assigns it to *Number2*.
Sum = Number1 + Number2	Adds 123 and 456 to get 579 and assigns it to *Sum*.
txtSum.Text = Sum	Converts 579 to a string and assigns it to *txtSum.Text*.

TABLE 7-3 *A Step-by-Step Description of Event Procedure cmdAdd_Click Doing Its Task* ▼

7.6

*B*UILD BETTER CALCULATING MACHINES

Project Calculator #2's adding machine also has a minor problem. If you enter a string that can't be converted to a number, and then click the + button, you will see the Type Mismatch error message box. The same thing happens if one of the text boxes contains the empty string. Project Calculator #5 - Adding Machine, Integer detects this situation and prints a message in the txtSum box:

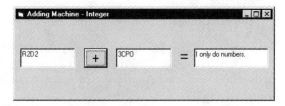

Event procedure cmdAdd_Click is modified to detect a string that can't be converted to a number. This task is accomplished by using the **IsNumeric** function in an **If...Then...Else** structure:

```
If IsNumeric(txtNumber1.Text) Then
  Number1 = txtNumber1.Text
Else
  txtSum.Text = "I only do numbers."
  Exit Sub
End If
```

If the string value of *txtNumber1.Text* can represent a number, then **IsNumeric**(*txtNumber1.Text*) is True. The string is converted to a number and assigned to *Number1*. If the string value of *txtNumber1.Text* cannot represent a number, then **IsNumeric**(*txtNumber1.Text*) is False, and the **Else** clause is executed. It displays "I only do numbers." in txtSum and then *exits the Sub procedure* by means of an **Exit Sub** statement.

Event procedure cmdAdd_Click contains two **If...Then...Else** structures that use the **IsNumeric** function and also contains two **Exit Sub** statements that can end the **Sub** procedure:

```
Private Sub cmdAdd_Click()

  Dim Number1 As Integer, Number2 As Integer, Sum As Integer

  ' If txtNumber1 contains a number, assign it to Number1.
  ' Otherwise display a message in txtSum and Exit Sub.
  If IsNumeric(txtNumber1.Text) Then
```

```
      Number1 = txtNumber1.Text
Else
   txtSum.Text = "I only do numbers."
   Exit Sub
End If

' If txtNumber2 contains a number, assign it to Number2.
' Otherwise display a message in txtSum and Exit Sub.
If IsNumeric(txtNumber2.Text) Then
   Number2 = txtNumber2.Text
Else
   txtSum.Text = "I only do numbers."
   Exit Sub
End If

Sum = Number1 + Number2
txtSum.Text = Sum

End Sub
```

Be sure to create project Calculator #5, make it work, try numbers and non-numbers in the text boxes. Try a number in one text box and leave the other one empty. Then truck on down to the exercises and build better calculating machines.

EXERCISES

1. Create project Calculator #6 - Number Cruncher, Double. This is the visual interface:

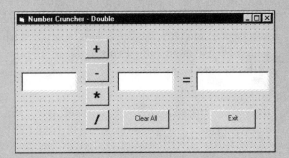

Enter numbers into the text boxes and then click + to add, − (minus) to subtract, * to multiply, or / to divide. Use variables of data type 5, Double.

2. Add an exponentiation (^) button to project Calculator #6 and save the modified project as Calculator #7 - Number Cruncher, Double.

7.7 CREATE COMPUTER "ART" IN THE STYLE OF ZAPPY ARTIST

Zappy Artist likes to create computer "art" by zapping around the screen, plotting random dots, and drawing random lines, boxes, and circles. Most of Zappy's zappings use the **Rnd** and **Fix** functions to calculate *random integers*, so we'll begin this section by using the Debug window to demonstrate these functions. Start a new project, run it, and click the Break tool to get the Debug window.

Rnd is a numeric function. It returns a random number between 0 and 1. Actually, the numbers generated by the **Rnd** function are not truly random, as are numbers obtained by rolling dice or spinning a roulette wheel. Instead, the numbers produced by the **Rnd** function are generated by code that uses a mathematical procedure, an *algorithm*. Such numbers are called *pseudorandom numbers*. Enter the following immediate statement in the Debug window and see some pseudorandom numbers:

```
Print Rnd, Rnd, Rnd
 0.7055475      0.533424       0.5795186
```

Unfortunately, these numbers are not really random. If you do this tomorrow, you will see the same three numbers. If you do it again next week or next month or next year, you will see the same three numbers. If you are skeptical, stop the run, run the project again, and click the Break tool to get the Debug window. Enter the same immediate **Print** statement again and see the same three numbers:

```
Print Rnd, Rnd, Rnd
 0.7055475      0.533424       0.5795186
```

Rnd begins with the same sequence of numbers each time you run the project. To avoid this replication, use the **Randomize** statement. Stop the run, run the project again, and click the Break tool to get the Debug window. Enter a **Randomize** statement and a **Print** statement to print three random numbers. We saw this in our Debug window:

```
Randomize
Print Rnd, Rnd, Rnd
 0.698208      0.7898175      0.1072133
```

You probably saw a different set of numbers. The **Randomize** statement starts the **Rnd** function at a value determined by the value of **Timer**. **Timer** ticks at the rate of 18.2 ticks per second and there are 86,400 seconds in a day, so there are more than 1.5 million different values of **Timer**, each starting a different sequence of **Rnd** numbers.

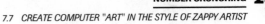
The **Rnd** function returns a number between 0 and 1. Its value is greater than 0 and less than 1:

```
0 < Rnd < 1
```

To obtain numbers in another range, multiply **Rnd** by an appropriate number. For example, *10 * Rnd* is a number between 0 and 10, greater than 0 and less than 10:

```
0 < 10 * Rnd < 10
```

Check this out in the Debug window:

```
Print 10 * Rnd, 10 * Rnd, 10 * Rnd
 8.158533      3.949503      4.801082
```

You most likely see a different set of numbers in your Debug window. Try a few more to gather evidence that *10 * Rnd* is probably between 0 and 10.

Zappy's projects require integer random numbers; he uses the **Fix** function to get them. **Fix** is a numeric function of a numeric argument. The returned value of **Fix**(*number*) is the integer part of the value of *number*. Here are some examples of the **Fix** function:

Non-negative Numbers	Negative Numbers
Fix(0) = 0	Fix(-1) = -1
Fix(3.14) = 3	Fix(-3.14) = -3
Fix(0.99) = 0	Fix(-0.99) = 0

You can use the **Fix** function and the **Rnd** function together to obtain integer random numbers:

Fix and Rnd Expression	Possible Values
Fix(2 * Rnd)	0, 1
Fix(6 * Rnd)	0, 1, 2, 3, 4, 5
Fix(6 * Rnd) + 1	1, 2, 3, 4, 5, 6
Fix(10 * Rnd)	0, 1, 2, 3, 4, 5, 6, 7, 8, 9
Fix(10 * Rnd) + 1	1, 2, 3, 4, 5, 6, 7, 8, 9, 10

Try it in the Debug window. For example, simulate rolling two dice like this:

```
Print Fix(6 * Rnd) + 1; Fix(6 * Rnd) + 1
 5   2
```

Zappy Artist uses the **Fix** and **Rnd** functions in his projects to calculate random coordinates, random color numbers, and other random stuff. You can use project

Zappy Artist Plots Dots to plot dots on the form. In the run shown here, someone has clicked the Dot button several times. Each time Dot is clicked, its event procedure plots one dot in a random place on the form. Usually the dot is visible, but sometimes it is under a button and you don't see it. The size of the dot is determined by the setting of the form's DrawWidth property, which is set to 8 in this run. You can click the Clear Form button to erase all the dots.

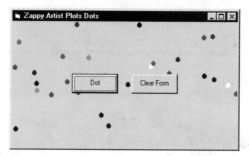

Tables 7-4 and 7-5 list the specifications for project Zappy Artist Plots Dots. Be sure to notice the settings of the form's Height, ScaleHeight, ScaleLeft, ScaleMode, ScaleTop, ScaleWidth, and Width properties. Zappy's projects depend on these settings.

Object	Property	Setting	Comment
Form1	Caption	Zappy Artist Plots Dots	
	Name	frmZappy01	
	DrawWidth	8	Determines the size of the dots.
	Height	3600	Determines the ScaleHeight.
	ScaleHeight	3195	When you set Height, VB sets ScaleHeight.*
	Width	6000	Determines the ScaleWidth.
	ScaleWidth	5880	When you set Width, VB sets ScaleWidth.*
	ScaleMode	1 - Twip	Default value. Exactly what we want.
	ScaleLeft	0	Left edge of form's internal coordinate system.
	ScaleTop	0	Top of form's internal coordinate system.
Command1	Caption	Dot	
	Name	cmdDot	
Command2	Caption	Clear Form	
	Name	cmdClearForm	

*When you set the Height and Width, Visual Basic sets ScaleHeight and ScaleWidth. If you use different settings of Width and Height, your ScaleHeight and ScaleWidth settings may be different than those shown. That's okay—Zappy's project will still work.

TABLE 7-4   *Visual Interface Specifications for Project Zappy Artist Plots Dots* ▼

Object Name	Event	Response
frmZappy01	Load	Randomizes the **Rnd** function.
cmdDot	Click	Plots a dot at random coordinates in a random color. The size of the dot is determined by the DrawWidth setting.
cmdClearForm	Click	Clears the form.

TABLE 7-5 *Event Procedure Specifications for Project Zappy Artist Plots Dots* ▼

Following are the event procedures for project Zappy Artist Plots Dots. Notice that the **Randomize** statement is in event procedure Form_Load and not in event procedure cmdDot_Click. Usually, we want to randomize only once at the beginning of a run, so Form_Load is a good place to put the **Randomize** statement.

```
Private Sub Form_Load()
  Randomize
End Sub

Private Sub cmdDot_Click()

Dim x As Integer, y As Integer, Color As Integer

  x = Fix(ScaleWidth * Rnd)      ' Random horizontal coordinate
  y = Fix(ScaleHeight * Rnd)     ' Random vertical coordinate
  Color = Fix(16 * Rnd)          ' Random color number
  PSet (x, y), QBColor(Color)    ' Plot a dot

End Sub

Private Sub cmdClearForm_Click()
  Cls
End Sub
```

The statement

```
Randomize
```

starts the **Rnd** function at a value determined by the value of **Timer**. Therefore, you see different patterns of dots if you run the project at different times of day.

cmdDot_Click

To understand event procedure cmdDot_Click, you must understand ScaleHeight, ScaleLeft, ScaleTop, ScaleWidth, and **Pset**. Let's start with ScaleHeight and ScaleWidth.

ScaleHeight and ScaleWidth

The settings of a form's Height and Width properties are the form's *external* dimensions in twips. The height includes the caption bar and the upper and lower borders. The width includes the left and right borders. The ScaleHeight and ScaleWidth of a form are its *internal* dimensions. We hope that the following picture is worth lots of words:

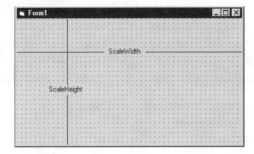

ScaleHeight and ScaleWidth can be in twips or another measure determined by the setting of the ScaleMode property. Instead of the default setting (1 - Twips) you can choose other measures such as Pixel, Inch, Millimeter, or Centimeter. Zappy is staying with the default setting, 1 - Twip.

Zappy set the Width to 6000 and the Height to 3600. Visual Basic automatically set the ScaleHeight to 3195 and the ScaleWidth to 5880. We'll use Zappy's settings in the discussion of event procedure cmdDot_Click that follows. If your settings are different, that's okay—just rethink the discussion to suit yourself.

ScaleLeft and ScaleTop

The settings of ScaleLeft and ScaleTop are the coordinates of the origin of the form's *internal* coordinate system used to position things inside the form. The coordinates of the upper-left inside corner of the form are (0, 0). If ScaleWidth is 5880 and ScaleHeight is 3195, then the coordinates of the lower-right inside corner of the form are (5879, 3194). The next picture shows the coordinates of the four corners:

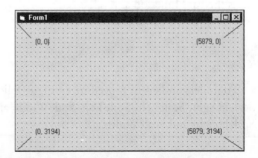

The statement

```
x = Fix(ScaleWidth * Rnd)
```

computes a random integer and assigns it to *x*. Zappy's ScaleWidth is 5880, so the value of *x* is a random integer in the range 0 to 5879. The value of *x* is used later as the horizontal coordinate of a dot.

The statement

```
y = Fix(ScaleHeight * Rnd)
```

computes a random integer and assigns it to *y*. Zappy's ScaleHeight is 3195, so the value of *y* is a random integer in the range 0 to 3194. The value of *y* is used later as the vertical coordinate of a dot.

The statement

```
Color = Fix(16 * Rnd)
```

computes a random integer in the range 0 to 15 and assigns it to *Color*. The value of *Color* is used later as the argument of the **QBColor** function.

Pset

The statement

```
PSet (x, y), QBColor(Color)
```

plots one dot at horizontal coordinate *x* and vertical coordinate *y* in color **QBColor**(*Color*). The coordinates are measured from (0, 0) in the upper-left corner of the form. This origin is determined by the settings of the ScaleLeft and ScaleTop properties. The size of the dot is determined by the setting of the DrawWidth property.

Project Zappy Artist Does Dots and Lines allows you to plot a dot or draw a line between random endpoints. Here is a sample run with some dots and lines:

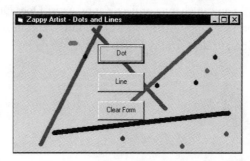

Click the Line button to draw a line between two random endpoints. Modify project Zappy Artist Plots Dots to get project Zappy Artist Does Dots and Lines and install event procedure cmdLine_Click:

```
Private Sub cmdLine_Click()

  Dim X1 As Integer, Y1 As Integer
  Dim X2 As Integer, Y2 As Integer, Color As Integer

  ' Random endpoints and color number
  X1 = Fix(ScaleWidth * Rnd)
  Y1 = Fix(ScaleHeight * Rnd)
  X2 = Fix(ScaleWidth * Rnd)
  Y2 = Fix(ScaleHeight * Rnd)
  Color = Fix(16 * Rnd)

  ' Draw a line
  Line (X1, Y1)-(X2, Y2), QBColor(Color)

End Sub
```

A line requires two endpoints and each endpoint requires two coordinates. The statements

```
X1 = Fix(ScaleWidth * Rnd)
Y1 = Fix(ScaleHeight * Rnd)
X2 = Fix(ScaleWidth * Rnd)
Y2 = Fix(ScaleHeight * Rnd)
```

compute random coordinates (X1, Y1) and (X2, Y2) for the endpoints of the line.
The statement

```
Line (X1, Y1)-(X2, Y2), QBColor(Color)
```

draws a line from (X1, Y1) to (X2, Y2) in color **QBColor**(*Color*).

You can change project Zappy Artist Does Dots and Lines slightly and get project Zappy Artist Does Dots, Lines, and Boxes, which lets you plot dots, draw lines, or draw empty boxes:

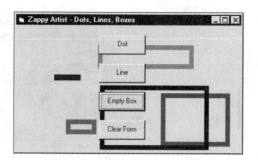

The code inside event procedure cmdEmptyBox_Click is almost the same as in event procedure cmdLine_Click. The only difference is the **B** at the right end of the **Line** statement.

```
Private Sub cmdEmptyBox_Click()

  Dim X1 As Integer, Y1 As Integer
  Dim X2 As Integer, Y2 As Integer
  Dim Color As Integer

  ' Random corner points and color number
  X1 = Fix(ScaleWidth * Rnd)
  Y1 = Fix(ScaleHeight * Rnd)
  X2 = Fix(ScaleWidth * Rnd)
  Y2 = Fix(ScaleHeight * Rnd)
  Color = Fix(16 * Rnd)

  ' Draw a box (B)
  Line (X1, Y1)-(X2, Y2), QBColor(Color), B

End Sub
```

The statement

```
Line (X1, Y1)-(X2, Y2), QBColor(Color), B
```

tells Visual Basic to draw a box with opposite corners at (X1, Y1) and (X2, Y2). The **B** at the right end changes this statement from a line-drawing statement to a box-drawing statement.

You can put **BF** instead of **B** at the end of a **Line** statement to draw filled boxes instead of empty boxes. The following run of project Zappy Artist Does Dots, Lines, and Filled Boxes shows some filled boxes:

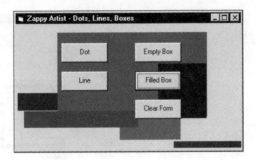

Solid-color filled boxes are drawn by event procedure cmdFilledBox_Click:

```
Private Sub cmdFilledBox_Click()

    Dim X1 As Integer, Y1 As Integer
    Dim X2 As Integer, Y2 As Integer
    Dim Color As Integer

    ' Random corner points and color number
    X1 = Fix(ScaleWidth * Rnd)
    Y1 = Fix(ScaleHeight * Rnd)
    X2 = Fix(ScaleWidth * Rnd)
    Y2 = Fix(ScaleHeight * Rnd)
    Color = Fix(16 * Rnd)

    ' Draw a filled box (BF)
    Line (X1, Y1)-(X2, Y2), QBColor(Color), BF

End
```

Instead of dots, lines, and boxes, Zappy next shows how to draw circles. Here is project Zappy Artist Draws Dots and Shapes after a few clicks of the Circle button.

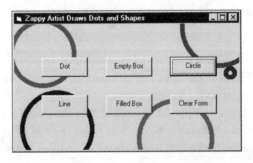

Circles can be drawn by event procedure cmdCircle_Click:

```
Private Sub cmdCircle_Click()

  Dim x As Integer, y As Integer
  Dim r As Integer, Color As Integer

  ' Random center coordinates, radius, and color number
  x = Fix(ScaleWidth * Rnd)
  y = Fix(ScaleHeight * Rnd)
  r = Fix(1000 * Rnd) + 1
  Color = Fix(16 * Rnd)

  ' Draw a circle
  Circle (x, y), r, QBColor(Color)

End
```

Event procedure cmdCircle_Click computes random coordinates (x, y) for the center of the circle, random radius r, and random color number *Color*. These are all used in a **Circle** statement to draw a circle.

The statement

```
Circle (x, y), r, QBColor(Color)
```

draws a circle with center at (x, y) and radius r in the color specified by **QBColor(***Color***)**. The width of the circle's border is determined by the setting of the form's DrawWidth property, set to 8 for the run shown above.

Now zoom along with Zappy and zap these exercises.

EXERCISES

1. Complete each of the following:

    a. _____ < **Rnd** < _____

    b. _____ < 100 * **Rnd** < _____

    c. _____ < 20 * **Rnd** – 10 < _____

    d. Possible values of **Fix**(16 * **Rnd**) are

       _____.

    e. Possible values of **Fix**(256 * **Rnd**) are integers in the range _____ to _____.

    f. Possible values of **Fix**(21 * **Rnd**) – 10 are integers in the range _____ to _____.

2. Rewrite event procedure cmdDot_Click. Use the **RGB** function instead of the **QBColor** function to determine the color of the dot. Recall that the **RGB** function requires three arguments, perhaps called *red*, *green*, and *blue*.

3. Start a new project and make the form the size you want. Make DrawWidth the width you want—we suggest a value in the range 1 to 8. Write a Form_Click event procedure to do the following:

   a. Set the form's BackColor to **QBColor**(15), bright white.

   b. Draw a bright white box around the inside of the form.

   c. Draw a blue horizontal line and a green vertical line that together divide the form into approximately equal quadrants (fourths).

   d. Draw an empty cyan box in the upper-left quadrant of the form.

   e. Draw a red circle centered in the lower-right quadrant of the form.

   f. Draw a filled magenta box in the upper-right quadrant of the form.

   g. Draw seven dots in random colors in the lower-left quadrant of the form.

   Run the project, click the form, and see something similar to this:

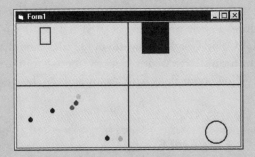

mastery
skills check

1. In a lottery, you pick *r* numbers, all different from one another, from a larger set of numbers. For example, in one lottery, you choose six integers

from the integers 1 to 49. How many ways are there to do this? You can calculate the number of ways like this:

$$NumberOfWays = \frac{49 \times 48 \times 47 \times 46 \times 45 \times 44}{1 \times 2 \times 3 \times 4 \times 5 \times 6}$$

Use the Debug window to calculate the number of ways to pick six integers from the integers 1 to 49. Also calculate the number of ways to choose six integers in the 6/53 lottery, in which you pick six integers from integers in the range 1 to 53.

2. Congratulations! You are the big winner on a TV game show. To select your prize, an integer from 1 to 1,000 is chosen at random. Call it n. You then have 30 seconds to select one, and only one, of these prizes:

Prize #1: You receive n dollars.

Prize #2: You receive $1.01 \char`\^ n$ dollars.

For some values of n, Prize #1 is larger; for other values of n, Prize #2 is larger. Quickly consult Visual Basic on your wrist computer, open the Debug window, and calculate $1.01\char`\^n$. Which prize will you take if $n = 100$? $n = 300$? $n = 500$? $n = 700$? $n = 900$? For what integer value of n are the two prizes about equal?

3. A student's grade point average (GPA) is the total number of grade points divided by the total number of units. Grade points are assigned like this: 4 points for each unit of A, 3 points for each unit of B, 2 points for each unit of C, 1 point for each unit of D, and 0 points for each unit of F. Design project Grade Point Average #1:

   a. Use labeled text boxes to acquire the number of units of A, B, C, D, and F.

   b. Calculate the total number of grade points and display it in a labeled text box.

   c. Calculate the total number of units and display it in a labeled text box.

   d. Calculate the grade point average and display it in a labeled text box.

4. Electrical energy is measured in *kilowatt-hours*. The cost of electrical energy is the number of kilowatt-hours times the electric rate in dollars per kilowatt-hour. Our electric rate is $0.1195 per kilowatt-hour. Design project Energy #1 - Cost of Electricity:

   a. In the Form_Load event procedure, put our electric rate (0.1195) or your own electric rate into a labeled text box.

b. Use a labeled text box to acquire the number of kilowatt-hours used.

c. In a command button event procedure, calculate the cost of electricity and display it in a labeled text box.

d. Include a command button to clear the text boxes containing the number of kilowatt-hours and the cost of energy.

5. Perhaps the easiest way you can help save the planet, and save money at the same time, is to replace your energy-gobbling incandescent light bulbs with energy-miserly compact fluorescent bulbs, or *Gaea bulbs*, as we call them. An 18-watt Gaea bulb produces about the same amount of light as a 75-watt incandescent bulb. Table 7-6 compares the power consumption, light output, and lifetime of Gaea and incandescent bulbs. The life expectancy of a Gaea bulb is about 10 thousand hours. You will burn out 10 to 13 incandescent bulbs in that time.

Design project Energy #2 - Cost, Gaea vs. Incandescent Bulbs. It compares the energy costs of incandescent and Gaea bulbs for 10 thousand hours of usage:

a. Use labeled text boxes to acquire the wattages of comparable incandescent and Gaea bulbs, for example, a 75-watt incandescent bulb and an 18-watt Gaea bulb.

b. Use a command button event procedure to calculate the energy costs for both bulbs and display these costs in labeled text boxes. If the electric rate is $0.1195 per kilowatt-hour, the energy cost for 10 thousand hour's use of a 75-watt incandescent bulb is $89.63 and the cost for an 18-watt Gaea bulb is $21.51.

6. Millions of people carry and use credit cards. Some people pay off their credit card balances every month. Others pay only part of their balances and accumulate interest charges on the unpaid amounts. Some people

Bulb Type	Power (watts)	Light Output (lumens)	Lifetime (hours)
Incandescent	60	860	1,000
Gaea	15	900	10,000
Incandescent	75	1,220	1,000
Gaea	18	1,100	10,000
Incandescent	100	1,710	750
Gaea	27	1,550	10,000

TABLE 7-6 *Comparison of Incandescent Bulb and Gaea Bulb* ▼

procrastinate, make late or infrequent payments, and accrue large interest penalties.

What if someone charged $1,000 on a credit card and didn't make a payment for one year? What would that person owe at the end of the year? How would different interest rates affect the debt? Project Credit #1 - Cost of Credit Card Procrastination computes the amount owed for values of the starting balance, the monthly interest rate, and the number of months someone procrastinates. Design the project:

a. Use labeled text boxes to acquire the starting balance, the monthly interest rate, and the number of months you wish to procrastinate. For example, these values might be entered as 1000 for $1000, 1.5 for 1.5 percent per month, and 12 for 12 months.

b. Calculate the amount owed at the end of the number of months you entered and display it in a labeled text box. For a starting balance of $1,000, a monthly interest rate of 1.5 percent, and a flagrant procrastination of 12 months, the procrastinator will gnash his teeth at a debt of $1,195.62.

7. Your energy company may charge for electrical energy at two rates—a low rate for kilowatt-hours up to a baseline quantity and a higher rate for kilowatt-hours above the baseline quantity. Assume that the low rate is $0.1195 per kilowatt-hour up to the baseline number of kilowatt-hours, and the high rate is $0.1374 per kilowatt-hour above the baseline. The rates remain the same for a long time, but the baseline value may be different each month. Project Energy #3 - Cost of Electricity compares the number of kilowatt-hours that you enter with the baseline value that you enter and calculates your cost according to your usage:

a. In the Form_Load event procedure, put the low rate (0.1195) and the high rate (0.1374) in labeled text boxes.

b. Use labeled text boxes to acquire the number of kilowatt-hours used and the baseline number of kilowatt-hours.

c. In a command button event procedure, calculate the cost of electricity and display it in a labeled text box. Use an **If...Then...Else** structure to calculate the cost.

d. Include a command button to clear the text boxes containing the number of kilowatt-hours used, the baseline number of kilowatt-hours, and the cost of energy.

Suppose that the baseline value is 368 kilowatt-hours. Your project should calculate a cost of $38.72 for 324 kilowatt-hours, $43.98 for 368 kilowatt-hours, and $101.82 for 789 kilowatt-hours. Drag out some of your energy company monthly statements and use project Energy #3 to check their calculations.

8. Modify your project Energy #3 of Exercise 7 to get project Energy #4 - Cost of Electricity. The only difference: To calculate the cost, use a **Select Case** structure instead of an **If...Then...Else** structure.

9. Create project Inspired by Zappy Artist #1. Your form will have five check boxes, one text box, and three command buttons captioned Draw, Clear, and Exit. The user can click any combination of check boxes to select things to draw: dots, lines, empty boxes, filled boxes, and circles. In the text box, the user can enter the number of things to be drawn when someone clicks the Draw button. Draw the artistic entities in a large picture box or on another form.

10. To project Inspired by Zappy Artist #1 (Exercise 9) add option buttons to select the DrawWidth setting. We suggest the options: 1, 2, 4, 8, and Random (1 to 8). Save this project as Inspired by Zappy Artist #2.

11. In a lottery, you pick r numbers, all different from one another, from a set of n numbers. How many ways are there to do this? You can calculate the number of ways like this:

$$Number\ Of\ Ways = \frac{n(n-1)(n-2)\dots(n-r+1)}{1(2)(3)\dots r}$$

Create project Lottery #1 to calculate the number of ways. Use text boxes to acquire the values of n and r, then click a button to calculate and display the number of ways to pick r numbers, all different from one another, from a set of n numbers. May dragons of good fortune bring you lotsa luck!

8

String Munching

chapter objectives

8.1 Experiment with strings in the Debug window

8.2 Experiment with string variables in the Debug window

8.3 Use input boxes to acquire values of variables

8.4 Use LCase and UCase in an easy quiz

8.5 Get acquainted with ANSI codes and characters

8.6 Use the Mid, Left, and Right functions to munch strings within strings

8.7 Sample a flock of functions

8.8 Relax with WordsWorth

VISUAL Basic has many data types, including Date/Time, Boolean, String, several types of numbers, and the ultra-flexible Variant, which can represent any type of data. You learned a little bit about strings in previous chapters, and you learned how to handle numbers and numeric variables in Chapter 7. In this chapter, you will learn more about strings and ways to munch them.

Several Visual Basic functions come in two varieties, a Variant version and a String version. For example, **Time** returns a Variant data type and **Time$** returns a String data type. Both work just fine for this chapter's string munching, so we'll describe the Variant type of each function (for those functions that have both String and Variant versions). We encourage you to experiment with the String versions as well.

| **8.1** | **EXPERIMENT WITH STRINGS IN THE DEBUG WINDOW** |

Remember that a string is just a bunch of characters strung together. A string can be any of these things:

A name, such as	Laran Stardrake
A telephone number, such as	707-555-1212
A message, such as	Reality expands to fill the available fantasies.
A date, such as	11-17-1995
A time, such as	13:26:38
A number, such as	123
Gibberish, such as	12#3bZ@m%W&

In Chapter 7, you used the Debug window to experiment with numbers. Now use it to experiment with strings. Start a new project with only Form1, run the project, and click the Break tool to get the Debug window. You can use an immediate **Print** statement to print a string:

```
Print "Laran"
Laran

Print "707-555-1212"
707-555-1212
```

In these statements, quotation marks enclose the strings. They tell Visual Basic where each string begins and ends. These quotation marks are not printed. What happens if you omit the quotation marks? Try it and see. Print Laran's name without enclosing it in quotation marks and also print the **VarType** of *Laran*:

```
Print Laran, VarType(Laran)
            0
```

Nothing is printed for Laran's name. What happened? The value printed for **VarType**(*Laran*) is a clue. Visual Basic did not recognize *Laran*, so it created a variable of Variant type called *Laran*. This variable has not been assigned a value, so **VarType**(*Laran*) is 0, Empty.

To really confuse Visual Basic, try these statements one at a time:

```
Print Laran Stardrake
Print VarType(Laran Stardrake)
```

The first statement prints nothing, or perhaps it prints the empty string—you see the cursor move down two lines. The second statement causes Visual Basic to trot out the "Expected:)" error message box. The space between *Laran* and *Stardrake* is the problem. **VarType** is a function of one argument, so it requires a parenthesis following *Laran*.

Next try the telephone number without the quotation marks:

```
Print 707-555-1212
-1060
```

Aha! Visual Basic thinks that you want to do arithmetic, so it evaluates this as a numeric expression. Try to print a time without enclosing the time in quotation marks:

```
Print 13:26:47
```

This invokes the "Expected: statement or end of statement" error message box. Visual Basic doesn't understand what you want it to do. Remember to enclose strings in quotation marks in a **Print** statement.

A **Print** statement can contain two or more items separated by commas or semicolons. The comma causes items to be printed in *standard print zones*. Each standard print zone is 14 characters wide:

```
Print "Zone1", "Zone2", "Zone3"
Zone1         Zone2         Zone3
```

Instead of commas, you may use semicolons (;) as separators, which causes items to be *concatenated* (joined). The next **Print** statements demonstrate the use of semicolons first with numbers and then with strings:

```
Print 1; 22; 333
 1  22   333

Print "1"; "22"; "333"
122333
```

The numbers 1, 22, and 333 are each printed with a leading space and a trailing space, so you see two spaces between numbers. The strings "1", "22", and "333" are concatenated without leading or trailing spaces.

The **Print** statement shown next mixes strings and numbers with semicolons as separators:

```
Print "Cost of electricity:"; 789 * 0.1195; "dollars."
Cost of electricity: 94.2855 dollars.
```

You can also use a plus sign (+) or an ampersand (&) to concatenate items in a **Print** statement. First, try plus signs with strings and numbers:

```
Print "1" + "2" + "3"
123

Print 1 + 2 + 3
 6
```

The strings "1", "2", and "3" are concatenated as a single string. In the second statement, Visual Basic interpreted 1 + 2 + 3 as a numeric expression, evaluated it, and printed its numeric value.

Try ampersands with strings and numbers:

```
Print "1" & "2" & "3"
123

Print 1 & 2 & 3
123
```

Clever! Because of the ampersand, Visual Basic interpreted 1, 2, and 3 as strings instead of as numbers and concatenated them as a single string. We will use the ampersand, not the plus sign, to concatenate strings.

What happens if you try to subtract a string from another string? Try it:

```
Print "456" - "123"
```

Visual Basic displays the Type Mismatch error message box. It can subtract numbers, but not strings. We'll suggest some other experiments in the exercises.

EXERCISES

1. What happens when you execute the following immediate **Print** statements? Try them and find out.

   a. Print 11-17-1995

   b. Print "123" + "45"

   c. Print "123" - "45"

   d. Print "123" * "45"

   e. Print "123" / "45"

2. What is printed by each immediate **Print** statement?

   a. Print "Laran", "Stardrake"

   b. Print "Laran"; "Stardrake"

   c. Print "Laran" & "Stardrake"

   d. Print "Stardrake"; ", "; "Laran"

   e. Print "Stardrake" & ", " & "Laran"

   f. Print "3 * 4 ="; 3 * 4

   g. Print "3 * 4 =" & 3 * 4

   h. Print "Mariko is"; 5 * 12 + 6; "inches tall."

8.2

EXPERIMENT WITH STRING VARIABLES IN THE DEBUG WINDOW

A string variable is a variable whose values are strings. You can use the String type designator, a dollar sign ($), to designate a variable as a string variable. Here are several examples of designated string variables:

```
Word$     Letter$     FirstName$     City$     Agent007$
```

Instead of a type designator, you can use a **Dim** statement to define variables as String type:

```
Dim Word As String, Letter As String, FirstName As String
```

Visual Basic's reserved words may not be used as variables. For example, you may not use *Name* or *Caption* as variables because they are the names of properties, and therefore are reserved words. You may not use *String* or *String$* as variables because **String** and **String$** are Visual Basic functions. However, you may use *FirstName$*, *NewCaption$*, *Strng$*, or *String1$* as designated string variables, and you may define *FirstName*, *NewCaption*, *Strng*, or *String1* as string variables in a **Dim** statement.

The following immediate statements assign a string value to the string variable *FirstName$* and then print the value of *FirstName$*:

```
FirstName$ = "Twinkle"
Print FirstName$
Twinkle
```

The following **Print** statements demonstrate several ways to print the values of two string variables. You may omit the comment on each line when you try these in the Debug window:

```
FirstName$ = "Twinkle"                  ' Assign a value to FirstName$
LastName$ = "Starr"                     ' Assign a value to LastName$
Print FirstName$, LastName$             ' Comma: standard print positions
Twinkle        Starr
Print FirstName$; LastName$             ' Use ; to concatenate 2 strings
TwinkleStarr
Print FirstName$ & LastName$            ' Use & to concatenate 2 strings
TwinkleStarr
Print FirstName$; " "; LastName$        ' Use ; to concatenate 3 strings
Twinkle Starr
Print FirstName$ & " " & LastName$      ' Use & to concatenate 3 strings
Twinkle Starr
Print LastName$; ", "; FirstName$       ' Name in reverse order with ;
Starr, Twinkle
Print LastName$ & ", " & FirstName$     ' Name in reverse order with &
```

It is again time for you to show off your skills as you wend your way through this short string of exercises.

EXERCISES

1. Assign string values to string variables as follows:

```
FirstName$ = "Stephen"
MiddleName$ = "Michael"
LastName$ = "Hasenpfeffer"
```

Describe the appearance of the information printed by each **Print** statement:

  a. Print FirstName\$, MiddleName\$, LastName\$

  b. Print FirstName\$; MiddleName\$; LastName\$

  c. Print FirstName\$ & MiddleName\$ & LastName\$

2. Assume that values have been assigned to *FirstName\$*, *MiddleName\$*, and *LastName\$* as in Exercise 1. Use these three variables in **Print** statements to produce the following results:

  a. Stephen Michael Hasenpfeffer

  b. Hasenpfeffer, Stephen Michael

  c. Stephen is 100 centimeters tall.

  d. Stephen is *Age%* years old. (Print the value of the integer variable *Age%*.)

8.3 USE INPUT BOXES TO ACQUIRE VALUES OF VARIABLES

You can use the **InputBox** function to acquire values of numeric variables:

```
Dim Number As Double
Number = InputBox("Enter a number.")
```

InputBox returns a Variant of type 8, String. If you enter a string that can be converted to a number, such as 123 or 3.14, Visual Basic cheerfully converts the string to a number and assigns it to the numeric variable *Number*. You can use the event procedures shown below to experiment with **InputBox**. We saved the project as Input Box #1. Because *String* and *Variant* are reserved words, we used *Strng* and *Varyant* as variables.

```
Private Sub cmdNumber_Click()

  Dim Number As Double

  Number = InputBox("Enter a number.")
  Print "Value of Number:"; Number

End Sub
```

```
Private Sub cmdString_Click()

  Dim Strng As String

  Strng = InputBox("Enter a string.")
  Print "Value of String: "; Strng

End Sub

Private Sub cmdVariant_Click

  Dim Varyant As Variant

  Varyant = InputBox("Enter a variant.")
  Print "Value of Variant: "; Varyant

End Sub
```

Put three command buttons on a form, install these event procedures, and run the project. Click a command button to get its input box, enter what it requests, and see your entry printed on the form. Be sure to enter a non-number in cmdNumber's input box and see what happens.

Event procedure Form_Click uses input boxes to acquire someone's name and a phrase to go with the name. It then prints three lines with a name and a phrase side by side on each line with a space between them. The name is printed in a random foreground color and the phrase is printed in another random foreground color. These colors are usually different, but can be the same. A **Dim** statement defines *Naym* and *Phrase* as string variables and *k* as an integer variable.

```
Private Sub Form_Click()

  Dim Naym As String, Phrase As String, k As Integer
  Randomize

  Naym = InputBox("Enter your name.")
  Phrase = InputBox("Enter a phrase to go with your name.")
  Cls

  For k = 1 To 3
    DoEvents
    Form1.ForeColor = QBColor(Int(15 * Rnd))
    Form1.Print Naym & " ";
    Form1.ForeColor = QBColor(Int(15 * Rnd))
```

```
    Form1.Print Phrase
  Next k

End Sub
```

The statement

```
Form1.Print Naym & " ";
```

prints the value of *Naym* and a space. The semicolon at the statement's right end holds the cursor in place so that the phrase is printed on the same line by the statement

```
Form1.Print Phrase
```

Install this event procedure. (Remember, it is a Form_Click procedure, not a Form_Load procedure.) Run the project and click the form. Enter your name in the first input box and your phrase in the second input box. Aurora saved this tiny project as Name and Phrase #1 - Random Colors, ran it, entered her name and the phrase "is A-OK!!!", and saw the following in random colors:

```
Aurora is A-OK!!!
Aurora is A-OK!!!
Aurora is A-OK!!!
```

Now do these exercises until you feel A-OK with input boxes and the values of variables.

EXERCISES

1. What happens when you enter a non-number such as "qwerty" or "Please do my homework" or "R2D2" in an input box and then try to assign the value to a numeric variable?

2. In project Input Box #1, event procedure cmdNumber_Click is:

```
Private Sub cmdNumber_Click()

   Dim Number As Double

   Number = InputBox("Enter a number.")
   Print "Value of Number:"; Number

End Sub
```

Modify the event procedure so that it detects an entry that cannot be converted to a number, displays an appropriate message box, and then displays the input box again. Save the project as Input Box #2.

3. Complete the following code so that the input box displays the prompt string "Enter a phrase to go with your name." and displays "Phrase" in the title bar:

```
Msg = _____
Title = _____
Phrase = InputBox(Msg, Title)
```

8.4 USE LCASE AND UCASE IN AN EASY QUIZ

Suppose that you are creating a trivia game. One of the questions is "What are the colors of a rainbow?" Red is one answer. People might enter it as **red** or **RED** or **Red**, or perhaps even as **ReD**. This could make it a bit difficult to determine if the answer is correct. You can use the **LCase** and **UCase** functions to solve this problem.

LCase and UCase are functions of a string argument. **LCase** returns a Variant type 8, String with all of the letters converted to lowercase. **UCase** returns a Variant type 8, String with all of the letters converted to uppercase. Here are examples of the values returned by these two functions:

Function and Argument	Value Returned	Data Type of Value
LCase("ABC 123")	abc 123	Variant type 8, String
UCase("abc 123")	ABC 123	Variant type 8, String

Install event procedure Form_Click, save the project as LCase and UCase #1, and then use it to learn more about **LCase** and **UCase**:

```
Private Sub Form_Click()

  Dim Msg As String, Title As String

  Cls
  Beep
```

```
    Msg = "Enter a string."
    Title = "LCase and Ucase"
    Strng = InputBox(Msg, Title)
    Print "Your string is: "; Strng
    Print "The LCase is: "; LCase(Strng)
    Print "The UCase is: "; UCase(Strng)
    Print

End
```

Run it and click the form. It beeps and an input box appears with the message "Enter a string." Enter a string with a mixture of lowercase and uppercase letters, digits, punctuation, and whatever else you want. We entered a bunch of nonsense and saw this:

```
Your string is: Qwerty 123.45 @#$%^& ABRAcadabra
The LCase is: qwerty 123.45 @#$%^& abracadabra
The UCase is: QWERTY 123.45 @#$%^& ABRACADABRA
```

Now try a really easy quiz. Install this event procedure in project LCase and UCase #2 - Rainbow Color Quiz:

```
Private Sub Form_Click()

  Dim Msg As String, Title As String
  Dim Color As String, ColorLC As String

  Beep
  Msg = "Enter a rainbow color."
  Title = "Rainbow Quiz"
  Color = InputBox(Msg, Title)
  ColorLC = LCase(Color)
  Select Case ColorLC
    Case "red", "orange", "yellow", "green", "blue", "violet"
      Print "Yes, "; Color; " is in my rainbow."
    Case Else
      Print "Sorry, "; Color; " is not in my rainbow."
  End Select

End Sub
```

Click the form and respond to the quiz in creative ways as a warmup for the following easy exercises.

EXERCISES

1. What are the data types of variables Msg, Title, Color, and ColorLC in the rainbow color quiz Form_Click event procedure?

2. Modify the rainbow color quiz event procedure to use **UCase** instead of **LCase**. Call this project LCase and UCase #3 - Rainbow Color Quiz.

8.5 G*ET ACQUAINTED WITH ANSI CODES AND CHARACTERS*

Visual Basic has a built-in set of characters called *ANSI* (short for *American National Standards Institute*). Some of these characters are visible on the keyboard, and you can use the keyboard to enter them. For example, these characters can all be entered from the keyboard:

Uppercase letters:	A	B	C	D
Lowercase letters:	a	b	c	d
Digits:	1	2	3	4
Punctuation:	.	,	;	:
Special characters:	@	#	$	*

There are also characters that you don't see on the keyboard. Some of these are shown here:

Spanish letters:	á	í	ó	ñ
Symbols:	£	¥	©	®

Every character has an *ANSI code*, which is an integer in the range 0 to 255. Here are some examples:

▼ The ANSI code for A is 65.

▼ The ANSI code for B is 66.

▼ The ANSI code for a is 97.

▼ The ANSI code for * is 42.

▼ The ANSI code for ñ is 241.

You have probably guessed that the ANSI code for C is 67. For the uppercase letters A to Z, the ANSI codes are 65 to 90. For the lowercase letters a to z, the ANSI codes are 97 to 122. Digits have ANSI codes 48 to 57. Codes 128 to 255 are codes for special characters, such as foreign alphabets and assorted other symbols. There are no characters for ANSI codes 0-7, 11, 12, and 14-31. ANSI codes 8, 9, 10, and 13 are control codes for backspace, tab, line feed, and carriage return, respectively. See Appendix A for a list of ANSI codes and characters.

You can use the **Chr** function to print ANSI characters. **Chr** is a string function of one numeric argument. The argument must be an ANSI code, an integer in the range 0 to 255. The value returned by **Chr** is a one-character Variant. Experiment with **Chr** in the Debug window:

```
Print Chr(65), Chr(97), Chr(42), Chr(241)
A         a         *         ñ
```

Chr(13) causes a *line feed* and **Chr**(10) causes a *carriage return*. A line feed moves the cursor down one line and a carriage return moves the cursor to the left margin. You can use them together to start a new line, like this:

```
Print "Blah, blah, blah,..." & Chr(13) & Chr(10) & "Mumble, mumble,..."
Blah, blah, blah,...
Mumble, mumble,...
```

Typing **Chr**(13) & **Chr**(10) uses lots of space, so it might be better to create and use a new line variable called *NL* as shown here:

```
NL = Chr(13) & Chr(10)
Print "Line 1" & NL & "Line 2" & NL & "Line 3"
Line 1
Line 2
Line 3
```

A message box or input box prints one message or prompt string. Perhaps you would like the message to appear on two or more lines. You can create a message string with embedded line feeds and carriage returns to do this task. Event procedure Form_Click constructs a string, assigned to *Msg*, that has embedded carriage returns and line feeds, and displays this message in a message box:

```
Private Sub Form_Click()

  Msg = "Visual Basic Backpack" & Chr(13) & Chr(10)
  Msg = Msg & "P.O. Box 478" & Chr(13) & Chr(10)
  Msg = Msg & "San Lorenzo, CA 94580" & Chr(13) & Chr(10)
  Msg = Msg & "On the net: Karl25 @ aol.com"
  MsgBox Msg, 64, "Our Newsletter"

End Sub
```

The statement

```
MsgBox Msg, 64, "Our Newsletter"
```

prints the value of *Msg* in a message box. Because of the embedded new line characters, the message will appear in four lines. The **MsgBox** statement is of type 64, information box. It displays the letter "i" as an icon. The third item in the statement, "Our Newsletter," is the title that appears in the message box's title bar.

Install the event procedure in project Message Box #2 - Multiline Message, run the project, click the form, and see the address of our newsletter for beginners:

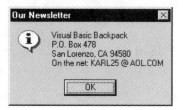

Send your request for a free copy of *Visual Basic Backpack* (tell us that you heard about it in *Teach Yourself Visual Basic*) and then munch on these exercises.

1. Try each of these **Print** statements:

    a. Print "Twinkle" & Chr(32) & "Starr"

    b. Print "She jumped up and exclaimed, " & Chr(34) & "Eureka!" & Chr(34)

    c. Print Chr(65.3), Chr(65.7)

    d. Print Chr(Fix(26 * Rnd) + 97)

    e. Print Chr(256)

    f. Print Chr(-1)

2. Modify project Message Box #2's Form_Click event procedure. Assign the line feed and carriage return characters to the variable *NL* and then use *NL* in the code lines that construct the value of *Msg*. Call this project Message Box #3 - Multiline Message.

8.6 USE THE MID, LEFT, AND RIGHT FUNCTIONS TO MUNCH STRINGS WITHIN STRINGS

The **Mid** function is a function of three arguments—one string argument and two numeric arguments. When a function has more than one argument, the arguments are separated by commas. You use **Mid** to select a portion of a string (a *substring*) from within a string. For example, the word "proverb" contains these shorter words:

pro prove prover rove rover over verb

You can use **Mid** to select these substrings of "proverb." Try the following **Print** statement in the Debug window to select and print two substrings of "proverb":

```
Print Mid("proverb", 1, 5), Mid("proverb", 2, 4)
prove          rove
```

The value returned by **Mid** is a substring of the function's first argument. The second argument is numeric; it specifies the position within the string to begin selecting characters. The third argument is also numeric; it specifies how many characters to select, counting from where the substring begins, as illustrated here:

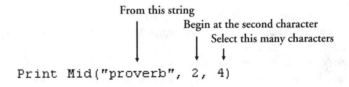

Suppose that you want to name a new product, or even a new company. Perhaps you are writing a novel and want to create unusual names for characters or places. You can use your computer to help you invent names. How would you write code to print names that are pronounceable, but seem exotic or even fantastic?

Project Word Maker #1 generates five-letter random words of the form: consonant, vowel, consonant, vowel, consonant (*cvcvc*). The letter "y" can appear as either a consonant or a vowel. A sample run shows some possible words:

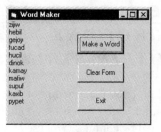

Design the visual interface and install the event procedures. Event procedures Form_Load and cmdMakeWord_Click are shown here:

```
Private Sub Form_Load()
  Randomize
End Sub

Private Sub cmdMakeWord_Click()

  Dim Consonant As String, Vowel As String, Word As String

  Consonant = "bcdfghjklmnpqrstvwxyz"   ' 21 consonants
  Vowel = "aeiouy"                       ' 5 vowels and y

  Word = ""            ' Start with the empty string ("")

  ' Concatenate a consonant, vowel, consonant, vowel, consonant
  Word = Word & Mid(Consonant, Int(21 * Rnd) + 1, 1)
  Word = Word & Mid(Vowel, Int(6 * Rnd) + 1, 1)
  Word = Word & Mid(Consonant, Int(21 * Rnd) + 1, 1)
  Word = Word & Mid(Vowel, Int(6 * Rnd) + 1, 1)
  Word = Word & Mid(Consonant, Int(21 * Rnd) + 1, 1)

  ' Display the word on the form
  Print Word

End Sub
```

Project Word Maker #1 uses the **Mid** function to select random consonants from the value of *Consonant* and random vowels from the value of *Vowel*. The string variables *Consonant* and *Vowel* are assigned values at the beginning of the event procedure. The statement

```
Word = Word & Mid(Consonant, Int(21 * Rnd) + 1, 1)
```

tells the computer to select one random letter from the value of *Consonant* and concatenate it to the value of *Word*. The letter is selected like this:

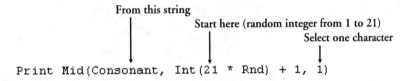

A similar code line selects a random vowel from the value of the string variable *Vowel* and concatenates it to the value of the string variable *Word*.

You can think of the **Left** and **Right** functions as specialized versions of **Mid**. **Left** extracts a substring from the left end of a string and **Right** extracts a substring from the right end of a string. **Left** and **Right** are functions of two arguments, a string argument followed by a numeric argument. Here are examples of both functions:

Function	Value of Function
Left("abc", 1)	a
Left("abc", 2)	ab
Left("abc", 3)	abc
Left("abc", 4)	abc
Right("abc", 1)	c
Right("abc", 2)	bc
Right("abc", 3)	abc
Right("abc", 4)	abc

The value of **Left**(*string, number*) is a Variant string consisting of the leftmost *number* of characters of *string* and the value of **Right**(*string, number*) is a Variant string consisting of the rightmost *number* of characters of *string*. Project Reverse a Word #1 uses **Left**, **Right**, and **Mid** to display a three-letter word with the letters reversed. Event procedure cmdReverse_Click reverses the string in text box txtWord and displays the result in text box txtReverse:

```
Private Sub cmdReverse_Click()

  Dim Word As String, Reverse As String

  Word = txtWord.Text
  Reverse = Right(Word, 1) & Mid(Word, 2, 1) & Left(Word, 1)
  txtReverse.Text = Reverse

End Sub
```

The following sample run displays a *semordnilap*, a word whose reverse is also a word:

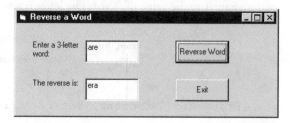

Modifying code is a good way for you to make sure that you understand how the code works. The best way to learn how to code is to write code and modify it until it works the way you want it to work. You can usually do things in more than one way. Try writing your own versions of the code that you see in this book.

EXERCISES

1. Modify project Word Maker #1 so that your new version prints random words of the form *vccvcv*. Examples of such words are: athena, ursula, and otsuko, although you probably won't see these when you run your program. Save this as project Word Maker #2.

2. Modify project Reverse a Word #1 to reverse a four-letter word. Call this project Reverse a Word #2.

3. In the following statements, describe the set of possible values assigned to the variables *CoinFlip* and *Letter*:

   a. CoinFlip = Mid("HT", Fix(2 * Rnd) + 1, 1)

   b. CoinFlip = Mid("HHHTT", Fix(5 * Rnd) + 1, 1)

   c. Consonant = "bcdfghjklmnpqrstvwxyz"
      Letter = Mid(Consonant, Fix(21 * Rnd) + 1, 1)

8.7 *S*AMPLE A FLOCK OF FUNCTIONS

The **String** function is a function of two numeric arguments or one numeric argument followed by a string argument. The value returned is a Variant string with up to 65,535 characters, all the same character. The first argument is numeric and specifies the length of the string (the number of characters). The second argument can be a single string character enclosed in quotation marks or the ANSI code of a character. The value returned by **String** is this character repeated the number of times specified by the first argument. In the Debug window, try these two ways to print a string of 23 asterisks (*). The ANSI code for the asterisk is 42.

```
Print String(23, 42)
***********************

Print String(23, "*")
***********************
```

The **Spc** function is a function of one numeric argument that can be used only with the **Print** method. **Spc** skips the number of spaces specified by the numeric argument. Try these **Print** statements:

```
Print "Twinkle"; Spc(1); "Starr"
Twinkle Starr

Print "Twinkle"; Spc(2); "Starr"
Twinkle  Starr
```

The **Len** function is a numeric function of a string argument. Its value is the number of characters, including spaces, in a string argument. For example, **Len**("abc") is 3, and **Len**("a b c") is 5. Project Sum of Digits of a Positive Integer #1 uses **Len** in event procedure Form_Click:

```
Private Sub Form_Click()

  Dim NumberString As String
  Dim Digit As Integer, SumDigits As Integer, k As Integer

  Msg = "Enter a long integer."
  NumberString = InputBox(Msg)
  SumDigits = 0

  For k = 1 To Len(NumberString)
    Digit = Mid(NumberString, k, 1)
    SumDigits = SumDigits + Digit
  Next k


  Print NumberString, SumDigits

End Sub
```

The **Len** function computes the number of digits in *NumberString* as the upper limit of the **For** statement:

```
For k = 1 TO Len(NmbrStrng)
```

Install the event procedure and try it. It works for zero or positive integers. If you wish to enjoy a view of an error message box, try a negative number, a noninteger, or a non-number. This presents a splendid opportunity for you to modify the code to detect these entries, display a message box, and let the user try again.

The **InStr** function is a numeric function of two string arguments. **InStr** returns a numeric value that depends on whether the second argument is a substring of the first argument. If there is not a match, the value of **InStr** is 0; if there is a match, the value of **InStr** is the position in the first argument where the second argument matches. Here are some examples:

Function	Value	Comment
InStr("abc", "a")	1	Match at position 1 of first argument.
InStr("abc", "b")	2	Match at position 2 of first argument.
InStr("abc", "*")	0	No match; no asterisk in first argument.
InStr("abc", "A")	0	No match; no A in first argument.
InStr("abc", "ab")	1	Match at position 1 of first argument.
InStr("abc", "bc")	2	Match at position 2 of first argument.
InStr("abc", "abc")	1	Match at position 1 of first argument.
InStr("abc", "abcd")	0	No match; abcd is not in first argument.

InStr appears in another version of the rainbow color quiz called project InStr #1 - Rainbow Color Quiz. Install event procedure Form_Click and try it:

```
Private Sub Form_Click()

    Dim Rainbow As String, Msg As String, Title As String
    Dim Color As String, ColorLC As String

    Rainbow = "red orange yellow green blue violet"

    Beep
    Msg = "Enter a rainbow color."
    Title = "Rainbow Quiz"
    Color = InputBox(Msg, Title)
    ColorLC = LCase(Color)

    If InStr(Rainbow, ColorLC) <> 0 Then
        Print "Yes, " & ColorLC & " is in my rainbow."
    Else
```

```
    Print "Sorry, " & ColorLC & " is not in my rainbow."
  End If

End Sub
```

In Chapter 7, we calculated the miles per gallon on an auto trip with the following immediate statement:

```
Print (72219 - 71832) / 9.3
 41.6129032258064
```

In displaying this information, it would be nice to round off the miles per gallon calculation to one decimal place. You can use the **Format** function to do this and a multitude of other formatting tasks. **Format** returns a Variant that is formatted as specified by a format string. The **Format** functions shown below have the syntax **Format**(*NumericExpression, FormatString*):

```
Print Format((72219 - 71832) / 9.3, "##.#")
 41.6
```

The function

```
Format((72219 - 71832) / 9.3, "##.#")
```

evaluates the numeric expression and formats it as a Variant number with up to two digits, then a decimal point, then one digit rounded at the first decimal place.

Experiment and learn more about the **Format** function. Table 8-1 shows examples of **Format** functions. Try them in immediate **Print** statements in the Debug window.

The **Asc** function is the opposite of the **Chr** function. **Asc** is a numeric function of a string argument—it returns the ANSI code of the first character of the

Format Function	Formatted Value	Comment
Format(123.456, "###.##")	123.46	Rounded to two decimal places.
Format(-123.456, "###.##")	–123.456	The minus sign is printed in its proper place.
Format(0123.000, "###.##")	123.	Using "#", leading and trailing zeros are ignored.
Format(0123.000, "0###.00")	0123.00	Use "0" to include leading and trailing zeros.
Format(1234, "#,###")	1,234	Insert a comma.
Format(123.45, "$###.00")	$123.45	Add a dollar sign.
Number = 1234.567 FrmtStrng = "$#,###.00" Format(Number, FrmtStrng)	$1,234.57	Use variables for the number to be formatted and the format string that specifies the format.

TABLE 8-1 *Examples of Format Functions* ▼

argument. For example, **Asc**("A") is 65 and **Asc**("*") is 42. If the argument consists of two or more characters, **Asc** returns the ANSI code of the first character. For example, **Asc**("abc") is 97. **Asc**("") is illegal because there is no ANSI code for the empty string. Try this immediate **Print** statement:

```
Print Asc("@"), Asc(" "), Asc("123")
 64          32          49
```

You will use several functions in the next section, so do these exercises to improve your functionality.

EXERCISES

1. What is printed by each **Print** statement?

   a. Print String(20, "@")

   b. Print String(12, 32)

   c. Print "a"; Spc(1); "b"; Spc(2); "c"

   d. Print Len("12345")

   e. Print Len(12345)

   f. Print Instr("proverb", "over")

   g. Print Instr("proverb", "raver")

   h. Print Format(123.453, "###.##")

   i. Print Format(123.456, "###.##")

   j. Print Format(123, "###.00")

   k. Print Format(123456789, "$###,###,###")

2. Describe the set of possible values assigned to the variables *CoinFlip* and *RandomChr*:

   a. Strng = "HT"
      CoinFlip = Mid(Strng, Fix(Len(Strng) * Rnd) + 1, 1)

   b. Strng = "HHHTT"
      CoinFlip = Mid(Strng, Fix(Len(Strng) * Rnd) + 1, 1)

   c. Strng = "bcdfghjklmnpqrstvwxyz"
      RandomChr = Mid(Strng, Fix(Len(Strng) * Rnd) + 1, 1)

8.8   *R*ELAX WITH WORDSWORTH

Take a break, grab a dictionary, and enjoy a recreational activity called *WordsWorth*. Assign a numeric score to each letter of the alphabet, A through Z, as follows:

A = 1	B = 2	C = 3	D = 4	E = 5	F = 6	G = 7
H = 8	I = 9	J = 10	K = 11	L = 12	M = 13	N = 14
O = 15	P = 16	Q = 17	R = 18	S = 19	T = 20	U = 21
V = 22	W = 23	X = 24	Y = 25	Z = 26		

For any dictionary word you choose, compute two numbers, called *WWsum* and *WWproduct*. *WWsum* is the numerical value of a word obtained by adding numeric scores of all the letters in the word. A letter's score is the same for uppercase or lowercase letters. Characters other than letters are ignored. Here are some examples:

▼   dragon is worth 4 + 18 + 1 + 7 + 15 + 14 = 59 points.

▼   Dragon is worth 4 + 18 + 1 + 7 + 15 + 14 = 59 points.

▼   R2D2 is worth 18 + 4 = 22 points.

WWproduct is the numerical value of a word obtained by multiplying the numeric scores of all the letters in the word. A letter's score is the same for uppercase or lowercase letters. Characters other than letters are ignored. Here are some examples:

▼   dragon is worth 4 * 18 * 1 * 7 * 15 * 14 = 105,840 points.

▼   Dragon is worth 4 * 18 * 1 * 7 * 15 * 14 = 105,840 points.

▼   R2D2 is worth 18 * 4 = 72 points.

In other words, *WWsum* is the sum of the numeric scores of all the letters in a word and *WWproduct* is the product of the numeric scores of all the letters in a word.

You can use project WordsWorth #1 to compute and display *WWsum* and *WWproduct* for a word entered into a text box. Tables 8-2 and 8-3 list the specifications for project WordsWorth #1. Here is a sample run:

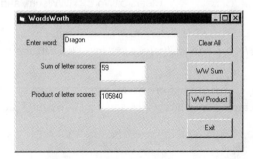

Object	Property	Setting
Form1	Caption	WordsWorth
	Name	frmWordsWorth
Label1	Caption	Enter word:
	Name	lblWord
Text1	Name	txtWord
	Text	
Label2	Caption	Sum of letter scores:
	Name	lblWWsum
Text2	Name	txtWWsum
	Text	
Command1	Caption	WW Sum
	Name	cmdWWsum
Label3	Caption	Product of letter scores:
	Name	lblWWproduct
Text3	Name	txtWWproduct
	Text	
Command2	Caption	WW Product
	Name	cmdWWproduct
Command3	Caption	Clear All
	Name	cmdClearAll
Command4	Caption	Exit
	Name	cmdExit

TABLE 8-2 *Visual Interface Specifications for Project WordsWorth #1* ▼

Object Name	Event	Response
txtWord	click	Clears itself and accepts focus.
cmdWWsum	click	Computes WWsum and displays it in txtWWsum.
cmdWWproduct	click	Computes WWproduct and displays it in txtWWproduct.
cmdClearAll	click	Clears txtWord, txtWWsum, and txtWWproduct.
cmdExit	click	Ends the run.

TABLE 8-3 *Event Procedure Specifications for Project WordsWorth #1* ▼

Most of the work in this project is done by event procedures cmdWWproduct_Click and cmdWWsum_Click:

```
Private Sub cmdWWproduct_Click()

    ' Product of letter scores (a = 1, b = 2, ...)
```

```
   Dim Product As Double, k As Integer
   Dim Word As String, Letter As String

   Word = txtWord.Text
   Product = 1
   For k = 1 To Len(Word)
     DoEvents
     Letter = LCase(Mid(Word, k, 1))
     If Letter >= "a" And Letter <= "z" Then
       Product = Product * (Asc(Letter) - 96)
     End If
   Next k

   txtWWproduct.Text = Product

End Sub

Private Sub cmdWWsum_Click()

   ' Sum of letter scores (a = 1, b = 2, ...)
   Dim Sum As Integer, k As Integer
   Dim Word As String, Letter As String

   Word = txtWord.Text
   Sum = 0
   For k = 1 To Len(Word)
     DoEvents
     Letter = LCase(Mid(Word, k, 1))
     If Letter >= "a" And Letter <= "z" Then
       Sum = Sum + Asc(Letter) - 96
     End If
   Next k
   txtWWsum.Text = Sum

End
```

Words can be entered in all uppercase letters, all lowercase letters, or a mixture of both. The statement

```
Letter = LCase(Mid(Word, k, 1))
```

converts any uppercase letter to lowercase and assigns it to *Letter*. If the value of *Letter* is a lowercase letter, then the **If...Then...Else** structure adds its numeric score to *Sum*. The statement

```
If Letter >= "a" And Letter <= "z" Then
```

has a *compound condition* consisting of two simple conditions connected by **And**. The compound condition is true when *both* simple conditions are true, but false if *either* simple condition is false, as shown in Table 8-4.

Now move on to this wordworthy exercise.

EXERCISE

1. Use project WordsWorth #1 to help you answer one or more of these questions. Each answer must be a dictionary word.

   a. What three-letter word has the smallest *WWsum*? What three-letter word has the smallest *WWproduct*? Four-letter word? Five-letter word? Et cetera, et cetera.

   b. What three-letter word has the largest *WWsum*? What three-letter word has the largest *WWproduct*? Four-letter word? Five-letter word? Et cetera, et cetera.

   c. What is the first word (alphabetically) to have a *WWsum* of exactly 100? What is the first word (alphabetically) to have a *WWproduct* of exactly 100?

   d. What is the last word (alphabetically) to have a *WWsum* of exactly 100? What is the last word (alphabetically) to have a *WWproduct* of exactly 100?

   e. In the entire dictionary, what word has the largest *WWsum*? *WWproduct*?

   f. What is the longest word (most letters) that has a *WWsum* equal to the number of weeks in a year?

   g. What word has a *WWproduct* closest to 1 million?

   Most of the work involved in answering these questions is people play: perusing a dictionary, thinking about what to do, creating strategies—most enjoyable! People do this well. Some of the work, such as looking up letter scores and calculating, is tedious. Let the computer do those tasks.

Letter >= "a"	Letter <= "z"	Letter >= "a" And Letter <= "z"
True	True	True
True	False	False
False	True	False
False	False	False

TABLE 8-4 *Truth Values of Two Simple Conditions and a Compound Condition Constructed from the Simple Conditions* ▼

mastery
skills check

1. The following table shows an argument or arguments and the value produced by a function operating on the argument or arguments. String arguments and string function values are enclosed in quotation marks. Complete the table by naming the function that operated on the argument or arguments to produce the function value.

Argument(s)	Function Value	Function
"abcdefg"	7	
"r2d2"	"R2D2"	
"Z"	90	
"proverb", 4	"verb"	
"proverb", 2, 5	"rover"	
"PROVERB"	"proverb"	
"proverb", "over"	3	
7, "*"	"*******"	
"proverb", 3	"pro"	
123.499, "###.00"	123.50	

2. What title and message will be printed in the information message box by the following chunk of code?

```
NL = Chr(13) & Chr(10)
Title = "Tourist Information"
Msg = "Tom, Forrest, and Teal Torres invite you " & NL
Msg = Msg & "to visit beautiful Belleview, Idaho." & NL & NL
Msg = Msg & "From Belleview, you can go anywhere." & NL
Msg = Msg & "Sun Valley is an easy 32 kilometer hike."
MsgBox Msg, 64, Title
```

3. Write event procedure Form_Click to display an information message box with the title "Scenic Trek" and the following multiline message:

```
Grab your backpack and hike around scenic
Coeur d'Alene Lake with famous guides
Aurora and Aidan Bennett.

Sign up now! We go tomorrow at first light.
```

4. Create project Sentence Maker #1. Use a Form_Click event procedure to do the following:

   a. Display an input box with the title "Make a Sentence" and the prompt message "Enter a noun."

   b. Display an input box with the title "Make a Sentence" and the prompt message "Enter a verb."

   c. Display an input box with the title "Make a Sentence" and the prompt message "Enter an adjective."

   d. Make a sentence using the three entries and print it on the form.

5. In flipping two fair coins, the possible outcomes, HH, HT, TH, and TT, are equally likely. Each possible outcome has a probability of $\frac{1}{4}$—that is, each outcome has 1 chance in 4 of occurring. Create project Coin Flip #1 - Flip Two Fair Coins. Put command button cmdFlipCoins with the caption "Flip Coins" on Form1. Click the button to "flip" the two coins and print the outcome (HH, HT, TH, or TT) on the form. Include another command button to clear the form and include event procedure Form_Load to **Randomize** the **Rnd** function. Five clicks of "Flip Coins" might show this:

```
TH
HT
HH
TH
TH
```

6. Use **Left** and **Right** to munch the value of *Strng* so that the value of *Gnrts* becomes "Flop Flip".

```
Strng = "Flip Flop"
Gnrts = _____
```

7. You can use project Great American Novel #1 to write the great American novel, if you run the project billions of times and do a great job of editing:

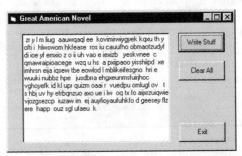

When you click the Write Stuff button, the button's event procedure creates a string of random characters, including spaces, and displays it in the multiline text box (set the text box's MultiLine property to True). The characters are selected from the value of *Alphabet*, which has been assigned a string such as:

```
Alphabet = String(12, " ") & "aaabcdeeefghiiijklmnooopqrstuuuvwxyz"
```

The value of *Alphabet* shown here has 12 spaces and 36 letters. Each vowel appears three times. Feel free to change the value of *Alphabet*. For example, the relative frequencies of letters used in the game of *Scrabble* might be better. Include a Form_Load event procedure to **Randomize** the **Rnd** function.

8. Create project Reverse a Word #3. Enter a word or string *of any length* into a text box and click the Reverse button to reverse the string and display the reversed string in another text box. For example, Lewis Carroll coined the word "semordnilap." A semordnilap is a word whose reverse is also a word. If you enter "semordnilap" as the word to be reversed, event procedure cmdReverse_Click should dutifully produce and display "palindromes" as the reversed word.

9. Use the Help system to learn more about the **InStr** function. Then use it in project Frequency of a Substring #1. At run time you enter a string of any length into text box txtString. You enter another string into text box txtSubstring. Click the Count Substrings button to count the number of occurrences of the substring within the string. You might use this, for example, to count the number of occurrences of the letter "a" or the number of times "you know" appears. The number of spaces in a string of text is usually a good approximation to the number of words in the text. Use this project to count the spaces.

10. Project Word Maker #1 generates random words of the form *cvcvc*. Project Word Maker #2 generates random words of the form *ccvcv*. Create project Word Maker #3. At run time, you enter the consonant-vowel structure and the number of words that you want. For example, for the consonant-vowel structure, you might enter "cvc" or "vcv" or "cvcvc" or "ccvcv." Click the Make Words button and soon you see your words displayed on the form, in a text box, or however you want to display them.

11. You can use **Or** to connect two simple conditions to form a compound condition. Look up **Or** in the Help system and then complete Table 8-5.

Condition1	Condition2	Condition1 Or Condition2
True	True	
True	False	
False	True	
False	False	

TABLE 8-5 *Truth Values of the Compound Condition Condition1 Or Condition2 for Given Truth Values of the Simple Conditions* ▼

9

Use Procedures to Make Your Own Tools and Toys

chapter objectives

9.1 Put **Public Function** procedures in the form module

9.2 Create a random backpack in a standard module

9.3 Add tools to the random backpack

9.4 Stuff your backpack with sub procedures

9.5 Use **Sub** procedures to arrange data in text boxes

9.6 Put a pack of subs in a standard module

EACH project discussed in chapters 1 through 8 has one or more *form modules*. A form module contains the visual elements of the form, including the form's controls, and all code associated with the form. Projects are saved as one or more form files with the filename extension .frm and a project file with the filename extension .vbp. Projects that contain pictures also have a file with the filename extension .frx.

Previous projects contain **Private Sub** event procedures such as Form_Load and Form_Click for the form and Command1_Click and Text1_Click for controls. Each private procedure is self-contained within its object and is not used by other objects in the project.

You have learned how to use many of Visual Basic's tools. In this chapter you'll learn how to use two more tools—called **Public Function** procedures and **Public Sub** procedures—to make new tools, stuff them into your Visual Basic backpack, and whip them out when you need them.

Public Function and **Public Sub** procedures are available throughout a project. Such procedures are called *general procedures* in Visual Basic's documentation. We'll begin slowly by putting **Public Function** procedures in the form and using them in the form's **Private Sub** event procedures.

A great way to build collections of tools is to put them into *standard modules* that are available to all the modules in a project. You can create lots of tools, put them into a standard module, save the module, and then load it into any project for which those tools are useful. A standard module is saved with the filename extension .bas, indicating that it contains Basic code. As you cruise this chapter, you can begin building backpack stuffers that you can use in your present and future projects.

9.1 *P*UT PUBLIC FUNCTION PROCEDURES IN THE FORM MODULE

Board games such as *Monopoly* use six-sided dice to determine the outcomes of events. In *Monopoly*, you roll two six-sided dice (2D6) to determine the number of squares to move your game token. Oops! Bad roll—go to jail.

In a role-playing game such as *Dungeons & Dragons*, you might use three six-sided dice (3D6) to roll a character. Relax--no mugging intended. Millions of game players know that "rolling a character" means creating a character by rolling 3D6 for each of several characteristics that define the character and his or her abilities. In one game system, a character has these seven characteristics: intelligence, intuition, size, strength, constitution, dexterity, and appearance.

Start a new project and create project Dice #1 - Roll Dice. It has one form module with four command buttons and their private event procedures. The form contains a **Private Sub** procedure to **Randomize** the **Rnd** function and a **Public Function** procedure that simulates rolling one six-sided die. Three of the command button event procedures use the **Public Function**. At run time you see this:

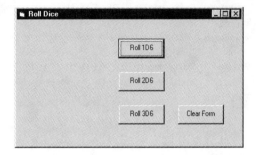

Click the Roll 1D6 button to print a simulated six-sided die roll on the form, click the Roll 2D6 button to roll two six-sided dice, or click the Roll 3D6 button to roll three six-sided dice. Click the Clear Form button to clear the clutter from the form after clicking the other buttons a bunch of times. We clicked the Roll 3D6 button seven times and got:

```
10
9
8
13
13
14
11
```

Table 9-1 lists project Dice #1's event procedures.

Object Name	Event	Response
Form1	Load	Randomizes the **Rnd** function.
cmdRollD6	Click	Prints a simulated roll of one six-sided die on the form.
cmdRoll2D6	Click	Prints a simulated roll of two six-sided dice on the form.
cmdRoll3D6	Click	Prints a simulated roll of three six-sided dice on the form.
cmdClearForm	Click	Clears the form.

TABLE 9-1   *Event Procedures for Project Dice #1 - Roll Dice* ▼

Draw the visual interface and install the event procedures:

```
Private Sub Form_Load()
  Randomize
End Sub

Private Sub cmdRollD6_Click()
  Print RollD6
End Sub

Private Sub cmdRoll2D6()
  Print RollD6 + RollD6
End Sub

Private Sub cmdRoll3D6_Click()
  Print RollD6 + RollD6 + RollD6
End Sub

Private Sub cmdClearForm_Click()
  Cls
End Sub
```

Event procedure cmdRollD6_Click uses a **Public Function** procedure called *RollD6* to roll one die. RollD6 returns a random integer in the range 1 to 6. Event procedure cmdRoll2D6_Click uses RollD6 twice and adds the values returned by the function. Event procedure cmdRoll3D6_Click uses RollD6 three times and adds the values returned by the function. In order for this to work, you'll need to create **Public Function** RollD6 and install it in the form:

```
Public Function RollD6()

  ' Returns a random integer, 1 to 6
  RollD6 = Fix(6 * Rnd) + 1

End Function
```

This **Public Function** procedure begins with a **Public Function** statement and ends with an **End Function** statement. The name of the procedure, RollD6, appears in the **Public Function** statement. The empty parentheses at the right end of the statement tell you that this procedure has no *arguments*. Later in this chapter you will encounter procedures that require arguments.

Install **Public Function** RollD6 in Form1 with these steps:

1. Start in Form1's code window. Double-click Form1 to open the code window.

2. Click the Insert menu and then click the Procedure command:

The Insert Procedure dialog box appears, ready to accept the name of a procedure:

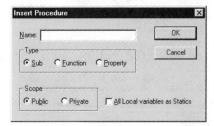

The **Public** choice is selected in the Scope box (good) and the **Sub** choice is selected in the Type box (oops). You want a **Function** procedure, not a **Sub** procedure.

3. Click **Function** in the Type box. Now you are ready to enter the name of the procedure.

4. Click the Name box and type the procedure's name: **RollD6**.

5. Click OK or press ENTER. That's it. The code window's Object box displays "general," the Procedures box displays "RollD6," and a **Public Function** procedure template appears:

```
Public Function RollD6()
|
End Function
```

6. Complete the procedure so that it looks like this:

```
Public Function RollD6()

   ' Returns a random integer, 1 to 6
   RollD6 = Fix(6 * Rnd) + 1


End Function
```

After completing the procedure see if it works. Run it and try all the buttons. Let the games begin!

Although the values of RollD6 are integers in the range 1 to 6, its data type is 4, Single. You can make RollD6 return values of data type 2, Integer, by using an integer type designator (RollD6%) or by appending an **As Integer** clause in the **Public Function** statement:

```
Public Function RollD6%()

  ' Returns a random integer, 1 to 6
  RollD6% = Fix(6 * Rnd) + 1

End Function

Public Function RollD6() As Integer

  ' Returns a random integer, 1 to 6
  RollD6 = Fix(6 * Rnd) + 1

End Function
```

When we wish to designate the value returned by a **Function** procedure as a particular data type, we will use the second method shown above (**As Integer**, **As Double**, **As String**, and so on).

EXERCISES

1. Add a command button captioned "Roll 4D6" to project Dice #1 and write event procedure cmdRoll4D6_Click. Call this project Dice #2 - Roll Dice.

2. In a game system, the outcome of an event might be determined by making a *percentage roll* that returns an integer in the range 0 to 99. Zero might be interpreted as zero or as 100. Let D100 be a percentage roll that returns an integer in the range 0 to 99. Add a command button captioned "Roll D100" to your project Dice #2 of Exercise 1 and write its event procedure. Also write **Public Function** RollD100. Call this project Dice #3 - Roll Dice.

3. Add text box Text1 and a RollnD6 button to your project Dice #3 of Exercise 2. Install event procedure cmdRollnD6_Click to simulate rolling *n* six-sided dice, where the value of *n* is in text box Text1. This is the event procedure:

```
Private Sub cmdRollnD6_Click()

  ' Roll n 6-sided dice
  Dim k As Integer, Total As Long

  Total = 0
  For k = 1 To Text1.Text
    Total = Total + RollD6
  Next k
  Print Total

End Sub
```

Run the project, enter a value of *n* in the text box, and roll dice. Call this project Dice #4 - Roll Dice.

9.2   *CREATE A RANDOM BACKPACK IN A STANDARD MODULE*

In this section, you will begin building tool collections that you can use in present and future projects. Each collection consists of a bunch of public procedures that reside in a standard module. You can use a standard module and its tools in any project for which the tools are useful. In this way you customize Visual Basic by adding tools that we suggest and by creating your own portfolio of tools.

Project Random Backpack #1 has one form module with the filename Random Backpack #1.frm and one standard module with the filename Random Backpack #1.bas. The form module contains nine command buttons and their event procedures. The standard module contains **Public Function** procedures RollD6, FlipCoin, and RndLetter that are used by the form module's event procedures. At run time, project Random Backpack #1 looks like this:

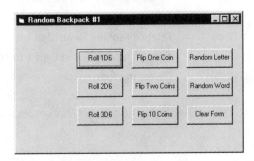

Click the Roll 1D6 button to roll one six-sided die, click the Roll 2D6 button to roll two six-sided dice, and click the Roll 3D6 button to roll three six-sided dice. Click the Flip One Coin button to print H or T on the form and click the Flip Two Coins button to see H H or H T or T H or T T. We clicked the Flip 10 Coins button three times and got this:

```
T H T H H T T H H H
H T H H H H T T H T
H H T H H T H T T T
```

Click the Random Letter button to get a random lowercase letter. We clicked the Random Word button five times and got the following strange-looking "words":

```
thwkz
edf
bxgeigxjry
c
xvngl
```

Start a new project and name it Random Backpack #1. Draw the visual interface, install the form's event procedures, and then create a standard module containing the **Public Function** procedures. Form1's caption is Random Backpack #1. Table 9-2 lists the project's event procedures.

Object Name	Event	Response
Form1	Load	Randomizes the **Rnd** function.
cmdRollD6	Click	Prints a simulated roll of one six-sided die on the form.
cmdRoll2D6	Click	Prints a simulated roll of two six-sided dice on the form.
cmdRoll3D6	Click	Prints a simulated roll of three six-sided dice on the form.
cmdFlipCoin	Click	Prints a simulated coin flip (H or T) on the form.
cmdFlipTwoCoins	Click	Prints a simulated flip of two coins (H H, H T, T H, T T) on the form.
cmdFlip10Coins	Click	Prints a simulated flip of 10 coins on the form.
cmdRandomLetter	Click	Prints a random lowercase letter on the form.
cmdRandomWord	Click	Prints a random word with 1 to 10 letters on the form.
cmdClearForm	Click	Clears the form.

TABLE 9-2 *Event Procedure Specifications for Project Random Backpack #1* ▼

Install event procedures Form_Load, cmdRollD6_Click, cmdRoll2D6_Click, cmdRoll3D6_Click, and cmdClearForm_Click, which are the same as in project DICE01. These procedures all use **Public Function** RollD6, which is in the standard module, not in the form module.

The coin flipping event procedures all use **Public Function** FlipCoin, which is in the standard module:

```
Private Sub cmdFlipCoin_Click()
  Print FlipCoin
End Sub

Private Sub cmdFlipTwoCoins_Click()
  Print FlipCoin & Chr(32) & FlipCoin
End Sub

Private Sub cmdFlip10Coins_Click()

  Dim TenCoins As String, Coin As Integer

  TenCoins = FlipCoin
  For Coin = 1 To 9
    TenCoins = TenCoins & Chr(32) & FlipCoin
  Next Coin
  Print TenCoins

End Sub
```

Event procedures cmdRandomLetter_Click and cmdRandomWord_Click both use **Public Function** RndLetter, which is in the standard module:

```
Private Sub cmdRandomLetter_Click()
  Print Chr(32) & RndLetter
End Sub

Private Sub cmdRandomWord_Click()

  Dim WordLength As Integer, Letter As Integer, Word As String

  WordLength = Fix(10 * Rnd) + 1
  Word = ""
  For Letter = 1 To WordLength
    Word = Word & RndLetter
  Next Letter
  Print Chr(32) & Word

End Sub
```

Most of the work is done. All that's left is to write **Public Functions** RollD6, FlipCoin, and RndLetter, and put them in a standard module. Here are the procedures, each with a comment that briefly describes what it does:

```
Public Function RollD6() As Integer

    ' Returns a random integer, 1 to 6
    RollD6 = Fix(6 * Rnd) + 1

End Function

Public Function FlipCoin() As String

    ' Simulates a coin flip. Returns random H or T.
    FlipCoin = Mid("HT", Fix(2 * Rnd) + 1, 1)

End Function

Public Function RndLetter() As String

    ' Returns a random lowercase letter
    RndLetter = Chr(Fix(26 * Rnd) + 97)

End Function
```

Ready to insert a module into the project? Of course you are. Insert a new module like this:

1. Click the Insert menu and then click Module.

2. Visual Basic inserts a module called Module1 into the project. It looks like a code window:

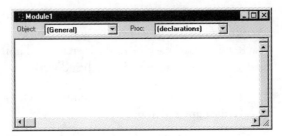

If you have not yet named and saved the project, you now see the following in the Project window:

▼ Project1 in the title bar

▼ Form1 in the files list

▼ Module1 in the files list

A module has one property, its Name. You can see the module's name, Module1, in the Properties window. Change the setting of the Name property to modRndPak1.

You can close the module by clicking its close button. If a module is not visible and you want to view it, double-click its name in the Project window, or click the module's name once to highlight it and then click View Code.

Install each of the three **Public Function** procedures in the module in the same way that you installed **Public Function** RollD6 in the form's code window in the previous section. In case you don't remember all the details, do it like this for each procedure:

1. Make sure that the module is active. Its title bar should be highlighted. If it isn't, click anywhere in the module to highlight its title bar.

2. Click the Insert menu and then click the Procedure command to obtain the Insert Procedure dialog box.

3. Click **Function** in the Type box.

4. Click the Name box and type the name of the procedure.

5. Click OK or press ENTER. The **Public Function** template appears in the module.

6. Complete the procedure. Add the **As Integer** or **As String** clause to the **Public Function** statement and add the two lines of code for each procedure.

That's it—the project is complete. After all that work, it's a good idea to save everything just in case something goes wrong at run time. Another reason: you will use Random Backpack #1 in the exercises and in the next section. So, as the Greek goddess of victory might advise, "Just do it."

1. Save the form file as Random Backpack #1. Visual Basic adds the .frm filename extension.

2. Save the module file as Random Backpack #1. Visual Basic adds the .bas filename extension.

3. Save the project file as Random Backpack #1. Visual Basic adds the .vbp filename extension.

 REMEMBER *You can use the Add File command on the File menu to add Random Backpack #1.frm or Random Backpack #1.bas to another project. You can create an enriched random backpack by adding more tools. We'll suggest a few in the following exercises.*

EXERCISES

1. Start a new project. Use the File menu's Add File command to add Random Backpack1.bas to your project. Add the following tools to module Random Backpack #1 and save the enriched module file as Random Backpack #2.bas:

   a. **Public Function** RollD100 simulates a percentage roll. It returns an integer in the range 0 to 99.

   b. **Public Function** RndUCLetter returns a random uppercase letter.

   c. **Public Function** RndConsonant returns a random lowercase consonant.

   d. **Public Function** RndVowel returns a random lowercase vowel.

2. Check out your new random backpack tools (from Exercise 1). Put command buttons on the form and install their event procedures to try each new **Public Function** procedure. Also put a command button on the form and install its event procedure to create random words of the form *cvcvc* or *vccvcv* or whatever consonant-vowel structure you like. Be sure to save Random Backpack #2 for use in the next section.

9.3   *ADD TOOLS TO THE RANDOM BACKPACK*

The **Public Function** procedures described so far are quite simple. Each procedure has the following syntax:

> Public Function *FunctionName*( ) [As *DataType*]
>   [*Statements*]
>   *FunctionName* = *Expression*
> End Function

The square brackets surrounding **As** *DataType* tell you that this clause is optional. If you omit it, the value returned is a **Variant** data type.

A **Function** procedure must always have a statement of the type

> *FunctionName* = *Expression*

which assigns the value returned by the **Function** to the name of the **Function**. Here are some examples:

```
RollD6 = Fix(6 * Rnd) + 1
RndLetter = Chr(Fix(26 * Rnd) + 97, 1)
```

The procedures shown so far are completely self-contained. Call 'em by name and they deliver. The empty parentheses () after *FunctionName* tells you that the procedure does not require arguments, as do built-in functions such as **Fix**, **Chr**, and **Mid**.

You can create more flexible, powerful, and useful **Function** procedures that do require arguments. Call 'em by name, supply the arguments, and reap the harvest. In this section, you will create **Public Function** procedures with this syntax:

> Public Function *FunctionName*(*Arguments*) [As *DataType*]
>   [*Statements*]
>   *FunctionName* = *Expression*
> End Function

We suggest that you begin with standard module Random Backpack #2, add tools that we describe, invent your own tools, and save the enriched random backpack as Random Backpack #3.bas. Feel free to add more tools, more tools, and more tools...

Our Random Backpack #2 module is named modRndPak2. Its contains the procedures whose first lines are

```
Public Function RollD6() As Integer
Public Function FlipCoin() As String
Public Function RndLetter() As String
Public Function RollD100() As Integer
Public Function RndUCLetter() As String
Public Function RndConsonant() As String
Public Function RndVowel() As String
```

We'll show you a bunch of **Public Function** procedures with arguments. Add one or two or more of these to the module. Put a command button on the form and write its event procedure to check out the new tool. When you are finished, save your enriched module with the filename Random Backpack #3.bas.

Public Function RndInteger has one argument called *Range* and returns an integer in the range 1 to *Range*. Use the Insert menu and the Insert Procedure dialog box to obtain the **Public Function** template shown here:

```
Public Function RndInteger()
|
End Function
```

Modify the first line and add the inside code so that the procedure looks like this:

```
Public Function RndInteger(Range) As Integer

  ' Returns a random integer, 1 to Range.
  RndInteger = Fix(Range * Rnd) + 1

End Function
```

The argument *Range* is enclosed in parentheses following the name of the procedure in the **Public Function** statement. To call this procedure, use its name and supply a value for the argument. For example, the following statement prints a random integer in the range 1 to 52 (a random week? A random card?):

```
Print RndInteger(52)
```

This statement passes the value 52 to RndInteger where it becomes the value of the argument *Range*. The procedure returns a random integer, 1 to 52, as the value of RndInteger.

```
Print RndInteger(52)
```
                                    ╱
Public Function RndInteger(Range) As Integer

The **As Integer** clause declares RndInteger to be an **Integer** procedure. What might happen if the value of *Range* is larger than 32,767? Instead of 52, try an outrageous value such as 65,534 (two times 32,767) in event procedure cmdRndInteger. RndInteger *might* return a value or it *might* display the Overflow dialog box. You can restrict *Range* to integer values by adding an **As Integer** clause:

```
Public Function RndInteger(Range As Integer) As Integer

   ' Returns a random integer, 1 to Range
   RndInteger = Fix(Range * Rnd) + 1

End Function
```

The argument *Range* **As Integer** declares *Range* to be an **Integer** variable, exactly right for this **Integer** procedure. If you try to call the procedure with an argument that is not in the range of integers, you will see the Overflow dialog box.

   Public Function RndLoHiInt has two integer arguments called *Lo* and *Hi*. It returns a random integer in the range *Lo* to *Hi*.

```
Public Function RndLoHiInt(Lo As Integer, Hi As Integer) As Integer

   ' Returns a random integer in the range Lo to Hi
   RndLoHiInt = Fix((Hi - Lo) * Rnd) + Lo

End Function
```

The arguments *Lo* and *Hi* are separated by a comma and both declared to be of integer type by the **As Integer** clause. To call this procedure, use its name and supply values for the two arguments. For example, use this statement to print a random integer in the range –60 to 120 (A random temperature in North Dakota?):

```
            Print RndLoHiInt(-60, 120)
```

Public Function RndLoHiInt(Lo As Integer, Hi As Integer) As Integer

   Our collection of gameplayer's dice has four-sided, six-sided, eight-sided, 10-sided, 12-sided, 20-sided, and other-sided dice. We can replace them all with **Public Function** RollnDs, which rolls *n* dice, each with *s* sides.

```
Public Function RollnDs(n As Integer, s As Integer) As Integer

  ' Simulates rolling n dice, each with s sides
  Dim Total As Integer, k As Integer, Die As Integer

  Total = 0
  For k = 1 To n
    Die = Fix(s * Rnd) + 1
    Total = Total + Die
  Next k
  RollnDs = Total

End Function
```

Want to roll 3D6? Easy—use this statement:

```
Print RollnDs(3, 6)
```

Total, k, and *Die* are *local variables* in RollnDs—they exist only while the procedure is executing. When you call the procedure, it creates and uses these local variables, and then discards them when the procedure ends. You can use the same variable as a local variable in two or more procedures without its use in one procedure affecting its use in another procedure.

Public Function RndWord returns a random word that conforms to the consonant-vowel structure you supply as its argument. For example, if you want a word of the form *cvcvc,* you call the procedure like this: RndWord(*"cvcvc"*). In turn, RndWord calls **Public Functions** RndConsonant and RndVowel to supply consonants and vowels as needed. Here is RndWord:

```
Public Function RndWord(CVstructure As String) As String

  ' Returns a random word with a consonant-vowel
  ' structure defined by the value of CVstructure.

  Dim Word As String, CorV As String, k As Integer

  CVstructure = LCase(CVstructure)   ' Make it lowercase

  Word = ""   ' Start with the empty string

  ' Add vowels or consonants as specified by CVstructure
  For k = 1 To Len(CVstructure)
    CorV = Mid(CVstructure, k, 1)
```

```
      If CorV = "c" Then
        Word = Word & RndConsonant
      ElseIf CorV = "v" Then
        Word = Word & RndVowel
      End If
      RndWord = Word
   Next k

End Function
```

Well now, here is a new tool that uses other new tools. You can get lots of leverage this way! Remember, RndWord uses RndConsonant and RndVowel, so they must all be available for the following event procedure to work:

```
Private Sub cmdRandomSentence_Click()

  Dim Sentence As String

  Sentence = RndWord("vccvcv")
  Sentence = Sentence & " " & RndWord("cvc")
  Sentence = Sentence & " " & RndWord("cvcvc")
  Print Sentence

End Sub
```

Random Backpack #3 now has quite a bunch of new tools. Now indulge yourself in some tool-building exercises.

EXERCISES

1. The first lines of several procedures are shown below in the order in which they appear in this chapter. Identify the arguments and local variables in each of these procedures:

   a. Private Sub Form_Click()

   b. Private Sub Roll3D6_Click()

   c. Public Function RollD6() As Integer

   d. Private Sub cmdFlip10Coins_Click()

    e.   Private Sub cmdRandomWord_Click()

    f.   Public Function RndInteger(Range As Integer) As Integer

    g.   Public Function RndWord(CVstructure As String) As String

2. Write **Public Function** RndLoHiLong. It returns a long integer in the range *Lo* to *Hi*. Use **As Long** clauses to declare *Lo*, *Hi*, and RndLoHiLong as data type **Long** so they may have values up to 2,147,483,647.

3. Write **Public Function** FlipCoins to Flip *n* coins and return the number of heads that occurred. Use **As Long** clauses to declare *n* and FlipCoins as data type **Long** so they may have values up to 2,147,483,647.

9.4   *S*TUFF YOUR BACKPACK WITH SUB PROCEDURES

You already know how to write **Private Sub** event procedures. You can easily transfer your know-how to writing **Public Sub** procedures. Start with this simple syntax:

    Public Sub *ProcedureName* [(*Arguments*)]
      [*Statements*]
    End Sub

You can put a **Public Sub** procedure in a form or in a standard module. Start a new project with Form1, install a **Public Sub** in Form1, and check it out. Call this project Swap #1 - Swap Two Variants.

    Microsoft did not include in Visual Basic the **Swap** statement from older Basics such as QBasic and GW-BASIC. **Swap** swapped the values of two variables of the same type. For example, the QBasic statement

```
Swap Variable1, Variable2
```

swaps the values of *Variable1* and *Variable2*. The old value of *Variable1* becomes the new value of *Variable2* and the old value of *Variable2* becomes the new value of *Variable1*. We found **Swap** quite useful and used it a lot. This presents a splendid opportunity to add an old tool from an old language to Visual Basic. Here is **Public Sub** Swap:

```
Public Sub Swap(Variant1, Variant2)

   ' Swaps the values of Variant1 and Variant2

   Dim Temp

   Temp = Variant1
   Variant1 = Variant2
   Variant2 = Temp

End Sub
```

Public Sub Swap has two arguments, *Variant1* and *Variant2*, and local variable *Temp*. **Swap** swaps the values of any two variables of the same type. Because the arguments are not declared to be a specific type, they are **Variant** by default. The **Dim** statement declares *Temp* without specifying a type, so *Temp* is **Variant** by default. Install **Public Sub** Swap in Form1 like this:

1. Start in Form1's code window. If the code window's title bar is not highlighted, click anywhere in the code window.

2. Click the Insert menu and then click the Procedure command to obtain the Insert Procedure dialog box. The **Public** choice is selected in the Scope box and the **Sub** choice is selected in the Type box:

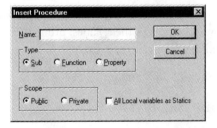

3. In the Name box, type the name of the procedure: **Swap**

4. Click OK or press ENTER.

That's it. Module1's Object box displays "general," the Proc box displays the procedure's name "Swap," and a **Public Sub** procedure template appears in the code window:

```
Public Sub Swap()
|
End Sub
```

Complete the procedure so that it looks like this:

```
Public Sub Swap(Variant1, Variant2)

    ' Swaps the values of Variant1 and Variant2

    Dim Temp

    Temp = Variant1
    Variant1 = Variant2
    Variant2 = Temp

End Sub
```

You can call **Sub** Swap and supply the required arguments in two ways:

▼ Put the name of the Sub in a Call statement and enclose the arguments in parentheses:

```
Call Swap(Variable1, Variable2)
```

▼ Use the **Sub**'s name by itself followed by the arguments not enclosed in parentheses:

```
Swap Variable1, Variable2
```

Event procedure Command1_Click assigns values to *Variable1* and *Variable2*, prints them, swaps their values, prints them again, swaps their values, and prints them once more:

```
Private Sub Command1_Click()

    Dim Variable1, Variable2

    Cls
    Print VarType(Variable1), VarType(Variable2)
    Variable1 = "abc"
    Variable2 = "xyz"
    Print Variable1, Variable2       ' Print Original values
    Call Swap(Variable1, Variable2)  ' Use Sub Swap
    Print Variable1, Variable2       ' Print values after swap
    Swap Variable1, Variable2        ' Use Sub Swap
    Print Variable1, Variable2       ' Print values after swap

End Sub
```

Install event procedure Command1_Click and try it to see:

```
 0               0
abc             xyz
xyz             abc
abc             xyz
```

How does it work? Let's take a leisurely stroll through event procedure
Command1_Click and **Public Sub** Swap and see what happens as selected
statements do their work. The statement

```
Dim Variable1, Variable2
```

invents variables *Variable1* and *Variable2*. Because there are no **As** *DataType*
clauses, these variables are **Variant** by default. The statement

```
Print VarType(Variable1), VarType(Variable2)
```

prints the data types of *Variable1* and *Variable2*. They have not yet been assigned
values, so they are empty. **VarType**(*Variable1*) and **VarType**(*Variable2*) both
return data type 0, **Empty**, and these numbers are printed on the form. The
statements

```
Variable1 = "abc"
Variable2 = "xyz"
Print Variable1, Variable2
```

assign string values to *Variable1* and *Variable2* and print their values on the form.
The statement

```
Call Swap(Variable1, Variable2)
```

calls **Sub** Swap. The argument *Variable1* is passed to **Sub** Swap argument *Variant1*
and the argument *Variable2* is passed to **Sub** Swap argument *Variant2* :

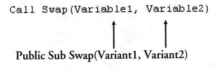

How is this done? Well, you can think of *Variable1* and *Variable2* as the names
of memory locations that contain data. The **Call** statement passes these memory
locations to **Sub** Swap as the locations of its arguments *Variant1* and *Variant2*.
After this brief burst of communication,

▼ *Variable1* and *Variant1* refer to the same memory location, which contains the value "abc".

▼ *Variable2* and *Variant2* refer to the same memory location, which contains the value "xyz".

Call Statement Argument	Sub Swap Argument	Memory Location Contains
Variable1	Variant1	"abc"
Variable2	Variant2	"xyz"

This is called *passing arguments by reference*. There are several consequences to this arrangement:

▼ Any change to *Variant1* in **Sub** Swap changes *Variable1* in Command1_Click.

▼ Any change to *Variant2* in **Sub** Swap changes *Variable2* in Command1_Click.

The **Call** statement turns over control to **Sub** Swap, which begins its work. Table 9-3 shows the values of *Variant1*, *Variant2*, *Temp*, *Variable1*, and *Variable2* after execution of each statement in **Sub** Swap.

Temp is a local variable. It is created by the **Dim** statement and is empty until assigned a value. It disappears at the end of the procedure. Every call to the procedure reincarnates *Temp* for a brief but useful life. At the end of the procedure, control passes back to Command1_Click and the statement

```
Print Variable1, Variable2
```

Sub Swap Statement	Variant1	Variant2	Temp	Variable1	Variable2
Sub Swap(Variant1, Variant2)	"abc"	"xyz"		"abc"	"xyz"
Dim Temp	"abc"	"xyz"	(empty)	"abc"	"xyz"
Temp = Variant1	"abc"	"xyz"	"abc"	"abc"	"xyz"
Variant1 = Variant2	"xyz"	"xyz"	"abc"	"xyz"	"xyz"
Variant2 = Temp	"xyz"	"abc"	"abc"	"xyz"	"abc"
End Sub	"xyz"	"abc"		"xyz"	"abc"

TABLE 9-3 *Values of* Variant1, Variant2, Temp, Variable1, *and* Variable2 *During Execution of* **Sub** *Swap* ▼

prints the new values of *Variable1* and *Variable2*. The statement

```
Swap Variable1, Variable2
```

calls **Sub** Swap again. It swaps the values of *Variable1* and *Variable2* again—they are now back in their original memory locations before all this swapping began. The statement

```
Print Variable1, Variable2
```

prints the values of Variable1 and Variable2 once more and the event procedure ends. Save the project as Swap #1 - Swap Two Variants and call upon your skills to hack your way through these exercises.

EXERCISES

1. Change event procedure Command1_Click so that input boxes are used to acquire the values of *Variable1* and *Variable2*, as shown below. Call this project Swap #2 - Swap Two Variants.

```
Variable1 = InputBox("Enter value of Variable1.", "Variable1")
Variable2 = InputBox("Enter value of Variable2.", "Variable2")
```

2. Create project Sort #1 - Sort Two Currency Amounts. Write **Public Sub** Sort2Money(*Money1* As Currency, *Money2* As Currency). This procedure sorts the values of *Money1* and *Money2* so that the smaller value ends up in *Money1* and the larger value in *Money2*. Write an event procedure to check out Sort2Money using either of these **Call** statements:

```
Call Sort2Money(Amount1, Amount2)
Sort2Money Amount1, Amount2
```

3. Create project Sort #2 - Sort Three Currency Amounts. Write **Public Sub** Sort3Money(*Money1* As Currency, *Money2* As Currency, *Money3* As Currency). This procedure sorts the values of *Money1*, *Money2*, and *Money3* so that the smallest value ends up in *Money1*, the middle value in *Money2*, and the largest value in *Money3*. Write an event procedure to check out Sort3Money using either of these **Call** statements:

```
Call Sort3Money(Amount1, Amount2, Amount3)
Sort3Money Amount1, Amount2, Amount3
```

9.5

USE SUB PROCEDURES TO ARRANGE DATA IN TEXT BOXES

Project Swap #3 - Swap the Contents of Two Text Boxes has text boxes Text1 and Text2, and command button cmdSwap on Form1:

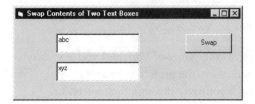

Click a text box to clear it and then enter data. In the above illustration, "abc" and "xyz" have been entered into the text boxes. Click the Swap button to swap the contents of the text boxes:

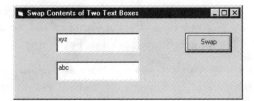

Draw the visual interface and write event procedures Text1_Click and Text2_Click to clear the text boxes and accept focus. Install **Public Sub** Swap in Form1. All that is left to do is to write event procedure cmdSwap_Click for the command button. "Easy," you're thinking. "We can call **Sub** Swap with *Text1.Text* and *Text2.Text* as the arguments—either of the following calls should do the job."

```
Call Swap(Text1.Text, Text2.Text)
Swap Text1.Text, Text2.Text
```

We installed this:

```
Private Sub cmdSwap_Click()
  Swap Text1.Text, Text2.Text
End Sub
```

Alas, it didn't work. We entered **abc** in the upper text box and **xyz** in the lower text box, clicked the Swap button, and nothing happened—"abc" and "xyz" remained steadfastly in place. We clicked again and again, a little more assertively each time, but nothing moved. **Sub** Swap seems to ignore *Object.Property* variables such as *Text1.Text* and *Text2.Text*. Of course! The procedure was written to use **Variant** variables.

What to do? We know that Swap works with **Variant** variables such as *Variable1* and *Variable2*. Let's try assigning the contents of the text boxes, the values of *Text1.Text* and *Text2.Text*, to variables and then use the variables as arguments in calling Swap. That should work—then, after the swap, we can assign the values of the variables back to *Text1.Text* and *Text2.Text*. Let's try it:

```
Private Sub cmdSwap_Click()

  Dim Variable1, Variable2

  Variable1 = Text1.Text
  Variable2 = Text2.Text

  Swap Variable1, Variable2

  Text1.Text = Variable1
  Text2.Text = Variable2

End Sub
```

It worked. Install it yourself and try it. One of the nicest things about Visual Basic is that there is usually another way and another way and another way to solve a problem. Project Swap #4 - Swap the Contents of Two Text Boxes demonstrates another way. The visual interface is the same as Swap #3's interface. These are the new procedures:

```
Private Sub cmdSwap_Click()
  SwapTextBoxes Text1, Text2
End Sub

Public Sub SwapTextBoxes(txtBox1 As Control, txtBox2 As Control)

  ' Swaps the contents of text boxes txtBox1 and txtBox2

  Dim Temp

  Temp = txtBox1.Text
  txtBox1.Text = txtBox2.Text
  txtBox2.Text = Temp

End Sub
```

In event procedure cmdSwap_Click, the statement

```
SwapTextBoxes Text1, Text2
```

has arguments *Text1* and *Text2* that are the *names of controls,* text boxes in this case. These names of text boxes are passed to **Public Sub** SwapTextBoxes. The **Public Sub** statement's argument list contains **As Control** clauses that declare arguments *txtBox1* and *txtBox2* as control objects:

```
Public Sub SwapTextBoxes(txtBox1 As Control, txtBox2 As Control)
```

Call statement argument *Text1* is passed to **Sub** SwapTextBoxes argument *txtBox1* and **Call** statement argument *Text2* is passed to **Sub** SwapTextBoxes argument *txtBox2*:

```
SwapTextBoxes Text1, Text2
```

Public Sub SwapTextBoxes(txtBox1 As Control, txtBox2 As Control)

Text1 and *txtBox1* refer to the same text box, so *Object.Property* variables *Text1.Text* and *txtBox1.Text* refer to the same value, the contents of the text box. The arguments *Text2* and *txtBox2* refer to the same text box, so *Object.Property* variables *Text2.Text* and *txtBox2.Text* refer to the same value, the contents of the text box.

Call Statement Argument	Object.Property Variable
Text1	Text1.Text
Text2	Text2.Text

Sub SwapTextBoxes Argument	Object.Property Variable
txtBox1	txtBox1.Text
txtBox2	txtBox2.Text

▼ Any change to *txtBox1.Text* in **Sub** SwapTextBoxes changes *Text1.Text*.

▼ Any change to *txtBox2.Text* in **Sub** SwapTextBoxes changes *Text2.Text*.

Assume that someone has entered **abc** into text box Text1, **xyz** into text box Text2, and then clicked the Swap button. Event procedure cmdSwap calls **Sub** SwapTextBoxes and passes the arguments *Text1* and *Text2* to *txtBox1* and *txtBox2*. **Sub** SwapTextBoxes's inside code goes to work as shown in Table 9-4.

Sub SwapTextBoxes Statement	Text1.Text	Text2.Text	Temp	txtBox1.Text	txtBox2.Text
Dim Temp	"abc"	"xyz"		"abc"	"xyz"
Temp = txtBox1.Text	"abc"	"xyz"	"abc"	"abc"	"xyz"
txtBox1.Text = txtBox2.Text	"xyz"	"xyz"	"abc"	"xyz"	"xyz"
txtBox2.Text = Temp	"xyz"	"abc"	"abc"	"xyz"	"abc"

TABLE 9-4   *Values of Variables as* **Sub** *SwapTextBoxes Performs Its Task* ▼

Sort Three Text Boxes

Project Sort #3 - Sort Three Text Boxes, ANSI sorts the contents of three vertically arranged text boxes. The "least" value is moved to the top text box, the "middle" value to the middle text box, and the "greatest" value to the bottom text box. The three values are sorted according to their ANSI codes. Therefore, any uppercase letter (ANSI code 65 to 90) is "less than" any lowercase letter (ANSI code 97 to 122). For this demonstration, we set the font size in each text box to 18 points. In the sample run shown here, someone has just entered **Z** in the top text box (Text1), **a** in the middle text box (Text2), and a snail (@) in the bottom text box (Text3):

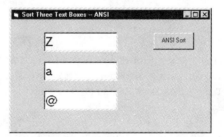

Click the ANSI Sort button and its event procedure sorts the three characters from top to bottom in order of their ANSI codes with "@" in the top text box, "Z" in the middle box, and "a" in the bottom box:

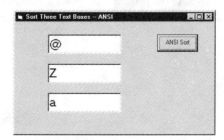

Event procedure cmdANSIsort is shown below. Notice that three of its statements call **Sub** SwapTextBoxes:

```
Private Sub cmdANSIsort_Click()

    ' First put the ANSI "least" value in Text1
    If Text1.Text > Text2.Text Then SwapTextBoxes Text1, Text2
    If Text1.Text > Text3.Text Then SwapTextBoxes Text1, Text3

    ' Then put the contents of Text2 and Text3 in ANSI order
    If Text2.Text > Text3.Text Then SwapTextBoxes Text2, Text3

End Sub
```

Complete project Sort #3 and give it a good workout. Use Appendix A, "ANSI Codes and Characters," to verify that the contents of the text boxes are sorted into ANSI order.

Because all uppercase letters have ANSI codes that are less than the ANSI code of any lowercase letter, project Sort #3 may not sort mixed-case text into alphabetical order. Project Sort #4 - Sort Three Text Boxes Alphabetically adds a command button captioned "Alpha Sort" that you can click to sort the contents of the three text boxes alphabetically. Here is event procedure cmdAlphaSort_Click:

```
Private Sub cmdAlphaSort_Click()

    ' First put the alphabetically first in Text1
    If LCase(Text1.Text) > LCase(Text2.Text) Then SwapTextBoxes Text1, Text2
    If LCase(Text1.Text) > LCase(Text3.Text) Then SwapTextBoxes Text1, Text3

    ' Then put the contents of Text2 and Text3 in alphabetical order
    If LCase(Text2.Text) > LCase(Text3.Text) Then SwapTextBoxes Text2, Text3

End Sub
```

Complete the project, take it for a walk, and add some convolutions to your gray matter with the following innocuous exercises.

EXERCISES

1. Create project Sort #5 - Sort Currency in Two Text Boxes. Write **Public Sub** Sort2TxtMoney(*txtBox1* As Control, *txtBox2* As Control). This procedure treats the values of *txtBox1.Text* and *txtBox2.Text* as **Currency** and sorts them so that the smaller value ends up in *txtBox1* and the larger value in *txtBox2*. Write an event procedure to exercise the **Sub** procedure using either of these **Call** statements:

```
Call Sort2TxtMoney(Text1, Text2)
Sort2txtMoney Text1, Text2
```

2. Create project Sort #6 - Sort Currency in Three Text Boxes. Write **Public Sub** Sort3TxtMoney(*txtBox1* As Control, *txtBox2* As Control, *txtBox3* As Control). This procedure treats the values of *txtBox1.Text*, *txtBox2.Text*, and *txtBox3.Text* as **Currency** and sorts them so that the smallest value ends up in *txtBox1*, the middle value in *txtBox2*, and the largest in *txtBox3*. Stack the text boxes vertically on Form1. Write an event procedure to check out the **Sub** procedure using either of these **Call** statements:

```
Call Sort3TxtMoney(Text1, Text2, Text3)
Sort3txtMoney Text1, Text2, Text3
```

9.6 *PUT A PACK OF SUBS IN A STANDARD MODULE*

In the previous two sections, we supplied and you may have created six **Public Sub** procedures and installed them in forms. We have these procedures installed:

▼ **Public Sub** Swap is in Form1 of project Swap #1 - Swap Two Variants.

▼ **Public Sub** Sort2Money is in Form1 of project Sort #1 - Sort Two Currency Amounts.

▼ **Public Sub** Sort3Money is in Form1 of project Sort #2 - Sort Three Currency Amounts.

▼ **Public Sub** SwapTextBoxes is in Form1 of project Swap #4 - Swap the Contents of Two Text Boxes.

▼ **Public Sub** Sort2TxtMoney is in Form1 of project Sort #5 - Sort Currency in Two Text Boxes.

▼ **Public Sub** Sort3TxtMoney is in Form1 of project Sort #6 - Sort Currency in Three Text Boxes.

Install these procedures in a standard module and save it as Sub Backpack #1.bas. To save wear and tear on your fingers, you can install these procedures by copying them from their forms and pasting them into Module1. We'll demonstrate by copying **Public Sub** Swap from project Swap #1's Form1. Follow these steps:

1. Start a new project with Form1 and change its caption to "Sub Backpack #1."

2. Change Form1's name to frmSubPak1. This is **very important** because you will soon add Form1 from project Swap #1. Visual Basic won't let you add a file Form1 if there is already a file by that name in the current project.

3. Use the Insert menu's Module command to insert Module1 into the project. The Project window should now display "frmSubPak1" and "Module1."

4. Now you are ready to copy **Sub** Swap from project Swap #1 to Module1. Use the File menu's Add File command to add form file Swap #1.frm to the project. You should then see its name in the Project window.

5. Open Swap #1.frm's code window, highlight the entire **Public Sub** Swap procedure, and use the Edit window's Copy command to copy **Sub** Swap to the Clipboard.

6. Select Module1 and use the Edit menu's Paste command to paste **Public Sub** Swap into Module1.

7. Select Swap #1.frm and then use the File menu's Remove File command to remove the form from the project.

If all goes well, a copy of **Sub** Swap now resides in Module1. Repeat steps 4 through 7 to copy **Sub** SwapTextBoxes from project Swap #4's Form1 to Module1. Then copy to Module1 the rest of the **Subs** from the previous two sections: **Sub** Sort2Money, **Sub** Sort3Money, **Sub** Sort2TxtMoney, and **Sub** Sort3TxtMoney.

Well, that's a great start. If you did all of the above, Module1 now has six **Subs**. Change the name of Module1 to modSubPak1 and save the project as Sub Backpack #1 with the filenames *Sub* Backpack #1.frm for the form file, Sub Backpack #1.bas for the module file, and Sub Backpack #1.vbp for the project file. Now we'll describe more **Public Sub** procedures that you may wish to add to the module.

Public Sub MinMax finds the minimum and maximum of three **Double** variables, assigns the minimum value to *Minimum,* and assigns the maximum value to *Maximum.* Although the **Public Sub** statement is shown here broken into two lines, enter it as a single line:

```
Public Sub MinMax(Number1 As Double, Number2 As Double,
   Number3 As Double, Minmum As Double, Maximum As Double)

  ' Assign the smallest number To Minimum
  Minimum = Number1
  If Minimum > Number2 Then Minimum = Number2
  If Minimum > Number3 Then Minimum = Number3

  ' Assign the largest number To Maximum
  Maximum = Number1
  If Maximum < Number2 Then Maximum = Number2
  If Maximum < Number3 Then Maximum = Number3

End Sub
```

Because the **Public Sub** statement has five arguments, the **Call** statement must have five arguments. For example, suppose you call **Sub** MinMax like this:

```
Call MinMax(4.56, 1.23, 7.89, Smallest, Largest)
```

The values 4.56, 1.23, and 7.89 are passed to **Sub** MinMax as the values of its arguments *Number1, Number2,* and *Number3.* The **Sub** returns 1.23 as the value of *Smallest* and 7.89 as the value of *Largest.* Use event procedure cmdMinMax_Click to give **Sub** MinMax a good workout:

```
Private Sub cmdMinMax_Click()

  Dim Number1 As Double, Number2 As Double, Number3 As Double
  Dim Smallest As Double, Largest As Double

  Cls
  Number1 = InputBox("Number, please.", "1st Number")
  Number2 = InputBox("Number, please.", "2nd Number")
  Number3 = InputBox("Number, please.", "3rd Number")

  Print Number1, Number2, Number3
  Print

  Call MinMax(Number1, Number2, Number3, Smallest, Largest)
```

```
Print "The smallest number is "; Smallest
Print "The largest number is "; Largest

End Sub
```

Visual Basic has no built-in method for causing a time delay. You might find a time delay procedure useful for slowing down activity on the screen or timing a response to a question or whatever. **Public Sub** Dally dallies the number of seconds specified by its argument:

```
Public Sub Dally(Seconds As Single)

  ' Dallies the number of seconds specified by Seconds
  ' Caution: Totally ties up your computer during the delay

  Dim StartTime As Single

  ' Here's the time delay
  StartTime = Timer
  If StartTime + Seconds < 86400 Then
    ' Does not go through midnight
    Do Until Timer > StartTime + Seconds: Loop
  Else
    ' Adjust for going through midnight
    Do Until Timer > StartTime + Seconds - 86400: Loop
  End If

End Sub
```

Does it work? Use your event procedure to try **Sub** Dally or use ours shown below. Be sure to test it while the time passes through midnight and the value of **Timer** is reset to zero. Leave a note (quietly, please) by our pillow to tell us what happened.

```
Private Sub cmdThreeBeeps_Click()

  Beep
  Call Dally(0.5)
  Beep
  Dally 0.5
  Beep

End Sub
```

Well, that's a good start. We'll suggest more **Subs** in the exercises; your brain is probably subdurally scintillating with ideas.

EXERCISES

1. Modify **Public Sub** Dally so that it can be used for long time delays without totally tying up the computer. To do so, add a DoEvents statement inside each Do...Loop.

2. Write **Public Sub** ReverseSort(*Money1* As Currency, *Money2* As Currency, *Money3* As Currency). This procedure sorts the values of *Money1*, *Money2*, and *Money3* so that the largest value ends up in *Money1*, the middle value in *Money2*, and the smallest value in *Money3*.

**mastery
skills check**

1. Define, describe, explain, or write a short essay about each of the following. Look up these items in the Visual Basic manuals or use the Help system:

   a. **Private Sub** procedure

   b. **Public Function** procedure

   c. **Public Sub** procedure

   d. Argument

   e. Passing an argument by reference

   f. Passing an argument by value

   g. Local variable

   h. Form-level variable

   i. **As** *DataType* (Integer, Long, Single, et cetera)

2. **Public Function** FlipCoin returns H or T with equal probability, thus simulating a fair coin. An individual with execrable ethics might imbed nanotech robots inside a coin to influence the coin's trajectory as it tumbles through the air. In your continuing study of despicable behavior, appropriate tools might be:

   a. **Public Function** FlipCoinA returns H with a probability of 3/5 and T with a probability of 2/5.

   b. **Public Function** FlipCoinB returns H with probabilty p and T with probability $1 - p$, where p is FlipCoinB's argument. For example, FlipCoinB(0.43) returns H with a probability of 0.43 and T with a probability of 0.57.

3. **Function** RollD6 returns an integer in the range 1 to 6 with equal probability, thus simulating the roll of a fair die. In the real world, unsavory individuals might use an unfair (loaded) die that favors a certain number or numbers. As a student of such antisocial behavior, you might enjoy the use of **Function** procedures that simulate these deviant dice. We suggest:

   a. **Public Function** RollD6A returns an integer in the range 1 to 6 in which 2 is twice as likely to occur as 1, 3, 4, 5, or 6. A blatantly loaded die!

   b. **Public Function** RollD6B returns an integer in the range 1 to 6 in which 5 is twice as likely to occur as 1, 2, 3, 4, or 6. RollD6A + RollD6B rolls so many sevens that you will surely be caught. (While doing time, enhance the lives of fellow inmates by teaching them Visual Basic.)

   c. Be subtle. Write **Public Function** RollD6C to return an integer from 1 to 6 with one value only slightly more probable than the other values.

4. In a lottery, you pick a set of numbers from a larger set of numbers. For example, you might pick six integers from the integers 1 to 53. In how many ways can you pick r different integers from the integers 1 to n? Suppose that $n = 4$ and $r = 2$. In this case, it is easy to list the possible choices:

1 and 2	1 and 3	1 and 4
2 and 3	2 and 4	
3 and 4		

   There are six ways to pick two integers from four integers if order doesn't matter. Choosing 2 and 1 is the same as choosing 1 and 2; choosing 3 and 1 is the same as choosing 1 and 3; and so on. This is a problem in combinations. In an algebra, finite math, or statistics book, the number of ways is usually represented by the symbol $_nC_r$. This calculation is available on many scientific and financial calculators and in spreadsheets such as Microsoft Excel. Here is a formula for computing $_nC_r$:

$$_nC_r = \frac{n(n-1)(n-2)...(n-(r-1))}{1(2)(3)...(r)}$$

Write **Public Function** Combinations(r As Long, n As Long) As Double. It returns the number of ways to pick *r* objects from a set of *n* objects.

5. Counting the number of spaces in a string gives you a rough idea of the number of words in the string. Design **Public Function** Spaces that returns the number of spaces in its string argument. Here is a suggested first line:

```
Public Function Spaces(Strng As String) As String
```

6. Create project Energy #5 - Cost of Energy. Use Public **Sub** EnergyCost to calculate the cost of electricity and use it again to calculate the cost of gas. Although the **Public Sub** statement is shown here broken into two lines, enter it as a single line:

```
Public Sub EnergyCost(Amount As Long, BaseLine As Long,
   LoRate As Currency, HiRate As Currency, Cost As Currency)
```

You may wish to review projects Energy #1 through Energy #4 in Chapter 7 for ideas. Use your energy company's low and high rates for electricity and gas. Our electric rates are $0.1195 and $0.1374 per kilowatt-hour. Our gas rates are $0.5265 and $0.7107 per therm.

7. What is the most tedious topic in elementary school math? Fractions, definitely. Fraction-crunching is a mechanical operation that frequently interferes with the enjoyment of learning math and using math as a modeling tool. You study a problem, figure out how to solve it, and set up your solution. Alas, the solution requires time-consuming fraction-crunching. Fortunately, enlightened schools provide tools such as the *Texas Instruments Math Explorer*, an inexpensive fraction calculator. In these schools, teachers and students can spend more time on math and less time in fraction-crunching busywork.

Project Fraction Cruncher #1 is a fraction calculator. After you create it, you can use it to add, subtract, multiply, and divide fractions, obtaining fractions as answers. In the sample run shown below, someone entered the fraction 3/8 in the two left text boxes, the fraction 5/12 in the middle two text boxes, and then clicked the Add (the plus sign) button. Fraction

Cruncher added the two fractions and displayed the result, 76/96, in the right two text boxes:

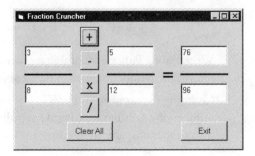

8. Fraction Cruncher #1 of Exercise 8 may not produce a result in *simplest terms*. For example, the fraction 76/96 can be simplified to 19/24. For anyone out there who is not adept at handling fractions, we suggest a scenario. Suppose that you are at a party and you are having a major attack of pizza lust. Fortunately, someone brought two medium pizzas, one multi-meat cut into eight slices and one veggie cut into 12 slices. Unable to control yourself, you eventually consume three slices of the multi-meat and five slices of the veggie. There in plain sight of everyone, you have eaten 76/96 of a medium pizza. Project Fraction Cruncher #2 adds a Simplify button that you can click to simplify the result to 19/24, which doesn't sound quite so gluttonous. In the meantime, have a Rolaid.

Create project Fraction Cruncher #2. It has a Simplify button that you can click to reduce the fraction to its simplest terms. For example, click Simplify to reduce 76/96 to 19/24:

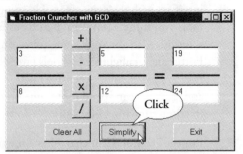

To simplify a fraction, you first compute the *greatest common divisor* (GCD) of the fraction's numerator and denominator, and then divide the numerator and denominator by the GCD. We suggest that you create **Public Function** GCD to handle this task.

10

Up, Up, and Array!

chapter objectives

10.1 Get acquainted with data arrays and array variables

10.2 Create the random fortune cookie project

10.3 Flashcard projects are handy homework helpers

10.4 Use option buttons to opt for sequential or random study

10.5 The people's poll uses control arrays to tally answers

10.6 Dynamic arrays enable better ways

10.7 Sort an array

10.8 Pass arrays to **Public Sub** procedures

10.9 Use control arrays in project High, Low, and Average

YOU can leap over tall heaps of data by using a *data structure* called an *array*. An array is an ordered list of *array variables*. All members of an array have the same name, the name of the array. An individual member of the array is identified by an *index*, also called a *subscript*.

You can also create and use *control arrays* that consist of two or more controls of the same type. For example, you can create a command button array, a text box array, an image box array, or an option button array. All controls in a control array have the same Name property setting. An individual member of the control array is identified by its Index property setting.

Data arrays and control arrays add new dimensions to your set of Visual Basic tools. Using arrays, you can do things that would be impractical using only simple variables and individual controls. Arrays enable you to write compact, efficient code to manipulate many controls and process lots of data.

10.1 ▮ *G*ET ACQUAINTED WITH DATA ARRAYS AND ARRAY VARIABLES

You have used simple variables to represent numbers, strings, and variant data. Here are simple variables as they appeared in **Dim** statements:

Dim Msg As String, Title As String

Dim red As Integer, green As Integer, blue As Integer

An *array* is a set, or collection, of *array variables*. Each array variable in an array is an *element*, or *member*, of the array. An array variable consists of the name of the array followed by an *index* enclosed in parentheses:

Number(3)   Strng(1)   Varyant(7.3)

The index of an array variable is a number enclosed in parentheses following the variable name. Because an index must be an integer, Visual Basic rounds a noninteger index to the nearest integer:

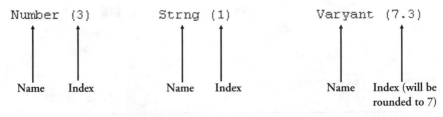

An index can be a number:	Temperature(3)
An index can be a variable:	Word(k)
An index can be an expression:	Fortune(Fix(7 * Rnd) + 1)

An array variable consists of these parts:

A variable name:	Number	Strng	Varyant
Left parenthesis:	Number(	Strng(	Varyant(
A numeric index:	Number(3	Strng(3	Varyant(3
Right parenthesis:	Number(3)	Strng(3)	Varyant(3)

An array is a list of array variables with indexes. Unless declared otherwise, the smallest index is zero (0). An array with four array variables has indexes 0, 1, 2, and 3:

Number(0)	Number(1)	Number(2)	Number(3)

An array with five array variables has indexes 0, 1, 2, 3, and 4:

Varyant(0)	Varyant(1)	Varyant(2)	Varyant(3)	Varyant(4)

An array name followed by an empty pair of parentheses refers to the entire array. This convention distinguishes an array from a simple variable or a single array variable.

Simple variable:	Number	Strng	Varyant
Single array variable:	Number(13)	Strng(13)	Varyant(13)
Entire array:	Number()	Strng()	Varyant()

You must declare an array before you use it. One way to do this is to use a **Dim** statement to specify the range of indexes in the array. A **Dim** statement reserves memory space for a specified number of array variables and assigns values as follows:

▼ Numeric array: Each array variable is assigned zero (0).

▼ String array: Each array variable is assigned a zero-length string (the empty string).

▼ Variant array: Each array variable is assigned data type 0, Empty.

The statement

```
Dim Number(12) As Double
```

declares a double-precision numeric array with 13 array variables, *Number(0)* through *Number(12)*. Each array variable represents a double-precision number. The **Dim** statement reserves memory space for 13 array variables and assigns to each the value zero (0) with data type 5, Double.

We will not use this form of the **Dim** statement. Instead, we will use a **Dim** statement with the keyword **To** and specify both the smallest and the largest index of the array:

The statement

```
Dim Tally(3 To 18) As Long
```

declares a long integer array with 16 array variables, *Tally(3)* through *Tally(18)*, and assigns to each the value zero (0) with data type 3, Long. Each array variable represents a long integer.

The statement

```
Dim Word(1 To 100) As String
```

declares a string array with 100 array variables, *Word(1)* through *Word(100)*, and assigns to each a zero-length string (empty string) with data type 8, String. Strings can vary in length from 0 bytes (the empty string) to a maximum of 32,767 bytes. Additional memory space is allocated later when string array variables are assigned values.

The statement

```
Dim Varyant(-273 To 1000) As Variant
```

declares a variant array with 1274 array variables, *Varyant(–273)* through *Varyant(1000)*, and assigns to each array variable a value of data type 0, Empty.

Let's verify some of the claims just given. Start a new project called Arrays #1 and open the form's code window. Enter the following **Dim** statements in the declarations section of the code window and then enter event procedure Form_Load.

```
Dim Tally(3 To 18) As Long
Dim Word(0 To 100) As String
Dim Varyant(-273 To 1000) As Variant

Private Sub Form_Load()
  AutoRedraw = True
  Print "The VarType of Tally(3) is "; VarType(Tally(3))
```

```
   Print "The VarType of Word(1) is "; VarType(Word(1))
   Print "The VarType of Varyant(-273) is "; VarType(Varyant(-273))
End Sub
```

The **Dim** statements declare arrays *Tally()*, *Word()*, and *Varyant()*. Event
procedure Form_Load prints the **VarType** of the value of the first array variable
(smallest index) in each array. Run the project to see this:

```
The VarType of Tally(3) is  3

The VarType of Word(0) is  8

The VarType of Varyant(-273) is  0
```

With a mighty leap you are up, up, and array! With confidence, bound over the
following exercise. Nothing can go awry.

EXERCISE

1. For each set of array variables, write a **Dim** statement to declare the array:

    a. Integer array variables *CoinFlips(0)* and *CoinFlips(1)*.

    b. Double-precision array variables *NationalDebt(1994)*,
       NationalDebt(1995), and *NationalDebt(1996)*.

    c. Long integer array variables *Inventory(1000)*, *Inventory(1001)*, and so
       on, up to *Inventory(9999)*.

    d. Single-precision array variables *QuizAverage(1)*, *QuizAverage(2)*, and so
       on, up to *QuizAverage(32)*.

    e. String array variables *Filename(1)*, *Filename(2)*, and so on, up to
       Filename(500).

    f. Variant array variables *Potpourri(–100)*, *Potpourri(–99)*, and so on, up
       to *Potpourri(200)*.

10.2 *C*REATE THE RANDOM FORTUNE COOKIE PROJECT

Way back in Chapter 2 or thereabouts, we promised you a project that would
display fortune cookie messages selected at random. Here is project is Fortune
Cookie #6 after someone clicked the Fortune button:

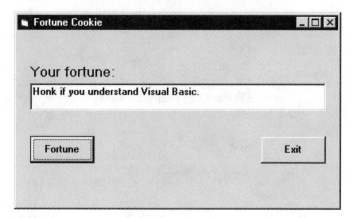

Each time you click the Fortune button, its event procedure selects a string randomly from string array *Fortune( )* and displays it in the text box. Some of the strings are fortunes, and others are suggestions that might be used, say, as bumper stickers. Start a new project and create Fortune Cookie #6's visual interface as shown in the illustration. Table 10-1 lists the project's module-level specifications and Table 10-2 lists its event procedure specs.

Open the form's code window, make sure that the Object box displays "(General)" and the Procedures box shows "declarations," then enter the following **Dim** statement to declare *Fortune( )* as a form-level string array:

```
Dim Fortune(1 To 100) As String
```

This declares *Fortune( )* as a string array with array variables *Fortune(1)* through *Fortune(100)*. You can store up to 100 strings in this array. Event procedure Form_Load assigns strings to the first seven array variables:

```
Private Sub Form_Load()
  Randomize
  Fortune(1) = "Dragons of good fortune will dance on your keyboard."
  Fortune(2) = "Reality expands to fill the available fantasies."
  Fortune(3) = "Your computer will understand you today."
  Fortune(4) = "Trust your psychic tailwind."
  Fortune(5) = "Be nice to the driver who just cut across your bow."
  Fortune(6) = "Honk if you understand Visual Basic."
  Fortune(7) = "Dance, sing, and whistle to banish the blues."
End Sub
```

Module Name	Declaration	Comment
frmFortune	Dim Fortune(1 To 100) As String	Array of up to 100 fortune cookie messages.

TABLE 10-1 *Module-level Specifications for Project Fortune Cookie #6* ▼

Object Name	Event	Response
frmFortune	Load	Randomizes the **Rnd** function and assigns values to array variables.
cmdFortune	Click	Selects a fortune randomly from *Fortune( )* and displays it in txtFortune.

TABLE 10-2 *Event Procedure Specifications for Project Fortune Cookie #6* ▼

At run time, Form_Load first randomizes the **Rnd** function, and then assigns string values to array variables *Fortune(1)* through *Fortune(7)*. Because *Fortune( )* is a form-level array, it is available to any procedure in the form. Event procedure cmdFortune_Click picks a random fortune from *Fortune( )* and displays it in text box txtFortune:

```
Private Sub cmdFortune_Click()

  ' Display a random fortune from array Fortune()

  Dim RandomIndex As Integer

  RandomIndex = Fix(7 * Rnd) + 1
  txtFortune.Text = Fortune(RandomIndex)

End
```

Install event procedures Form_Load and cmdFortune_Click, add event procedure cmdExit_Click, and run the project. Click the Fortune button until you have seen each message stored in array *Fortune( )* at least once.

While dragons of good fortune dance on your keyboard, try your luck with these exercises.

EXERCISES

1. Add the following two messages to the string array *Fortune( )*:

   When tools become toys, then work becomes play.

   Everything you do is practice for what you do next.

   a. Modify event procedure Form_Load to assign the additional messages to string array *Fortune( )*. The array now has nine messages.

   b. Modify event procedure cmdFortune_Click so that any of the nine messages can be selected randomly.

2. Project Fortune Cookie #7 is similar to project Fortune Cookie #6, except that the form-level **Dim** statements and event procedure Form_Load are as listed here:

```
Dim Fortune(1 To 100) As String
Dim NumberFortunes As Integer

Private Sub Form_Load()
  Randomize
  NumberFortunes = 7
  Fortune(1) = "Dragons of good fortune will dance on your keyboard."
  Fortune(2) = "Reality expands to fill the available fantasies."
  Fortune(3) = "Your computer will understand you today."
  Fortune(4) = "Trust your psychic tailwind."
  Fortune(5) = "Be nice to the driver who just cut across your bow."
  Fortune(6) = "Honk if you understand Visual Basic."
  Fortune(7) = "Dance, sing, and whistle to banish the blues."
End Sub
```

Complete project Fortune Cookie #7 by writing event procedure cmdFortune_Click so that it uses the form-level variable *NumberFortunes* to compute the value of local variable *RandomIndex*.

10.3 *F*LASHCARD PROJECTS ARE HANDY HOMEWORK HELPERS

Have you ever used flashcards to study a language or another subject? You can use project Flashcards #1 - Sequential to learn some Japanese words and phrases. Or you can modify the project to study another subject by changing event procedure Form_Load, which assigns values to arrays *SideA( )* and *SideB( )*. At run time you see the following screen:

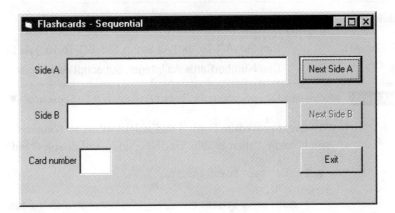

At the beginning of a run, the Next Side A is enabled. The Next Side B button is disabled—it appears dimmed. Click the Next Side A button to display Side A of the first card in the text box labeled "Side A" and the card number (1) in the text box labeled "Card number." This click enables the Next Side B button and disables the Next Side A button. Click the Next Side B button to see Side B of the first card. The run now looks like this:

You can now run through the cards by repeatedly clicking the Next Side A and Next Side B buttons. After displaying Side B of the last card, the run starts over with the first card. Table 10-3 lists project Flashcards #1's module-level specifications and Table 10-4 shows the event procedure specs.

Arrays *SideA( )* and *SideB( )* and integer variables *NumberCards* and *Subscript* are declared in the General declarations area of frmFlashcard1's code window:

```
Dim SideA(1 To 100) As String, SideB(1 To 100) As String
Dim NumberCards As Integer, Subscript As Integer
```

Module Name	Declaration
frmFlashcard1	Dim SideA(1 To 100) As String, SideB(1 To 100) As String
	Dim NumberCards As Integer, Subscript As Integer

TABLE 10-3 *Module-level Specifications for Project Flashcards #1 - Sequential* ▼

Event procedure Form_Load assigns values to *NumberCards* and arrays *SideA( )* and *SideB( )*, then enables cmdNextSideA and disables cmdNextSideB:

```
Private Sub Form_Load()

    ' Assign values to arrays SideA() and SideB()
    NumberCards = 7
    SideA(1) = "Nihon'go"
    SideB(1) = "Japanese language"
    SideA(2) = "Ohayo gozaimasu"
    SideB(2) = "Good morning"
    SideA(3) = "Kon'nichi wa"
    SideB(3) = "Hello or Good day"
    SideA(4) = "Kon'ban wa"
    SideB(4) = "Good evening"
    SideA(5) = "Oyasumi nasai"
    SideB(5) = "Good night"
    SideA(6) = "Ja, mata ashita"
    SideB(6) = "Well, I'll see you again tomorrow"
    SideA(7) = "Sayonara"
    SideB(7) = "Goodbye"

    ' Enable NextSide A button and disable NextSide B button
    cmdNextSideA.Enabled = True
    cmdNextSideB.Enabled = False

End Sub
```

Object Name	Event	Response
frmFlashcard1	Load	Randomizes **Rnd**, assigns values to array variables, enables cmdNextSideA, and disables cmdNextSideB.
cmdNextCardA	Click	Displays Side A, enables cmdNextSideB, and disables cmdNextSideA.
cmdNextCardB	Click	Displays Side B, enables cmdNextSideA, and disables cmdNextSideB.
cmdExit	Click	Ends the run.

TABLE 10-4 *Event Procedure Specifications for Project Flashcards #1 - Sequential* ▼

Because cmdNextSideA is enabled by event procedure Form_Load at run time, event procedure cmdNextSideA_Click is ready to use:

```
Private Sub cmdNextSideA_Click()

  ' Display Side A of the next flashcard

  ' Increase the current subscript and test to see
  ' if it in the range 1 to NumberCards
  Subscript = Subscript + 1
  If Subscript < 1 Or Subscript > NumberCards Then
    ' If Subscript is out-of-range, then start over
    Subscript = 1
  End If

  ' Display Side A and card number, clear Side B
  txtCardNumber.Text = Subscript
  txtSideA.Text = SideA(Subscript)
  txtSideB.Text = ""

  ' Disable Side A button and enable Side B button
  cmdNextSideA.Enabled = False
  cmdNextSideB.Enabled = True

End Sub
```

If the run has just begun, the value of *Subscript* has been set to zero (0) by the **Dim** statement in the declarations section. If the last card has just been displayed, the value of *Subscript* will be greater than the value of *NumberCards*. In either of these cases, the value of *Subscript* is set to 1, ready to show the first card.

The procedure then clears txtSideA and txtSideB, displays the card number (value of *Subscript*) in txtCardNumber, and shows Side A of that card. After doing all this work quick as a wink, the procedure disables cmdNextSideA and enables cmdNextSideB so that you can click the Next Side B button to see Side B of the current card:

```
Private Sub cmdNextSideB_Click()

  ' Display Side B of the current card
  txtSideB.Text = SideB(Subscript)

  ' Enable Side A button and disable Side B button
  cmdNextSideA.Enabled = True
  cmdNextSideB.Enabled = False

End Sub
```

After seeing Side B of the current card, you no doubt want to see Side A of the next card, so the procedure obligingly enables cmdNextSideA and disables cmdNextSideB.

Now flash your new know-how by sidling up to this exercise.

1. Project Flashcards #1 displays cards sequentially from the first card to the last card, and then starts over. Create project Flashcards #2 - Random. When you click the Next Side A button, event procedure cmdNextSideA_Click selects a flashcard at random and displays Side A. Click the Next Side B button to display Side B of the same card.

10.4 *U*SE OPTION BUTTONS TO OPT FOR SEQUENTIAL OR RANDOM STUDY

Instead of separate projects for sequential or random study, wouldn't you rather have a single project that lets you opt for one or the other at any time? If you said yes, project Flashcards #3 - Sequential or Random is at your service. It has option buttons that you can click to select sequential or random access. You can click at any time to switch from one to the other mode of study. The option buttons are drawn inside a frame so that you can move the frame and its option buttons as a unit. At run time you see this:

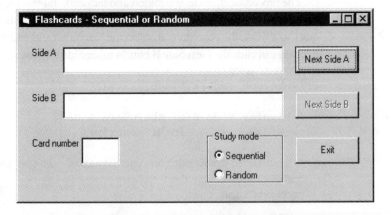

Project Flashcards #3 has option buttons captioned "Sequential Study" and "Random Study." At the beginning of a run, the Sequential Study button is selected--its circle contains a bullet (•). You can go with sequential study or click the Random Study button at any time to change mode. You can return to sequential mode any time by clicking "Sequential Study." Table 10-5 lists project Flashcards #3's frame and option button specifications, Table 10-6 shows the module-level specifications, and Table 10-7 displays the event procedure specs.

Object	Property	Setting	Comment
Frame1	Caption	Study Mode	
	Name	fraStudyMode	
Option1	Caption	Sequential Study	
	Name	optSequential	
	Value	True	This button is selected at run time.
Option2	Caption	Random Study	
	Name	optRandom	
	Value	False	This button is not selected at run time.

TABLE 10-5   *Option Button Specifications for Project Flashcards #3 - Sequential or Random*   ▼

Module Name	Declaration
frmFlashcard3	Dim SideA(1 To 100) As String, SideB(1 To 100) As String
	Dim NumberCards As Integer, Subscript As Integer

TABLE 10-6   *Module-level Specifications for Project Flashcards #3 - Sequential or Random*   ▼

Object Name	Event	Response
frmFlashcard3	Load	Randomizes **Rnd**, assigns values to array variables, enables cmdNextSideA, and disables cmdNextSideB.
cmdNextCardA	Click	Displays Side A, enables cmdNextSideB, and disables cmdNextSideA.
cmdNextCardB	Click	Displays Side B, enables cmdNextSideA, and disables cmdNextSideB.
cmdExit	Click	Ends the run.

TABLE 10-7 *Event Procedure Specifications for Project Flashcards #3 - Sequential or Random* ▼

This project is similar to projects Flashcards #1 and Flashcards #2. You can modify one of them to get this one. Most of the work is done by event procedure cmdNextSideA_Click:

```
Private Sub cmdNextSideA_Click()

  ' Display Side A sequentially or randomly

  ' Option buttons select sequential or random card
  If optSequential.Value = True Then

    ' Sequential card. If past last card, start over.
    Subscript = Subscript + 1
    If Subscript > NumberCards Then Subscript = 1

  ElseIf optRandom.Value = True Then

    ' Random card. Random subscript, 1 to NumberCards
    Subscript = Fix(NumberCards * Rnd) + 1

  End If

  ' Display card number and Side A, clear Side B
  txtCardNumber.Text = Subscript
  txtSideA.Text = SideA(Subscript)
  txtSideB.Text = ""

  ' Disable Side A button and enable Side B button
  cmdNextSideA.Enabled = False
  cmdNextSideB.Enabled = True

End Sub
```

An **If...Then...Else** structure checks the option button settings and calculates a sequential or random subscript. In a set of option buttons, only one button can have a Value setting of True; all other buttons in the set have a Value setting of False:

▼   If option button optSequential is selected, then the setting of optSequential.Value is True, the setting of optRandom.Value is False, and the value of *Subscript* is increased by 1. If the new value is greater than the number of cards, then *Subscript* is set to 1 and the first card is selected.

▼   If option button optRandom is selected, then the setting of optRandom.Value is True, the setting of optSequential.Value is False, and *Subscript* is assigned a random value in the range 1 to *NumberCards*.

Now study these exercises sequentially or randomly.

EXERCISES

1. Modify project Flashcards #3 to obtain project Flashcards #4 - Sequential, Random, or Selected. This project has a third option button captioned "Selected Card" as shown here:

You can click text box txtCardNumber and enter the number of the next card that you want to see, and then click option button Selected Card and command button Next Card to see the selected card. What tasks should event procedure txtCardNumber_Click perform? What happens if you click txtCardNumber and enter 0, or –1, or a number greater than the number of cards (value of *NumberCards*)?

2. Oh, you don't want to learn Japanese? How about Spanish? If yes, grab a good Spanish-English dictionary and load arrays *SideA( )* and *SideB( )* with the words or phrases that you want to learn. Or pick another subject.

THE PEOPLE'S POLL USES CONTROL ARRAYS TO TALLY ANSWERS

Imagine that you are assigned the task of polling people at a computer fair to obtain and tally answers to these questions:

1. Does your computer understand you?

2. What languages do you understand?

You can use project People's Poll #1 to obtain and tally answers to the first question. At run time, it begins like this:

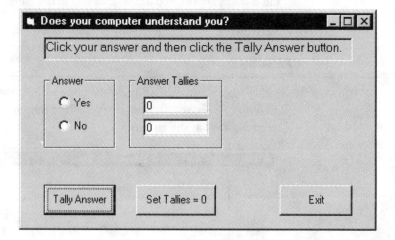

Text boxes display the number of yes and no responses, (initially zero for both). Click the Yes option button in the Answer box and then click the Tally Answer button to increase the affirmative tally by one. Click the No option button in the Answer box and then click the Tally Answer button to increase the negative tally by one. Click the Set Tallies = 0 button to start over with zero in both text boxes. Project People's Poll #1 uses option button and text box control arrays to accomplish its task.

A *control array* is a set of controls of the same type. All controls in the array have the same Name property setting. An individual member of the control array is identified by its Index property setting. In Visual Basic code, a member of a control array is identified by the name of the control array and an index enclosed in parentheses. Project People's Poll #1's option button and text box control arrays are listed in Table 10-8.

Control Type	Name	Index	Name(Index)
Option button	optAnswer	0	optAnswer(0)
Option button	optAnswer	1	optAnswer(1)
Text box	txtTally	0	txtTally(0)
Text box	txtTally	1	txtTally(1)

TABLE 10-8   *Control Arrays for Project People's Poll #1* ▼

Draw the project's visual interface. Change the form's caption to "Does your computer understand you?" and draw a label with the caption "Click your answer and then click the Tally Answer button." Add the three command buttons. We named them cmdTallyAnswer, cmdZeroTallies, and cmdExit.

The option button and text box control arrays are inside frames. Draw the frame captioned "Answer" and then create the option button control array:

1. Draw option buttons Option1 and Option2 inside the frame.

2. Change the name of Option1 to optAnswer.

3. Change the name of Option2 to optAnswer. This is the same name as the other option button, so Visual Basic asks if you want to create a control array:

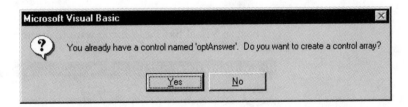

4. Click the Yes button to create the option button control array.

You have created a control array with elements optAnswer(0) and optAnswer(1). Finish designing this array so that the two option buttons have the property settings shown in Table 10-9.

Option Button	Property	Setting	Comment
Upper button	Caption	Yes	
	Name	optAnswer	
	Index	0	
	TabIndex	1	See note below.
	Value	False	Not selected at run time.
Lower button	Caption	No	
	Name	optAnswer	
	Index	1	
	TabIndex	2	See note below.
	Value	False	Not selected at run time.

TABLE 10-9   *Option Button Array Specifications for Project People's Poll #1* ▼

 NOTE *If an option button's TabIndex property setting is 0, then it will be selected at run time even though its Value property setting is False. Therefore, make sure that neither option button has a TabIndex setting of 0.*

Draw the frame captioned "Answer Tallies" and then create the text box control array:

1. Draw text boxes Text1 and Text2 inside the frame.

2. Change the name of Text1 to txtTally.

3. Change the name of Text2 to txtTally. This is the same name as the other text box, so Visual Basic asks if you want to create a control array:

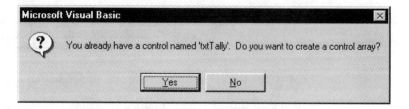

4. Click the Yes button to create the text box control array.

You have created a control array with elements txtTally(0) and txtTally(1). Finish designing this array so that the two text boxes have the property settings shown in Table 10-10. Table 10-11 lists the event procedure specifications for the form and the command buttons.

Event procedure Form_Load uses a **For...Next** loop to set *txtTally(0).Text* and *txtTally(1).Text* to zero:

```
Private Sub Form_Load()

  ' Set tallies to zero
  For k = 0 To 1
    txtTally(k).Text = 0
  Next k

End Sub


For k = 0 To 12
```

Event procedure cmdTallyAnswer_Click uses a **For...Next** loop to examine the option button array. If an option button is selected, the procedure increases the corresponding tally:

```
Private Sub cmdTallyAnswer_Click()

  ' Increase tally for the selected option button (if any)
  For k = 0 To 1
    If optAnswer(k).Value = True Then
      txtTally(k).Text = txtTally(k).Text + 1
    End If
  Next k

End Sub
```

Option Button	Property	Setting	Comment
Upper text box	Name	txtTally	
	Index	0	
	Text		Set to 0 by the Form_Load procedure.
Lower text box	Name	txtTally	
	Index	1	
	Text		Set to 0 by the Form_Load procedure.

TABLE 10-10   *Text Box Array Specifications for Project People's Poll #1* ▼

Object Name	Event	Response
frmPoll01	Load	Sets txtTally(0).Text and txtTally(1).Text to 0.
cmdTallyAnswer	Click	If an option button is selected, increases the corresponding tally by 1.
cmdZeroTallies	Click	Sets txtTally(0).Text and txtTally(1).Text to 0.
cmdExit	Click	Ends the run.

TABLE 10-11 *Event Procedure Specifications for Project People's Poll #1* ▼

Event procedure cmdTallyAnswer_Click uses a **For...Next** loop to set the tallies to zero:

```
Private Sub cmdZeroTallies_Click()

  ' Set tallies to zero
  For k = 0 To 1
    txtTally(k).Text = 0
  Next k

End Sub
```

Project People's Poll #2 has the right stuff for obtaining and tallying answers to the second question, "What languages do you understand?" At run time, it begins like this:

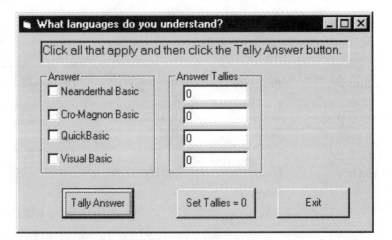

This project has a check box array and a text box array. Click the Tally Answer button to increase the tallies corresponding to all checked check boxes. Table 10-12 lists the control array specifications and Table 10-13 lists the event procedure specs for the project.

Object Name	Property	Setting	Comment
chkAnswer(0)	Caption	Neanderthal Basic	
	Name	chkAnswer	
	Index	0	
	Value	0 - Unchecked	Not checked at run time.
chkAnswer(1)	Caption	Cro-Magnon Basic	
	Name	chkAnswer	
	Index	1	
	Value	0 - Unchecked	Not checked at run time.
chkAnswer(2)	Caption	QuickBasic	
	Name	chkAnswer	
	Index	2	
	Value	0 - Unchecked	Not checked at run time.
chkAnswer(3)	Caption	Visual Basic	
	Name	chkAnswer	
	Index	3	
	Value	0 - Unchecked	Not checked at run time.
txtTally(0)	Name	txtTally	
	Index	0	
	Text		Set to zero during Form_Load.
txtTally(1)	Name	txtTally	
	Index	1	
	Text		Set to zero during Form_Load.
txtTally(2)	Name	txtTally	
	Index	2	
	Text		Set to zero during Form_Load.
txtTally(3)	Name	txtTally	
	Index	3	
	Text		Set to zero during Form_Load.

TABLE 10-12   *Control Array Specifications for Project People's Poll #2* ▼

Object Name	Event	Response
frmPoll02	Load	Sets txtTally(0).Text through txtTally(3).Text to 0.
cmdTallyAnswer	Click	If a check box is checked, increases the corresponding tally by 1.
cmdZeroTallies	Click	Sets txtTally(0).Text through txtTally(3).Text to 0.
cmdExit	Click	Ends the run.

TABLE 10-13 *Event Procedure Specifications for Project People's Poll #2* ▼

Event procedures Form_Load and cmdZeroTallies_Click should look familiar. They are the same as in project People's Poll #1 except for the upper limit of the **For** statement.

```
Private Sub Form_Load()

  ' Set tallies to zero
  For k = 0 To 3
    txtTally(k).Text = 0
  Next k

End Sub

Private Sub cmdZeroTallies_Click()

  ' Set tallies to zero
  For k = 0 To 3
    txtTally(k).Text = 0
  Next k

End Sub
```

Event procedure cmdTallyAnswer_Click increases the tallies that correspond to checked check boxes. If a check box is checked, then its Value property setting is 1, as shown here:

```
Private Sub cmdTallyAnswer_Click()

  ' Increase tally for every checked (Value = 1) check box
  For k = 0 To 3
    If chkAnswer(k).Value = 1 Then
```

```
        txtTally(k).Text = txtTally(k).Text + 1
    End If
Next k

End Sub
```

Your best option now is to check out these exercises.

1. Add another question or two to project People's Poll #1. To do so, add appropriate option buttons and text boxes to the project's control arrays. New answers that occurred to us are "Sometimes," "None of your business," and "None of the above." Call this project People's Poll #3.

2. Add another language or two or more to project People's Poll #2. To do so, add appropriate check boxes and text boxes to the project's control arrays. Visual C? Esperanto? Call this project People's Poll #4.

10.6 **D**YNAMIC ARRAYS ENABLE BETTER WAYS

The data arrays used in the fortune cookie and flashcard projects are *static arrays*. They are dimensioned by **Dim** statements that use specific numeric values for the smallest and largest indexes:

```
Dim SideA(1 To 100) As String, SideB(1 To 100) As String
```

Each of these static arrays can have up to 100 elements. If you try to assign a value to *Fortune(101)* or *SideA(101)* or *SideB(101),* you will see a "Subscript out of range" error message. When you use static arrays, you sometimes must guess at the maximum number of elements in the array. If your guess is too small—trouble. If your guess is too large, you may waste precious memory space.

As usual, Visual Basic provides a better way. Instead of using static arrays, you can create *dynamic arrays* that grow or shrink as required to get the work done. To dimension an array as a dynamic array, you use the array's name followed by empty parentheses in a **Dim** statement. For example, the statement

```
Dim SideA() As String, SideB() As String
```

dimensions *SideA( )* and *SideB( )* as dynamic string arrays.

Once you have created a dynamic array, you can use a **ReDim** statement in a procedure to *redimension* the array to the size that is just right for that procedure. You can even use variables to specify the smallest or largest index, or both. For example, these statements

```
NumberCards = 7
ReDim SideA(1 To NumberCards) As String
ReDim SideB(1 To NumberCards) As String
```

redimension *SideA( )* as a string array with elements *SideA(1)* to *SideA(7)* and *SideB( )* as a string array with elements *SideB(1)* To *SideB(7)*. Want a bigger or smaller array? Easily done—just change the value of *NumberCards*.

Let's redesign project Flashcards #1 using dynamic arrays. Project Flashcards #5 - Sequential has essentially the same visual interface as project Flashcards #1. The changes are in the form's module-level declarations and event procedure Form_Load. Here are the module-level declarations:

```
Dim SideA() As String, SideB() As String    ' Dynamic arrays
Dim NumberCards As Integer, Subscript As Integer
```

Event procedure Form_Load redimensions dynamic duo *SideA( )* and *SideB( )* using integer variable *NumberCards*:

```
Private Sub Form_Load()

    ' Redimension dynamic arrays SideA() and SideB()
    NumberCards = 7
    ReDim SideA(1 To NumberCards) As String
    ReDim SideB(1 To NumberCards) As String

    ' Assign values to arrays SideA() and SideB()
    SideA(1) = "Nihon'go"
    SideB(1) = "Japanese language"
    SideA(2) = "Ohayo gozaimasu"
    SideB(2) = "Good morning"
    SideA(3) = "Kon'nichi wa"
    SideB(3) = "Hello or Good day"
    SideA(4) = "Kon'ban wa"
    SideB(4) = "Good evening"
    SideA(5) = "Oyasumi nasai"
    SideB(5) = "Good night"
    SideA(6) = "Ja, mata ashita"
    SideB(6) = "Well, I'll see you again tomorrow"
    SideA(7) = "Sayonara"
```

```
SideB(7) = "Goodbye"

' Enable Side A button and disable Side B button
cmdNextSideA.Enabled = True
cmdNextSideB.Enabled = False

End Sub
```

That's all. The command button event procedures remain the same. Make the changes and Nihon'go o naraimasu (study Japanese). You can modify this project to create the next project.

Project Flashcards #2 - Random picks flashcards randomly from arrays. Thus it is possible to see the same card more than once. Another way to design a random flashcard project is to first shuffle the flashcard arrays and then select flashcards from the shuffled array sequentially. In this way, no card is repeated during one pass through the cards. Project Flashcards #6 - Random has a Shuffle button that shuffles the cards.

You can quickly modify project Flashcards #5 to get this project. Add a **Randomize** statement to event procedure Form_Load. Event procedures cmdNextSideA_Click, and cmdNextSideB_Click remain the same as before. Add the Shuffle button and its event procedure:

```
Private Sub cmdShuffle_Click()

  ' Shuffle the arrays SideA() and SideB()
  Dim k As Integer RandomIndex As Integer, Temp As String

  For k = 1 To NumberCards
```

```
' Swap card k with a random card
RandomIndex = Fix(NumberCards * Rnd) + 1

' Swap side A
Temp = SideA(k)
SideA(k) = SideA(RandomIndex)
SideA(RandomIndex) = Temp

' Swap side B
Temp = SideB(k)
SideB(k) = SideB(RandomIndex)
SideB(RandomIndex) = Temp

' Enable the SideA button and disable the Side B button
cmdNextSideA.Enabled = True
cmdNextSideB.Enabled = False

    Next k

End Sub
```

After saving project Flashcards #6, shuffle on down to the exercises.

EXERCISES

1. Suppose that you want to study the names and symbols of elements in the periodic table of elements by assigning names of elements (Hydrogen, Helium, Lithium, Beryllium, Boron, Carbon, and so on) to array *SideA( )* and symbols (H, He, Li, Be, B, C, etc.) to array *SideB( )*. A periodical table in a 1995 high school chemistry book lists 109 elements. How can you modify project Flashcards #5 or Flashcards #6 for this task?

2. How does event procedure cmdShuffle_Click work?

10.7 SORT AN ARRAY

You may want to arrange the values in an array into a specific order, such as alphabetical. A *sort* is a procedure that orders an array. For example, a small array of four elements might be in the order shown here:

Elements(1)	Hydrogen
Elements(2)	Helium
Elements(3)	Lithium
Elements(4)	Beryllium

We want to sort the array alphabetically.

Elements(1)	Beryllium
Elements(2)	Helium
Elements(3)	Hydrogen
Elements(4)	Lithium

The *selection sort* is a simple sort that begins with the first element of an array, compares its value with each of the other elements, and swaps their values if they are out of order. The second element is then compared with each element that has a higher index. Out of order values are swapped. This process keeps going and going and going until the list is completely ordered. The steps for each pass through an array of four elements are shown here. This is the original array:

Elements(1)	Hydrogen
Elements(2)	Helium
Elements(3)	Lithium
Elements(4)	Beryllium

Compare the first array value and the second array value. Are they in alphabetical order? No, so swap them. The array now looks like this:

Elements(1)	Helium
Elements(2)	Hydrogen
Elements(3)	Lithium
Elements(4)	Beryllium

Compare the first array value and the third array value. Are they in alphabetical order? Yes, so don't swap them.

Compare the first array value and the fourth array value. Are they in alphabetical order? No, so swap them.

Elements(1)	Beryllium
Elements(2)	Hydrogen
Elements(3)	Lithium
Elements(4)	Helium

The alphabetically first value is now in *Elements(1)*. Use the same process to put the alphabetically second string in *Elements(2)*.

Compare the second array value and the third array value. Are they in alphabetical order? Yes, so don't swap them.

Compare the second array value and the fourth array value. Are they in alphabetical order? No, so swap them.

Elements(1)	Beryllium
Elements(2)	Helium
Elements(3)	Lithium
Elements(4)	Hydrogen

The alphabetically first string is now in *Elements(1)* and the alphabetically second string is in *Elements(2)*. Use the same process to put the alphabetically third string in *Elements(3)*.

Compare the third array value and the fourth array value. Are they in alphabetical order? No, so swap them.

Elements(1)	Beryllium
Elements(2)	Helium
Elements(3)	Hydrogen
Elements(4)	Lithium

The array is now in alphabetical order.

Project Sort #7 - Sort an Array has command buttons that you can click to print, shuffle, or sort an array. Run the project and click the Print Array button to see the following screen:

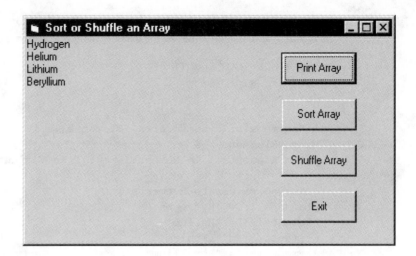

Click the Sort Array button and then click the Print Array button to see the array sorted into alphabetical order. Click the Shuffle Array button and then click the Print Array button to see the shuffled array. Table 10-14 lists the project's event procedure specifications. The project has module-level declarations that dimension *Elements( )* as a dynamic variant array and *NumberElements* as an integer variable:

```
Dim Elements() As Variant    ' Dynamic array
Dim NumberElements As Integer
```

Object Name	Event	Response
frmSort07	Load	Randomizes **Rnd**, redimensions Elements( ), and Assigns values to the array.
cmdPrintArray	Click	Prints Elements( ) on the form.
cmdSortArray	Click	Sorts Elements( ) into alphabetical order.
cmdShuffleArray	Click	Shuffles Elements( ) into random order.
cmdExit	Click	Ends the run.

TABLE 10-14 *Event Procedure Specifications for Project Sort #7 - Sort an Array* ▼

Event procedure Form_Load randomizes the **Rnd** function, redimensions *Elements( )*, and assigns values to the array variables, as shown here:

```
Private Sub Form_Load()

    Randomize

    ' Redimension dynamic array Elements()
    NumberElements = 4
    ReDim Elements(1 To NumberElements) As Variant

    ' Assign values to Elements()
    Elements(1) = "Hydrogen"
    Elements(2) = "Helium"
    Elements(3) = "Lithium"
    Elements(4) = "Beryllium"

End Sub
```

Event procedure cmdPrintArray_Click prints the elements of *Elements( )* from its smallest subscript to its largest subscript:

```
Private Sub cmdPrintArray_Click()

    ' Print array Elements() from its smallest index (1)
    ' to its largest index, UBound(Elements)

    Dim k As Integer

    Cls

    For k = 1 To UBound(Elements)
      Print Elements(k)
    Next k

End Sub
```

The **UBound** function is a numeric function of an array argument; it returns the largest index of the array. **UBound**'s argument is the name of the array without parentheses. In the Form_Load procedure, *Elements( )* is redimensioned to have indexes 1 to 4, so the value of **UBound***(Elements)* is 4.

Event procedure cmdShuffleArray_Click shuffles *Elements( )* from its smallest index (1) to its largest index, which is calculated by the **UBound** function:

```
Private Sub cmdShuffleArray_Click()

  ' Shuffle array Elements() from its smallest index (1)
  ' to its largest index, UBound(Elements)

  Dim k As Integer, Temp As Variant

  For k = 1 To UBound(Elements)
    RndIndex = Fix(UBound(Elements) * Rnd) + 1
    Temp = Elements(k)
    Elements(k) = Elements(RndIndex)
    Elements(RndIndex) = Temp
  Next k

End Sub
```

Event procedure cmdSortArray_Click sorts array *Elements( )* into alphabetical order from its smallest index (1) to its largest index, which is calculated by the **UBound** function.

```
Private Sub cmdSortArray_Click()

  ' Sort array Elements() from its smallest index (1)
  ' to its largest index, UBound(Elements)
  ' Sort is alphabetical regardless of upper- or lowercase

  Dim i As Integer, j As Integer, Temp As Variant

  For i = 1 To UBound(Elements) - 1

    For j = i + 1 To UBound(Elements)

      If LCase(Elements(j)) < LCase(Elements(i)) Then

        ' Swap values of Elements(i) and Elements(j)
        Temp = Elements(i)
        Elements(i) = Elements(j)
        Elements(j) = Temp
      End If

    Next j

  Next i

End Sub
```

The procedure sports nested **For...Next** loops. The outer loop controls the number of passes through the array. The inner loop controls the number of comparisons made for each pass of the outer loop. An **If...End If** structure in the inner **For...Next** loop contains the comparison and swaps the compared elements if they are out of order. Notice the use of the **LCase** function in the comparisons to ensure that strings are compared alphabetically, regardless of case.

EXERCISE

1. Create project Sort #8 - Long Integers. Use input boxes to acquire the values of the long integer array *LongInt( )*, which has elements *LongInt(1)* through *LongInt(n)*. We suggest command buttons captioned "Enter Array," "Print Array," "Sort Array," and "Shuffle Array."

   a. Event procedure cmdEnterArray_Click displays an input box to acquire the number of elements (*n*) in the array and then redimensions the array. It then displays input boxes to acquire the values of *LongInt(1)* through *LongInt(n)*.

   b. Event procedure cmdPrintArray_Click prints the array on the form or in a picture box—your choice.

   c. Event procedure cmdSortArray_Click sorts the array.

   d. Event procedure cmdShuffleArray_Click shuffles the array.

10.8 *P*ASS ARRAYS TO PUBLIC SUB PROCEDURES

Let's generalize. Let's create form-level **Public Sub** procedures to print, shuffle, and sort an array and then call them from event procedures. Project Sort #9 - Public Procedures looks and works like project Sort #7. At run time you see the same visual interface:

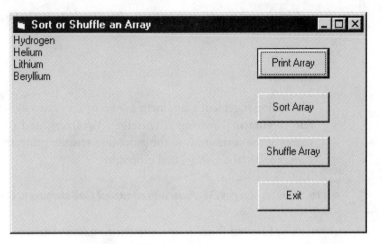

The project's form-level declarations and Form_Load procedure are the same as those of project Sort #7. Click the Print Array button and its event procedure calls form-level **Public Sub** PrintArray, which prints the *Elements( )* array. This is event procedure cmdPrintArray_Click:

```
Private Sub cmdPrintArray_Click()

  ' Call PrintArray procedure to print array Elements()

  PrintArray Elements()

End Sub
```

The statement

```
PrintArray Elements()
```

calls **Public Sub** PrintArray and passes the array *Elements( )* to the procedure. *Elements( )* is passed by reference to PrintArray. The calling statement passes the memory location and other information about the array to the procedure, which then goes to work:

```
Public Sub PrintArray(VarArray() As Variant)

  ' Print VarArray() from LBound(VarArray) to UBound(VarArray)

  Dim k As Integer

  Cls
```

```
    For k = LBound(VarArray) To UBound(VarArray)
      Print VarArray(k)
    Next k

End Sub
```

The calling statement's argument *Elements( )* is passed by reference to the **Public Sub**'s argument *VarArray( )*. Therefore, *VarArray( )* and *Elements( )* are both names of the same array, so the procedure actually prints the values assigned to *Elements( )* in the Form_Load procedure.

 NOTE *You can also call PrintArray with an explicit **Call** statement: **Call** PrintArray (Elements( )).*

The **LBound** function is a numeric function of an array argument; it returns the smallest index of the array. **LBound**'s argument is the name of the array without parentheses. In the Form_Load procedure, *Elements( )* is redimensioned to have subscripts 1 to 4, so the value of **LBound**(*VarArray*) is 1, the same as **LBound**(*Elements*).

Click the Sort Array button and its event procedure calls form-level **Public Sub** AlphaSortArray, which sorts the *Elements( )* array alphabetically. Here is event procedure cmdSortArray_Click:

```
Private Sub cmdSortArray_Click()

  ' Call AlphaSortArray procedure to sort array Elements()

  AlphaSortArray Elements()

End Sub
```

The statement

```
AlphaSortArray Elements()
```

calls **Public Sub** AlphaSortArray and passes the array *Elements( )* to the procedure. *Elements( )* is passed by reference to AlphaSortArray. The calling statement passes the memory location and other information about the array to the procedure, which then goes to work:

```
Public Sub AlphaSortArray(VarArray() As Variant)

  ' Sort VarArray() from LBound (VarArray) to UBound (VarArray)
  ' Sort is alphabetical regardless of upper- or lowercase
```

```
Dim i As Integer, j As Integer, Temp As Variant

For i = LBound(VarArray) To UBound(VarArray) - 1

  For j = i + 1 To UBound(VarArray)

    If LCase(VarArray(j)) < LCase(VarArray(i)) Then
      ' Swap the values of VarArray(i) and VarArray(j)
      Temp = VarArray(i)
      VarArray(i) = VarArray(j)
      VarArray(j) = Temp
    End If

  Next j

Next i

End Sub
```

Click the Shuffle Array button and its event procedure calls **Public Sub ShuffleArray**. Both procedures are shown here:

```
Private Sub cmdShuffleArray_Click()

  ' Call ShuffleArray procedure to shuffle array Elements()

  ShuffleArray Elements()

End Sub

Public Sub ShuffleArray(VarArray() As Variant)

  ' Shuffle VarArray() into random

  Dim k As Integer, Lo As Integer, Hi As Integer
  Dim Temp As Variant

  For k = LBound(VarArray) To UBound(VarArray)

    ' Calculate random index in the range, Lo to Hi
    Lo = LBound(VarArray)
    Hi = UBound(VarArray)
    RndIndex = Fix((Hi - Lo + 1) * Rnd) + Lo

    ' Swap the values of VarArray(k) and VarArray(RndIndex)
```

```
        Temp = VarArray(k)
        VarArray(k) = VarArray(RndIndex)
        VarArray(RndIndex) = Temp

    Next k

End Sub
```

Hark—the sound you hear is the next exercise calling to you.

EXERCISE

1. Modify project Sort #9 to create project Sort #10 - Public Procedures. Create an appropriate version of **Public Sub** Swap (see Chapter 9) and install it in the form. Modify **Public Subs** ShuffleArray and AlphaSortArray to call Swap to do the swapping. In our project Sort #10, **Public Sub** Swap's first line is this:

```
Public Sub Swap(Variable1 As Variant, Variable2 As Variant)
```

In **Public Sub** ShuffleArray, we call **Public Sub** Swap this way:

```
Swap VarArray(k), VarArray(RndIndex)
```

In **Public Sub** AlphaSortArray, we call **Public Sub** Swap this way:

```
Swap VarArray(i), VarArray(j)
```

10.9 # *U*SE CONTROL ARRAYS IN PROJECT HIGH, LOW, AND AVERAGE

Project High, Low, Average #1 finds and displays the high, low, and average of a week's worth of temperatures. Here is a sample run after someone has entered seven temperatures and then clicked the High, Low, and Average buttons:

Temperatures for Sunday through Saturday are entered into text box array txtDay(), which has a corresponding array of labels, lblDay(). The high, low, and average temperatures are displayed in individual textboxes txtHigh, txtLow, and txtAverage. We called the command buttons cmdHigh, cmdLow, cmdAverage, cmdClearAll, and cmdExit.

Start a new project and put the text box array on the form. To do this, you will draw the first text box and set its properties, and then use the Edit menu's Copy and Paste commands to make six copies of this text box. Do it with these steps:

1. Draw the first text box. Make it the size you want, set its Name property to txtDay and its Text property to empty. Move it to where you want it.

2. While txtDay is selected, click the Edit menu and then click its Copy command to copy txtDay to the clipboard.

3. Click the Edit menu and then click its Paste command to paste a copy of txtDay on the form. Visual Basic displays a dialog box with the message: You already have a control named 'txtDay'. Do you want to create a control array?

4. Click the Yes button. A copy of txtDay appears in the upper-left corner of the form. Move it to its place below the original txtDay. Control array elements txtDay(0) and txtDay(1) are now in place. They are identical except for their Index property settings.

5. Use the Edit menu's Paste command to make five more copies and move them to their places.

Control array txtDay() is now in place. Next, create control array lblDay() with these steps:

1. Draw the first label. Make it the size you want, set its Name property to lblDay and its Alignment property to 1 - Right Justify. Move it to the left of txtDay(0).

2. While lblDay is selected, click the Edit menu and then click its Copy command to copy lblDay to the clipboard.

3. Click the Edit menu and then click its Paste command to paste a copy of lblDay on the form. Visual Basic displays a dialog box with the message: You already have a control named 'lblDay'. Do you want to create a control array?

4. Click the Yes button. A copy of lblDay appears in the upper-left corner of the form. Move it to its place below the original lblDay. Control array elements lblDay(0) and lblDay(1) are now in place. They are identical except for their Index property settings. For example, both captions are "Label1."

5. Use the Edit menu's Paste command to make five more copies and move them to their places.

6. Click each element of lblDay() and set its Caption property to the appropriate day of the week: Sunday, Monday, and so on.

Complete the visual interface by drawing the individual command buttons, text boxes, and labels. Table 10-15 lists the project's event procedure specifications.

Object Name	Event	Response
txtDay	Click	Clears itself and accepts focus (any element of array).
cmdHigh	Click	Finds the highest number in txtDay() and displays it in txtHigh.
cmdLow	Click	Finds the lowest number in txtDay() and displays it in txtLow.
cmdAverage	Click	Calculates the average of the numbers in txtDay() and displays it in txtAverage.
cmdClearAll	Click	Clears all text boxes.
cmdExit	Click	Ends the run.

TABLE 10-15 *Event Procedure Specifications for Project High, Low, Average #1* ▼

Control array txtDay has one event procedure that works when you click any of the seven boxes. In the Design screen, double-click any element of txtDay() to obtain its event procedure template.

```
Private Sub txtDay_Change(Index As Integer)
|
End Sub
```

Because this event procedure is for a control array, Visual Basic displays the argument *Index As Integer* in the **Private Sub** template. This argument is the setting of the Index property of the selected text box, 0 to 6 for array txtDay( ). The default event for a text box is Change, not the one you want. Change "Change" to "Click" and complete the event procedure so that it looks like this:

```
Private Sub txtDay_Click(Index As Integer)

  txtDay(Index).Text = ""

End Sub
```

We'll show event procedures cmdHigh_Click and cmdAverage_Click, but leave cmdLow_Click and cmdClearAll_Click for you to do in the exercises. Here are cmdHigh_Click and cmdAverage_Click:

```
Private Sub cmdHigh_Click()

  ' Display highest value in txtDay() in txtHigh

  Dim High As Single, Day As Integer

  High = txtDay(0).Text

  For Day = 1 To 6
    If txtDay(Day) > High Then
      High = txtDay(Day).Text
    End If
  Next Day

  txtHigh.Text = High

End Sub
```

```
Private Sub cmdAverage_Click()

  ' Calculate the average of the numbers in txtDay()

  Dim Total As Single, Average As Single, Day As Integer

  Total = 0

  For Day = 0 To 6
    Total = Total + txtDay(Day)
  Next Day

  Average = Total / 7

  txtAverage.Text = Average

End Sub
```

After you do these exercises with your usual high level of work, project High, Low, and Average #1 will be complete.

---

1. Write event procedure cmdLow_Click.

2. Write event procedure cmdClearAll_Click. It should clear all 10 text boxes.

mastery

skills check

1. List the individual array variable defined by each **Dim** statement. For c, d, and e, list the first two array variables, an ellipsis (...), and the last array variable:

   a. Dim TallyD6(6) As Integer

   b. Dim TallyD6(1 To 6) As Long

   c. Dim Tally3D6(3 To 18) As Long

    d. Dim AtomicMass(1 To 109) As Single

    e. Dim IRS(1990 To 2001) As Currency

2. For each set of array variables, write a **Dim** statement to dimension the array:

    a. Integer array: MonthDays(1), MonthDays(2), ..., MonthDays(12)

    b. Long integer array: TwoCoins(0), TwoCoins(1), TwoCoins(2), TwoCoins(3)

    c. Double-precision array: PrimeNumber(1), PrimeNumber(2), ..., PrimeNumber(100000)

    d. Currency array: Price(1000), Price(1001), ..., Price(9999)

    e. String array: MonthName(1), MonthName(2), ..., MonthName(12)

    f. Variant array: ThisNThat(–1), ThisNThat(0), ThisNThat(1), ..., ThisNThat(37)

3. Projects in this chapter have used these types of control arrays: option button arrays, check box arrays, text box arrays, and label arrays. Create project QBColor #4 - Button Array. It has a control array of 16 command buttons, cmdQBColor(0) through cmdQBColor(15), captioned "QBColor 0," QBColor 1," QBColor 2," and so on, up to "QBColor 15." Click a button and event procedure cmdQBColor_Click sets the form's BackColor to the QBColor number on the button.

4. You can pass a data array to a **Function** procedure the same way that you pass an array to a **Sub** procedure. The **Function** procedure processes the array and returns a result. For example, a **Function** procedure called Maximum returns the largest number in a double-precision array. This is the first line of **Public Function** Maximum:

```
Public Function Maximum(NumberArray() As Double) As Double
```

Once Maximum is installed, you can use it to obtain the maximum value in a double-precision array that you create. For example, you can create a double-precision array called *NumberArray( )* and print its maximum value like this:

```
Print Maximum(NumberArray())
```

    a. Start a new project, write **Public Function** Maximum, and install it in the form.

    b. Write **Public Function** Minimum and install it in the form. Minimum returns the smallest number in a double-precision array.

   c. Write **Public Function** Average and install it in the form. Average returns the average of the numbers in a double-precision array.

   d. Create project MaxMinAvg #1 to test your Function procedures.

5. An anagram is a scrambling of the letters in a word. For example, here are 10 anagrams of "anagram":

nmaarga	agamarn	gaaramn	nagmaar	armnaga
agnmara	gaanmar	nrgaama	nmargaa	gnramaa

Create project Anagram #1 to print anagrams of a word. Use a text box to acquire the word to be scrambled and then click the Anagram button to display an anagram of the word in another text box. Each time you click, you see another anagram.

6. If you roll three six-sided dice (3D6), the possible outcomes for one roll are 3 to 18. If you roll three dice 1000 times, or 2000 times, or 10,000 times, will each possible outcome occur about the same number of times? Investigate this problem by simulating the number of rolls you want and tallying the outcomes. Statisticians call this a *frequency distribution*. Create project Frequency Distribution #2 - 3D6. You enter the number of simulated rolls of 3D6 that you want, click the Roll Dice button and see the results printed on the form, in a picture box, or wherever you want them to appear. Here are some of the results that we saw for 5000 simulated rolls:

Outcome	Frequency
3	30
4	68
5	139
.	.
.	.
.	.
17	64
18	18

11

Add Tools to Your Visual Basic Backpack

chapter objectives

11.1 Use built-in constants and constants that you define

11.2 Graph some math functions

11.3 Use list boxes to manage lists of items

11.4 Use combo boxes to manage lists of items

11.5 Step through code and watch expressions

11.6 Anticipate and trap errors

11.7 Use the drive, directory, and file list boxes to find files

11.8 Look onward

Y OUR journey on the road to Visual Basic literacy is going well. You are approaching the summit of the first range of mountains and you will soon see what lies beyond. In this chapter, you will sample a variety of tools and techniques. This chapter has no exercises. Instead, we'll encourage you to browse the Help system for more information. Grab your backpack and move strongly onward.

11.1 *U*SE BUILT-IN CONSTANTS AND CONSTANTS THAT YOU DEFINE

Visual Basic provides built-in *mnemonic* (memory-assisting) constants that you can use in place of cryptic numbers. For example, you can use *True* instead of –1 and *False* instead of 0 as the value of a variable that can be true or false. Now you will learn about more built-in constants and how to use the **Const** statement to define constants that you can use in your projects.

You can display message boxes that contain icons to indicate the type of message being displayed, from simple information to an emphatic warning that something dire might happen. Here are four types of message box statements:

Statement	Description of Message Box
MsgBox Msg, 16, Title	Critical box (Danger!). Displays a stop sign icon.
MsgBox Msg, 32, Title	Question box. Displays a question mark icon.
MsgBox Msg, 48, Title	Exclamation box. Displays an exclamation point icon.
MsgBox Msg, 64, Title	Information box. Displays the letter *i* as an icon

The numbers 16, 32, 48, and 64 specify the icon displayed in the message box. When you write a **MsgBox** statement, you can look up the number or guess and try. There's an easier way—use built-in, easy-to-remember constants instead of enigmatic numbers:

Constant	Value	Description
vbCritical	16	Displays stop sign icon.
vbQuestion	32	Displays question mark icon.
vbExclamation	48	Displays exclamation point icon.
vbInformation	64	Displays the letter *i* as an icon.

Use these constants to write less cryptic, more readable code:

Cryptic Code	More Readable Code
MsgBox Msg, 16, Title	MsgBox Msg, vbCritical, Title
MsgBox Msg, 32, Title	MsgBox Msg, vbQuestion, Title
MsgBox Msg, 48, Title	MsgBox Msg, vbExclamation, Title
MsgBox Msg, 64, Title	MsgBox Msg, vbInformation, Title

Built-in constants are always there when you need them. You can use the **Const** statement to create your own mnemonic constants. A **Const** statement assigns a poor approximation of π to the constant named *pi* in this event procedure:

```
Private Sub Command1_Click()
  Const pi = 3.14
  Print pi, VarType(pi)
End Sub
```

Install this procedure and try it. It prints the value of *pi* and its data type. You can see that the default data type is 5, Double, even though the assigned value has only three digits. If you really want to use this poor approximation, you can save a little memory space by using an **As** clause to declare *pi* as data type 4, Single:

```
Const pi As Single = 3.14
```

We recommend that you use a much better approximation of π as the value of *pi* :

```
Const pi As Double = 3.14159265358979
```

Let's declare *pi* as a constant and use it to calculate the circumference and area of a circle, and the surface area and volume of a sphere, all of radius *r*. The following code acquires the value of *r* from a text box and displays the calculated values in text boxes:

```
Private Sub Command1_Click()

  Dim r As Double
  Const pi As Double = 3.14159265358979

  r = txtRadius.Text

  txtCircumference.Text = 2 * pi * r
  txtAreaCircle.Text = pi * r ^ 2
  txtAreaSphere.Text = 4 * pi * r ^ 2
  txtVolume.Text = (4 / 3) * pi * r ^ 3

End Sub
```

In event procedure Command1_Click, *pi* is private to the procedure and not available to another procedure. To make a constant more available, you can put it in the General area of a form module and use **Private** to declare its availability. In a module, the statement

```
Private Const pi As Double = 3.14159265358979
```

declares *pi* to be available to all procedures in that module. (It is not available to other modules in the project.) To make a constant even more available, you can put it in a standard module and use **Public** to declare its availability to all modules in the project.

The statement

```
Public Const pi As Double = 3.14159265358979
```

makes *pi* available to all procedures in all modules of the project.

Here are some **Public** constants that we find useful now and then. Because the default data type for numbers is Double, we omit **As** Double for numbers that we want to be double-precision numbers:

```
Public Const eLogBase = 2.71828182845905   ' Natural log base

Public Const Gravity = 6.673E-11   ' Gravitational constant
Public Const gEarth = 9.78         ' Acceleration, Earth
Public Const gMars = 3.71          ' Acceleration, Mars

Public Const Alphabet As String = "abcdefghijklmnopqrstuvwxyz"
Public Const Consonants As String = "bcdfghjklmnpqrstvwxyz"
Public Const Vowels As String = "aeiou"
```

Visual Basic has a large set of built-in constants. You can use the Object Browser tool to obtain information about them:

1. Click the Object Browser tool on the toolbar to open the Object Browser dialog box.

2. Click the button on the right end of the Libraries/Projects box to drop down its list of items. One of the items in the list is "VB - Visual Basic objects and procedures."

3. Click "VB - Visual Basic objects and procedures." Its list appears in the Classes/Modules box. One of the items is "Constants".

4. In the Classes/Modules box, click Constants. You will see a list of constants in the Methods/Properties list box.

5. Click the question mark button directly below the Classes/Modules box to open the help window called Visual Basic Constants.

6. Browse. Click any topic to view information about that topic.

You can also use the Help system to get information about built-in constants:

1. Click Help on the menu bar and then click Contents to get the Visual Basic Help table of contents.

2. Click Reference Information to get the Reference Information window.

3. In the Reference Information window, scroll down to the Other Information section and click Visual Basic Constants to open the help window called Visual Basic Constants.

4. Browse. Click any topic to view information about that topic.

Perhaps you wonder if you can use a **Const** statement to change one of Visual Basic's built-in constants. Yes, you can, but we recommend that you don't. It's easy to avoid changing a built-in constant. They all begin with "vb," so simply refrain from using "vb" as the first two letters of your constant.

11.2   *GRAPH SOME MATH FUNCTIONS*

Visual Basic has a rich repertoire of functions, including several math functions. Table 11-1 is a short list of math functions.

In Chapter 7, you learned how to use immediate statements in the Debug window. Use immediate statements in the Debug window to try the functions in Table 11-1. For example:

```
Print Exp(1)
 2.71828182845905
```

Function	Description	Example
Abs	Returns the absolute value of its argument.	Abs(–1) = 1
Sqr	Returns the positive square root of its argument.	Sqr(64) = 8
Exp	Returns *e* raised to the power of its argument.	Exp(1) = 2.71828182845905
Log	Returns the logarithm, base e, of its argument.	Log(2.71828182845905) = 1
Cos	Returns the cosine of a radian argument.	Cos(pi / 6) = 0.866025403784439
Sin	Returns the sine of a radian argument.	Sin(pi / 6) = 0.5
Tan	Returns the tangent of a radian argument.	Tan(pi / 6) = 0.577350269189625

TABLE 11-1 *A Short List of Math Functions* ▼

If *pi* is defined by a **Const** statement in the form's General area, you can use it in the Debug window:

```
Print Cos(pi / 6)
 0.866025403784439
```

If *pi* is *not* defined by a **Const** statement in the form's General area, you can assign a value to *pi* as an ordinary variable in the Debug window:

```
pi = 3.14159265358979
Print Cos(pi / 6)
 0.866025403784439
```

 NOTE *You cannot use a **Const** statement in the Debug window. If you do, you will see an exclamation box with the message, "Invalid in the Immediate Pane."*

Project Graphs #1 - Sin, Cos, and Tan has buttons that you can click to draw graphs of the trigonometric functions **Sin**, **Cos**, and **Tan**. The graphs are drawn in picture box Picture1. After you click all three buttons, the form looks like this:

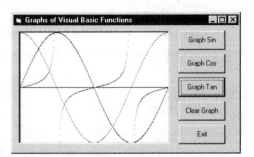

The event procedures use the form-level constant *pi*, which is declared in the General area of the form:

```
Private Const pi As Double = 3.14159265358979
```

The Graph Sin button's event procedure is shown here:

```
Private Sub cmdSin_Click()

  Dim x As Double, y As Double

  ' Coordinates of left-upper and right-lower corners
  Picture1.Scale (0, 1)-(2 * pi, -1)

  ' Draw x- And y-axes
  Picture1.Line (0, 0)-(2 * pi, 0)   ' x-axis
  Picture1.Line (0, -1)-(0, 1)       ' y-axis

  DeltaX = 1 / 64    ' Step size of x in For...Next

  ' Plot graph from left edge to right edge of Picture1
  for x = 0 To 2 * pi Step DeltaX
    y = Sin(x)
    picture1.PSet (x, y), vbBlue
  Next x

End Sub
```

This procedure uses the **Scale** method to define the coordinate system of picture box Picture1. The statement

```
Picture1.Scale (0, 1)-(2 * pi, -1)
```

defines the coordinates of the left-upper corner of Picture1 to be (0, 1) and the coordinates of the right-lower corner to be (2 * *pi*, –1). These coordinates are appropriate for graphing trigonometric functions.

The graph is plotted by a **For...Next** loop with the variable *x*. The step size is predetermined by assigning 1/64 as the value of *DeltaX*. Try other values, such as 1/32, which produces a graph with fewer plotted points, and 1/128, which produces a graph with more plotted points. **Sin**(*x*) is assigned to *y*, and then *x* and *y* are used to plot a point using the **PSet** method. The statement

```
Picture1.PSet (x, y), vbBlue
```

plots one point at coordinates (x, y) in a color specified by the Visual Basic constant, *vbBlue*. We find *vbBlue* much easier to remember than its numeric equivalent, 1.

The event procedure that graphs the **Cos** function is quite similar to the one that graphs the **Sin** function. It uses **Cos**(x) instead of **Sin**(x) to calculate the value of y:

```
Private Sub cmdCos_Click()

  Dim x As Double, y As Double

  ' Coordinates of left-upper and right-lower corners
  Picture1.Scale (0, 1)-(2 * pi, -1)

  ' Draw x- and y-axes
  Picture1.Line (0, 0)-(2 * pi, 0)   ' x-axis
  Picture1.Line (0, -1)-(0, 1)       ' y-axis

  DeltaX = 1 / 64    ' Step size of x in For...Next

  ' Plot graph from left edge to right edge of Picture1
  For x = 0 To 2 * pi Step DeltaX
    y = Cos(x)
    Picture1.PSet (x, y), vbGreen
  Next x

End Sub
```

The procedure for graphing the tangent is a little more complicated. The tangent is undefined and unbounded (some say *infinite*) at $pi / 2$ and $3 * pi / 2$. These values would produce an overflow error and so must be avoided. An **If...End If** structure in event procedure cmdTan_Click avoids this problem:

```
Private Sub cmdTan_Click()

  Dim x As Double, y As Double

  ' Coordinates of left-upper and right-lower corners
  Picture1.Scale (0, 10)-(2 * pi, -10)

  ' Draw x- and y-axes
  Picture1.Line (0, 0)-(2 * pi, 0)   ' x-axis
  Picture1.Line (0, -10)-(0, 10)     ' y-axis
```

```
DeltaX = 1 / 64    ' Step size of x in For...Next

' Plot graph from left edge to right edge of Picture1
For x = 0 To 2 * pi Step DeltaX
   If x <> pi / 2 And x <> 3 * pi / 2 Then
     y = Tan(x)
     Picture1.PSet (x, y), vbRed
   End If
Next x

End Sub
```

Two petite procedures complete the project:

```
Private Sub cmdClearGraph_Click()
  Picture1.Cls
End Sub

Private Sub cmdExit_Click()
  End
End Sub
```

Try graphing **Abs, Sqr, Exp**, or **Log**. Table 11-2 suggests **Scale** statements for these functions.

11.3   USE LIST BOXES TO MANAGE LISTS OF ITEMS

Life is full of lists: grocery lists, to-do lists, and even lists of lists. Always helpful Visual Basic provides the ListBox tool especially designed for creating and managing lists. Look for it in the toolbox:

You can draw a list box on the form, put a list into it, and write code to use the list in various ways. Use the ListBox tool to draw a list box on the form. Make its width 1215 twips and its height about 1785 twips. (That's tall enough to hold the list we have in mind.) List box List1 might look like this on the form:

Function	Scale Statement	Comment
Abs	Picture1.Scale (−2, 2)−(2, −2)	
Sqr	Picture1.Scale (0, 8)−(64, −1)	**Sqr**(x) is undefined for $x < 0$.
Exp	Picture1.Scale (−1, 8)−(2, −1)	
Log	Picture1.Scale (0, 3)−(8, −3)	**Log**(x) is undefined for $x <= 0$.

TABLE 11-2   *Suggested **Scale** Statements for Graphing **Abs**, **Sqr**, **Exp**, and **Log*** ▼

The list box has a short list consisting of one item, "List1." That's not the list we want. Let's put a short list of atomic elements in the list box. The first item in the list is "Elements," the second item is "Hydrogen," the third item is "Helium," and so on to "Carbon." After we enter the list, the list box looks like this:

A list is an array of items. Each item in the list has a ListIndex number. ListIndex numbers are integers, beginning with zero (0) at the top of the list. The following shows the ListIndex numbers for our list:

Item	ListIndex Number
Elements	0
Hydrogen	1
Helium	2
Lithium	3
Beryllium	4
Boron	5
Carbon	6

When designing you can enter a list into a list box by using the list box's List property. List1 now contains only the item "List1." Let's replace that list with the list of elements. Follow these steps:

1. Click the List property and then click its properties button. An empty text box appears with the cursor in its upper-left corner.

2. Type **Elements** and press ENTER. The List property's text box disappears and your entry immediately appears as the first entry in the list box, replacing "List1."

3. Click the List property and then click its properties button. Its text box appears with "Elements" at the top and the cursor on the second line.

4. Type **Hydrogen** and press ENTER. The List property's text box disappears and your entry immediately appears as the second entry in the list box, which now has two items, "Elements" and "Hydrogen."

5. Enter the rest of the items in the list: Helium, Lithium, Beryllium, Boron, and Carbon. The list box should now contain seven items whose ListIndex numbers are 0 to 6.

Add text boxes Text1 and Text2 to the form. Put them to the right of the list box. Together, they look like this in project List Box #1:

The project has three controls, list box List1 and text boxes Text1 and Text2. Next, we want a double-click event procedure for the list box. At run time, when you *double-click* an item in the list box, its ListIndex appears in Text1 and the item itself appears in Text2. Install this code:

```
Private Sub List1_DblClick()
  Text1.Text = List1.ListIndex
  Text2.Text = List1.List(List1.ListIndex)
End
```

Run the project. Click an item in List1 to highlight it—nothing else happens. Double-click an item; its ListIndex number appears in Text1 and the item itself appears in Text2. For example, double-click "Elements." Its ListIndex number, 0, appears in Text1 and "Elements" appears in Text2. Double-click "Hydrogen." Its ListIndex number, 1, appears in Text1 and "Hydrogen" appears in Text2. The statement

```
Text1.Text = List1.ListIndex
```

assigns the ListIndex number of the double-clicked item to Text1.Text. The statement

```
Text2.Text = List1.List(List1.ListIndex)
```

assigns the double-clicked item to Text2.Text. This statement uses *Object.Property* variables *List1.ListIndex* and *List1.List* to select the double-clicked item. Here are some examples:

Item Double-clicked	List1.ListIndex	List1.List(List1.ListIndex)
Elements	0	Elements
Hydrogen	1	Hydrogen
Carbon	6	Carbon

Stop the run, return to the design screen, and decrease the height of the list box so that only the top five items are showing. As soon as you do this, a scroll bar automatically appears on the right side of the list box:

Single-clicking an item selects it (highlights it), but does not cause event procedure List1_DblClick to respond. You can click an item to select it, and then use the Text property (not shown in the Properties window) or the List and ListIndex properties to pluck the selected item. Put Command1 and Command2 on the form and try these event procedures:

```
Private Sub Command1_Click()
  Print List1.Text
End Sub

Private Sub Command2_Click()
  Print List1.List(List1.ListIndex)
End Sub
```

At the beginning of a run, no list item is selected (highlighted). If no item is selected, the value of ListIndex is –1. You can use an **If...End If** structure to determine if an item has been selected:

```
Private Sub Command3_Click()

  If List1.ListIndex <> -1 Then
    Print List1.List(List1.ListIndex)
  Else
    Beep
  End If

End Sub
```

The number of items in the list is available as the value of the ListCount property (not shown in the Properties window). Because ListIndex values begin at zero, the value of ListCount is one more than the ListIndex of the last item in the list. Event procedure Command4_Click prints the entire list:

```
Private Sub Command4_Click()

  Cls
  For Item = 0 To List1.ListCount - 1
    Print List1.List(Item)
  Next Item

End Sub
```

When designing, instead of entering a list manually, you can write code to enter the list at run time. Project List Box #2 has list boxes named lstElements and lstSymbols (the standard prefix for a list box name is *lst*). There are three text boxes named txtListIndex, txtElement, and txtSymbol. Here is the project at run time after someone scrolled down to "Carbon" and double-clicked it:

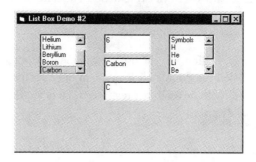

You can click an entry in either list box to display the ListIndex, element name, and element symbol in the three text boxes. Items are entered into the list boxes at run time by event procedure Form_Load:

```
Private Sub Form_Load()

    ' Enter elements list into lstElements
    lstElements.Clear
    lstElements.AddItem "Elements", 0
    lstElements.AddItem "Hydrogen", 1
    lstElements.AddItem "Helium", 2
    lstElements.AddItem "Lithium", 3
    lstElements.AddItem "Beryllium", 4
    lstElements.AddItem "Boron", 5
    lstElements.AddItem "Carbon", 6

    ' Enter symbols list into lstSymbols
    lstSymbols.Clear
    lstSymbols.AddItem "Symbols", 0
    lstSymbols.AddItem "H", 1
    lstSymbols.AddItem "He", 2
    lstSymbols.AddItem "Li", 3
    lstSymbols.AddItem "Be", 4
    lstSymbols.AddItem "B", 5
    lstSymbols.AddItem "C", 6

End Sub
```

The procedure uses the **Clear** method to clear the list boxes and the **AddItem** method to add items to the list boxes. The statement

```
lstElements.Clear
```

clears any list from lstElements. The statement

```
lstElements.AddItem "Helium", 2
```

adds "Helium" to the list in lstElements as the item with ListIndex = 2.

You can double-click any item in either list box to display corresponding items from both boxes in the text boxes. Here are the event procedures that perform that handy task:

```
Private Sub lstElements_DblClick()
  txtListIndex.Text = lstElements.ListIndex
  txtElement.Text = lstElements.List(lstElements.ListIndex)
  txtSymbol.Text = lstSymbols.List(lstElements.ListIndex)
End Sub

Private Sub lstSymbols_DblClick()
  txtListIndex.Text = lstSymbols.ListIndex
  txtElement.Text = lstElements.List(lstSymbols.ListIndex)
  txtSymbol.Text = lstSymbols.List(lstSymbols.ListIndex)
End Sub
```

You can easily create a list and then have Visual Basic automatically sort it alphabetically at run time. To do this, set the Sorted property to True. When you run the project, Visual Basic will sort the list alphabetically.

To remove an item from a list at run time, use the **RemoveItem** method. The statement shown here removes the item whose ListIndex is 3 from list box List1:

```
List1.RemoveItem(3)
```

To learn more about list boxes, search the Help system for ListBox Control, AddItem Method, List Property, ListCount Property, ListIndex Property, RemoveItem Method, Sorted Property, and Text Property.

11.4   U*SE COMBO BOXES TO MANAGE LISTS OF ITEMS*

Combine a list box and a text box and what have you got? A combo box. It has many properties and methods that are the same as those of a list box. You use the toolbox's ComboBox tool to put a combo box on the form:

Combo boxes come in three styles determined by the setting of the Style property: Dropdown Combo (Style 0), Simple Combo (Style 1), and Dropdown List (Style 2). A Dropdown Combo box (Style 0) is shown here at run time before and after clicking its detached arrow button:

Before clicking, you see the text box part of the combo box. After clicking, you see the text box and the list of choices. You can click a choice to enter it into the text box, or type whatever you want directly into the text box.

A Simple Combo box (Style 1) displays its list at all times. If the box's height is too short to show the entire list, a scroll bar is attached to the box:

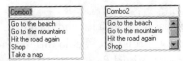

You can click a choice to enter it into the text box, or type whatever you want directly into the text box.

A Dropdown List box (Style 2) is similar to a Dropdown Combo box, except that you can't type text into the text box. You can only select an item from the list.

Project Combo Box #1 - Traveler's Choice provides a Simple Combo box (Style 1) with five choices and a command button that you can click to copy the choice in the combo box's text box to a text box labeled "We will:". Here's the project at run time after someone decided that it was time to move on, clicked "Hit the road again" in the combo box, and then clicked the Copy Combo Box Choice button to copy the choice from the combo box's text box to the "We will:" text box:

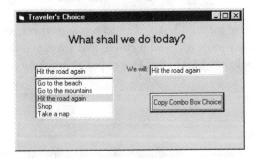

Design the visual interface. Change the combo box's Style property setting to 1 - Simple Combo and enter the list of items as you did in the preceding section for a list box. Install the command button's event procedure:

```
Private Sub Command1_Click()
  Text1.Text = Combo1.Text
End Sub
```

The statement

```
Text1.Text = Combo1.Text
```

copies the item in Combo1's text box into text box Text1.

You generally use a list box to present a list of the *only* choices available to the user. You can use a Dropdown List combo box (Style 2) for this purpose. You usually use a Dropdown Combo box (Style 0) or Simple Combo box (Style 1) to present a list of *suggested* choices. The user can select an item from the list or type another choice into the text box.

Learn more. Search the Help system for the following topics: Combo Box, AddItem Method, List Property, ListCount Property, ListIndex Property, RemoveItem Method, Sorted Property, and Text Property.

11.5 STEP THROUGH CODE AND WATCH EXPRESSIONS

Bugs are pesky critters, especially when they prevent your code from doing what you want it to do. Bugs come in many forms, but perhaps the worst kind are *logic error* bugs. Your code looks correct, runs without invoking any error messages, but produces incorrect results. Oh well, back to the drawing board, or mouse and keyboard in this case.

Fortunately, Visual Basic has a set of handy debugging tools that you can use to find and exterminate bugs. Look for these anti-bug buttons on the toolbar:

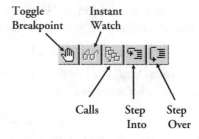

The Step Into tool provides a handy way for you to study the behavior of code by executing one statement at a time. Try it. Start a new project and install this Form_Load procedure:

```
Private Sub Form_Load()
  Form1.Show
  Print Date
  Print Time
  Print "Laran Stardrake"
  Beep
End Sub
```

Starting in the design screen, use the Step Into tool to run this procedure *one step at a time*, with these steps:

1. Click the Step Into button on the toolbar. This runs the project and displays the code window for the Form_Load procedure. The **Private Sub** statement is boxed (enclosed in a rectangular box).

2. Click Step Into. The box moves down to the next statement: **Form1.Show**. This statement is selected (boxed) and ready to be executed.

3. Click Step Into. This executes the **Form.Show** statement and the form appears. If the code window covers the form, move it so you can see the form. In the code window, the box moves to **Print Date**.

4. Click Step Into. The **Print Date** statement is executed and the date appears on the form. The box moves to **Print Time**.

5. Click Step Into. The **Print Time** statement is executed and the time appears on the form. The box moves to the **Print "Laran Stardrake"** statement.

6. Click Step Into. The **Print "Laran Stardrake"** statement is executed and **"Laran Stardrake"** appears on the form. The box moves to **Beep.**

7. Click Step Into. The computer beeps. The box moves to **End Sub.**

8. Click Step Into. The box disappears and the Step Into tool is disabled (dimmed) because there is no more code to step into.

You can *watch* a variable or expression in the Debug window as you step through code. To do so, you use the Add Watch command in the Tools menu:

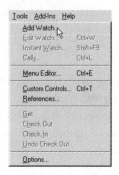

Let's watch the value of the **Time** function in event procedure Form_Load. Follow these steps:

1. In the Form_Load procedure, select **Time**:

   ```
   Print Time
   ```

2. Click the Tools menu and then click Add Watch to open the Add Watch dialog box:

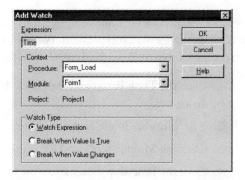

   If all goes well, you'll see "Time" highlighted in the Expression box, "Form_Load" in the Procedure box, and "Form1" in the Module box. If this is not so, you can enter **Time** in the Expression box, select Form1 in the Module box, and select Form_Load in the Procedure box. The Watch Expression button should be selected in the Watch Type box; if it isn't, select it.

3. When everything is as it should be, click OK.

Now step through the Form-Load procedure. As soon as you begin by clicking Step Into, the Debug window appears displaying the *watch expression*. Our expression is as follows:

Expression	Value	Context
Time	12:57:36	Form1.Form_Load

Step through the procedure. Each time you click Step Into, Visual Basic updates the value of the watch expression. Time marches on, so you will see a new value of **Time** each time you click Step Into.

Add command button Command1 and text box Text1 to the form. Install this event procedure:

```
Private Sub Command1_Click()

  Dim Number As Integer

  For Number = 1 To 3
    Text1.Text = Number
  Next Number
  Beep

End Sub
```

Let's watch *Number* while stepping through Command1_Click. Try a different way of adding the watch expression, *Number*. Don't select *Number* in event procedure Command1_Click. Instead, do this:

1. Click the Tools menu and then click Add Watch to open the Add Watch dialog box.

2. Type **Number** in the Expression box.

3. Click the Module box's arrow button and select Form1 from its list.

4. Click the Procedure box's arrow button and select Command1 from its list.

5. Click OK.

You can now watch two expressions, **Time** and *Number*. First step through the Form_Load procedure (think of this as review):

▼ Click the Step Into button on the toolbar. The Debug window should show these two watch expressions:

Expression	Value	Context
Number	Out of context	Form1.Command1
Time	13:05:28	Form1.Form_Load

You are stepping through the Form_Load procedure; it is the current *context*. *Number* is in Command1_Click, so its value is "Out of context." After stepping through the entire Form_Load procedure, step through the Command1_Click procedure. Follow these steps:

1. Click the Command1 button. Its event procedure appears in the code window. The **Private Sub** statement is boxed. The new watch expressions are given here:

Expression	Value	Context
Number	0	Form1.Command1
Time	Out of context	Form1.Form_Load

2. Click Step Into. The box jumps over the **Dim** statement and lands on the **For...Next** statement. The watch value of *Number* changes to 1.

3. Click Step Into. The box moves down to **Text1.Text** = *Number*.

4. Click Step Into. **Text1.Text** = *Number* is executed and 1 appears in the text box. The box moves to **Next** *Number*.

5. Click Step Into. **Next** *Number* is executed and the watch value of *Number* changes to 2. The box jumps up to **Text1.Text** = *Number* and the **For...Next** loop continues.

6. Click Step Into. **Text1.Text** = *Number* is executed and 2 appears in the text box. The box moves to **Next** *Number*.

7. Click Step Into. **Next** *Number* is executed and the watch value of *Number* changes to 3. The box jumps up to **Text1.Text** = *Number* and the **For...Next** loop continues.

8. Click Step Into. **Text1.Text** = *Number* is executed and 3 appears in the text box. The box moves to **Next** *Number*.

9. Click Step Into. **Next** *Number* is executed and the watch value of *Number* changes to 4. This ends the **For...Next** loop. The box moves to **Beep**.

10. Click Step Into. The computer beeps and the box moves to **End Sub**.

11. Click Step Into. The box disappears and the Step Into tool is disabled (dimmed) because there is no more code to step into. The watch window now displays the following expressions:

Expression	Value	Context
Number	4	Form1.Command1
Time	Out of context	Form1.Form_Load

You can use the Tools menu's Edit Watch command to delete a watch expression:

1. Click the Tools menu and then click its Edit Watch command to get the Edit Watch dialog box.

2. Enter the watch expression that you want to delete in the Expression box.

3. Click the Delete button.

Now is a good time to search the Help system for more information about Step Into and Add Watch.

If you'd like more practice, watch *OuterLoop* and *InnerLoop* while stepping through this procedure:

```
Private Sub Command1_Click()

  Dim OuterLoop As Integer, InnerLoop As Integer

  For OuterLoop = 1 To 3
    For InnerLoop = 1 To 2
      Print OuterLoop, InnerLoop
    Next InnerLoop
  Next OuterLoop
  Beep

End Sub
```

There are more debugging tools. Search the Help system for break mode, breakpoint, Calls dialog box, Debug window, Instant Watch, Step Over, and Toggle Breakpoint.

11.6 ANTICIPATE AND TRAP ERRORS

When your perfect code is used by the ideal user, everything runs smoothly and no errors occur. Alas, in the real world code can be imperfect, users make mistakes, and runs come to a crunching halt. The good news is that you can include chunks of code to trap errors and do something about them.

Create project Error Trap #1 - Oops. Put text box Text1 and command buttons cmdPrintNumber and cmdClearForm on the form. Install the following code:

```
Private Sub cmdClearForm_Click()
  Cls
End Sub

Private Sub cmdPrintNumber_Click()

  Dim ShortInteger As Integer

  ShortInteger = Text1.Text
  Print Text1.Text, ShortInteger

End Sub

Private Sub Text1_Click()
  Text1.Text = ""
End Sub
```

This code looks okay. What can go wrong when someone runs the project, enters a number into Text1, and clicks the Print Number button? Lots! First notice that *ShortInteger* is dimensioned as a variable of **Integer** type and then run the project. Try these entries in text box Text1:

▼   Enter **123** and click the Print Number button. It works just fine and your entry is printed on the form.

▼   Enter **123.45** and click the Print Number button. Because *ShortInteger* is dimensioned **As** Single, the entry is rounded to the nearest integer and assigned to *ShortInteger*, then printed as 123.

▼   Enter **123.56** and click the Print Number button. The text box entry is rounded to the nearest integer and assigned to *ShortInteger*, then printed as 124.

▼   Enter **1234567** and click the Print Number button. This is too big to be of **Integer** type, so the Overflow error box appears.

▼   Enter **qwerty** and click the Print Number button. Oops, that's no number! The Type mismatch error box appears. Visual Basic can't assign a non-numeric string to an integer variable.

▼   Click the text box and don't enter anything so that the text box remains empty. Click the Print Number button, and the Type Mismatch Error box appears. Visual Basic can't assign the empty string to an integer variable.

The second and third entries listed above may or may not be problems. Only the code writer knows. The project continues to run and no nasty error box appears. The fourth, fifth, and sixth entries are definite problems. An error box appears and the run ends.

The problems in the fourth, fifth, and sixth entries above are *trappable errors*. Overflow is error number 6 and Type mismatch is error number 13. You can find a list of trappable errors in the Help system (search for *trappable errors*). One way to handle these errors is to include an **On Error** statement in the code that, in the event of an error, sends control to a chunk of code that does something about the error. The statement

```
On Error GoTo FixIt
```

sends control to a *line label* called *FixIt*. Following *FixIt*, you write the code to, well, fix it. Modify project Error Trap #1 to get project Error Trap #2 - Fix It. It's easy to do—you just modify event procedure cmdPrintNumber_Click so that it looks like this:

```
Private Sub cmdPrintNumber_Click()

  Dim ShortInteger As Integer, Msg As String, Title As String

  On Error GoTo FixIt

  ShortInteger = Text1.Text
  Print ShortInteger
  Exit Sub

FixIt:
  If Err = 13 Then
    Msg = "Please enter a number."
    Title = "Type Mismatch"
    MsgBox Msg, vbExclamation, Title
  ElseIf Err = 6 Then
    Msg = "Must be an integer in the" & Chr(13) & Chr(10)
    Msg = Msg & "range -32768 to 32767."
    Title = "Overflow"
    MsgBox Msg, vbExclamation, Title
  End If

End Sub
```

Install this procedure and run it through its paces. The **On Error** statement near the beginning of the procedure tells Visual Basic that, if an error occurs, go to *FixIt* and execute the code that follows. If you enter a number in the range of an integer, all goes well, no error occurs, and this chunk of code is executed:

```
ShortInteger = Text1.Text
Print ShortInteger
Exit Sub
```

The text number in Text1 is converted to an integer, assigned to *ShortInteger*, and printed. An exit from the procedure occurs. The **Exit Sub** statement is necessary so that code below this code is not executed.

If the text in Text1 cannot be converted to a number of data type **Integer**, an error occurs in the execution of the statement:

```
ShortInteger = Text1.Text
```

In this case, execution jumps to *FixIt* and the code following it is executed:

```
FixIt:
  If Err = 13 Then
    Msg = "Please enter a number."
    Title = "Type Mismatch"
    MsgBox Msg, vbExclamation, Title
  ElseIf Err = 6 Then
    Msg = "Must be an integer in the" & Chr(13) & Chr(10)
    Msg = Msg & "range -32768 to 32767."
    Title = "Overflow"
    MsgBox Msg, vbExclamation, Title
  End If

End Sub
```

When an error has occurred, the **Err** function returns the number of the error. This code does something about a Type mismatch error (**Err** = 13 is True) or an Overflow error (**Err** = 6 is True). In either case, a message box is displayed. The user clicks OK to dismiss the message box, and the **End Sub** statement is executed. The procedure ends, but the run continues. Our user, now better informed, can try again.

Someone might click the text box, enter nothing, and then click the Print Number button. A Type mismatch error occurs in trying to convert the empty string to an integer and assigning it to *ShortInteger*. Project Error Trap #3 - FixIt has a version of event procedure PrintNumber_Click that detects this situation, inserts a text zero ("0") in the text box, and resumes executing code with the statement that caused the error, *ShortInteger* = Text1.Text:

```
Private Sub cmdPrintNumber_Click()

  Dim ShortInteger As Integer, Msg As String, Title As String

  On Error GoTo FixIt

  ShortInteger = Text1.Text
  Print ShortInteger
  Exit Sub

FixIt:
  Select Case Err
    Case 13
      If Text1.Text = "" Then
        Text1.Text = "0"
        Resume
      Else
        Msg = "Please enter a number."
        Title = "Type Mismatch"
        MsgBox Msg, vbExclamation, Title
      End If
    Case 6
      Msg = "Must be an integer in the" & Chr(13) & Chr(10)
      Msg = Msg & "range -32768 to 32767."
      Title = "Overflow"
      MsgBox Msg, vbExclamation, Title
  End Select

End Sub
```

If the error was a type mismatch (**Err** = 13), then **Case** 13 is executed. If the type mismatch occurred because Text1 contains the empty string, the **If...End If** structure inserts a text zero ("0") into the text box. The statement

```
Resume
```

causes execution to resume (continue) with the statement that caused the error, *ShortInteger* = Text1.Text in this case. Because there is now a text zero ("0") in Text1, this statement will be executed successfully and the run continues.

A variation of the **If...End If** structure demonstrates the **Resume Next** statement:

```
FixIt:
  Select Case Err
    Case 13
      If Text1.Text = "" Then
        Text1.Text = "0"
        ShortInteger = 0
        Resume Next
      Else
        Msg = "Please enter a number."
        Title = "Type Mismatch"
        MsgBox Msg, vbExclamation, Title
      End If
    Case 6
      Msg = "Must be an integer in the" & Chr(13) & Chr(10)
      Msg = Msg & "range -32768 to 32767."
      Title = "Overflow"
      MsgBox Msg, vbExclamation, Title
  End Select
```

This version of the *FixIt* code puts a text zero in the text box and also assigns a numeric zero to *ShortInteger*. The statement

```
Resume Next
```

causes execution to resume (continue) with the statement *that follows* the statement where the error occurred, **Print** *ShortInteger* in this example.

Error trapping is a big subject. This section has only exposed the tip of the iceberg. So don your scuba gear, dive into the Help system, and search for Trappable Errors, On Error Statement, Err Object, Line Label, Resume Statement, Error Function, and Error Statement.

11.7   *U*SE THE DRIVE, DIRECTORY, AND FILE LIST BOXES TO FIND FILES

The FileListBox, DirListBox, and DriveListBox controls are a coder's delight, powerful tools that you can use to locate files anywhere on your computer system:

▼   A FileListBox control locates and lists files in the folder specified by the setting of its Path property at run time. Its list consists of the names of files in the current path. On our system, Visual Basic is in the Vb folder on disk drive C, so our current path is c:\Vb.

▼ A DirListBox control displays folders and paths at run time. Why is it called "DirListBox" instead of "FolderListBox?" Because that's what it was called in previous versions of Visual Basic, in those days of yore when files were located in directories instead of folders.

▼ A DriveListBox control lists the disk drives on your system and enables you to clickly select a disk drive at run time.

You can use all three of these special-purpose list boxes in harmonious concert to locate a file in any folder on any disk drive. Look for these power tools in the toolbox:

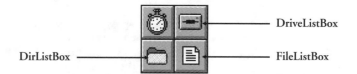

The FileListBox, DirListBox, and DriveListBox controls have many properties that are the same as ListBox and ComboBox properties. They have additional properties specifically designed for locating files. Table 11-3 shows some run-time properties that we will use a lot. (Run-time properties do not appear in the Properties window. They are set by code at run time.)

Let's build projects slowly. We'll begin with only a FileListBox, then add a DirListBox, then add a DriveListBox. Project File Path Boxes #1 has one FileListBox named File1 and command buttons that you can click to print the values of the FileListBox's Path, Pattern, ListCount, and ListIndex properties. You can click a filename in the list to select it and then click the Print Selection button to print that filename. After someone has clicked merrily away, it might look like this:

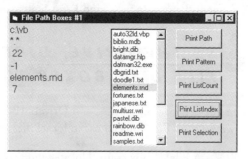

We clicked the top four buttons in order from top to bottom, selected (clicked) the "elements.rnd" filename in the FileListBox, clicked the Print Selection button to print the selected filename, and clicked the Print ListIndex button to print the

Property	Possible Setting	FileListBox	DirListBox	DriveListBox
List	List (array) of items	Yes	Yes	Yes
ListCount	Number of items in the list	Yes	Yes	Yes
ListIndex	Item number: 0, 1, 2, …, ListCount −1	Yes	Yes	Yes
Path	c:\Vb	Yes	Yes	No
Pattern	All types of files: *.*	Yes	No	No

TABLE 11-3   *Some Run-Time Properties of the FileListBox, DirListBox, and DriveListBox Controls* ▼

selected filename's ListIndex number. Table 11-4 is a step-by-step description of all this clicking. Table 11-5 lists event procedure specifications for project File Path Boxes #1.

As soon as you put file list box File1 on the form, its Path property is assigned the value of the current path, *c:\Vb* on our system. Event procedure cmdPrintPath_Click prints the value of *File1.Path* on the form:

```
Private Sub cmdPrintPath_Click()
  Print File1.Path
End Sub
```

The type of files displayed in the list depends on the setting of the Pattern property. The default setting is "*.*" and specifies that all files of all types in the path are listed. You could change the setting of the Pattern property to "*.vbp" to display only project files or "*.frm" to display only form files. Event procedure cmdPrintPattern_Click prints the value of *File1.Pattern* on the form:

```
Private Sub cmdPrintPattern_Click()
  Print File1.Pattern
End Sub
```

Event procedure cmdPrintListCount_Click prints the value of *File1.ListCount*, which is the number of items in the list:

```
Private Sub cmdPrintListCount_Click()
  Print File1.ListCount
End Sub
```

Each item in the list has an index number ranging from zero (0) for the first item to ListCount −1 for the last item. The value of the ListIndex property is the index of the currently selected item. If no item is selected, the value of ListIndex is −1.

We Clicked	Printed on Form	Property Value Printed	Comment
Print Path	c:\Vb	File1.Path	Current drive and folder.
Print Pattern	*.*	File1.Pattern	All file types are listed.
Print ListCount	22	File1.ListCount	The list has 22 items.
Print ListIndex	–1	File1.ListIndex	No item is selected yet.
Elements.rnd			We selected a list item.
Print Selection	elements.rnd	File1.List(File1.ListIndex)	Our selection is printed.
Print ListIndex	7	File1.ListIndex	Elements.rnd's ListIndex number.

TABLE 11-4   *Step-by-Step Clicking in Project File Path Boxes #1* ▼

Object Name	Event	Response
cmdPrintPath	Click	Prints the value of File1.Path on the form.
cmdPrintPattern	Click	Prints the value of File1.Pattern on the form.
cmdPrintListCount	Click	Prints the value of File1.ListCount on the form.
cmdPrintListIndex	Click	Prints the value of File1.ListIndex on the form.
cmdPrintSelection	Click	Prints the selected list item on the form.

TABLE 11-5   *Event Procedure Specifications for Project File Path Boxes #1* ▼

Event procedure cmdPrintListIndex_Click prints the value of *File1.ListIndex*:

```
Private Sub cmdPrintListIndex_Click()
  Print File1.ListIndex
End Sub
```

You click an item in the list to select it. This action highlights the item and sets the ListIndex to the item's index number. For example, "elements.rnd" is the eighth item in our list of files, so its index number is 7. Event procedure cmdPrintSelection_Click prints the value of the selected item, if an item is selected. If no item is selected, the procedure prints an empty line:

```
Private Sub cmdPrintSelection_Click()
  Print File1.List(File1.ListIndex)
End Sub
```

You can greatly improve the usefulness of this project by adding a DirListBox that lets you select any folder on the current disk drive and automatically change the Path setting of both the DirListBox and the FileListBox. We call this project File Path Boxes #2. At design time, it looks like this:

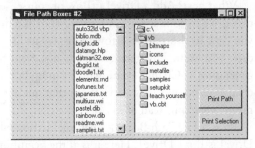

As soon as you add a DirListBox, it displays a hierarchical list of folders in the current path. At run time, you can double-click a folder to select it and generate a Change event. The Change event procedure can update the Path setting of a FileListBox so that it then displays a list of files in the selected folder. We ran the project and double-clicked the *icons* folder. The DirListBox (named Dir1) displayed the folders within the *icons* folder, such as *elements*. We double-clicked *elements* and its list of filenames appeared in the FileListBox. What's the path? We clicked the Print Path button to find out and saw "c:\Vb\icons\elements" printed on the form. We then selected the Earth.ico filename and clicked the Print Selection button to print it on the form. Table 11-6 summarizes our activities.

Event procedures cmdPrintPath_Click and cmdPrintSelection_Click are the same as in project File Path Boxes #1. The default name of the DirListBox is Dir1 and its Change event procedure is shown here:

```
Private Sub Dir1_Change()

   ' If Dir1's path changes, update File1's path
   File1.Path = Dir1.Path

End Sub
```

Action	Result
Double-click Icons in DirListBox Dir1.	Its list of folders appears. The FileListBox is empty.
Double-click Elements in Dir1.	The list of filenames in Elements appears in the FileListBox.
Click the Print Path button.	The path is printed. Our path is C:\Vb\Icons\Elements.
Click Earth.ico in the FileListBox.	It is selected and highlighted.
Click the Print Selection button.	"earth.ico" is printed on the form.

TABLE 11-6 *Step-by-Step Clicking in Project File Path Boxes #2* ▼

If you double-click Dir1, you change its Path property setting and generate its Change event, which then updates File1's Path property. Simple, neat, and elegant!

What next? Add a DriveListBox, of course, so that you can locate files on any disk drive in your system. A DriveListBox is a drop-down list box. At run time, you click its drop-down arrow to display its list of disk drives and then click the drive you want. This generates a Change event that can change a DirListBox, thus generating its Change event, which can update a FileListBox. A veritable change-reaction. Oops, sorry about that unclear reactor pun. Oops again, we meant *nuclear* instead of *unclear*.

Project File Path Boxes #3 has FileListBox File1, DirListBox Dir1, and DriveListBox1 Drive1. Here it is at the beginning of a run, just after someone clicked Drive1's drop-down button:

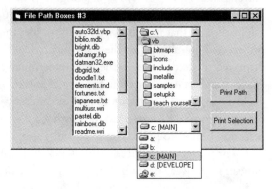

Click a drive to select it and you trigger event procedure Drive1_Change:

```
Private Sub Drive1_Change()

  ' If Drive1 changes, update Dir1's path
  Dir1.Path = Drive1.Drive

End Sub
```

This procedure changes Dir1's Path setting and triggers event procedure Dir1_Change:

```
Private Sub Dir1_Change()

  ' If Dir1's path changes, update File1's path
  File1.Path = Dir1.Path

End Sub
```

This procedure sets File1's Path property to the disk drive selected in Drive1 and the folder selected in Dir1. This path's list is displayed in File1, awaiting your filename selection.

 NOTE *Changing the Path property in File1 triggers its PathChange event. Because no PathChange event procedure was written, this has no affect in project File Path Boxes #3.*

A modest amount of work converts project File Path Boxes #3 into Project Slide Show #1. You can use this new project to view "slides" of picture files. While exercising the project, we saw the familiar picture shown in Figure 11-1. (Remember that "freeway" metafile we used in earlier chapters?)

We named the forms frmSlideShow1 and frmScreen. From top to bottom on frmSlideShow1 the command buttons are called cmdShowScreen, cmdHideScreen, cmdNextSlide, and cmdExit. In the same order, here are their event procedures:

```
Private Sub cmdShowScreen_Click()
   frmScreen.Show
End Sub


Private Sub cmdHideScreen_Click()
    frmScreen.Hide
End Sub


Private Sub cmdNextSlide_Click()

   ' If more slides remain in list, show next slide
   If File1.ListIndex < File1.ListCount - 1 Then
     File1.ListIndex = File1.ListIndex + 1
     PicturePath = File1.Path & "\" & File1.List(File1.ListIndex)
     frmScreen.Caption = PicturePath
     frmScreen.Picture = LoadPicture(PicturePath)
   Else
     Beep
     MsgBox "That was the last slide."
   End If

End Sub


Private Sub cmdExit_Click()
   End
End Sub
```

You can use project Slide Show #1 to view pictures stored in your computer.

▼

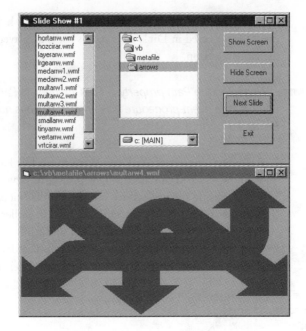

Design the project, install the event procedures, run the project, and browse Visual Basic's myriad images. You can also browse picture files in other applications. We recently enjoyed a slide show from the path C:\Winword\Clipart. It's loaded with a multitude of metafiles that we can use in future projects.

Be sure to search the Help system for FileListBox, DirListBox, DriveListBox, Path Property, PathChange Property, Pattern Property, Change Event, and PatternChange Event.

11.8 *L*OOK ONWARD

You have trekked well on the road to Visual Basic literacy. You have reached the summit of the first range of mountains. What do you see? Another range of mountains. Beyond that range, another range, and so on. Another adventure beckons!

Look back on your travels and prepare to move on with confidence. Browse the Help System. Read helpful books. Especially, create your own Visual Basic projects. We bid you farewell and we hope that you fare well.

A

ANSI Characters

T ABLES A-1 and A-2 list the ANSI codes and characters supported by Microsoft Windows and Visual Basic. Table A-1 lists ANSI codes 0 through 127, and Table A-2 lists ANSI codes 128 through 255. You can use Visual Basic's online Help system to display the information in these tables. Just follow these steps:

1. Click Help on the menu bar to open the Help menu.

2. Click Search For Help On to open the Search window.

3. In the Search window text box, type ANSI and then click the Show Topics button.

4. In the list of topics, click Character Set (0-127) or Character Set (128-255), and then click the Go To button to display the character set you've chosen.

In Table A-1, no characters are assigned to ANSI codes 0-7, 11-12, 14-31, and 127. In Table A-2, no characters are assigned to ANSI codes 128-144 and 147-159. These codes are not supported by Microsoft Windows.

 NOTE   *The Visual Basic Help system displays square bullets (■) to designate ANSI codes that do not have characters assigned to them. Here we've simply left those character spaces blank.*

0		32	(space)*	64	@	96	`
1		33	!	65	A	97	a
2		34	"	66	B	98	b
3		35	#	67	C	99	c
4		36	$	68	D	100	d
5		37	%	69	E	101	e
6		38	&	70	F	102	f
7		39	'	71	G	103	g
8	(backspace)*	40	(	72	H	104	h
9	(tab)*	41	)	73	I	105	i
10	(linefeed)*	42	*	74	J	106	j
11		43	+	75	K	107	k
12		44	,	76	L	108	l
13	(carriage return)*	45	-	77	M	109	m
14		46	.	78	N	110	n
15		47	/	79	O	111	o
16		48	0	80	P	112	p
17		49	1	81	Q	113	q
18		50	2	82	R	114	r
19		51	3	83	S	115	s
20		52	4	84	T	116	t
21		53	5	85	U	117	u
22		54	6	86	V	118	v
23		55	7	87	W	119	w
24		56	8	88	X	120	x
25		57	9	89	Y	121	y
26		58	:	90	Z	122	z
27		59	;	91	[	123	{
28		60	<	92	\	124		
29		61	=	93	]	125	}
30		62	>	94	^	126	~
31		63	?	95	_	127	

*These ANSI codes have no graphical representation, but depending on the application, may affect the visual display of text.

TABLE A-1　*ANSI Character Set 0-127* ▼

128		160	(space)*	192	À	224	à
129		161	¡	193	Á	225	á
130		162	¢	194	Â	226	â
131		163	£	195	Ã	227	ã
132		164	¤	196	Ä	228	ä
133		165	¥	197	Å	229	å
134		166	¦	198	Æ	230	æ
135		167	§	199	Ç	231	ç
136		168	¨	200	È	232	è
137		169	©	201	É	233	é
138		170	ª	202	Ê	234	ê
139		171	«	203	Ë	235	ë
140		172	¬	204	Ì	236	ì
141		173	-	205	Í	237	í
142		174	®	206	Î	238	î
143		175	‾	207	Ï	239	ï
144		176	°	208	Ð	240	∂
145	'	177	±	209	Ñ	241	ñ
146	'	178	²	210	Ò	242	ò
147		179	³	211	Ó	243	ó
148		180	´	212	Ô	244	ô
149		181	µ	213	Õ	245	õ
150		182	¶	214	Ö	246	ö
151		183	°	215	×	247	÷
152		184	¸	216	Ø	248	ø
153		185	¹	217	Ù	249	ù
154		186	º	218	Ú	250	ú
155		187	»	219	Û	251	û
156		188	¼	220	Ü	252	ü
157		189	½	221	Ý	253	ý
158		190	¾	222	þ	254	þ
159		191	¿	223	ß	255	ÿ

*This ANSI code has no graphical representation, but depending on the application, may affect the visual display of text.

TABLE A-2 *ANSI Character Set 128-255* ▼

B

Answers

T HIS appendix contains answers to selected exercises that appear throughout this book. Answers or hints for *all* of the exercises are available on our *Teach Yourself Visual Basic* disk, which you can order by filling out the coupon located near the back of the book (just after the Index).

CHAPTER 1

1.1 Exercises

1. Compare your answers with Figure 1-2.

3. The size of Form1 in twips is:

    Width = 6810 and Height = 6345.

    On your screen, you can find Form1's size in the object size box.

4. To exit Visual Basic, click the Visual Basic close button in the upper-right corner of the title bar.

1.2 Exercises

2. To make Form1 reappear, double-click Form1's name in the project window.

3. To see the Properties window, click the Properties tool on the toolbar.

5. To resize Form1, the Properties window, or the project window, click and drag a border to the desired size.

1.3 Exercises

2. Default settings of Form1's properties (800 × 600 screen resolution) are:

    Caption property: Form1
    Height property: 6345
    Left property: 1080
    Name property: Form1
    Picture property: (none)
    Top property: 1170
    Width property: 6810

3. To change the setting of the Caption property, click the Caption property in the Properties window and then type the desired setting.

1.4 Exercises

1. To run a project, click the Start tool on the toolbar.

2. To stop a project that is running, click the End tool on the toolbar.

1.5 Exercises

1. Visual Basic filename extensions are:

   a. Form file: .frm

   b. Project file: .vbp

1.6 Exercises

2. To open a project called Doodle.vbp:

   a. Click the Open tool on the toolbar.

   b. If you are not in the Teach Yourself Visual Basic folder then make your way there.

   c. Select Doodle.vbp (the .vbp extension may not appear on your screen) from the file list box.

   d. Click the Open command button.

3. We mentioned the following properties associated with Form1: Caption, Height, Left, Name, Picture, Top, and Width.

5. To make these screen elements disappear and reappear:

   a. For Form1:

▼ Click its close button on the right end of its caption bar to make it disappear.

▼ To make it reappear, double-click Form1 in the project window.

b. For the Properties window:

▼ Click its close button on the right end of its caption bar to make it disappear.

▼ To make it reappear, click the Properties tool on the toolbar.

c. For the project window:

▼ Click its close button on the right end of its caption bar to make it disappear.

▼ To make it reappear, click the Project tool on the toolbar.

8. To change the setting of the Caption property, click the Caption property in the Properties window and then type the desired setting.

11. To start or stop a project, perform the following actions:

▼ To run a project, click the Start tool on the toolbar.

▼ To stop a project that is running, click the End tool on the toolbar.

12. To save a project:

a. Click the Save Project button on the toolbar.

b. The Save File As dialog box appears. Type the name of the form file in the File name box and press ENTER .

c. The Save Project As dialog box appears. Type the name of the project file in the File name box and press ENTER.

14. To open a project called My Project.vbp:

a. Click the Open tool on the toolbar.

b. If you are not in the Teach Yourself Visual Basic folder then make your way there, or make your way to where you saved this project.

c. Select My Project.vbp (the .vbp extension may not appear on your screen) from the file list box.

d. Click the Open command button

e. The form will not be visible, so double-click the form's name in the project window to make it appear.

*C*HAPTER 2

2.2 Exercises

4. Project Beep #1 has one event procedure.

   a. Click (a mouse click) is the event.

   b. The command button named Command1 and captioned "Beep" responds to the Click event.

   c. Command1_Click is the name of the event procedure.

   d. Event procedure Command1_Click is:

```
Private Sub Command1_Click()
  Beep
End Sub
```

2.3 Exercises

2. The **End** statement ends a run and returns to the design screen.

3. Double-click Command1 to open the code window with the event procedure template:

```
Private Sub Command1_Click()
|
End Sub
```

2.4 Exercises

1. The actions performed by statements are shown here in a neat table:

	Statement	Action Performed	Example
a.	Cls	Clears the form.	
b.	Print Date	Prints the date on the form.	12/13/95
c.	Print Time	Prints the time on the form.	10:54:38 AM
d.	Print Now	Prints the date and time on the form.	12/13/95 10:54:38 AM
e.	Print Timer	Prints the number of seconds since midnight on the form.	39496.04
f.	End	Ends the run.	

2.5 Exercises

2. Design the visual interface with a form and two command buttons as specified in the visual interface table. The event procedures for buttons cmdLetterhead and cmdQuit are shown here:

```
Private Sub cmdLetterhead_Click()
  Cls
  Print "Laran Stardrake"
  Print "P.O. Box 1635"
  Print "Sebastopol, CA 95473-1635"
  Print "707-555-1212"
End Sub

Private Sub cmdQuit_Click()
  End
End Sub
```

2.6 Exercises

1. These properties control run-time appearance and behavior of the form:

Property	Setting	Action or Result at Run Time
AutoRedraw	True	Text printed in the Form_Load procedure is visible.
	False	Text printed in the Form_Load procedure is not visible.
ControlBox	True	The form has a control-menu icon.
	False	The form does not have a control-menu icon.
CurrentX	2400	Sets the horizontal coordinate of the cursor.
CurrentY	1200	Sets the vertical coordinate of the cursor.
MaxButton	True	The form has a maximize button.
	False	The form does not have a maximize button.
MinButton	True	The form has a minimize button.
	False	The form does not have a minimize button.

3. The BorderStyle property settings affect the control-menu icon. The control-icon menu commands for BorderStyle setting 2 - Sizable assume that ControlBox, MaxButton, and MinButton are set to True.

BorderStyle Setting	Control Icon Commands
0 - None	There is no control-menu icon!
1 - Fixed Single	Move, Minimize, Maximize, Close, Switch To...
2 - Sizable	Restore, Move, Size, Close, Switch To...
3 - Fixed Dialog	Move, Close, Switch To...
4 - Fixed ToolWindow	Move, Close, Switch To...
5 - Sizable ToolWindow	Move, Size, Close, Switch To...

4. Project Form Load #4 - Click and DblClick has event procedures
Form_Load, Form_Click, and Form_DblClick, shown here:

```
Private Sub Form_Load()
  AutoRedraw = True
  Print "Experiment! Click me and double-click me."
End Sub

Private Sub Form_Click()
  Print "You clicked."
  Beep
End Sub

Private Sub Form_DblClick()
  Print "You double-clicked."
  Beep
End Sub
```

When you click the form, you hear one beep and see this:

```
You clicked.
```

When you double-click the form, you hear two beeps and see this:

```
You clicked.
You double-clicked.
```

The first click of the double-click triggers event procedure Form_Click,
which does its task. Completing the double-click signals event procedure
Form_DblClick, which responds in its way.

mastery
skills check

2. The two types of objects used are forms and command buttons.

3. You can use the Properties window to change any of the requested items.
You can also change the size of an object by clicking and dragging its border.

   a. Click the object to select it, click the Caption property in the Properties
   window, type the new caption, and press ENTER.

   b. Click the object to select it, click the Name property in the Properties
   window, type the new name, and press ENTER.

c. Click the form to select it and then change the Width and Height property settings in the Properties window. Click each property, type the new setting, and press ENTER. Or click and drag the form's border.

d. Click the command button to select it and then change the Width and Height property settings in the Properties window. Click each property, type the new setting, and press ENTER. Or click and drag a selection handle on the command button's border.

5. The name of an event procedure consists of the name of an object, the underscore character, and the name of an event. For example, Command1_Click. Exception: the name of an event procedure for a form consists of the word *Form,* the underscore character, and the name of an event. For example, Form_Load or Form_Click.

6. The visual interface specifications for project Kronos #4 - Start and Stop Times are listed here:

Object	Property	Default Setting	Final Setting
Form1	Caption	Form1	Start Time and Stop Time
	Name	Form1	frmKronos4
Command1	Caption	Command1	Start Time
	Name	Command1	cmdStartTime
Command2	Caption	Command2	Stop Time
	Name	Command2	cmdStopTime
Command3	Caption	Command3	Clear Form
	Name	Command3	cmdClearForm
Command4	Caption	Command3	The End
	Name	Command3	cmdEnd

The project's event procedure specifications are listed here:

Object Name	Event	Response
frmKronos4	None	None.
cmdStartTime	Click	Prints "Start time:" and value of **Timer**.
cmdStopTime	Click	Prints "Stop time:" and value of **Timer**.
cmdClearForm	Click	Clears the form.
cmdEnd	Click	Ends the run and returns to the design screen.

Finally, here are the project's event procedures:

```
Private Sub cmdStartTime_Click()
  Print "Start time:"
  Print Timer
End Sub

Private Sub cmdStopTime_Click()
  Print "Stop time:"
```

```
    Print Timer
End Sub

Private Sub cmdClearForm_Click()
  Cls
End Sub

Private Sub cmdEnd_Click()
  End
End Sub
```

9. The visual interface specifications for project Kronos #6 - Hour, Minute, and Second are listed here:

Object	Property	Default Setting	Final Setting
Form1	Caption	Form1	Hour, Minute, and Second
	Name	Form1	frmKronos6
Command1	Caption	Command1	Time
	Name	Command1	cmdTime
Command2	Caption	Command2	Hour
	Name	Command2	cmdHour
Command3	Caption	Command3	Minute
	Name	Command3	cmdMinute
Command4	Caption	Command4	Second
	Name	Command4	cmdSecond
Command5	Caption	Command5	Clear Form
	Name	Command5	cmdClearForm
Command6	Caption	Command6	Quit
	Name	Command6	cmdQuit

The event procedure specifications for project Kronos #5 - Year, Month, Day, and Weekday are listed here:

Object Name	Event	Response
frmKronos6	None	None.
cmdTime	Click	Prints the value of **Time**.
cmdHour	Click	Prints the hour (0 to 23) in the value of **Time**.
cmdMinute	Click	Prints the minute (0 to 59) in the value of **Time**.
cmdSecond	Click	Prints the second (0 to 59) in the value of **Time**.
cmdClearForm	Click	Clears the form.
cmdQuit	Click	Ends the run and returns to the design screen.

Finally, the event procedures cmdHour_Click, cmdMinute_Click, and cmdSecond_Click are shown here:

```
Private Sub cmdHour_Click()
  Print Hour(Time)
End Sub
```

```
Private Sub cmdMinute_Click()
  Print Minute(Time)
End Sub

Private Sub cmdSecond_Click()
  Print Second(Time)
End Sub
```

CHAPTER 3

3.1 Exercises

1. The standard prefix for a label is "lbl." The standard prefix for a text box is "txt."

3. Draw the visual interface as specified by the illustration and the specification tables. Install event procedure cmdNow_Click:

```
Private Sub cmdNow_Click()
  txtNow.Text = Now
End Sub
```

3.2 Exercise

1. Add these specifications to Table 3-5:

Object	Property	Setting
Label1	Alignment	1 - Right Justify
Label2	Alignment	1 - Right Justify

3.4 Exercises

3. The visual interface specifications for project Experiment #2 - Show Text Box Location and Size are listed here:

Object	Property	Setting
Form1	Caption	Show Text Box Location and Size
	Name	frmExperiment2
Text1	Text	Text1
	Name	Text1
Command1	Caption	Show Left
	Name	cmdShowLeft
Command2	Caption	Show Top

Object	Property	Setting
	Name	cmdShowTop
Command3	Caption	Show Width
	Name	cmdShowWidth
Command4	Caption	Show Height
	Name	cmdShowHeight

The project's event are listed here:

Object	Event	Response
cmdShowLeft	Click	Prints the value of Text1's Left property on the form.
cmdShowTop	Click	Prints the value of Text1's Top property on the form.
cmdShowWidth	Click	Prints the value of Text1's Width property on the form.
cmdShowHeight	Click	Prints the value of Text1's Height property on the form.

Finally, here are the project's event procedures:

```
Private Sub cmdShowLeft_Click()
  Print Text1.Left
End Sub

Private Sub cmdShowTop_Click()
  Print Text1.Top
End Sub

Private Sub cmdShowWidth_Click()
  Print Text1.Width
End Sub

Private Sub cmdShowHeight_Click()
  Print Text1.Height
End Sub
```

3.5 Exercises

2. Because txtCopyEntry's Multiline property is False, only one line of text is visible. The rest of the text is there, but out of sight. You can click the text that is showing and drag to the right to see the rest of the text. Or you can click the text and use the right arrow key to access the rest of the text.

3.6 Exercises

2. Here are partial specifications for project Copycat #4's text boxes:

Object	Property	Setting	Comment
Text1	Text	(Text)	Indicates Multiline box.
	Name	txtEnter	
	Multiline	True	
	ScrollBars	2 - Vertical	
Text2	Text	(Text)	Indicates Multiline box.
	Name	txtCopyEntry	
	Multiline	True	
	ScrollBars	1 - Horizontal	

Here are event procedures cmdEnter_Click and cmdCopyEntry_Click:

```
Private Sub cmdEnterText_Click():
  txtEnter.Text = ""    ' Clear txtEnter
  txtEnter.SetFocus     ' Select txtEnter (cursor appears)
End Sub


Private Sub cmdCopyEntry_Click()
  txtCopyEntry.Text = txtEnter.Text    ' Copy the string
End Sub
```

3.7 Exercises

1. 1440 twips equals one inch and 72 points equals one inch, so there are 20 twips (1440 / 72) per point.

2. Only part of the caption shows. We saw two lines with "Alas, this caption is too long to fit" and the top half of a third line with (we think) "in a default-size." When we changed the Autosize property to True, the label's width expanded to hold the entire caption on one line and the height shrunk to just tall enough to hold the line. The object size box displayed 4260×195 (Width = 4260 and Height = 195).

3.8 Exercises

1. Here are the additional visual interface specifications for project QBColor #2 - Text Box Colors Using Scroll Bars:

Object	Property	Setting	Comment
Label2	Caption	ForeColor:	
	Alignment	1 - Right Justify	
	AutoSize	True	
	Name	lblForeColor	
HScrollBar2	Name	hsbForeColor	The standard prefix is hsb.
	Max	15	Maximum value - scroll button far right.
	Min	0	Minimum value - scroll button far left.
	Value	0	Position of the scroll button.
Text2	Text		
	Name	txtForeColor	

Here is event procedure hsbForeColor_Scroll:

```
Private Sub hsbForeColor_Scroll()
  txtForeColor.Text = hsbForeColor.Value
  txtShowColors.ForeColor = QBColor(hsbForeColor.Value)
End Sub
```

3.9 Exercises

2. Event procedures txtRedBC_Click and cmdShowColors_Click are shown here:

```
Private Sub txtRedBC_Click()
  txtRedBC.Text = ""    ' Clear txtRedBC
End Sub

Private Sub cmdShowColors_Click()

  ' Declare variables. They are Variant by default.
  Dim redBC, greenBC, blueBC
  Dim redFC, greenFC, blueFC
```

```
' Assign values to variables
redBC = txtRedBC.Text
greenBC = txtGreenBC.Text
blueBC = txtBlueBC.Text
redFC = txtRedFC.Text
greenFC = txtGreenFC.Text
blueFC = txtBlueFC.Text

' Set txtShowColors BackColor and ForeColor
txtShowColors.BackColor = RGB(redBC, greenBC, blueBC)
txtShowColors.ForeColor = RGB(redFC, greenFC, blueFC)

End Sub
```

3. Event procedure hsbRed_Scroll is shown here. Use it as a model to write event procedures hsbGreen_Scroll and hsbBlue_Scroll.

```
Private Sub hsbRed_Scroll()

    Dim red, green, blue

    red = hsbRed.Value
    green = hsbGreen.Value
    blue = hsbBlue.Value
    txtRedNumber.Text = red
    txtRedBC.BackColor = RGB(red, 0, 0)
    frmRGB03.BackColor = RGB(red, green, blue)

End Sub
```

mastery
skills check

1. No. These are controls: command button, text box, label, horizontal scroll bar, and vertical scroll bar.

5. An Object.Property name consists of the name of an object, a period, and the name of a property.

   a. txtFortune.Text

   b. frmExperiment1.Width

   c. Text1.Left

     d. txtShowColors.BackColor

     e. hsbBackColor.Value

7. These statements appeared in project Kronos #11 - Stopwatch.

     a. Assigns the value of **Timer** to txtStart.Text. This value appears in the text box.

     b. Assigns the value of **Timer** to txtStop.Text. This value appears in the text box.

     c. Subtracts the value in text box txtStart from the value in text box txtStop and assigns the result (difference) to txtElapsed.Text.

9. These statements appeared in project Copycat #1.

     a. Gives the focus to txtEnter. The cursor appears in the text box.

     b. Assigns the value of txtEnter.Text to txtCopyEntry.Text. The text in txtEnter is copied into txtCopyEntry.

10. To change the alignment of text in a text box, first set the Multiline property to True and then set the Alignment property to the setting you want (0 - Left Justify, 1 - Right Justify, and 2 - Centered). To make a text box wordwrap, set its Multiline property to True.

*C*HAPTER 4

4.1 Exercises

1. The path is C:\Vb\Icons\Misc. Load the binocular icon (filename Binoculr.ico) onto Form1.

     a. It's as easy as 1-2-3-4:

          1) Double-click Form1's Picture property to open the Load Picture dialog box.

          2) Double-click the Icons folder.

          3) Double-click the Misc folder.

          4) Double-click Binoculr.

     b. If you have just displayed an icon from the Elements folder, the current path is C:\Vb\Icons\Elements.

1) Double-click Form1's Picture property to open the Load Picture dialog box.

2) Double-click the Icons folder.

3) Double-click the Misc folder.

4) Double-click Binoculr.

c. If you have just displayed an icon from the Misc folder, the current path is C:\Vb\Icons\Misc.

1) Double-click Form1's Picture property to open the Load Picture dialog box.

2) Double-click Binoculr.

2. If you have just displayed an icon from the Misc folder on drive C, the current path is C:\Vb\Icons\Misc.

a. Double-click Form1's Picture property to open the Load Picture dialog box.

b. Double-click the Vb folder.

c. Double-click the Bitmaps folder.

d. Double-click the Assorted folder.

e. Double-click Camcord.

4.2 Exercises

2. After you have been on the road for awhile, limber up with some stretches.

a. The icon remains nestled in the upper-left corner of the image box and adamantly refuses to change its size.

b. The icon grows to fill the box. As it grows, it becomes grainier.

3. Remove a picture from Image1 like this:

a. Click Image1 to select it.

b. Click the Picture property to select it. The Properties button appears.

c. *Don't* click the Properties button. Instead, click anywhere in the Settings box *except* the Properties button.

d. Press DELETE.

4.3 Exercises

2. Here are the event procedures for project Storm #1:

```
Private Sub Form_Load()
   imgCloud.Visible = True        ' Makes imgCloud visible
   imgLitening.Visible = False    ' Makes imgLitening invisible
   imgRain.Visible = False        ' Makes imgRain invisible
End Sub


Private Sub imgCloud_Click()
   imgCloud.Visible = True        ' Makes imgCloud visible
   imgLitening.Visible = True     ' Makes imgLitening visible
   imgRain.Visible = False        ' Makes imgRain invisible
End Sub


Private Sub imgLitening_Click()
   imgCloud.Visible = False       ' Makes imgCloud invisible
   imgLitening.Visible = False    ' Makes imgLitening invisible
   imgRain.Visible = True         ' Makes imgRain visible
End Sub


Private Sub imgRain_Click()
   imgCloud.Visible = True        ' Makes imgCloud visible
   imgLitening.Visible = False    ' Makes imgLitening invisible
   imgRain.Visible = False        ' Makes imgRain invisible
End Sub
```

4.4 Exercises

2. We sized the image boxes 1500×900 and set their Stretch property settings to True.

   a. We loaded the lightning icon (Litening.ico) into Image1. The icon expanded to the size of Image1 (1500×900). The outline of the lightning bolt looked grainy.

   b. We loaded the bell bitmap (Bell.bmp) into Image2. The bitmap expanded to the size of Image2 (1500×900). The bell looked a bit ragged.

   c. We loaded the freeway intersection metafile (Multarw4.wmf) into Image3. The metafile shrunk to the size of Image3 (1500 x 900) and all of it was visible.

4.5 Exercises

2. We set AutoSize to True for each picture box. Here is what happened on our screen:

   a. Picture1 expanded to 2775×525. Now we can see the entire thermometer.

   b. Picture2 shrunk to the size of the icon. The size of Picture2, including its border, is 510×510. The default BorderStyle of a picture box is 1 - Fixed Single. If you change BorderStyle to 0 - None, the size of Picture2 will be 480×480.

   c. Picture3 expanded to the size of the metafile, very big. We could see only a little of the upper-left corner of the picture. Picture3's size is 7080×4920.

4.6 Exercises

1. If no object name is specified, then the form is the object of a method.

   a. Clears the form.

   b. Prints "Be nice to the driver who just cut across your bow." on the form.

   c. Clears Form1.

   d. Prints "Dance, sing, and whistle to banish the blues." on Form1.

   e. Clears picture box Picture1.

   f. Prints "Honk if you understand Visual Basic." in picture box Picture1.

   g. Prints the value of the **Time** function on the form.

   h. Prints the value of the **Time** function on Form1.

   i. Prints the value of the **Time** function in picture box Picture1.

4.7 Exercises

1. We used the Shape control to draw Eve's head (3 - Circle) and we used the Line control to draw her body, arms, and legs. We encourage you to draw a much better picture of Eve!

2. First put the picture box on the form and then draw the control inside the picture box. For example, draw a shape like this:

   a. Click the Shape tool once to select it.

b. Move the mouse pointer to the picture box. The pointer changes to a cross-hair.

c. Move the cross-hair to the place in the picture box where you want to draw the shape.

d. Click and drag to draw it the size you want.

e. Click the Shape property and select the shape you want.

4.8 Exercises

1. The center of the resized pool table is at 1500, 1200 and the *radius* of the ball is 90 twips. When centered on the pool table, the ball is at Left = 1500 − 90 = 1410 and Top = 1200 − 90 = 1110.

   a. Here is event procedure lblCenter_Click for Project Move It #1:

   ```
   Private Sub lblCenter_Click()
     ' Move the ball to the center of picPoolTable
     shpBall.Left = 1410
     shpBall.Top = 1110
   End Sub
   ```

   b. Here is event procedure lblCenter_Click for Project Move It #2:

   ```
   Private Sub lblCenter_Click()
     ' Move the ball to the center of picPoolTable
     shpBall.Move 1410, 1110
   End Sub
   ```

2. Set the ball's Left property to half the picture box's ScaleWidth minus half the ball's Width. Set the ball's Top property to half the picture box's ScaleHeight minus half the ball's Height.

   a. Here is event procedure lblCenter_Click for project Move It #1:

   ```
   Private Sub lblCenter_Click()
     ' Move the ball to the center of picPoolTable
     shpBall.Left = picPoolTable.ScaleWidth / 2 - shpBall.Width / 2
     shpBall.Top = picPoolTable.ScaleHeight / 2 - shpBall.Height / 2
   End Sub
   ```

   b. Here is event procedure lblCenter_Click for project Move It #2:

   ```
   Private Sub lblCenter_Click()
   ```

```
    Dim NewLeft, NewTop As Integer

    ' Move the ball to the center of picPoolTable
    NewLeft = picPoolTable.ScaleWidth / 2 - shpBall.Width / 2
    NewTop = picPoolTable.ScaleHeight / 2 - shpBall.Height / 2
    shpBall.Move NewLeft, NewTop
End Sub
```

mastery

skills check

2. An image box's Stretch property and a picture box's AutoSize property determine what happens when you load a picture.

   a. Stretch = False. Image1 resizes to the size of the icon or bitmap.

   b. Stretch = False. Image1 resizes to the size of the metafile.

   c. Stretch = True. The bitmap or icon resizes to the size of Image1.

   d. Stretch = True. The metafile resizes to the size of Image1.

   e. AutoSize = False. Picture1's size does not change. It the picture is smaller than Picture1, it appears in Picture1's upper-left corner. If the picture is larger than Picture1, it is clipped and only part of it appears in Picture1.

   f. AutoSize = False. A metafile is drawn to fit its container, so the entire metafile appears in Picture1.

   g. AutoSize = True. Picture1 resizes to the size of the bitmap or icon.

   h. AutoSize = True. Picture1 resizes to the size of the metafile.

4. The following table of *Object.Property* variables shows a possible value for each variable:

Object Name	Property Name	Object.Property Variable	Possible Value
Form1	DrawStyle	Form1.DrawStyle	4 - Dash - Dot - Dot
frmIcons01	BackColor	frmIcons.BackColor	&H00FFFFFF&

Image1	Stretch	Image1.Stretch	False
imgEmpty	BorderStyle	imgEmpty.BorderStyle	1 - Fixed Single
Picture1	Picture	Picture1.Picture	(Metafile)
picEarth	Visible	picEarth.Visible	True
Line1	BorderWidth	Line1.BorderWidth	2
linLeftArm	X1	linLeftArm.X1	1200
Shape1	Shape	Shape1.Shape	1 - Square
shpAnyShape	FillStyle	shpAnyShape.FillStyle	7 - Diagonal Cross

6. We expect that you are now quite adept at doing this type of task.

   a. imgLightOff.Visible = True

   b. imgLightOn.Visible = False

   c. imgLitening.Enabled = True

   d. imgCloud.Enabled = False

   e. picDisplay.Picture = LoadPicture ("c:\vb\icons\elements\earth.ico")

   f. picDisplay.AutoSize = True

   g. Laran Stardrake's statement: Form1.Print "Laran Stardrake"

   h. Laran Stardrake's statement: Picture1.Print "Laran Stardrake"

   i. picDisplay.Cls

   j. frmCanvas.DrawWidth = 4

   k. This requires four statements:

      1) Line1.X1 = 240

      2) Line1.Y1 = 360

      3) Line1.X2 = 1200

      4) Line1.Y2 = 1320

   l. Shape1.Shape = 5

   m. Shape1.Move 960, 1440

CHAPTER 5

5.2 Exercises

1. Command buttons cmdShowForm2 and cmdExit are unchanged. Delete command button cmdHideForm2 and its event procedure from Form1. Put command cmdHideForm2 on Form2 and install its event procedure:

```
Private Sub cmdHideForm2_Click()
  Form2.Hide
End Sub
```

5.3 Exercises

1. Form1's event procedures are shown here:

```
Private Sub cmdShowForm2_Click()
  Form2.Show    ' Show Form2 as a modeless form
End Sub

Private Sub cmdShowForm3_Click()
  Form3.Show 1    ' Show Form3 as a modal form
End Sub

Private Sub cmdExit_Click()
  End
End Sub
```

Form2 is an ordinary, run-of-the-mill modeless form. Its event procedures are given here:

```
Private Sub cmdPrintMode_Click()
  Cls
  Print "I'm a modeless form. You can use"
  Print "other forms while I am showing."
End Sub

Private Sub cmdCancel_Click()
  Form2.Hide
End Sub
```

Form3 is a modal form. When it is open, it hogs the show. No other form can be used until you close or cancel Form3. Its event procedures are shown here:

```
Private Sub cmdPrintMode_Click()
  Cls
  Print "I'm a modal form. You can't use another"
  Print "form until you close or cancel me."
End Sub

Private Sub cmdCancel_Click()
  Form3.Hide
End Sub
```

5.4 Exercises

1. The event procedures for project Light Bulb and Storm #2 are shown here:

```
Private Sub Form_Load()

  ' Position and size frmLtBlbStorm2
  frmLtBlbStorm2.Left = 1200
  frmLtBlbStorm2.Top = 1200
  frmLtBlbStorm2.Width = 6000
  frmLtBlbStorm2.Height = 2400

  ' Position cmdLightBulb, cmdStorm, and cmdExit
  cmdLightBulb.Left = 600
  cmdLightBulb.Top = 720
  cmdStorm.Left = 2280
  cmdStorm.Top = 720
  cmdExit.Left = 3960
  cmdExit.Top = 720

End Sub

Private Sub cmdLightBulb_Click()

  ' Size and position frmLtBulb2
  frmLtBulb2.Width = 3000
  frmLtBulb2.Height = 2400
  frmLtBulb2.Left = 1200
  frmLtBulb2.Top = 3600

  frmLtBulb2.Show

End Sub

Private Sub cmdStorm_Click()

  ' Size and position frmStorm01
  frmStorm01.Width = 3000
```

```
    frmStorm01.Height = 2400
    frmStorm01.Left = 4200
    frmStorm01.Top = 3600

    frmStorm01.Show

End Sub
```

5.5 Exercises

1. The Cancel button properties for the light bulb form are listed here:

```
Begin VB.Command Button cmdCancel
    Cancel          =   -1   'True
    Caption         =   "Cancel"
    Height          =   495
    Left            =   1320
    TabIndex        =   2
    Top             =   1320
    Width           =   1215
```

5.6 Exercise

1. We saw "Go, Team, Go!!" printed in 24-point, italic Arial font.

5.7 Exercises

1. Open project Light Bulb and Storm #1. Pull down the File menu and select the Make EXE File command to get the Make EXE File dialog box. Enter the name of the folder where you want to save the EXE file into the Save In box. Enter the filename into the File name box. When everything is A-OK, click the OK button and Visual Basic does the rest.

5.8 Exercises

1. Here is event procedure cmdQuestion_Click:

```
Private Sub cmdQuestion_Click()

    Dim Msg As Variant, Title As Variant

    Msg = "Are you sure you want to do that?"
```

```
Title = "Question"
MsgBox Msg, 64, Title

End Sub
```

mastery
skills check

1. To add a new form, click the Form tool on the left end of the toolbar. To add a previously saved form, click the File menu and then click the Add File command to open the Add File dialog box. In the Add File dialog box, find the filename you want and double-click it.

3. Refer to an object on another form by using the name of the form followed by an exclamation point.

   a. Two statements are required:

      1) Form2!Text1.Left = 600 and

      2) Form2!Text1.Top = 360

   b. Form3!Image1.Move 720, 240

   c. frmPlanets!imgEarth.Picture = LoadPicture("c:\vb\icons\elements\earth.ico")

   d. frmCongestion!picFreeway.Picture = LoadPicture("c:\vb\metafile\arrows\multarw4.wmf")

5. Feel free to print what you want to print. Also try other fonts and styles.

```
Private Sub Command1_Click()
   Printer.Font = "Times New Roman"
   Printer.FontSize = 24
   Printer.FontBold = True
   Printer.FontItalic = True
   Printer.Print "Visual Basic is AOK!"
   Printer.EndDoc
End Sub
```

6. Open the project for which you want to make an EXE file. Click the File menu and then click the Make EXE File command to get the Make EXE File dialog box. Enter the name of the folder where you want to save the EXE file into the Save In box. Enter the filename in the File name box. When everything is AOK, click the OK button and Visual Basic does the rest.

To run the EXE file:

a. Click the start button on your task bar.

b. Click the Programs icon to open File Manager.

c. Find the Windows Explorer icon and click it.

d. Using the folder tree, find the folder in which you saved the .EXE file.

e. Double-click the file's icon to load the file and then run it.

CHAPTER 6

2. Here are the event procedures for Project Metronome #3:

```
Private Sub cmdStartTimer_Click()
  Timer1.Interval = txtInterval.Text
  Timer1.Enabled = True
End Sub

Private Sub cmdStopTimer_Click()
  Timer1.Enabled = False
End Sub

Private Sub cmdExit_Click()
  End
End Sub

Private Sub txtInterval_Click
  txtInterval.Text = ""
End Sub

Private Sub Timer1_Timer()
  Beep
End Sub
```

6.2 Exercises

1. Here's a handy table of answers:

Condition	Statement Executed if Condition Is True
Text1.Text $<$ 0	Print "Negative"
Text1.Text $=$ 0	MsgBox "Zero"
Text1.Text $>$ 0	Text2.Text $=$ "Positive"

2. Project Negative, Zero, or Positive #2, event procedures cmdNegZerPos_Click and txtEnter_Click.

```
Private Sub cmdNegZerPos_Click()
  If txtEnter.Text < 0 Then txtNegZerPos.Text = "Negative"
  If txtEnter.Text = 0 Then txtNegZerPos.Text = "Zero"
  If txtEnter.Text > 0 Then txtNegZerPos.Text = "Positive"
  Beep
End Sub

Private Sub txtEnter_Click()
  txtNegZerPos.Text = ""
  txtEnter.Text = ""
End Sub
```

6.4 Exercises

1. Check boxes and option buttons are both on/off (selected/unselected) controls and they have many of the same properties, events, and methods. If a check box or an option button is off, clicking it turns it on. If a check box or an option button is on, clicking it turns it off. Here's one important difference between check boxes and option buttons: Any number of check boxes on a form can be selected at the same time. Selecting or unselecting a check box has no effect on the other check boxes. However, only one option button on a form or in a container, such as a frame or a picture, box can be selected. Selecting one option button in a set of option buttons automatically turns off any other option buttons in that set that might have been on.

6.5 Exercise

1. Here is event procedure cmdIgniteLight_Click for project Negative, Zero, or Positive #5 - Ignite My Light.

```
Private Sub cmdIgniteLight_Click()

  Select Case txtNumber.Text

    Case Is = ""
      ' If txtNumber is empty, turn off the lights
      imgNegative.Picture = imgLightOff.Picture
      imgZero.Picture = imgLightOff.Picture
      imgPositive.Picture = imgLightOff.Picture
```

```
    Case Is < 0
      imgNegative.Picture = imgLightOn.Picture
      imgZero.Picture = imgLightOff.Picture
      imgPositive.Picture = imgLightOff.Picture

    Case Is = 0
      imgNegative.Picture = imgLightOff.Picture
      imgZero.Picture = imgLightOn.Picture
      imgPositive.Picture = imgLightOff.Picture

    Case Is > 0
      imgNegative.Picture = imgLightOff.Picture
      imgZero.Picture = imgLightOff.Picture
      imgPositive.Picture = imgLightOn.Picture

  End Select

End Sub
```

6.6 Exercises

2. Each **For** statement is of the form: **For** *firstnumber* **To** *lastnumber*
   Step *increment*:

	Sequence of Values	**For Statement**
a.	0, 3, 6, 9	For a = 0 To 9 Step 3
b.	10, 8, 6, 4, 2, 0	For b = 10 To 0 Step −2
c.	1000, 2000, 3000	For c = 1000 To 3000 Step 1000
d.	3, 2.5, 2, 1.5, 1	For d = 3 To 1 Step −0.5

3. Our event procedure clears the picture box before printing each number.
   What happens if you don't do this? Try it and find out.

```
Private Sub Command1_Click()
  For Number = 2000 To 1000 Step -1
    DoEvents
    Picture1.Cls
    Picture1.Print Number
  Next Number
End Sub
```

6.7 Exercises

2. Event procedures for cmdRed, cmdGreen, and cmdBlue are shown here:

```
Private Sub cmdRed_Click()

  Dim red As Variant

  For red = 0 To 255
    DoEvents
    frmRGB05.BackColor = RGB(red, 0, 0)
  Next red

End Sub

Private Sub cmdGreen_Click()

  Dim green As Variant

  For green = 0 To 255
    DoEvents
    frmRGB05.BackColor = RGB(0, green, 0)
  Next green

End Sub

Private Sub cmdBlue_Click()

  Dim blue As Variant

  For blue = 0 To 255
    DoEvents
    frmRGB05.BackColor = RGB(0, 0, blue)
  Next blue

End Sub
```

a. Because cmdRed_Click contains a **DoEvents** statement, clicking "Green" interrupts cmdRed_Click and runs through all 256 shades of green (unless you click another button). Then cmdRed_Click resumes displaying shades of red until it ends or you click again.

b. Because cmdGreen_Click contains a **DoEvents** statement, clicking "Green" a second time interrupts cmdGreen_Click and runs through all 256 shades of green (unless you click another button). Then the interrupted cmdGreen_Click resumes displaying shades of green until it ends or you click again.

6.8 Exercises

2. Here are your assorted **Do...Loop** structures:

   a. Using a **Do Until...Loop** structure:

   ```
   start = Timer
   Do Until Timer >= start + 0.125
   Loop
   ```

   b. Using a **Do...Loop While** structure:

   ```
   start = Timer
   Do
   Loop While Timer < start + 0.125
   ```

   c. Using a **Do...Loop Until** structure:

   ```
   start = Timer
   Do
   Loop Until Timer >= start + 0.125
   ```

   d. This version uses a **Do While...Loop** structure:

   ```
   start = Timer
   Do While Timer < start + 0.125
     DoEvents
   Loop
   ```

mastery

skills check

2. Form1's BackColor alternates once per second between bright red and bright green.

4. For these procedures to work, Form1's BackColor must first be set to one of the three colors. You can do this in the Form_Load procedure.

   a. Using an **If...Then...Else** structure:

   ```
   Private Sub Timer1_Timer()

     If Form1.BackColor = RGB(255, 0, 0) Then
       Form1.BackColor = RGB(0, 255, 0)
   ```

```
   ElseIf Form1.BackColor = RGB(0, 255, 0) Then
     Form1.BackColor = RGB(0, 0, 255)
   ElseIf Form1.BackColor = RGB(0, 0, 255) Then
     Form1.BackColor = RGB(255, 0, 0)
   End If

End Sub
```

b. Using a **Select Case** structure:

```
Private Sub Timer1_Timer()

  Select Case Form1.BackColor
    Case Is = RGB(255, 0, 0)
      Form1.BackColor = RGB(0, 255, 0)
    Case Is = RGB(0, 255, 0)
      Form1.BackColor = RGB(0, 0, 255)
    Case Is = RGB(0, 0, 255)
      Form1.BackColor = RGB(255, 0, 0)
  End Select

End Sub
```

6. Sometimes the last number is not attained, as in c, g, and h:

For Statement	Sequence of Values
a. For n = 0 To 5	0, 1, 2, 3, 4, 5
b. For x = 0.5 To 2.5	0.5 1.5, 2.5
c. For y = 1 To 2.5	1, 2
d. For z = 1 To 2.5 Step 0.5	1, 1.5, 2, 2.5
e. For w = 100 To 200 Step 10	100, 110, 120, …, 200
f. For f = 3000 To 1000 Step –100	3000, 2900, 2800, …, 1000
g. For a = 10 To 11 Step 0.333	10, 10.333, 10.666, 10.999
h. For b = 10 To 12 Step 0.667	10, 10.667, 11.334

7. Here are the requested **For...Next** statements:

Sequence of Values	For Statement
a. 0, 3, 6, 9	For a = 0 To 9 Step 3
b. 10, 8, 6, 4, 2, 0	For b = 10 To 0 Step -2
c. 1000, 2000, 3000	For c = 1000 To 3000 Step 1000
d. 1, 2, 3, 4,..., 365	For d = 1 To 365

e. 365, 364, 363, 362,..., 1   For e = 365 To 1 Step –1

f. 0, 0.125, 0.25, 0.375,..., 1   For f = 0 To 1 Step 0.125

g. 3, 2.5, 2, 1.5, 1, 0.5, 0   For g = 3 To 0 Step –0.5

h. 0.5, 1.5, 2.5, 3.5, 4.5   For 0.5 To 4.5

10. We started a new project, put Command1 and Text1 on the form, and installed these event procedures:

```
Private Sub Command1_Click()
  Cls
  n = 1
  Do While n <= Text1.Text
    DoEvents
    Print n
    n = n + 1
  Loop
End Sub

Private Sub Text1_Click()
  Text1.Text = ""
End Sub
```

Try it yourself and experiment by entering various values in the text box. Enter a positive integer, zero, a negative integer, and some positive non-integers (for example, try 3.14 and 4.99). While you are experimenting, rewrite Command1_Click using **Do Until...Loop**, **Do...Loop While**, and **Do...Loop Until** structures.

CHAPTER 7

7.1 Exercises

2. Each statement is of the form **Print** *Object.Property*:

Object	Property	Print Statement
a. Label1	Caption	Print Label1.Caption
b. Text1	Text	Print Text1.Text
c. Form1	Picture	Print Form1.Picture
d. Image1	Picture	Print Image1.Picture
e. Picture1	Picture	Print Picture1.Picture

f. Line1	X1 and Y1	Print Line1.X1, Line1.Y1
g. Line1	X2 and Y2	Print Line1.X2; Line1.Y2
h. Shape1	Shape	Print Shape1.Shape
i. Timer1	Interval	Print Timer1.Interval

7.2 Exercises

1. If Form1's properties are set to their default values, the **Print** statements print the following information on the form:

Printed on the Form	Data Type(s)
a. 2	Integer
b. 2 2 2	Integer, Integer, Integer
c. 4 11 11	Single, Boolean, Boolean
d. 11 11	Boolean, Boolean
e. 8	String
f. 4 4	Single, Single

3. Each number's data type is designated by a data type symbol:

Number	Symbol	Data Type
a. 3.14!	!	Single
b. 3.141592653589793#	#	Double
c. 365%	%	Integer
d. 234567.89@	@	Currency
e. −2147483648&	&	Long

7.3 Exercises

2. Parentheses to the rescue!

  a. Print (23 * 16 + 14) * 28.35

  b. Print (8 * 60 + 37) * 60 + 42

  c. Print (19 + 17 + 24) / 3

  d. Print 29 / (29 + 12 + 5)

3. Print 5.8 * (1 + 1.7 / 100) ^ 20

NOTE *The answer is in billions of people.*

7.4 Exercises

1. Floating-point notation is a handy shorthand for tiny or humongous numbers.

    a. Speed of light in meters per second: 299,790,000

    b. Mass of an electron in kilograms:
       .00000000000000000000000000000000911

    c. Mass of the Earth in kilograms: 5,970,000,000,000,000,000,000,000

3. The Currency data type allows up to 15 digits to the left of the decimal point and up to four digits to the right of the decimal point.

    a. This causes an overflow. There are too many digits to the left of the decimal point.

    b. The result is within the range of data type Currency:
       123456789876543.21

    c. The result is within the range of data type Currency:
       123456790098765.4321

7.5 Exercise

1. Change only the form's caption and the **Dim** statement in event procedure cmdAdd_Click.

    a. Project Calulator #3. Change the form's caption to: Adding Machine - Double. Change the **Dim** statement to: Dim Number1As Double, Number2 As Double.

    b. Project Calulator #4. Change the form's caption to: Adding Machine - Currency. Change the **Dim** statement to: Dim Number1 As Currency, Number2 As Currency.

7.6 Exercises

1. Project Calculator #6. We're sure that you know how to write event procedures cmdClearAll_Click, cmdExit_Click, txtNumber1_Click, and txtNumber2_Click. Event procedure cmdAdd_Click is shown here, along with modifications to obtain event procedures cmdSubtract_Click, cmdMultiply_Click, and cmdDivide_Click.

```
Private Sub cmdAdd_Click()

  Dim Number1 As Double, Number2 As Double, Sum As Double

  ' If txtNumber1 contains a number, assign it to Number1.
  ' Otherwise display a message in txtResult and Exit Sub.
  If IsNumeric(txtNumber1.Text) Then
    Number1 = txtNumber1.Text
  Else
    txtResult.Text = "I only do numbers."
    Exit Sub
  End If

  ' If txtNumber2 contains a number, assign it to Number2.
  ' Otherwise display a message in txtResult and Exit Sub.
  If IsNumeric(txtNumber2.Text) Then
    Number2 = txtNumber2.Text
  Else
    txtResult.Text = "I only do numbers."
    Exit Sub
  End If

  Sum = Number1 + Number2
  txtResult.Text = Sum

End Sub
```

To obtain the rest of the event procedures, you need only change the **Public Sub** statement and the two lines of code that calculate the result and assign it to a text box variable. In the following, vertical ellipses (three dots arranged vertically) indicate missing code that is the same as in event procedure cmdAdd_Click:

```
Private Sub cmdSubtract_Click()

  .
  .
  .

  Difference = Number1 - Number2
```

```
         txtResult.Text = Difference

     End Sub

     Private Sub cmdMultiply_Click()

         .
         .
         .


       Product = Number1 * Number2
       txtResult.Text = Product

     End Sub

     Private Sub cmdDivide_Click()

         .
         .
         .


       Quotient = Number1 / Number2
       txtResult.Text = Quotient

     End Sub
```

7.7 Exercises

1. The **Rnd** function returns a random number between 0 and 1. To get a random number in another range, you perform algebraic alakazams on **Rnd**.

   a. $0 < Rnd < 1$

   b. $0 < 100 * Rnd < 100$

   c. $-10 < 20 - Rnd * 10 < 10$

   d. Possible values of Fix(16 * Rnd) are integers in the range 0 to 15: 1, 2, 3, 4, 5, 6, 7, 8, 9, 10, 11, 12, 13, 14, and 15.

   e. Possible values of Fix(256 * Rnd) are integers in the range 0 to 255.

   f. Possible values of Fix(21 * Rnd) - 10 are integers in the range −10 to 10.

2. We installed this event procedure and saved the project as Zappy Artist Plots RGB Dots:

```
Private Sub cmdDot_Click()
```

```
Dim x As Integer, y As Integer
Dim red As Integer, green As Integer, blue As Integer
Dim Color As Long

x = Fix(ScaleWidth * Rnd)        ' Random horizontal coordinate
y = Fix(ScaleHeight * Rnd)       ' Random vertical coordinate
red = Fix(256 * Rnd)             ' Random RGB color number for red
green = Fix(256 * Rnd)           ' Random RGB color number for green
blue = Fix(256 * Rnd)            ' Random RGB color number for blue
Color = RGB(red, green, blue)    ' RGB color
PSet (x, y), Color               ' Plot a dot

End Sub
```

mastery

skills check

3. A run of project Grade Point Average #1 might go like this:

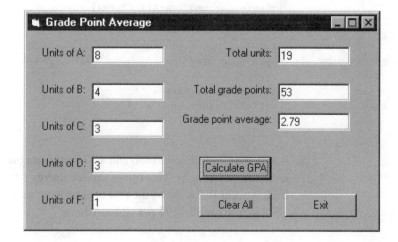

Event procedures cmdCalcGPA_Click and cmdClearAll_Click calculate and display the grade point average:

```
Private Sub cmdCalcGPA_Click()

  Dim A As Single, B As Single, C As Single
  Dim D As Single, F As Single
  Dim TotalUnits As Single, TotalPoints As Single
  Dim GPA As Single

  ' Assign units in text boxes to numeric variables
  A = txtA.Text
  B = txtB.Text
  C = txtC.Text
  D = txtD.Text
  F = txtF.Text

  ' Calculate total units, total points, and GPA
  TotalUnits = A + B + C + D + F
  TotalPoints = 4 * A + 3 * B + 2 * C + 1 * D + 0 * F
  GPA = TotalPoints / TotalUnits

  ' Stuff total units, total points, and GPA into text boxes
  txtTotalUnits.Text = TotalUnits
  txtTotalPoints.Text = TotalPoints
  txtGPA.Text = Format(GPA, "0.##")

End Sub

  Private Sub cmdClearAll_Click()
    txtA.Text = ""
    txtB.Text = ""
    txtC.Text = ""
    txtD.Text = ""
    txtF.Text = ""
    txtTotalUnits.Text = ""
    txtTotalPoints.Text = ""
    txtGPA.Text = ""
End Sub
```

5. A 100-watt incandescent bulb and a 22-watt Gaea bulb put out about the same amount of light. This run of project Energy #2 - Cost, Gaea vs. Incandescent Bulbs shows the cost of electricity using both bulbs for 10,000 hours at $0.1195 per kilowatt-hour:

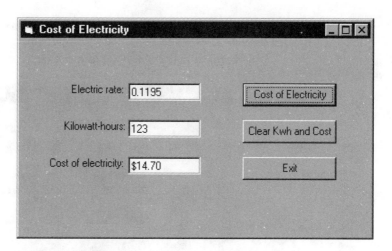

Switch to Gaea bulbs and save $119.5 − $26.29 = $93.21 in the cost of electricity per bulb! We are quite certain that you know how to write the event procedures for cmdClearAll, cmdExit, txtGaea, and txtIncan. Here's our version of the big one, event procedure cmdCalculate_Click:

```
Private Sub cmdCalculate_Click()

    Dim ElecRate As Currency, Hours As Currency
    Dim IncanWatts As Currency, GaeaWatts As Currency
    Dim IncanKw As Currency, GaeaKw As Currency
    Dim IncanCost As Currency, GaeaCost As Currency

    ' Assign electric rate and number of hours
    ElecRate = 0.1195
    Hours = 10000

    ' Assign text box wattages to numeric variables
    IncanWatts = txtIncanWatts.Text
    GaeaWatts = txtGaeaWatts.Text

    ' Calculate energy cost for each bulb
    IncanKw = IncanWatts / 1000            ' Kilowatts, Incan
    IncanCost = IncanKw * Hours * ElecRate
    GaeaKw = GaeaWatts / 1000              ' Kilowatts, Gaea
    GaeaCost = GaeaKw * Hours * ElecRate

    ' Display costs in text boxes
    txtIncanCost.Text = Format(IncanCost, "$##0.00")
    txtGaeaCost.Text = Format(GaeaCost, "$##0.00")

End Sub
```

7. We modified project Energy #1 by rearranging its objects, adding a baseline label and text box, and rewriting some of the code. Here's a sample run of project Energy #3 - Cost of Electricity:

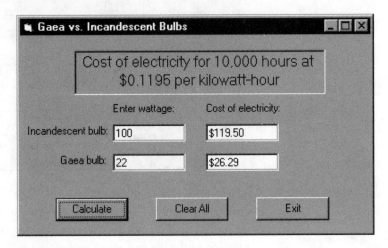

And here are the project's event procedures:

```
Private Sub txtBaseLine_Click()
  txtBaseLine.Text = ""
End Sub


Private Sub Form_Load()
  txtLowRate.Text = 0.1195   ' Low rate, $ per kilowatt-hour
  txtHighRate.Text = 0.1374  ' High rate, $ per kilowatt-hour
End Sub


Private Sub cmdElecCost_Click()

  Dim LowRate As Currency, HighRate As Currency
  Dim Kwh As Currency, Baseline As Currency
  Dim ElecCost As Currency

  ' Assign values to variables from text boxes
  LowRate = txtLowRate.Text
  HighRate = txtHighRate.Text
  Kwh = txtKwh.Text
  Baseline = txtBaseLine.Text

  ' Calculate cost of electricity
  If Kwh <= Baseline Then
    ElecCost = Kwh * LowRate
  ElseIf Kwh > Baseline Then
```

```
      ElecCost = (Kwh - Baseline) * HighRate + Baseline * LowRate
   End If

   txtElecCost.Text = Format(ElecCost, "$###,##0.00")

End Sub
```

CHAPTER 8

8.1 Exercises

2. The immediate **Print** statements produce these results:

a. `Laran          Stardrake`

b. `LaranStardrake`

c. `LaranStardrake`

d. `Stardrake, Laran`

e. `Stardrake, Laran`

f. `3 * 4 = 12`

g. `The Type mismatch error box appears.`

h. `Mariko is 66 inches tall.`

8.3 Exercises

2. We did it like this:

```
Private Sub cmdNumber_Click()

  Dim InputValue As Variant
  Dim Number As Double

  ' Loop until a number is entered
  Do
    InputValue = InputBox("Enter a Number.")
    If IsNumeric(InputValue) = True Then
      Exit Do
    Else
      MsgBox ("Oops! I want a number.")
```

```
    End If
Loop

' Convert InputValue to Double and assign it to Number
Number = InputValue
Print "Value of Number:"; Number

End Sub
```

8.4 Exercises

1. Since there is no **Dim** statement to define them otherwise, *Msg, Title,* and *Strng* are Variant by default.

2. Here is event procedure Form_Click for project LCase and UCase #3:

```
Private Sub Form_Click()

    Dim Msg As String, Title As String
    Dim Color As String, ColorUC As String

    Beep
    Msg = "Enter a rainbow color."
    Color = InputBox(Msg)
    ColorUC = UCase(Color)
    Select Case ColorUC
      Case "RED", "ORANGE", "YELLOW", "GREEN", "BLUE", "VIOLET"
        Print "Yes, "; Color; " is in my rainbow."
      Case Else
        Print "Sorry, "; Color; " is not in my rainbow."
    End Select

End Sub
```

8.5 Exercise

2. Here is event procedure Form_Click for project Message Box #3 - Multiline Message:

```
Private Sub Form_Click()

  Dim NL As String, Msg As String

  NL = Chr(13) & Chr(10)     ' New line characters
```

```
' Construct the message
Msg = "Visual Basic Backpack" & NL
Msg = Msg & "P.O. Box 478" & NL
Msg = Msg & "San Lorenzo, CA 94580" & NL
Msg = Msg & "On the net: KARL25 @ AOL.COM"

MsgBox Msg, 64, "Our Newsletter"    ' Display the message

End Sub
```

8.6 Exercises

1. Here is event procedure cmdMakeWord_Click for project Word Maker #2:

```
Private Sub cmdMakeWord_Click()

   Dim Consonant As String, Vowel As String, Word As String

   Consonant = "bcdfghjklmnpqrstvwxyz"    ' 21 consonants
   Vowel = "aeiouy"                        ' 5 vowels and y

   Word = ""              'Start with the empty string ("")

   ' Concatenate a consonant, vowel, consonant, vowel, consonant
   Word = Word & Mid(Vowel, Int(6 * Rnd) + 1, 1)
   Word = Word & Mid(Consonant, Int(21 * Rnd) + 1, 1)
   Word = Word & Mid(Consonant, Int(21 * Rnd) + 1, 1)
   Word = Word & Mid(Vowel, Int(6 * Rnd) + 1, 1)
   Word = Word & Mid(Consonant, Int(21 * Rnd) + 1, 1)
   Word = Word & Mid(Vowel, Int(6 * Rnd) + 1, 1)

   ' Display the word on the form
   Print Word

End Sub
```

8.7 Exercises

2. The **Len** function returns the length of a string:

   a. **Fix**(**Len**(*Strng*)) = 2. The possible values are "H" and "T". They are equally likely. Each occurs with a probability of 1/2. These statements simulate a "fair coin."

   b. **Fix**(**Len**(*Strng*)) = 5. The possible values are "H" and "T". They are *not* equally likely. "H" occurs with a probability of 3/5 and "T" occurs with a probability of 2/5. These statements simulate an "unfair coin" that turns up "H'" on about 60 percent of the flips.

c. **Fix**(**Len**(*Strng*)) = 21. The possible values are lowercase consonants. They are equally likely. Each consonant has 1 chance in 21 of occurring when the statements are executed.

8.8 Exercises

1. The answers depend on the dictionary you use, the search strategies you use, how much research time you spend, etc., etc. We've shared this recreation with hundreds of elementary school students. Many years ago, *Games* magazine ran a contest to find the word whose WW product is closest to 1 million in a dictionary they designated. They received more than 14,000 entries! We'd love to hear from you about *your* answers. Send them to Visual Basic Backpack, P.O. Box 478, San Lorenzo, CA 94580.

mastery

skills check

2. The title is "Tourist Information". The message is:

```
Tom, Forrest, and Teal Torres invite you
to visit beautiful Belleview, Idaho.

From Belleview, you can go anywhere.
Sun Valley is an easy 32 kilometer hike.
```

3. Here's the "Scenic Trek" Form_Click event procedure:

```
Private Sub Form_Click()

  ' Title As String, Msg As String

  NL = Chr(13) & Chr(10)    ' New line characters

  Title = "Scenic Trek"

  ' Construct multiline message
  Msg = "Grab your backpack and hike around scenic" & NL
```

```
Msg = Msg & "Coeur d'Alene Lake with famous guides" & NL
Msg = Msg & "Aurora and Aidan Bennett." & NL & NL
Msg = Msg & "Sign up now! We go tomorrow at first light."

MsgBox Msg, 64, Title

End Sub
```

5. Here is event procedure cmdFlipCoins_Click for project Coin Flip #1:

```
Private Sub cmdFlipCoins_Click()

Dim Flip As Integer

Flip = Fix(4 * Rnd) + 1
Print Mid("HHHTTHTT", 2 * Flip - 1, 2)

End Sub
```

6. Remember to put a space between "Flop" and "Flip":

```
Gnrts = Right(Strng, 4) & " " & Left(Strng, 4)
```

CHAPTER 9

9.1 Exercises

1. Here is event procedure cmdRoll4D6_Click for Project Dice #2:

```
Private Sub cmdRoll4D6_Click()
   Print RollD6 + RollD6 + RollD6 + RollD6
End Sub
```

9.2 Exercises

1. Here are the designated **Public Functions** for Project Random Backpack #2:

a. **Public Function** RollD100:

```
Public Function RollD100() As Integer

   ' Returns a random integer 0 to 99
   RollD100 = Fix(100 * Rnd)
```

```
         End Function
```

b. **Public Function** RndUCLetter:

```
Public Function RndUCLetter() As String

   ' Returns a random uppercase letter
   RndUCLetter = Chr(Fix(26 * Rnd) + 65)

End Function
```

c. **Public Function** RndConsonant:

```
Public Function RndConsonant() As String

   ' Returns a random lowercase consonant

   Dim Consonants As String

   Consonants = "bcdfghjklmnpqrstvwxyz"
   RndConsonant = Mid(Consonants, Int(21 * Rnd) + 1, 1)

End Function
```

d. **Public Function** RndVowel:

```
Public Function RndVowel() As String

   ' Returns a random lowercase vowel or y.

   Dim Vowels As String

   Vowels = "aeiouy"
   RndVowel = Mid(Vowels, Int(6 * Rnd) + 1, 1)

End Function
```

9.3 Exercises

1. Here are the arguments and local variables in the given procedures:

   a. No arguments; no local variables.

   b. No arguments; no local variables.

   c. No arguments; no local variables.

   d. No arguments; local variables *TenCoins* and *Coin*.

    e. No arguments; local variables *WordLength*, *Letter*, and *Word*.

    f. Argument *Range*; no local variables.

    g. Argument *CVstructure*; local variables *Word*, *CorV*, and *k*.

3. Here is **Public Function** FlipCoins:

```
Public Function FlipCoins(n As Long) As Long

  ' Returns the number of heads in n simulated coin flips

  Dim NumberHeads As Long, k As Long, Flip As Integer

  NumberHeads = 0

  ' Flip coin n times and tally heads
  For k = 1 To n
    Flip = Fix(2 * Rnd)    ' 0 = heads, 1 = tails
    If Flip = 0 Then NumberHeads = NumberHeads + 1
  Next k

  FlipCoins = NumberHeads

End Function
```

9.4 Exercises

2. Project Sort #1, **Public Sub** Sort2Money calls **Public Sub** Swap if a swap is required:

```
Public Sub Sort2Money(Money1 As Currency, Money2 As Currency)
  If Money1 > Money2 Then Swap Money1, Money2
End Sub
```

Event procedure Command1_Click calls **Public Sub** Sort2Money, which may call **Public Sub** Swap:

```
Private Sub Command1_Click()

  Dim Amount1 As Currency, Amount2 As Currency

  Cls
  Amount1 = InputBox("Enter amount #1.", "Amount1")
  Amount2 = InputBox("Enter amount #2.", "Amount2")

  Print "Before sort:"
  Print "Amount #1: "; Amount1
```

```
Print "Amount #2: "; Amount2
Print

Call Sort2Money(Amount1, Amount2)
' Or call Sub with: Sort2Money Amount1, Amount2

Print "After sort:"
Print "Amount #1: "; Amount1
Print "Amount #2: "; Amount2

End Sub
```

9.5 Exercises

1. Project Sort #5, **Public Sub** Sort2TextMoney calls **Public Sub** Swap if need be:

```
Public Sub Sort2TxtMoney(txtBox1 As Control, txtBox2 As Control)

  Dim Money1, Money2 As Currency

  Money1 = txtBox1.Text
  Money2 = txtBox2.Text
  If Money1 > Money2 Then SwapTextBoxes txtBox1, txtBox2

End Sub
```

Event procedure cmdSortMoney_Click calls **Public Sub** Sort2Money, which calls **Public Sub** Swap as needed:

```
Private Sub cmdSortMoney_Click()
  Call Sort2TxtMoney(Text1, Text2)
End Sub
```

9.6 Exercises

1. This version of **Public Sub** Dally has **DoEvents** statements in its **Do Until...Loop** structures:

```
Public Sub Dally(Seconds As Single)

  ' Dallies the number of seconds specified by Seconds
  ' Caution: Totally ties up your computer during the delay

  Dim StartTime As Single
```

```
' Here's the time delay
StartTime = Timer
If StartTime + Seconds < 86400 Then
  Do Until Timer > StartTime + Seconds: DoEvents: Loop
Else
  ' Adjust for going through midnight
  Do Until Timer > StartTime + Seconds - 86400: DoEvents: Loop
End If

End Sub
```

mastery
skills check

2. Embed these **Public Functions** in your lucky coins:

a. **Public Function** FlipCoinA:

```
Public Function FlipCoinA() As String

  ' Simulates an unfair coin: 3/5 H, 2/5 T
  FlipCoinA = Mid("HHHTT", Fix(5 * Rnd) + 1, 1)

End Function
```

b. **Public Function** FlipCoinB:

```
Public Function FlipCoinB(p As Double) As String

  ' Simulates an unfair coin:
  ' Probability of H = p, Probability of T = 1 - p

  Dim Flip As Double, HorT As String

  Flip = Rnd            ' Random number 0 to 1

  If Flip <= p Then
    HorT = "H"
  Else
    HorT = "T"
  End If

  FlipCoinB = HorT
```

```
     End Function
```

4. You can use **Public Function** Combinations to do lottery calculations. For
   the 6/49 lottery, call it like this:

```
Call Combinations(6, 49)
```

Install **Public Function** Combinations and try it for various values of *r*
and *n*:

```
Public Function Combinations(r As Long, n As Long) As Double

  ' Returns the number of ways to pick r objects
  ' from a set of n objects

  Dim k As Long, nCr As Double

  nCr = 1

  For k = 0 To r - 1
    nCr = nCr * (n - k) / (k + 1)
  Next k

  Combinations = nCr

End Function
```

5. Here is **Public Function** Spaces:

```
Public Function Spaces(Strng As String) As Integer

  ' Returns the number of spaces in Strng

  Dim NmbrSpaces

  NmbrSpaces = 0

  For k = 1 To Len(Strng)
    Character = Mid(Strng, k, 1)
    If Character = Chr(32) Then NmbrSpaces = NmbrSpaces + 1
  Next k

  Spaces = NmbrSpaces

End Function
```

CHAPTER 10

10.1 Exercise

1. These **Dim** statements with the keyword **To** specify both the smallest and largest index of the array:

   a. **Dim** CoinFlips(0 To 1) As Integer

   b. **Dim** NationalDebt(1994 To 1996) As Double

   c. **Dim** Inventory (1000 To 9999) As Long

   d. **Dim** QuizAverage(1 To 32) As Single

   e. **Dim** Filename(1 To 500) As String

   f. **Dim** Potpourri(-100 To 200) or **Dim** Potpourri(-100 To 200) As Variant

10.2 Exercises

1. Add two fortunes to the fortune cookie project:

   a. In event procedure Form_Load add these lines:

```
Fortune(8) = "When tools become toys, then work becomes play."
Fortune(9) = "Everything you do is practice for what you do next."
```

   b. In event procedure cmdFortune_Click change only the line that assigns a random integer to *RandomIndex*:

```
RandomIndex = Fix(9 * Rnd) + 1
```

10.3 Exercise

1. Project Flashcard #2. Event procedure cmdNextSideB_Click is the same as in project Flashcard #1. Here is event procedure cmdNextSideA_Click:

```
Private Sub cmdNextSideA_Click()

    ' Display Side A of a randomly selected card

    ' Random subscript in the range, 1 to NumberCards
```

```
Subscript = Fix(NumberCards * Rnd) + 1

' Display card number and Side A, clear Side B
txtCardNumber.Text = Subscript
txtSideA.Text = SideA(Subscript)
txtSideB.Text = ""

' Disable Side A button and enable Side B button
cmdNextSideA.Enabled = False
cmdNextSideB.Enabled = True

End Sub
```

10.4 Exercises

2. Easy! Change only the assignment of values to arrays *SideA()* and *SideB()* in the Form_Load procedure.

10.5 Exercises

1. Start with project People's Poll #1. Draw the third option button inside frame fraAnswer and change the button's name to the name of the option button control array (optAnswer in our project). Visual Basic recognizes that this button is a new member of an existing control array and sets its index to 2. Draw the third text box inside frame fraTallies and change the box's name to the name of the text box control array (txtTally in our project). Visual Basic recognizes that this box is a new member of an existing control array and sets its index to 2. In event procedures Form_Load, cmdTallyAnswer_Click, and cmdZeroTallies_Click, change the **For** statement to:

```
For k = 0 To 2
```

That's it. Project People's Poll #3 is ready to tally answers.

10.6 Exercises

1. In project Flashcards #5, modify event procedure Form_Load. Elements 1 (Hydrogen) through 92 (Uranium) occur naturally, except element 43 (Technetium), which is a *synthetic* element (created in the laboratory). Elements 93 (Neptunium) through 103 (Lawrencium) are synthetic

elements that have common names. Elements 104 through 109 currently have three-letter code names. The Form_Load procedure shown here assigns the number of elements (109) to *NumberCards* and shows selected element names and symbols assigned to arrays *SideA()* and *SideB()*:

```
Private Sub Form_Load()

    ' Redimension dynamic arrays SideA() and SideB()
    NumberCards = 109
    ReDim SideA(1 To NumberCards), SideB(1 To NumberCards)

    ' Assign values to arrays SideA() and SideB()
    SideA(1) = "Hydrogen"
    SideB(1) = "H"
    SideA(2) = "Helium"
    SideB(2) = "He"
    SideA(3) = "Lithium"
    SideB(3) = "Li"
    .
    .
    .
    SideA(92) = "Uranium"
    SideB(92) = "U"
    SideA(93) = "Neptunium"
    SideB(93) = "Np"
    SideA(94) = "Plutonium"
    SideB(94) = "Pu"
    .
    .
    .
    SideA(108) = "Uno"
    SideB(108) = "Uno"
    SideA(109) = "Une"
    SideB(109) = "Une"

    ' Enable Side A button and disable Side B button
    cmdNextSideA.Enabled = True
    cmdNextSideB.Enabled = False

End Sub
```

10.7 Exercise

1. Project Sort #8, form-level declaration and Form_Load procedure:

```
Dim LongInt() As Long    ' Dynamic array

Private Sub Form_Load()
```

```
      Randomize
End Sub
```

a. Event procedure cmdEnterArray_Click:

```
    Private Sub cmdEnterArray_Click()

      ' Enter values of the long integer array LongInt()
      ' from LongInt(1) to LongInt(n)

      Dim n As Integer, k As Integer, Msg As String

      ' Acquire value of n and redimension array
      n = InputBox("Enter value of n.")
      ReDim LongInt(1 To n) As Long

      ' Acquire values of LongInt(1) to LongInt(n)
      For k = 1 To n
        Msg = "Enter value of LongInt(" & k & ")."
        LongInt(k) = InputBox(Msg)
      Next k

    End Sub
```

b. After the array has been entered, event procedure cmdPrintArray_Click can print it. This procedure clears the form and then prints the array one number per line on the form:

```
    Private Sub cmdPrintArray_Click()

      ' Print array LongInt() from its smallest index (1)
      ' to its largest index, UBound(LongInt)

      Dim k As Integer

      Cls

      For k = 1 To UBound(LongInt)
        Print LongInt(k)
      Next k

    End Sub
```

c. Event procedure cmdSortArray_Click sorts the array into ascending numerical order:

```
    Private Sub cmdSortArray_Click()

      ' Sort array LongInt() from its smallest index (1)
      ' to its largest index, UBound(LongInt)
```

```
      Dim i As Integer, j As Integer, Temp As Long

      For i = 1 To UBound(LongInt) - 1
        For j = i + 1 To UBound(LongInt)

          If LongInt(j) < LongInt(i) Then
            ' Swap values of LongInt(i) and LongInt(j)
            Temp = LongInt(i)
            LongInt(i) = LongInt(j)
            LongInt(j) = Temp
          End If

        Next j
      Next i

    End Sub
```

d. Event procedure cmdShuffleArray_Click scrambles the array:

```
    Private Sub cmdShuffleArray_Click()

      ' Shuffle array LongInt() from its smallest index (1)
      ' to its largest index, UBound(LongInt)

      Dim k As Integer, RndIndex As Integer, Temp As Long

      For k = 1 To UBound(LongInt)
        RndIndex = Fix(UBound(LongInt) * Rnd) + 1
        Temp = LongInt(k)
        LongInt(k) = LongInt(RndIndex)
        LongInt(RndIndex) = Temp
      Next k

    End Sub
```

10.9 Exercises

1. Project High, Low, Average #1. Event procedure cmdLow_Click finds the smallest number in the text box control array and puts this number in txtLow:

```
    Private Sub cmdLow_Click()

      ' Display lowest value in txtDay() in txtLow

      Dim Low As Single, Day As Integer
```

```
Low = txtDay(0).Text

For Day = 1 To 6
  If txtDay(Day) < Low Then
    Low = txtDay(Day).Text
  End If
Next Day

txtLow.Text = Low

End Sub
```

mastery
skills check

2. We use **Dim** statements with the keyword **To** and specify both the smallest and largest index of the arrays. If the **Dim** statement does not have an **As** *DataType* clause, the array is Variant by default.

   a. **Dim** MonthDays(1 To 12) As Integer

   b. **Dim** TwoCoins(0 To 3) As Long

   c. **Dim** PrimeNumber(1 To 10000) As Double

   d. **Dim** Price(1000 To 9999) As Currency

   e. **Dim** MonthName(1 To 12) As String

   f. **Dim** ThisNThat(-1 To 37) As Variant or Dim ThisNThat(-1 To 37)

4. Project MaxMinAvg #1. A form-level **Dim** statement declares *NumberArray()* as a dynamic double-precision array:

```
Dim NumberArray() As Double    ' Dynamic array
```

Event procedure cmdEnterArray_Click prints each array value as it is acquired from an input box:

```
Private Sub cmdEnterArray_Click()

  ' Enter values of the double-precision array NumberArray()
  ' from NumberArray(1) to NumberArray(n)

  Dim n As Integer, k As Integer, Msg As String
```

```
' Acquire value of n and redimension array
n = InputBox("Enter value of n.")
ReDim NumberArray(1 To n) As Double

' Acquire values of NumberArray(1) to NumberArray(n)
' and print each value on the form
For k = 1 To n
  Msg = "Enter value of NumberArray(" & k & ")."
  NumberArray(k) = InputBox(Msg)
  Print NumberArray(k);
Next k
Print: Print    ' Return cursor and print line space

End Sub
```

a. Event procedure cmdMaximum_Click calls **Public Function** Maximum:

```
Private Sub cmdMaximum_Click()

  ' Print maximum number in NumberArray()
  Print "Maximum: "; Maximum(NumberArray())
  Print

End Sub

Public Function Maximum(NumberArray() As Double) As Double

  ' Returns the maximum number in NumberArray()

  Dim FirstIndex As Integer, LastIndex As Integer
  Dim Biggest As Double, k As Integer

  FirstIndex = LBound(NumberArray)
  LastIndex = UBound(NumberArray)

  Biggest = NumberArray(FirstIndex)    ' Tentative maximum

  For k = FirstIndex + 1 To LastIndex
    If NumberArray(k) > Biggest Then
      Biggest = NumberArray(k)
    End If
  Next k

  Maximum = Biggest

End Function
```

b. Event procedure cmdMinimum_Click calls **Public Function** Minimum:

```
        Private Sub cmdMinimum_Click()

          ' Print minimum number in NumberArray()
          Print "Minimum: "; Minimum(NumberArray())
          Print

        End Sub

        Public Function Minimum(NumberArray() As Double) As Double

          ' Returns the minimum number in NumberArray()

          Dim FirstIndex As Integer, LastIndex As Integer
          Dim Smallest As Double, k As Integer

          FirstIndex = LBound(NumberArray)
          LastIndex = UBound(NumberArray)

          Smallest = NumberArray(FirstIndex)      ' Tentative minimum

          For k = FirstIndex + 1 To LastIndex
            If NumberArray(k) < Smallest Then
              Smallest = NumberArray(k)
            End If
          Next k

          Minimum = Smallest

        End Function
```

c. Event procedure cmdAverage_Click calls **Public Function** Average:

```
        Private Sub cmdAverage_Click()

          ' Print the average of the numbers in NumberArray()
          Print "Average: "; Average(NumberArray())
          Print

        End Sub

        Public Function Average(NumberArray() As Double) As Double

          Dim FirstIndex As Integer, LastIndex As Integer
          Dim Sum As Double, k As Integer, n As Integer

          FirstIndex = LBound(NumberArray)
          LastIndex = UBound(NumberArray)

          ' Add the numbers in NumberArray()
          Sum = 0
```

```
For k = FirstIndex To LastIndex
   Sum = Sum + NumberArray(k)
Next k

' Calculate the average
n = LastIndex - FirstIndex + 1    ' Number of numbers
Average = Sum / n

End Function
```

Index

Symbols

$ (dollar sign), string variables, 275-277
& (ampersand), concatenating **Print** statement items, 274
+ (plus signs), concatenating **Print** statement items, 274
; (semicolons), standard print zones, 235, 273-274
, (commas), standard print zones, 242-243

A

Add File command, combining projects, 175-176
Add Watch command, debugging tools, 396-397, 398
AddItem method, List Box project #2, 392
Aligning
   labels, 76-77
   text in text boxes, 83
Alphabetic sorts, Sort project #4 - Sort Three Text Boxes
   Alphabetically, 328
Ampersands (!), concatenating **Print** statement items, 274
Anagrams, array exercise, 378
ANSI codes and characters, 282-284, 413-416
   Chr functions, 283-284
   MsgBox statements, 283-284
   Sort project #3 - Sort Three Text Boxes, ANSI, 327-328
Arguments, passing by reference, 322
Arithmetic calculations, 241-246
   exercises, 246
   order of operations, 245
Arrays, 337-378
   anagrams, 378
   Array project #1, 340-341
   control, 352-359, 372-376
   declaring, 339-341
   defined, 338
   Dim statements, 338-341
   dynamic, 359-362
   elements, 338
   Flashcards project #1 - Sequential, 344-348
   Flashcards project #2 - Random, 348
   Flashcards project #3 - Sequential or Random, 348-351
   Flashcards project #4 - Sequential, Random, or Selected,
     351
   Fortune Cookie project #6, 341-343

Fortune Cookie project #7, 344
frequency distribution, 378
Function procedures, 377
High, Low, Average project #1, 372-376
indexes, 338-339
LBound function, 370
mastery skills check, 376-378
option buttons, 348-351
passing to **Public Sub** procedures, 368-372
QBColor project #4 - Button Array, 377
ReDim statements, 360-361
selection sorts, 363
Sort project #7 - Sort an Array, 364-368
Sort project #8 - Long Integers, 368
Sort project #9 - Public Procedures, 368-372
Sort project #10 - Public Procedures, 372
sorting, 362-368
static, 359
UBound function, 366-367
variables overview, 338-341
Art. *See* Zappy Artist
As Integer clauses, **Integer** procedures, 315
Asc function, strings, 291-292
AutoRedraw property
   data types, 239
   forms, 59
   superimposing text over pictures, 116-117
AutoSize property, picture boxes, 130, 134

B

Background colors
   Check Box project #1 - Mix Colors, 207-209
   default, 92-93
   Option Button project #1 - Select BackColor, 209-210
   RGB project #1 - Form BackColor Using RGB, 102-104
Backpacks
   adding tools to, 379-412
   Public Sub procedures, 329-333
   Random Backpack project #1, 307-312
Bang project #1, firecrackers, 126-127
Basic. *See* Visual Basic

477
▼

Visual Basic Backpack

While writing this book and working with high school students who are learning Visual Basic, we noticed that there is no Visual Basic periodical for **beginners**. Aha! A splendid opportunity for two compulsive communicators! So we have started a modest newsletter called *Visual Basic Backpack: Tools and Toys for Beginners*. For a free copy, send your request to:

> Visual Basic Backpack
> P.O. Box 478
> San Lorenzo, CA 94580
>
> E-mail: Karl25@aol.com

Teach Yourself Visual Basic Disk Offer

Teach Yourself Visual Basic describes more than 200 Visual Basic projects. Many are small, and you can create them in a few minutes. Other projects are larger and might take many minutes to create—even longer if your fingers stumble on the keyboard and introduce pesky bugs.

Relax; help is available. Our *Teach Yourself Visual Basic* disk contains all of the larger projects described in this book. As you work and play your way through *Teach Yourself Visual Basic* (the book), you can save lots of time by loading projects from *Teach Yourself Visual Basic* (the disk). You can use this time well by customizing our projects on the disk to your style, walking in wonderful places, sitting under a tree, et cetera, et cetera.

The disk also contains the complete set of answers to all of the exercises in the book. Whereas Appendix B includes selected answers, you'll find the complete set here. All of the data files on the disk are in Microsoft *rich text format* (file extension: rtf). These files can be read by most word processors.

To get your copy, fill out the following order form and send it to the address below. Disks are $9.95 each, shipping and handling included. Please allow 2 weeks for delivery.

****

Quantity: _____ 5$\frac{1}{4}$" + _____ 3$\frac{1}{2}$" = _____ Total x $9.95 ea. = _____Total enclosed
Name: _____
Address: _____
City: _____ State: _____ ZIP: _____

Send check or money order to:

> TYVB Disk Offer
> P.O. Box 478
> San Lorenzo, CA 94580

****

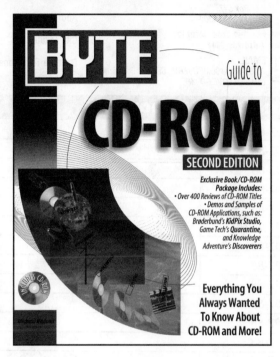

ORDER BOOKS DIRECTLY FROM OSBORNE/McGRAW-HILL

For a complete catalog of Osborne's books, call 510-549-6600 or write to us at 2600 Tenth Street, Berkeley, CA 94710

Call Toll-Free: 1-800-822-8158
24 hours a day, 7 days a week in U.S. and Canada

Mail this order form to:
McGraw-Hill, Inc.
Customer Service Dept.
P.O. Box 547
Blacklick, OH 43004

Fax this order form to:
1-614-759-3644

EMAIL
7007.1531@COMPUSERVE.COM
COMPUSERVE GO MH

Ship to:

Name _____

Company _____

Address _____

City / State / Zip _____

Daytime Telephone: _____
(We'll contact you if there's a question about your order.)

ISBN #	BOOK TITLE	Quantity	Price	Total
0-07-88				
0-07-88				
0-07-88				
0-07-88				
0-07-88				
0-07088				
0-07-88				
0-07-88				
0-07-88				
0-07-88				
0-07-88				
0-07-88				
0-07-88				
0-07-88				

Shipping & Handling Charge from Chart Below		
Subtotal		
Please Add Applicable State & Local Sales Tax		
TOTAL		

Shipping & Handling Charges

Order Amount	U.S.	Outside U.S.
Less than $15	$3.50	$5.50
$15.00 - $24.99	$4.00	$6.00
$25.00 - $49.99	$5.00	$7.00
$50.00 - $74.99	$6.00	$8.00
$75.00 - and up	$7.00	$9.00

Occasionally we allow other selected companies to use our mailing list. If you would prefer that we not include you in these extra mailings, please check here: ☐

METHOD OF PAYMENT

☐ Check or money order enclosed (payable to Osborne/McGraw-Hill)

☐ AMERICAN EXPRESS   ☐ DISCOVER   ☐ MasterCard.   ☐ VISA

Account No. ☐☐☐☐☐☐☐☐☐☐☐☐☐☐☐☐

Expiration Date _____

Signature _____

In a hurry? Call 1-800-822-8158 anytime, day or night, or visit your local bookstore.

Thank you for your order   Code BC640SL